Maria Gulovich,
OSS Heroine of
World War II

Maria Gulovich, OSS Heroine of World War II

The Schoolteacher Who Saved American Lives in Slovakia

SONYA N. JASON

Foreword by PAUL ROBERT MAGOCSI

McFarland & Company, Inc., Publishers
Jefferson, North Carolina, and London

LIBRARY OF CONGRESS CATALOGUING-IN-PUBLICATION DATA

Jason, Sonya, 1924–
    Maria Gulovich, OSS heroine of World War II : the schoolteacher who saved American lives in Slovakia / Sonya N. Jason ; foreword by Paul Robert Magocsi.
        p.   cm.
    Includes bibliographical references and index.

    ISBN 978-0-7864-3832-7
    softcover : 50# alkaline paper ∞

    1. Gulovich, Maria. 2. World War, 1939–1945 — Secret service — United States. 3. United States. Office of Strategic Services — Biography. 4. World War, 1939–1945 — Czechoslovakia. 5. Spies — Czechoslovakia — Biography. 6. Spies — United States — Biography. I. Title.
    D810.S8G85   2009
    940.54'8973092 — dc22 [B]   2008042002

British Library cataloguing data are available

©2009 Sonya N. Jason. All rights reserved

No part of this book may be reproduced or transmitted in any form or by any means, electronic or mechanical, including photocopying or recording, or by any information storage and retrieval system, without permission in writing from the publisher.

On the cover: Maria Gulovich (Museum of the Uprising Archives, Banska Bystrica, Slovakia); captured American soldiers (The Granger Collection). Front cover by TG Design

Manufactured in the United States of America

McFarland & Company, Inc., Publishers
    Box 611, Jefferson, North Carolina 28640
        www.mcfarlandpub.com

To the men in my family who have
served in the active military for the
United States of America.

Husband: Tech-Sgt John Joseph Jason, Sr.
(3 years in General George S. Patton's Special Forces)

Brother: Private Nicholas Negra
(died in combat in France, November 17, 1944)

Brother: Private Charles Negra
(United States Air Force)

Brother: Daniel Negra
(Seaman 1st class, United States Navy)

Son: John Joseph Jason, Jr
(Chief Warrant Officer, II, United States Air Force, Viet Nam)

Brother-in-law: Joseph Jason
(United States Air Force)

May their memory be eternal.

Acknowledgments

My heartfelt thanks to many kind individuals who lent their support in numerous ways. First of all, my husband, John Joseph Jason, Sr., who survived five years of Army service and helped me understand the complex world of the military during war; our sons, John, Jr., a commercial airline pilot, and Gary, a college professor, who had special insights to offer; grandson Zachary, who delved into demanding research; and my entire family who endured my roller coaster emotional ride that went into writing a story based on love, hope and tragedy, all of which this story has in abundance.

I am grateful for the assistance of Paul Robert Magocsi, renowned master of Ukrainian studies at the University of Toronto, who critiqued some of my work and made excellent suggestions.

A boatload of thanks to reliable marketing expert Nancy Akers for her guidance and assistance through some very rough spots; Maria Gulovich Liu, who patiently endured countless hours of interviews on the story of the Dawes mission; Slovak partisan Michael Fedornak, who explained the battle operations of partisans; Mira Mullen for her unforgettable tale of the Nazi brutality directed at commandos and anyone involved in espionage; Lazslo and Luba Macko for sifting out the misunderstood political history of the Slovak-German alliance in World War II; Barbara Podoski, former WAAC who admired Maria's heroism; and Dr. Andrew Cincura, Vavry Rysovy, Gary Gallo and Victor Frudenfeld, who contributed fascinating details of the Uprising that enhance the story.

A debt of gratitude to Slovak resident Jan Kristak and his daughter, Jana Marko, for their written accounts that clarified the heroic risk taken by his parents to rescue an unknown American agent from under the noses of Nazi troops quartered nearby.

Thanks to Kenneth Dunlevy for his riveting personal account of the mission; Steven Catlos, Sr., from whom I first heard the story; and Steve Catlos, Jr., for his input.

Immense appreciation to Anna Provotiakova, former mayor of Polomka, and Slovakian school teacher Viera Petrovicova, who learned English from a couple of textbooks, teaches it to her pupils and, during our brief visit, gave excellent translations of our conversations from Slovak to English and reverse.

A great warm thank you to Edward Bull for his hours of combing through OSS classified records that produced necessary and memorable research material that made all the difference, and Julia Bertonovich for her enthusiastic research on our behalf.

And thanks to good friends like Dorothy Ikach, Diane Grahovac and Estelle Dvorin, who bolstered me with their continued confidence.

Finally, thanks to Jerry Lopez and Maria Berbée, who filled my ears with spiritually uplifting reminders that nothing worth creating can be achieved without frustration, hard work and just soldiering through rough spots until it is complete.

Table of Contents

Acknowledgments — vii
Foreword by Paul Robert Magocsi — 1
Preface — 3
Introduction — 7
Prologue — 9

1. The Simmering Slovakian Revolt Erupts — 15
2. The OSS Mission Arrives on the Scene — 34
3. As the Uprising Collapses, the OSS Is Trapped — 52
4. A Resourceful Maria Joins the Team — 68
5. Maria's American Serenade — 78
6. Division, Debate, Departure — 94
7. Love Blossoms, Even in Hell — 106
8. A Real Thanksgiving — 119
9. Maria's Love Is Captured — 131
10. Waiting in Vain for Help — 143
11. A Christmas of Hope — 154
12. Betrayal: Attack and Capture — 165
13. Unlikely Shelter from the Storm — 176
14. Ultimate Horror at the Hands of the Nazis — 186
15. Maria and Company: Caught in the Crosshairs — 201
16. Desperate "Hail Mary" Escape Plan Works — 209

17. Freedom's High Price	218
18. Maria Departs for the United States	227
19. A Bronze Medal for Maria	237
Epilogue	248
Chapter Notes	265
Bibliography	275
Index	277

Foreword
by Paul Robert Magocsi

Europe is a fascinatingly complex continent inhabited by numerous peoples of differing languages, cultures and religions. On this diverse conglomeration have been grafted several states. For the past thousand years some of these states have had long lives and might even exist today; most, however, have disappeared as a result of the twists and turns of history. States have come and gone, but peoples have tended to remain in their ancestral homelands.

Central Europe has always been one of the more ethnically and linguistically complex regions of the continent. At the close of World War I, the peoples of Europe woke up one day in late 1918 to find themselves in several new countries. One of these was Czechoslovakia, whose borders encompassed the homelands of a wide range of ethnically diverse peoples: Czechs, Slovaks, Germans, Magyars, Jews and Gypsies, among others. Among those others were Carpatho-Rusyns, who lived primarily in the far eastern portion of the new Czechoslovak state.

Just 20 years later, on the eve of World War II, Hitler's Germany, in collaboration with Great Britain, France and Italy, destroyed Czechoslovakia without even firing a shot. Parts of the short-lived country were annexed to Nazi Germany and Hungary, while much of the region called Slovakia became an independent state closely allied to Nazi Germany. This was the political situation that was to prevail throughout World War II.

Despite its relatively short existence, for two decades during the interwar period Czechoslovakia did manage to imbue most of its citizens — especially those of Czech, Jewish and Carpatho-Rusyn ethnicity — with a sense of love and patriotism toward their country. Not unexpectedly, Czechs, Jews, and Carpatho-Rusyns were shocked by the destruction of Czechoslovakia in early 1939; they were opposed to the Nazi German, Slovak, and Hungarian regimes that ruled their land; and they lived on with the hope that at the close of World War II their country would be restored.

Among those with such hopes was the heroine of Sonya Jason's historic tale, Maria Gulovich. The daughter of a priest in the Greek Catholic Church (this is Eastern-rite Christians in union with Catholic Rome), she was working as an elementary school teacher when World War II broke out in 1939. Maria was of Carpatho-Rusyn ethnicity, and although born in northeastern Slovakia, she was raised to be a loyal citizen of Czechoslovakia. It is not surprising, then, that she was opposed to the Slovak state, under whose regime she found herself.

Maria's chance to do something on behalf of her former country — Czechoslovakia — came in August 1944, when discontented elements in Slovakia, urged by the western Allies and the Soviet Union, led an uprising against the Slovak states. Like several other Carpatho-Rusyns, Maria joined the Slovak underground, and during the uprising found herself in the role of a courier for an American-led intelligence mission operating at the time in Slovakia. The rest of the story forms the subject of Sonya Jason's wonderful true-life tale, which you are about to read.

Paul Robert Magocsi is a professor of history and political science at the University of Toronto. He is the president of the World Congress of Rusyns and author of many books on the people and history of the Ukraine and Carpatho-Rusyn nations.

Preface

There is an entire generation of men who were mere boys when they immigrated to the United States with their parents from various parts of the troubled countries of Europe, only to be forced to return a decade or so later as warriors, embroiled in World War II, the biggest war in history. Some were tapped for espionage assignments in the military because General William B.N. Donovan, chief of the Office of Strategic Services, or OSS (precursor to the Central Intelligence Agency), viewed each of them as especially valuable, given their knowledge of the mores of their country of origin, flawless language skills and an emotional tie that motivated them to give their all in defeating the Nazi enemy and to see their native land victorious.

I had no such reflective thoughts on a stiflingly hot August day as I sat with my husband and his friend Steven Catlos, who regaled us with a story about a recent incident in his life. Although these two men had known each other as neighborhood friends while they were growing up, and both were fluent in Hungarian, they had lost touch after the war when we moved to California. Steve had been sent by the U.S. State Department to Slovakia to participate in the 20th anniversary of the victory of communism over the Nazism that had tinged the previous state government.

Now as these friends shared war stories, I was struck again at how reluctant most genuine heroes of any war are to delve too deeply into their memories. My husband had survived three years of frontline combat under General George Patton. It was his unit that had opened up the Dachau concentration camp—a subject he could not bear to touch. And Steve had been selected for espionage as a member of the Dawes mission—the OSS mission that suffered the biggest loss of life of any OSS mission in World War II. With them was a war correspondent who suffered the same tragic fate as 14 of the 19 members of Dawes who had perished by the executioner's hand.

It was only when I idly asked Steve if there had been any women involved in the mission that I realized how deeply affecting his experience had to have been. Yes, he replied, there was a woman, a young schoolteacher named Mary. No, he didn't know where she was and had made no effort to contact her after the war. There was something, though, in his vibrant voice that hit me with the knowledge that here was a story that had to be told. His tone did not reflect a romantic interest per se — it was more one of near awe as he described what a beautiful, brave person she was and how she had saved his life and that of Kenneth Dunlevy, the other agent who eluded capture. He gave Mary full credit for their escape from specially trained pursuing Nazi forces that had been ordered to capture commandoes at any cost, and later, from the Soviet communists who were in the process of deploying them under guard to Russia where they would have vanished behind the Iron Curtain.

As a writer, I knew I had been privileged with a once-in-a-lifetime chance to tell the true story with all the ingredients that make for a riveting tale. Here was a beautiful woman who became part of the Underground after she hid a Jewish woman and her child — a capital offense. Later she would go on to become the guide and interpreter for the American OSS agents and downed flyers stranded behind enemy lines when the Nazis attacked, her only goal being to guide them to the approaching Red Army where they would be safe. The mission was tragic because of the loss of so many men, but it was also somehow miraculous in that any of them survived to tell the story. Had they all perished, doubtless no information about a large part of this critical mission would ever have been heard.

I always had a degree of fascination with Czechoslovakia because Ruthenia, the eastern part of the country until 1948, was the land of my parents' birth and the country from which they emigrated to the United States. In addition, my husband — also of Hungarian heritage — was born in the Slovakia part of the country of a Hungarian mother and an American father.

Of course, I had no idea how difficult researching such a story would be, and this one had mazes within mazes with seemingly no end. Until 1990, most documentation was in Top Secret files. And once I determined that it would be necessary to visit the country itself — a journey in 1978 on which my sister accompanied us — I saw firsthand that the region was under the rigid control of a Communist government and learned just how devastating such control can be where life becomes a gray existence and anyone can stumble into trouble. Additionally, since I spoke some Russian and was openly seeking information about the Slovakian revolt of 1944 — and especially the participation of any Americans — I soon learned how dangerous this could be. Any role in the revolt on the part of Americans was steadfastly denied, and vigilance was soon apparent. To know that your every move and word is being witnessed and listened to by unknown and less-than-friendly stalkers is a terror-inspiring experience indeed.

We made a second visit in 1995 after the division of Czechoslovakia into the Czech Republic and the Slovak Republic with Ruthenia ceded to Ukraine. The changes in the Czech and Slovakia parts of the region were amazing. We were free to move about, rent and drive a car and feel reasonably safe it would not be stolen, and enjoy the warmth of freedom. The children in the family who were helpful to us were eagerly learning English and living conditions in general were much improved.

It was only when we crossed the border to visit Uzgorod, capital city of Ukraine, that we knew communism was still alive and well. It suffered under the same constraints that the rest of Czechoslovakia had endured and now was mostly free from, and we witnessed firsthand what anarchy is like. There was little law and order, and we were warned by our hosts who escorted us, the bus driver and the furtive gazes of anyone who recognized us as American tourists not to venture any farther. We cancelled our overnight reservation and hurried back to the comparative safety of Slovakia.

My lifelong dream of visiting the villages where my parents and their families had lived was not to be. I was advised by our most knowledgeable escort that all records had been destroyed, people had shifted about, and it would not only be futile but also dangerous to pursue this hopeless goal. So I will live the rest of my life thinking of cousins whom I was never able to meet and whose fates are destined forever to remain a mystery.

Researching and writing the story of the Dawes Mission was a catharsis of sorts. I gained a more thorough understanding of the realities of war and how every war bequeaths to its survivors yet another war, as we are witnessing via Iraq and probably Iran.

Beyond that is the sometimes stunning realization of how brave ordinary men can be even under the direst of circumstances — and how strong and persistent women can be if called upon to perform a particular duty. On the other side, of course, is the viciousness of the hunt for the hated and how lonely the gallant, usually unknown secret service of espionage has to be. Yet how necessary is this oldest weapon of war.

Introduction

When I began to research and cover the Slovak Revolt of 1944, two decades after it ended and from a great geographical distance, for much of that time I had no idea that the heroine of this uprising lived only a hundred miles away from me. Understandably, at first she was not eager to participate in any book being written about a painful period of her life as well as that of her family and country. She agreed, however, when she realized how vital the event had been for the small nation that eventually became the Slovak Republic rather than be relegated to existence as one-half of Czechoslovakia, as it had been previously. The Uprising and post–World War II developments fulfilled the centuries-old dream of many Slovaks for a separate identity from the Czechs.

I discovered in Maria Gulovich Liu a woman of passion and zeal for causes she believed in and people in whom she believed. Just as she had defied the authorities by hiding a Jewish woman and her child, Maria supported the rebel band of Slovak State Army soldiers who were called the CzechSlovak Forces of the Interior (CFI). Their intent was to depose the German tainted government headed by President Monsignor Josef Tiso by staging a political and military coup and to reinstate the more democratic pre–World War II government in Slovakia.

Maria was serving as courier for the Underground based in the town of Banska Bystrica, located near the center of Slovakia. Initially she was somewhat dubious of the American OSS mission that flew in to spy on the revolt and rescue downed Allied airmen. But when the German army launched a fierce attack on the area held by the insurrectionists, she was forced to flee for her life and joined the Americans to escape into the lower Tatra mountains. When requested by the OSS commander to serve as guide and interpreter, she cast her lot with the Americans. And not once during the following months they spent evading pursuit by Nazi commando hunting experts did she consider abandoning them and saving herself as she was urged to do by concerned fellow Slovaks.

She emerged from the venture with great respect for the performance and courage exhibited by the entire OSS unit, from commander Lieutenant James Holt Green and next in command Lieutenant James Harvey Gaul to 37-year-old Private Jerry Mican and 19-year-old Private Charles Heller, both of Czech origin.

There have been stories about women spies but this one differs from those in that Maria was called upon to play many roles rather than consigned solely to gathering and passing on information. Her fluency in five languages was a solid plus that helped her operate as the buffer between uneasy Americans and hostile Russian guerrillas who did not welcome Yankees invading their turf. As courier, she knew all the leaders of various Slovak CFI partisan and Soviet guerrilla outfits. She was familiar with the rugged mountain terrain, and these were her people among whom she could more easily discern who was friend and who could be a foe, such as some Slovaks of German origin who were loyal to the enemy.

The Slovak revolt was a costly undertaking, as all such attempts to usurp a state government turn out to be. It affected every citizen and when the war ended, the country was bankrupt and overrun with undisciplined Russian-Siberian soldiers who raped, robbed and seized anything they could from terrified Slovak residents. Furthermore, it shattered the dreams of many Slovaks of worldwide recognition as a separate country. That reality was deferred until the fall of communism several decades later, when the country was again divided into the current Czech Republic and Slovak Republic, with Ruthenia once again part of Ukraine.

The easier way of telling such an active story line is through the two or three most prominent characters. Instead, I have endeavored to include all the men because every one of them is a hero and deserves recognition.

As for Maria, the unique attributes she possessed destined her to become the heroine of the OSS mission that suffered the biggest loss of life of any of its operations in World War II. She was honored as such in 1946, but at the cost of personal losses and of being banished from seeing her family and native country for the next 20 years.

Prologue

Against strong opposition from the Federal Bureau of Investigation, in 1942 President Franklin D. Roosevelt established the Office of Strategic Services (OSS), precursor to the current Central Intelligence Agency. He faced severe criticism when he appointed controversial General William B. N. Donovan as director. A strong critic was Nelson Rockefeller, chairman of the State Department's Committee to Coordinate Anti-American Affairs, who feared Donovan would interfere in his South American bailiwick.[1] An even stronger critic was J. Edgar Hoover, who was afraid that Donovan would steal the spotlight from the Federal Bureau of Investigation. In fact, Hoover had secret files on everyone and even President Roosevelt dared not challenge him when he tried to find derogatory information on Donovan, such as women, drugs, drink, or anything else.[2]

Roosevelt, a wily politician who charmed much of the nation, also had a secretive — some say Machiavellian — side. It raises the question: just how much did he confide in Donovan? For instance, at the Teheran Conference in November 1943, President Roosevelt, Prime Minister Winston Churchill and Premier Josef Stalin, the Big Three world movers and shakers, made a secret deal to turn over Czechoslovakia, Hungary and most of the Balkans to the Soviet sphere of influence after the war.[3]

Given this decision at the highest level, why did Donavan, despite possibly knowing that central Europe was lost to the West, send his biggest OSS unit behind enemy lines and onto Soviet turf into that area in September 1944 — almost a year later? And why, on a visit to Moscow in December 1943 to organize an OSS-NKVD co-operative plan for the war effort, did Donovan offer to provide identities of OSS agents in Nazi-occupied Europe that would endanger the missions and lives of those agents?[4] Therefore, was it a doomed mission operating in the same manner as the British Special Operations Executive (SOE) whose agents lasted an estimated sixty days? That intelligence agency regarded men and women who volunteered for heroic "gray" operations to be considered "forfeited" the moment they left England, liable to betrayal, capture, or execution.[5] Or was Donovan, like the members of the mission, unaware of the political fait accompli that predestined Czechoslovakia to post-war Soviet domination?

Why Czechoslovakia?

Prior to the end of World War I in 1918, much of central Europe was part of the Austro-Hungarian Empire. However, histories and cultures of the ethnic peoples forced to co-exist in such a vast empire are lengthy and diverse, with most of them long governed by monarchs.

Slovakia, for instance, experienced statehood already in the 9th century under her ruler King Svatopluk. In the custom of monarchs, he married a Czech princess and thereby acquired Bohemia as part of his realm, known as Greater Moravia. When he died in 895, Czech princes ceded the territory and agreed to become vassals of the Frankish ruler Arnuff. The rest of Greater Moravia fell victim to Hungarian excursions and Slovakia proper was soon integrated into the Hungarian kingdom. Thus, the history of the first 9th century state to include Czechs and Slovaks was to be repeated a thousand years later in 1918, but within less than two decades it was doomed to failure.

Czech-inhabited Bohemia and Moravia remained under the rule of Germanic kings and later was part of the Holy Roman Empire. In 1806, when Napoleon put a formal end to the Holy Roman Empire, the Czech lands remained under Habsburg rule as part of the Austro-Hungarian Empire. When World War I dismantled the Habsburg Empire, a second attempt would be made to conjoin the Czechs and Slovaks.[6]

Czechoslovakia was a phoenix among nations, arising from the ashes of the Austro-Hungarian Empire at the end of World War I. Some claimed the new republic to be one of the most satisfying products borne out of the war. The economy was balanced between agriculture and industry and was reputed to have the finest workmen with technical know-how in Europe. The state was formed when Czech leaders Thomas Masaryk, a master politician married to American Charlotte Garrigue, and Edvard Beneš persuaded a reluctant President Woodrow Wilson that, in the name of human rights and the rights of nations to self-determination, it was necessary to dismember Austria-Hungary and form a new central Europe. When they convinced President Wilson that a democracy in the heartland of Europe could succeed, the Czech-inhabited areas of Bohemia and Moravia were joined with Slovakia and

Ruthenia to form one state called Czechoslovakia. The West had high hopes for this new democratic country lying within the large buffer zone between Europe's ancient rivals, Germany and Russia.[7] Later, Thomas Masaryk's son, Jan Masaryk, would portray Czechoslovakia as a bridge between the East and West with a Switzerland-like neutrality.[8]

Had Czechoslovakia not been formed, the Czech area would have become part of Germany or Austria, Slovakia part of Hungary, and neither would be the independent republics they are today.[9]

Since the beginning of recorded history, small nations have been the hunting grounds of greater powers and political ideals seldom coincide with realities. The founders and supporters of Czechoslovakia failed to recognize how different the Czechs were from the Slovaks, let alone from other peoples in the new postwar state: Carpatho-Rusyns, Magyars, and Germans. As for the country's main peoples, Czechs and Slovaks, they had separate histories, languages, cultures and aspirations. The more westernized Czechs were free-minded and their area industrially developed, whereas the Slovak and Rusyn lands were more rural and their peoples politically unsophisticated. It was inevitable that the two views would clash. Also, the founders of Czechoslovakia did not perceive the depth of Slovak desire for autonomy as a separate nation, which had disappeared a thousand years before when it was submerged into and under the domination of the Austro-Hungarian Empire.[10] Nor did they understand the ire of the nearly three million Germans living in the part of the country known as Sudetenland at being incorporated into this new Czechoslovakia, a failure that would prove to be a fatal political error.

Who controls Prague, Czechoslovakia's capital, controls all of Europe, German statesman Otto Bismarck once stated. And so it seems to be. A cursory glance at the map of Central Europe in 1939 shows why Hitler was determined to break up the country. Hitler was a master at knowing how to divide groups and play them against each other in conquered countries; in this case, Czechs versus Slovaks, Germans versus Czechs, or Magyars versus Slovaks. Those who provided food and war materials for Germany would be given an orderly administration. The conquest-minded Hitler moved quickly to destroy Czechoslovakia by exploiting the ancient rivalries of the Czechs and Slovaks going back a century or more.[11]

The Sudetenland, without the consent of Czechoslovak leaders, was ceded to Germany by France and Britain in September 1938, as part of the infamous Munich Pact.[12]

The Munich Pact also compelled Slovakia to surrender some territory and population to Hungary, leaving the worried Slovaks trying to maintain what control over their destiny remained possible.[13] When Hitler summoned

Monsignor Josef Tiso, Slovakia's prime minister, to Berlin on March 10, 1939, Tiso was presented with a Shakespearean "to be or not to be" ultimatum. The choice was between several evils: (a) become a German protectorate; (b) be divided between Poland and Hungary; (c) be occupied by Hungarian troops massed on the border; or (d) declare Slovakia an independent state.[14]

A desperate Tiso conferred with the Slovak Diet and on March 14, 1939, the entire body unanimously voted to declare Slovakia an independent state as their only hope to escape being submerged into submission under German or Hungarian control. Slovakia was eventually recognized by 27 states, among them the Soviet Union, Great Britain, and France as well as the Holy See. However, since the Vatican did not approve of clergy assuming political interests for secular states, Rome did not support Tiso.[15]

The price demanded was that in exchange for Slovakia's international existence, the Nazi German line was to be followed. To avoid confrontation with its threatening neighbors, President Tiso signed a treaty of protection with Germany. There was as yet no war when Slovakia became a sovereign state and Slovakia had no army. That changed the next day. On March 15, 1939, the history of a thousand years earlier was repeated when the German army invaded Prague and annexed what remained of Bohemia and Moravia, bringing the 20-year-old democracy of Czechoslovakia to an end.[16]

There are divergent views on how the people of Slovakia reacted to the events. One was that the majority supported a separate Slovak state even with the help of Nazi Germany. Another is that the majority of Slovaks backed any movement that would resurrect Czechoslovakia to pre–Munich borders with close ties to the Soviets. Still another is that most citizens accepted the new state as the best means of survival.[17]

Slovak leaders sadly learned, as leaders of all small nations inevitably do, that solemn formalities mean little in international politics. In that arena, political and military power counts above all. Hitler immediately exercised German privileges under the protection treaty by which the new state had limited sovereignty. The treaty also created an international legal basis for further German interference in Slovakia. This would prove to be a crucial factor during the internal revolt brewing on the horizon. Until then, Germany regarded Slovakia as a mere "calling card" to other Eastern European states. The uprising of 1944 turned it into a strategic area.[18]

The OSS and the SOE were also interested in Czechoslovakia, since lack of access to that former country hindered their intelligence operations. Since the Czechoslovak president-in-exile, Beneš, was reluctant to deal with the West, the OSS felt it urgent to know what the Czech government in exile was up to. Had they sold out to the Soviets? With Yugoslavia taken by the Red

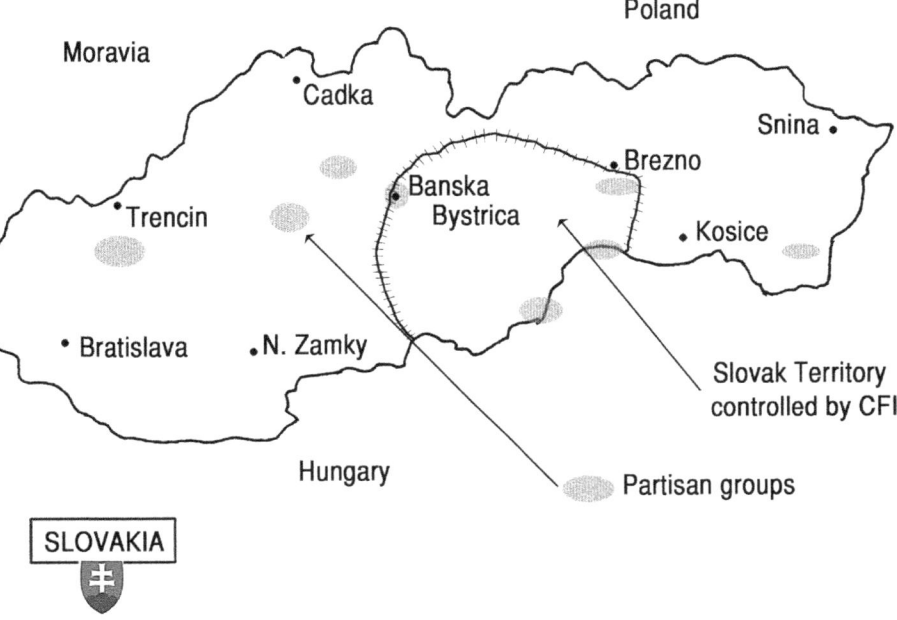

Army, Poland and Romania defecting, adjacent Hungary tottering on the brink of surrender, and with rumors rife of an impending revolution in Slovakia, the Allies decided the time was ripe for a mission into that area.[19] The Czechoslovak government-in-exile based in London failed to understand the conflict between the Office of Strategic Services (OSS) and England's Special Operations Executive (SOE), therefore leaving the SOE to deploy its own mission into the same area only days later.[20]

The decisions by the two major Allied powers to deploy separate intelligence missions into Slovakia catapulted that small, insignificant nation into a strategic area. And with the resistance of the Soviets to any Anglo-American presence in the area certain to stir up murky political waters, the cold war between the East and the West was underway.[21]

1

THE SIMMERING SLOVAKIAN REVOLT ERUPTS

Arrayed in a new sky blue dress, Maria Gulovich stood tall and straight on the parade grounds of West Point Academy. Flanking her on one side was OSS director General William B. N. Donovan, on the other General Maxwell Taylor and other dignitaries, and high above, the colors of the American flag floated in the breeze off the Hudson River. With pounding heart keeping rhythm to the drumbeats of the band playing Stars and Stripes Forever, she gazed in a near dream-like state at the sea of cadets in dress blue uniforms stepping smartly by in perfect cadence, faces turned her way. Maria was only a minute away from becoming the first woman in the history of the academy to be decorated for heroism in war. She had indeed, as her father feared, ventured a long way from Slovakia.

From the outset of World War II, Moscow looked beyond immediate war aims towards the long-term advancement of the communist cause. Following the Teheran Conference in November 1943, our State Department was made aware that Stalin, with agreements by President Roosevelt and Winston Churchill, had scoped out the spheres of Eastern Europe and the Balkans for their post war influence. It made the Soviet practice of intensive collection of information on American, British and French military and intelligence activities particularly dangerous in wartime.[1] Furthermore, anticipating Anglo-American interest and intervention, the Soviets moved quickly. In late 1943, trained Russian guerrillas began parachuting into the Carpathian Mountains of northern Slovakia to establish camps. Their goal was to foment chaos with acts of terrorism against the Slovak state. And by the spring of 1944, Slovakia was simmering with internal discord.[2]

The turmoil was to affect every Slovak citizen, but especially those who embraced democracy and resented the creeping fascist intervention into their lives. Maria Gulovic was one of that stripe, and her ideals and those of her family were to be tested to the utmost.

For a time, Jews who remained in Slovakia were comparatively secure. Then Slovak socialist Vojtech Tuka, with Nazi support but without the signature of President Tiso, pushed through the Jewish Codex that limited their property and employments rights. The codex initiated the deportation of Slovak Jews to Nazi-occupied Poland, ostensibly to work in factories.[3]

When two Slovak Jewish escapees informed Slovak bishop Vojitossak of the true fate of Jews in Polish concentration camps, he appealed to the Papal Nuncio. Pressure from the Vatican, worldwide Jewry and influential Lutherans enabled Tiso to soften the policy. In 1942 deportations ceased, with Hitler permitting Jews to be interred in camps in Slovakia. Tiso issued false baptismal certificates and granted work exemptions using the rationale that the materiel these provided was essential to war production.[4]

Because he operated a lumber mill, Julius Goldberger was one of those Jews who received an exemption. His crisis began when Nazi official Adolf Eichmann was sent to Hungary to speed up shipment of Jews to Poland. Until March of 1944, Regent Nicholas Horthy, with the help of Swedish ambassador Ben Wallenberg, had been able to stem the tide of deportations.[5] But Eichmann destroyed that safety net and Jews in Hungary were no longer safe. When Ben, the husband of Julius' sister Hannah, was taken off the street, her landlord hid her and her eight-year-old son until a smuggler managed to slip her and the child into Slovakia and Julius' home. He secreted Hannah and the boy in a walled-off area behind basement stairs until a friend warned Julius that someone had tipped off the Gestapo. He had to remove them at once.

Maria, like most Slovak citizens, had no knowledge of the fate of Jews sent to Poland until Holy Saturday, the day before Easter of 1944. Her ignorance was shattered that morning when she encountered a young Jewish man hiding in the hayloft of their barn. He'd escaped from a truck transporting a group of Jews from Hungary to Poland when they stopped briefly at Novacky, a Slovak internment camp.[6]

In cities like Bratislava, the black market flourished and, as one journalist had described it, Slovakia was an isle of plenty in hungry Europe.[7] But this was not the case in the villages. Rationing had tightened and coupons meant little. Because the Gulovich family had a cow, and vegetables in the root cellar, they fared moderately well with basics. Treats, however, were a luxury, such as the cookies her mother Anastasia was baking, thanks to Maria's allotment of sugar she had saved. Crossing herself, she warned Maria not to mention the refugee to another soul, especially her father. She filled a plate with

1. The Simmering Slovakian Revolt Erupts

Maria Gulovich waiting for female history to be made at West Point, May 16, 1944 (courtesy Roy Brunhart).

bread and creamy Brinza cheese slices and a few of the cookies. Maria covered the plate with a dish towel, filled a jar with water, and scurried to the barn. The emaciated man devoured the repast in seconds. Maria and her mother put the refugee in touch with his cousin in nearby Stara Lubovna, and a few days later, rested and fed, he slipped away in the dead of the night. The hunted-animal look in his eyes was to haunt Maria, a look she was to see in many others in the future.[8]

The word "crisis" in Greek also means judgment. Maria's father had taught his family and church flock that what one does in a crisis is how they will be judged by God. For Maria, his teachings were buffered by words from Dante's *Inferno* that captivated her at the teachers college: "The lowest depths of hell are reserved for those, who in time of crisis, do nothing." The two lessons were deeply imbedded in Maria's mind and heart and were to profoundly affect her reaction when confronted with her moment of truth that very day, resulting in her life taking an irreversible turn.[9]

It occurred when Julius and Maria's younger sister Marta, a close friend of Julius who was aware of the anti–Nazi views of the Gulovich family, appealed to Maria for help in hiding his sister. He had an ally in Marta. They reasoned that Hrinova, where Maria taught school, was two hundred kilometers distant and safer from the Gulovic home in Jakubiany near the Polish border and in a more remote area safer from scrutiny. And Julius promised it would only be for a few days at most. At first Maria demurred, pointing out that she was already in disfavor with the authorities for refusing to teach fascist propaganda to her third and fourth grade students. The outrage she felt at the increasing Nazi interference into their lives and, now, compassion at Julius' tearful plea, blew the lid off her simmering resentment and plunged Maria into a cauldron of emotions.[10]

She still bristled at the punishment meted out to her father for listing himself and twenty-five other clergyman priests as Carpatho-Rusyns rather than Slovaks in protest at the Jewish Codex. His salary was withheld for eighteen months, and with a wife and five daughters at home to support, it had been a difficult time. Also, Uniate priests, under the jurisdiction of the Vatican, were prohibited from expressing political views, whereas Roman Catholic clergy were steeped in such activities.[11]

Not long before, she had avoided stringent punishment for refusing to have her students use the Hlinka salute, which resembled the Nazi salute with upraised arm, only because her father was a highly respected pastor and supervisor of fourteen other priests. Instead, she was reassigned to "that godforsaken hole" of Hrinova, three hundred kilometers from her family. Anger and fear warred with compassion. If she did not help Julius, his sister might well be on the next truck to a Nazi concentration camp in Poland. She reluctantly agreed, having only a vague perception of how drastically her life would be changed. Certainly there was no inkling that this would be the last Easter she would spend with her family.[12]

* * *

Maria was always to remember how the spring of 1944 had arrived with a special glory. A warm spell caused buds to sprout on trees, shrubs to awaken from a wintry sleep to flourish, and the fragrant air caressed by soft breezes off the Carpathian Mountains blew fresh and sweet. There had been no indication that this holiday would be drastically different from previous holidays. She had spent pleasant days before Holy Saturday with her sisters Marta and Magda, decorating Saint Peter and Paul Uniate Church with pine branches and kitchen geraniums. Occasionally she paused to step outside and breathe in the tangy air and gaze at the faraway mountains, longing to see what lay behind them, never suspecting that before long she would find out.[13]

At the first rays of dawn on Sunday morning, the family trooped to the Resurrection service at Saint Peter and Paul's. Villagers carrying lighted candles were walking to the church from every direction, turning these myriad points of light converging on the small place of worship into a scene from a mystic world.

Basking in the mystery and beauty of the candlelit Mass at which her father presided, resplendent in the white and red ecclesiastical robes Anastasia had sewed, Maria was jolted back to reality when Marta whispered in her ear that she and Julius would bring his sister to Hrinova the next afternoon.

When the service ended, Maria and family "madcap" Magda were walking home ahead of the others when a stocky man blocked their path. He was the father of the student who had reported Maria and was one of the special Hlinka Guards trained in Germany by the Nazi SS. Although the influence of the guards had waned since 1942, they remained an element best handled with wariness.[14]

"*Na straz!*" (On guard.) He whipped his right hand up with palm thrust stiffly forward.

"Whatever happened to *Christos Voskrece*? (Christ Is Risen)?" Maria snapped.

Evidently sensing trouble, her mother intervened. "*Christos Voskrece*, Stefan," she said and extended the traditional greeting of kisses on both the man's cheeks.

"Your daughters would do well to show respect for the Slovak state," he said angrily.

"Of course, Stefan, but this is Easter, a time to forgive each other's shortcomings," Anastasia cajoled. And while her warmth did not soften him, he let the matter pass.

That afternoon, preparing for the return trip to Hrinova, Maria was treated to one of Magda's mischievous performances. Strutting around with hand upheld in imitation of pompous Stefan, she growled, "*Na straz!*" Maria's chuckles were interrupted by a rustle outside an open window. She tiptoed over to it and peeked out. Crouching in the brush was Stefan eavesdropping. Maria reached for the chamber pot used on frigid nights.

"Let's fill it up, and not with water!" she hissed to her sister.

They urinated into the pot, which Maria then emptied on the unsuspecting spy. He cursed and scrambled away while the perpetrators collapsed on the bed from stifled laughter.[15]

Before departing, Maria slipped away for a stroll around the village. Years later, she would remember that right over the mountains was the area in Poland from where Pope John Paul II came. One part of Maria loved the land, but another part was inquisitive and adventurous, like her father before he set aside philosophy and classical languages to study theology.[16]

With her blonde hair, lustrous blue eyes and tall, straight carriage, Maria strongly resembled her father. She also projected his aura of self-possession which registered with others when first meeting her.[17] At home, her anxious father awaited her at the door.

"One of these days those restless feet will take you far away from us," he gently chided, reaching out to touch three fingers of his right hand to her forehead to make the sign of the cross.

His blessing, as always, brought a sense of peace to Maria. It lasted until her mother brought up the irksome subject of Maria's unmarried state by telling her that another suitor had asked for her hand in marriage. Maria firmly resisted the accepted custom of arranged marriages, especially with candidates for the priesthood. Unlike regular Roman Catholic priests, clergy of the Byzantine rite are permitted by the Vatican to marry.[18] Maria had decided she did not want a provincial life such as her mother's after a visit during the summer of her fifteenth year with her Aunt Yolanda in Venice. It had opened her eyes to wider vistas of music, art museums, libraries, fashions and cosmopolitan people.

Frustrated by Maria's resistance, her mother threw up her hands and sighed. "Oh, who knows what will happen by summer? The whole world could go up in flames before this demonic war ends."[19]

Remote from the seats of worldly power, neither Anastasia nor Maria could imagine how true that presentiment was to be. Churchill's policy of "Set Europe ablaze!" with the code name of Arcadia was to engage in the world's oldest weapon, subversion. It would ignite fires of insurrection in Slovakia and neighboring countries. These were to be carried out in butcher and bolt raids, assassinations and any means to establish a fifth column that would weaken Germany's military strength in conquered countries.[20]

Maria might have been captivated by the romantic myths and heroes in internal uprisings had she read John Steinbeck's novel "The Moon Is Down" that glorified the notion. Or to know that secret couriers such as film stars Greta Garbo, Leslie Howard, Noel Coward, Sterling Hayden and other prominent celebrities had lent their acting talents to the shadow world of subversion.[21]

* * *

On Monday, alone and anxious in Hrinova, Maria dismissed her students early to await the arrival of Julius and Marta. She frowned at the portrait of black-haired, blue-eyed President Tiso on the wall, his Celtic appearance so unlike the more Slavic countenances of Edvard Beneš, Thomas Masyrk and Milan Stefanik. Maria did not regard Tiso as an image of "the people" but more that he symbolized the eradication of the democratic ideals upon which Czechoslovakia was founded.[22]

Moderate Tiso, however, was also a victim of events beyond his control. Opposed by the national socialist element in his administration, he was unable to stem the drift to one political party when the government tragically crossed the line from democracy to fascism.[23]

When Marta, Julius and his sister Hannah arrived late in the afternoon, to Maria's dismay, a boy the age of her students was with them. At first irate because she had not been told about the child, pity for the wan, pasty-faced lad and his attractive raven-haired mother replaced Maria's annoyance. She pushed aside her anxiety as she served the meager meal of sliced sausages, bread, and tea she had prepared. Too soon, Julius and Marta had to leave. At the door, Hannah clung to her brother and sobbed while the child clutched arms around his uncle's knees and wailed in fright. Heavy with the burden she had taken on, Maria watched her sister and Julius disappear into the dusk.

Two more people added to the 9 by 12 room furnished only by a Franklin stove, a bed and chifferobe, a small table and two chairs, was like a crowd. She instructed Hannah to sleep in her bed and the boy on blankets on the floor and to extinguish the kerosene lamp and lock the door as soon as she left. She would spend the night in the classroom. There, Maria removed her blouse, skirt, and shoes and lay down on the cot used for sick children. Alert and hyper, she listened to the sounds outside. Tree branches brushed against the sides of the building, crickets serenaded in rhythmic chirrups, interspersed with the mournful hooting of an owl. It was the ordinary music of the night, but she imagined unseen eyes observing her and lay awake for hours.[24]

At daybreak, Maria hurried to her room to again instruct a sleepy Hannah to not answer any knock at the door, talk only in whispers, keep the shades down, and stay out of sight. She'd remembered to bring pencils and paper for Zoltan to keep up with his schoolwork. Then after splashing cold water over her face and running a comb through tangled hair, she forced her reluctant legs to the door of her principal. The pale features of the alarmed man grew ashen as he listened gravely to her news.

"Maria, how reckless! This act could throw me into the Army or send me as laborer in a German factory! And what would happen to my family then?"[25]

His words took Maria aback. She had forgotten that men with skills were being deployed by the Central Employment Agency to Germany to work and even badly needed teachers who might be suspect were drafted into the military.[26] He finally relented, however, and ordered Maria to keep Hannah and Zoltan out of sight and to get rid of them as soon as possible. Maria knew that he would not betray her, but he was also too frightened to help. Her only hope was that Julius would return soon for his sister and her boy.

One week stretched into two, then a month. Maria's note to Marta to "come pick up your belongings" went unanswered. Then, one afternoon, she found her nine-by-twelve room empty. Panic subsided only when Hannah and Zoltan returned from a friendly visit to the Jewish village doctor. Hannah's recklessness infuriated Maria. Now that their presence was known, she would have to register Hannah and the boy at the post office, and she feared the worst.

Maria claimed Hannah and Zoltan as her aunt and cousin. When the postmistress raised no questions about their smudged documents, her fear subsided. It resurfaced the next afternoon when Igor, the village Casanova, paid Maria a surprise visit to her classroom. He leaned over the desk where she was correcting test papers and with a smirk and told her he knew who her visitors were. But if she was nice to him, he'd keep her secret. When she insisted that they were her aunt and nephew, he strode away tossing a remark back at her. "Think it over because you can be in big trouble, but I can help you."

Maria knew that Igor was a member of Internal Security and could carry out his threat. After he left — furious at her rejection — Maria's thoughts churned in search of a possible solution. Finally, one came to mind. Maria again cautioned Hannah to remain out of sight and then hurried off to consult the village priest.[27]

The aged cleric lived in two small rooms adjacent to his plain wooden church. His office space was so cluttered there was no place to even lay his spectacles. He listened gravely and then rubbed his eyes and asked what her father would say about this. When she admitted that she had not told him and was hoping there was some parish far away where Father Andrew could send Hannah to work as a housekeeper or something, he heaved a deep sigh and said he had to consult his bishop.

His words dashed Maria's hopes. The Vatican did not support Tiso and in any event, no bishop would allow his clerics to risk arrest and imprisonment like the hundreds of them who had already met that fate, leaving village flocks of the faithful with no shepherd.[28] The pope and Roman Catholic bishops were unlike the patriarch of Constantinople, titular head of the Eastern Orthodox Church, who had urged his bishops in the Balkans and Europe to aid Jews and to state from the pulpit that doing so was a sacred duty. In contrast, Pope Pius VI mouthed pious phrases but was much more cautious.[29]

Before Maria had time to devise a second plan, she had another visitor. It was Capt. Milan Polak, district head of Army Central Intelligence in Banska Bystrica, locale of the underground operations. Unknown to her, he was also an important figure in the dissident Underground Movement. Polak had been a

1. The Simmering Slovakian Revolt Erupts 23

teacher and was now liaison to General Ludvig Svoboda, but Maria did not know that most Slovak dissident leaders also were underground communists, guided from Moscow.[30]

The sandy-haired man of medium build had dark gypsy eyes and wore a plain jacket and pants, but had a certain presence about him. Maria was aware that this casual type could be more than a little dangerous as the Gestapo wore civilian clothes and often appeared benign, but they were never to be underestimated. Like Igor earlier, Polak had come to propose a resolution, albeit not an amorous one. Serve as courier in the underground and he'd take care of her problem. Refuse and expect arrest.[31]

Couriers were carefully selected; their entire backgrounds and sympathies known. Living in enemy territory, they were able to carry messages between two agents. And since the messages were coded, they would have no meaning for the courier and there were few leaks.[32]

Refusal not only meant placing her own life at risk, but that of Julius, his sister and her boy, the principal, his family, and her parents and five sisters, fourteen lives against her one. Her back-to-the-wall decision to accept Polak's offer was to catapult her into a maelstrom with an outcome she could not possibly envision.

* * *

It began on bright June day shortly after the Allied invasion of France. Natives were not permitted to move about freely but Polak reappeared with an official permit that allowed Maria to change her residence and provided a good cover story and new identity. Her code name would be Gita, her occupation a student in a clothing design class, her new location the small town of Banska Bystrica in central Slovakia. Polak advised her to make it look as though she would be returning. So Maria packed a suitcase only with her good clothing and necessities and boarded a bus to Hrinova and then a train to Banska Bystrica. Her sisters Marta and Magda would take turns staying with Hannah and Zoltan until Polak could relocate them.[33]

Her transition to Banska Bystrica was not as difficult as Maria feared. The bucolic old town was a mélange of the medieval and modern. A sprinkling of fashionably dressed women mingled on cobblestoned streets with peasants wearing dark, drab clothing. The population of twelve thousand had swelled by thousands more, men who came to work in the re-opened silver mines, CFI partisans, and refugees fleeing war-torn Poland and Nazi-occupied western Czechoslovakia.[34]

The house of Josef and Anne Krutel, in which she would live, was ideal. It was behind the railroad station where she could mingle with throngs and

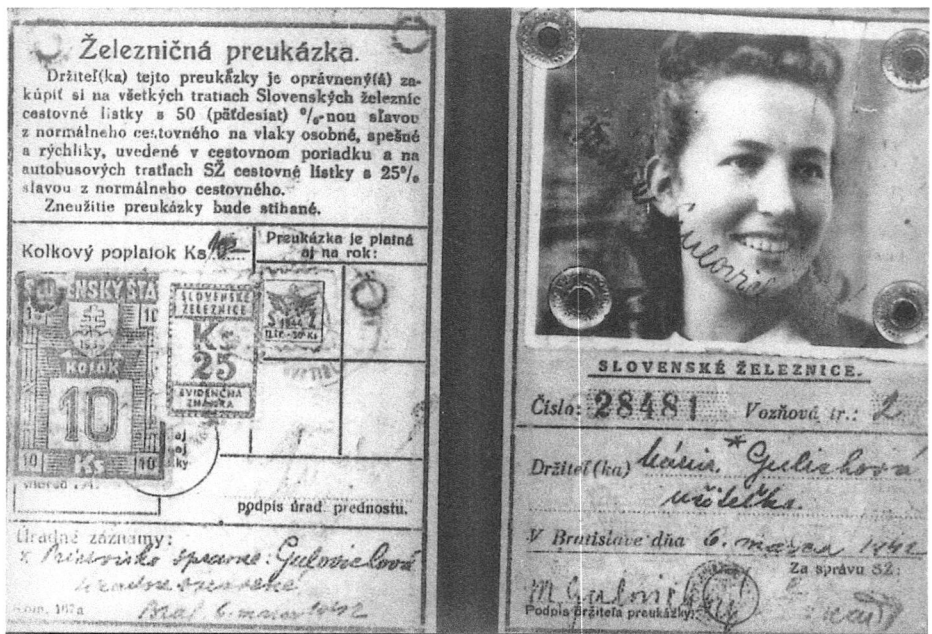

Maria's national identity card, a critical document for every Slovak citizen and especially important for Maria (courtesy the Museum of the Uprising Archives, Banska Bystrica, Slovakia).

not appear conspicuous, and since the window in her room faced the street, she could also covertly observe the comings and goings of anyone who might appear suspicious. Her schedule left Maria free to pick up Polak's instructions near the Krutels' mailbox, perform the designated courier duty, and return to her fashion designing class. There were no social contacts and life could have been deadly dull except for the fact that, as with any dangerous occupation, there is an element of excitement. And as the war drew closer to Slovakia, both danger and excitement escalated with her duties.

By July, large units of Soviet guerrillas who dropped down in parachutes were well entrenched in the Lower Tatra Mountains. They left their telltale trademark in bridges, roads and buildings blown up and railroad lines derailed. Overhead, flotillas of B-17s flying into East Germany from Allied air bases in Italy filled the skies.[35]

Day by day, Maria's assignments grew more daring. One was to take a train to Bratislava to pick up spare radio parts and where she was forced by the jealous wife of her contact to wait on a porch swing in the cold for three hours until her contact arrived. On the return train to Banksa Bystrica, two

Gestapo agents leaped aboard when it began to move out of the station, one at each end of the car, trapping her in the corridor with the bag they would search. She had only moments to act.[36]

The adjacent compartment was filled with young German officers. Maria flashed a flirtatious smile at one and he invited her to join them. Telling him she was a teacher and her suitcase filled with books, she held her breath until he stashed the bag overhead. When the Gestapo came by, they merely winked at the young officer and went on. But the danger was not over; at the station more Gestapo waited. Once more, she had to act fast. Assuming what she hoped was a coy expression, Maria smiled at the officer and asked how long he would be in Banska Bystrica.

Taking the bait, he replied, "Not long — will you have dinner with me tonight, fraulein?" With her acceptance, he picked up her bag and carried it past the Gestapo, and joined his companions, leaving Maria still shaken by the close calls at evading capture.

A week later, Czech partisan Captain Pavel Pavlovich sent for Maria. He had parachuted into the mountains some weeks earlier and Maria was sent to locate and escort him to a safe house where he set up operations. His assignment for her was to transport a CFI colonel, sought all over town by the Gestapo, to a guerrilla camp. The colonel was concealed in a battered truck under a load of odd bits of furniture and clothing on which Maria perched. Posing as a married couple, Maria and Jan finessed the first two checkpoints easily, but at the last one, the guards were older and more experienced. They stared hard at Maria while jabbing bayonets into various spots of the load, each thrust filling her with nauseous dread. Her obvious nervousness made her suspect, and when one of the guards suspicious demanded to know what was the matter with her, Jan was quick with the reply that she was in the family way, and rubbed his stomach to indicate morning sickness. The guard continued to study her through narrowed eyes before he finally let them proceed. They delivered the colonel and returned to Banska Bystrica without further incident.[37]

Not until late July was Polak to make good on his promise to relocate Hannah and her child in Rysava, the remote mountain home of Polak's Jewish grandmother. By then, Maria had learned the reason for Polak's delay in relocating Hannah. The average life of a courier was six weeks[38] and he evidently hoped he would not have to be bothered with Hannah.

In early August, rumors about an uprising against the government became open talk. Soviet guerrillas and Slovak partisans stealthily crept down from mountain hideouts at night to commit acts of sabotage and to ambush and kill political opponents. The disorder created rampant fear.[39] Unfortunately, the distrust and lack of cooperation between moderate and radical political elements would open the door for German intervention, a development President Tiso tried to prevent. He was dead set against Nazi occupation because it would ruin plans to turn his government over to the state army at a given time to form an interim government, which would then reach out to the West and later the United Nations. German occupation would obliterate all such hopes.[40]

As summer ebbed and the war in Europe went on, revolts, bloody plots and uprisings permeated Europe, including the failed German Black Orchestra plot to assassinate Hitler in which General Erwin Rommel played an integral part.[41] However, group resistance to the still considerable might of the Wehrmacht remained perilous business. For example, on D-Day, several thousand Free French Maquisards were cordoned off on the plains of Vercars, France, by the Nazis. Aided by an Allied Intelligence Jedburgh team consisting of one French agent, one American, and one British, a thousand planes loaded with weapons were sent to the trapped men. But it was not enough to overcome the powerful SS anti-partisan reinforcements brought in by glider landings. Parachute and glider landings are most dreaded because they produce confusion, leaving no flank or rear guard, and no escape. They surrounded the entrapped Maquisards and by July killed all of them.[42]

In another case, on August 1, 1944, under directions from the London-based Polish government, the Polish Home Army staged a fierce attack on German troop occupants in Warsaw while looking to the Red Army for assistance. Instead, General Konev's 1st Ukrainian Front holed up on the banks of the Vistula River and waited. A covert OSS action of a drop of supplies came too late and the Polish Home Army was decimated, along with two hundred thousand Polish civilians, and the city left in flames. Stalin viewed the Home Army as a threat to the Polish Communist Party and even refused facilities for British planes to supply arms to the insurgents, who were decimated.[43]

And in Greece, native partisan activity, aided by local communists, was punished so brutally by Germans it resulted in British Intelligence dissuading Greek activists from initiating further attacks.

Still, partisan warfare was flourishing under General Marshal Tito in Yugoslavia. Could Slovak dissidents, champing with unrest, utilize forested mountains from which to stage raids of hit and run and succeed in similar warfare?[44]

As the chaos escalated, two divisions refusing to fight against the Allies deserted the Slovak State Army and formed a rebel military force called the Czechoslovak Forces of the Interior (CFI), commanded by General Jan Golian.

1. The Simmering Slovakian Revolt Erupts 27

This non-communist and anti-fascist element was dedicated to restoring Czechoslovakia to its pre–Munich arrangement with closer ties to the West. Opposing them were Slovak communists, armed and commanded by Soviet guerrillas, who also wanted a reunited Czechoslovakia, but as a Soviet state. Their motive for a revolt was to coerce Germany into invading Slovakia and paving the way for the Red Army to enter as liberators, making for an easy takeover of Slovakia. It would also return Beneš and the deposed Czech exiled leaders to power. A third element of resistance wanted Slovakia restored to its pre–Munich democratic state but as a republic separate from the Czechs.

More civilians joined the CFI and units sprouted up in towns surrounding Banksa Bystrica until the insurrectionists numbered between 50,000 and 60,000 partisans under the command of Gen. Golian. Their hope was to join the Soviets after they achieved a successful uprising. The main stumbling block to any such unified Soviet-Slovak effort was enmity between the CFI partisans and Russian guerrilla commanders who distrusted and refused to aid each other.[45]

Maria's courier skills were put to their most severe test when Polak sent her to contact Soviet guerrilla captains Piotor Alexjenic Velichko and Alexia Semionovic Jegerov with urgent coded messages. Both men were top Russian military leaders and rivals for power.[46] Unfortunately, she would meet Velichko first, an encounter she would never forget.

Camps were secluded and studded with bunkers dug out of mountainsides with tops covered by vegetation of balsam pine and birch. This left the surrounding topography undisturbed so reconnaissance planes flying above could not detect hidden camps. The bunkers had dirt walls and ceilings with tree trunks for tables. The men slept on planks padded with blankets and clothing which became lice-infested after months of guerrilla warfare. Most guerrilla leaders had a "wife," a camp follower who cooked and slept with him in exchange for booze and a few cheap trinkets.[47]

Velichko's "wife" glared at Maria as she delivered the coded verbal message. Noticing that Velichko wore the symbol of a grain of wheat on his shirt that signified he was a high ranking communist,[48] Maria felt uneasy. When he insisted she take time for refreshments and dismissed the driver and then his female companion, her unease heightened. Clutching a bottle of vodka, glasses, and a plate of bread and bacon, he lumbered towards her, murmuring, "I like you." The oily tone was ominous and she moved aside. But refusing refreshments was considered rude, so Maria forced herself to nibble a bit of bacon and bread, but declined the vodka. She edged slowly to the bunker opening, intent on leaving. But Velichko had another intent. He lunged and grabbed her arms, twisting them behind her back. He pushed her to a cot and threw her down on it and tried to yank off her sweater. Maria, wriggling and struggling to escape his grip, cried out, hoping to stop him. "What will your girl think?"[49]

"Don't worry about that whore! It's just you and me," he snorted, her resistance only whetting his desire.

Maria was five feet eight inches tall and in excellent condition but was not strong enough to escape or fend off the heavy, jowly Russian with a body heavy as concrete. "You're a wild one! But then ... this can't be new to a pretty girl like you not afraid to come to our camps," he said with a devilish leer.

Maria burned with the desire to kill him. If she had a gun she would have used it, but mere possession of a gun meant imprisonment. Her voice was shrill and on the verge of hysteria as she demanded, "Let me go! I have to leave!"

Velichko scowled and said, "You're not going anywhere. You've seen too much in my camp."

His cunning expression brought a fresh surge of alarm. With an attempt at bravado, she tried to reason with him. "Captains Polak and Pavlovich ordered me to bring you and Captain Jergerov important messages. You will answer to them if I don't get back to Banksa Bystrica safely."

He suddenly pushed her aside and let her go. Maria moved to the entrance, unsure of what he'd do next. Something had changed and she didn't know what.[50]

Unknown to Maria, Jegerov was Velichko's superior[51] and he had no choice but to let her go. He offered her a glass of vodka and when she refused, belted it down, stalked to the opening and stuck his head out and whistled for his orderly who appeared out of the darkness.

"Take her to Jegerov's camp!"

"Now, Commandant?" the bewildered flunky blurted.

"Now!"

Until then, Maria had believed that her impressive credentials provided protection, but she learned that in war there are so such formalities as protective credentials and any woman is fair game to a rapacious soldier.[52]

* * *

The entrance to Jegerov's camp was guarded by several coarse looking men with straggly beards. Two of them jumped in front of the car, noses of submachine guns pointed at Maria and the driver, and studied the courier

1. The Simmering Slovakian Revolt Erupts

with eyes hard and cold and demanding the password. When Velichko's aide replied "Pushkin," the guards moved aside and they entered the camp.

Jegerov was already a Russian legend. He stood straight and tall, imposing as a preacher. His more elaborate unit near Stara Hory was decorated with the Red Star, hammer and sickle and a portrait of Stalin.[53] The captain was summoned and the wait allowed Maria to regain some of her composure. Glancing about, she noted a few civilized amenities. A couple of woven scatter rugs were on the dirt floor and a framed painting graced one wall. On a rustic table were two books of Russian classics. As she leaned over to catch the titles, she heard voices.

"You want to see her, Commandant?"

Wanted dead or alive, Jegerov usually talked to strangers from behind a partition; however, this time he evidently had no reservations. "She's only a woman, harmless I'm sure."

Maria was startled at how different he appeared from Velichko and other guerrilla commanders she had dealt with. Of slight build, his sandy hair was neatly trimmed and he wore casual slacks and shirt open at the throat. His features were refined but his shrewd, gray eyes flicked over Maria, missing nothing.[54]

As with any legend, lurid stories circulated about the man. He was said to have guerrillas shot if even suspected of dealing with the enemy, for failure to obey orders or for lying and stealing. He was driven, it was said, by a ferocious hatred of Germans since they killed his wife and small son.[55] He was known to be a stern disciplinarian, and Maria sat tense and apprehensive while he studied her.

His adjutant moved a chair close to her and Jegerov sank into it easily. His penchant for procuring attractive young women was also well known. Maria's qualms rose to an intolerable level as he listened to the message she had for him. To her astonishment, he asked no questions. Instead, he launched into a dissertation of philosophy and quoted Russian poets before he abruptly stood up and yawned. Maria noticed for the first time the lines of fatigue on his face.

"*Stranaya devochka*" (Strange girl), he commented. "Why are you in this?"

"For the free government I hope to see again when this is over."

He let out a cynical snort. "Free government! Your poor misguided girl, such Don Quixote ideas! It is not what you or I would want but what *Batuishka* (Little Father) Stalin has already decreed. Now..." and his voice shifted to a cajoling tone, "you have to stay the night ... do you want to sleep with me?"

"No, and I must go!" She stood up prepared to flee or resist.

"Oh well," he said with a shrug, "I'm too tired anyway. Maybe next time. But you have to stay the night. Even *I* can't guarantee your safety in these parts after dark."

His orderly made a bed of parachutes on the floor for her and she eased herself onto it. She lay wide awake, body rigid, half expecting Jegerov to reappear, and expected the worst. In the morning another orderly appeared to take her to Banska Bystrica. The fox-like Jegerov had already moved on to another lair. On the way to town she recalled the obvious enjoyment of his reputation as a cultured man.

"Hundreds of years ago," he had told her dreamily, "the Roman Emperor Trajan camped on this very spot and wrote poetry between battles. I might do the same."[56]

In her room, Maria experienced delayed shock and revulsion. She lathered her body with soap and water to scrub away anger and disgust, cursing Velichko and all such powerful, cruel men, determining that when she saw Polak, she would tell him she quit. She'd had enough. But she was not to have that opportunity.

At midnight, an agitated Capt. Pavlovich knocked at the window. He'd been betrayed. The Gestapo had located his radio transmitter, arrested the couple who hid him and set fire to their house, but he escaped. He informed Maria that they were looking for her, too. Maria hid him under the bed until morning when she escorted him to the Army Geographical Institute, eight kilometers out of town. Warning her that the revolution was going to start any minute, Pavlovich urged Maria to find new quarters and urged her to help the CFI by working as a translator for some special Russians arriving any moment.

"I hate communists as much as I do fascists," she declared. "I'll try to make it home."

"Home is the first place the Gestapo will look for you. And after all, you'll be working for General Golian and I'm sure he'll issue an official work permit for the CFI."

Maria had met the courteous general on several occasions, and she liked him. Furthermore, the signature of the supreme commander of the CFI on a document would provide the legitimacy she needed.[57]

Hour by hour the upheaval grew more volcanic. Guerrillas seized police stations, blew up bridges and tunnels, and took over villages, fomenting more confusion and chaos. On August 12, Tiso declared martial law, but since he lacked the power to enforce it, Hitler prepared to take over. Aware that German occupation meant the end of Slovakia, Tiso tried to delay by pleading for more time.[58]

1. The Simmering Slovakian Revolt Erupts

At the same time, Gen. Golian was trying to convince Velichko to wait until all CFI units were coordinated before striking a major blow. Ignoring his wishes, Velichko seized control of the uprising from Slovak nationalists in the same manner the communists had out-maneuvered Spanish nationalists in the 1938 civil war in Spain.[59] In mid–August, his guerrillas started requisitioning cars, robbing stores and farmers, and shooting Slovak army officers.[60] One Slovak partisan commander later wrote, "The revolt had all the markings of a Bolshevik revolution. Soviet and Slovak communist guerrillas wore red kerchiefs, some sported Lenin goatees and a rosary of grenades around belts. Robbers, rapists, plunderers and murderers were set loose, some of them singling out priests to be killed."[61] Communist underground leaders had attended Lenin's school in Moscow for subversion and sabotage of non-communist countries. There were no rules and no mercy.[62]

The revolt came to a head on August 27, in Turciansky St. Martin when Soviet guerrillas halted a train carrying General Otto and twenty-seven members of a German diplomatic group returning from Romania, which had just surrendered to the Red Army. Velichko ordered their execution, including the women and children. This act of terrorism was deliberately designed to entice the Germans into Slovakia. To quell the disorder, an enraged Hitler ordered troops to invade Slovakia and crush the uprising.[63] Until then, Slovakia had enjoyed the best economic period in the country's history. The rigors of war would bring grim changes.[64]

In nearby Zilina, on August 29, Vavro Rysovy, vice president of the Regional Underground Committee of northwest Slovakia, notified General Josef Dobrodsky that German troops had crossed the Slovakian border. The rapid move did not give the surprised Slovak partisan top command in Banska Bystrica time to issue necessary orders, so Rysovy pre-empted them by issuing the order to start the uprising. This made Zilina the first city to engage in the uprising and, at the end, the last city in Slovakia to be liberated from the Nazis.[65]

Shouting the slogan *"Mor Ho"* ("Crush him!") over Slovak Free Radio, rebels urged the bewildered people to join the revolt and to resist their government. Trying to coordinate with Moscow, the leftist Slovak National Council declared a provisional government called *Slovenska Narodne Rada* to be set up in Banska Bystrica. To gain the support of the people, Soviet guerrillas spread rumors that Tiso had been killed by the Germans when they took over the state government. It was not true but it added to civilian confusion and terror.[66]

By August 30, the insurgents had seized control of an area of one hundred miles around Banska Bystrica, reaching north to the River Vah, west to

Novacky, east to Spisska Nova, west to Levoc, and southwest to Depva, including the lower Tatra Mountains. Incoming German troops ordered Slovak village and farm youths to dig trenches or be deported to work in German factories. Instead, many slipped away to join the insurgents.[67]

On August 31, Slovak defense minister Gen. Ferdinand Catlos defected and appealed to all factions to support the uprising. There was no police or state army in the region held by the insurgents and Tiso's regime teetered as the German army poured into Slovakia from eleven points and encircled the area. Beneš promised assistance to the CFI but the Red Army was one hundred miles away, leaving the CFI doomed to be let down, as was the Polish Home Army earlier. They were also abandoned by the Slovak communists who did not man their assigned posts in Banska Bystrica, so their role in the revolt would be negligible.[68]

During the entire existence of the Slovak state and until the German occupation with the uprising, there had been no death sentences for political reasons and Tito had abolished the death penalty. With the loss of western Slovakia to the Germans and eastern Slovakia to the Soviets, the bloodletting would claim the lives of 30,000 Slovaks.[69]

The fallout would be staggering. Five thousand Jews released from the Novacky camp by insurrectionists fled to the mountains to hide or join the guerrillas. All Jews were to be especially pursued by Germans because they were suspected of being communists. Sadly, stranded Allied airmen would no longer find any place of refuge in Slovakia.[70]

When the revolt reached the boiling point, Maria's position turned exceedingly perilous. She could not endanger her family by returning home. Polak urged her to dye her blonde hair dark and go into hiding, but she refused. Helen, a gypsy girl in the underground, warned Maria that the Gestapo had questioned Madame Olga about her whereabouts and were looking for her. She hid for a couple of days with Helen's family, but that placed them, a despised ethnic element scheduled for the death camps, in grave danger.[71] Maria had to find another refuge.

On September 1, Russian Maj. Ivan Skripka-Studensky, accompanied by minor officials and a contingency of reporters, arrived in Banska Bystrica to establish a Soviet Intelligence operation. As first deputy commander of the Partisan Movement in Slovakia, he would liaise with Gen. Ivan Konev's First Ukrainian Army Front.[72]

The next morning, Maria reported to the Soviet Intelligence headquarters on the 3rd floor of the Infantry Building. Although it was early, Studensky was imbibing champagne, but she noted it did not impair his mental sharpness. Maria's linguistic abilities in German, Czech, Hungarian, Russian and Slovak languages were immediately put to use translating CFI war communications from the Western Roman script into the Russian Cyrillic alphabet. The Russians then relayed these reports via shortwave radio to guerrilla headquarters in Kiev.[73]

With that step into an opaque Russian domain, her father's fears were confirmed. Spiraling events would indeed carry Maria far away from their village home and family — farther than either of them could have imagined.

2

THE OSS MISSION ARRIVES ON THE SCENE

Until the uprising, Slovakia had the most balanced economy in wartime Europe. The uprising would reduce it to beggary. Eruption of the revolt and the inevitable German military occupation brought into Slovakia the grim realities of war, such as food shortages, bombings, bloodshed and battlefield terrors.[1] In their shadow would be a band of unforgettable Americans, but not before they overcame some formidable obstacles to get there.

Throughout the war, the Allies had maintained separate watch on developments in Central Europe, but this only led to distrt between England's SOE and America's OSS.[2] The SOE did not share their intelligence system with the OSS as they did with the Czechs and Poles. This inter-agency hostility influenced the Czech government-in-exile in seeking help from the British and Soviets rather than the United States.[3] An additional impediment was that, as a result of the Teheran agreement that changed the course of the war, the United States was required to formally request permission from the Soviets to enter Slovakia and Hungary, making any OSS mission into those areas touchy.[4]

Accordingly, the official State Department circles felt it not expedient to openly defy either England or Russia and refused overt help to Slovakia. They also did not want to acknowledge that the SOE and OSS were competitive, antagonistic organizations.[5] So England continued to support Yugoslavian nationalistic partisan leader Gen. Draga Mihailovich and his Chetniks, whereas, from 1943 onward, at the behest of Donovan's recommendation, the United States shifted support to General Marshal Tito's communist partisans. Another factor was the Friendship Treaty signed by exiled President Edvard Beneš with the Soviets on December 12, 1943, which gave the Soviets a relatively free hand in Slovakia.[6] To avoid further roiling of troubled waters the

2. The OSS Mission Arrives on the Scene

United States State Department urged only *unofficial* and covert OSS action since the Soviets would not cooperate in areas under their influence.[7]

However, following D-Day, the Americans took a very close look at Central Europe. Donovan's reports to President Roosevelt on deteriorating conditions in Germany, as well as the disillusionment of Slovaks with the Nazis, convinced the president to approve OSS plans to send a mission into the area, providing they bypassed two barriers — both of them Allies. These were England and Russia, between whom lasting distrust existed. The British were in a snit after Yugoslavian partisan leader General Marshal Tito turned from the SOE to the OSS and Soviets for aid. The Britons not only lost face, but also feared being left out of post-war plans for Central Europe. To preempt any such development, unknown to the OSS, the SOE carried out their own secret mission into the area held by the CFI in Slovakia.[8] From Banska Bystrica, the SOE alerted the London office and the OSS in Bari of guerrilla activity in the mountains and that insurgents had released a large number of American airmen from a POW camp for Allied captives in Granava and brought them to Banska Bystrica. If there was anything the OSS had to learn from the SOE it would be to dare to do what was expedient for them, regardless of the diplomatic consequences.[9]

A telling incident at the Teheran Conference reveals the disparate views of President Roosevelt and Prime Minister Churchill regarding encroaching Soviet control of post-war Europe. When Premier Stalin described his brutal intent to deal with German generals and staff by executing 50,000 of them, a shocked Churchill rose up in protest and left the room. Stalin and Vyacheslav Molotov, the Soviets' commissar of foreign affairs, followed Churchill, smiling and telling him it was just a joke. A dubious Churchill reminded Stalin that he was one-half American, on his mother's side, and respected Americans. Roosevelt, on the other hand, laughed and in jest suggested that Stalin shoot only 49,000 German officers and staff.[10]

In support of the Slovak revolt, President Roosevelt sent Beneš a wire stating, "We, the American people, greet our Czechoslovak friends in arms who have contributed to the liberation of their own and other countries." To officially establish the United States position, on September 2, 1944, Roosevelt further proclaimed that soldiers of the CFI in Czechoslovakia constituted a force operating against Germany and that any violations of the rules of war were at their peril and they would be held responsible for war crimes. They were part of the Allied armies, and he warned Hitler to abide by the Geneva conventions of war.[11]

Under the appealing (and concealing) public relations cover story of sending in a "military mission" for search and rescue of stranded American

Funeral of American pilots shot down in Slovakia (courtesy the Museum of the Uprising Archives).

airmen, the United States was reluctantly granted permission by the Russians to enter Slovakia.[12] The mission was set in motion as soon the intelligence branch (SI) of the 2677th Regiment of the Army in Bari, Italy, learned that the Tri Duby airstrip near Banska Bystrica could handle the United States' heavier B-17s.[13] The make-shift landing strip, now controlled by the insurgents, had been built by the Germans for training Czech pilots. When it was readied to receive the Dawes intelligence team, the first and biggest OSS mission of World War II was deployed behind enemy lines into Central Europe.[14]

The Dawes mission could have been appropriately named for William Dawes, a member of the patriotic Mechanics Intelligence organization and one of the "two lanterns," the other being Paul Revere, who galloped off to warn the Concord Minutemen that "the British are coming." In this case, it was not only the British coming, but also the Americans, and not as enemies, but as friends.[15]

* * *

During August 1944, OSS planners took a long, hard look at central and eastern European fronts. There was the August 2 uprising in Poland, and

2. The OSS Mission Arrives on the Scene

reports of partisan activity in the mountains of Slovakia. Something was brewing and they wanted to find out what it was, and now was the time to do so.

On September 17, 1944, at 0600 hours, three B-17s of the 15th Air Force based at Foggia, Italy, carrying six members of the mission, flew in formation with a number of B-24 bombers, headed for Austria and eastern Germany on bombing raids. The B-17s were loaded with medical supplies, 120 Marlin guns with 84,000 rounds of ammunition, and 12 bazookas with 16 rounds each for the CFI partisans. Wearing regulation uniforms, the OSS contingent arrived in Banska Bystrica in broad daylight and were cordially greeted and congratulated by partisan leaders for successfully landing in enemy territory.[16]

The mission commander, naval Lt. James Holt Green, code name Ocean, was from Charleston, South Carolina. The thirty-three-year-old Green had been exempt from military service because of his administration of a textile mill vital to the war effort. However, he champed with the desire to join his two brothers serving as naval officers. Some political persuasion and family influence were able to help facilitate his wish to play an active role in the war.[17] Following in the footsteps of his brothers, Walter and Robert, Green had enlisted in the Navy in February 1943, after which he spent nine months observing Tito's partisan warfare in Yugoslavia. Then consigned to a desk job that he found unsatisfactory, he requested a return to the field. His request was granted, and he was appointed commander of the Dawes unit. His duties as commander of the mission were to evacuate Allied airmen, act as liaison with the CFI and other insurrectionist groups, and report on military, political and economic intelligence activities within the scope of the mission. He and his men were to remain within the confines of Slovakian territory.[18]

All the men of Dawes were volunteers, including the youngest and the oldest of what would become a nineteen-man operation. Intelligence recruits are a rare breed: they must have cool nerves, be in good physical condition, be proficient in languages and think and act quickly under pressure. They were tested for memory and had to undergo 18 hours a day training in codes. Out of 4,000 examined for the mission, only 50 were accepted.

The first deployment of the mission consisted of two components, Dawes and Houseboat. Dawes was to arrange for evacuation of stranded airmen, but also to liaise with the CFI to report on battle intelligence, the situation with the insurgent's campaign, and to estimate arms, ammunition and needs of the CFI. Assisting Green were Staff Sgt. Joseph Horvath, born in Slovakia but reared in Cleveland; Master Sgt. Jerry Mican, born in Prague and now a resident of Illinois; and Corporal Robert Brown. Horvath and Mican, fluent in the Slovak and Czech languages, typified naturalized citizens, or those who had contact in countries of their origin, and were especially sought out by

Donovan as potentially ideal spies.[19] Corporal Robert Brown, who like Commander Green did not speak a foreign language, was the radio operator for Dawes.

The second operation, Houseboat, was headed by Lt. John Schwartz, code name Krizan, and was strictly a spying mission. He and his teammate were to infiltrate across the heavily guarded border of Bohemia and report directly back to Bari on economic and political intelligence. For twenty-four-year-old Schwartz, this was a homecoming after five years. A native of Slovakia, he'd been active in the underground until the Gestapo closed in, and he fled to France where he joined the Free French underground. He was captured by the Nazis, but escaped from a POW camp and managed to reach the United States where he immediately volunteered for the OSS. Swartz was described as being clever and canny. He spoke French and German fluently but his English had a heavy accent. His friend SPX/2/c Charles Heller, who was fluent in the Czech language, had volunteered to serve with Swartz and would be his radio operator.[20]

The youngest member of the mission, Heller had enlisted in the Navy at age seventeen and was now twenty. That morning of departure, his friend Czech partisan Richard Grey took special notice of Heller's attitude. He was cocksure with pride over his first intelligence commission as he strutted over to where Grey was watching the planes being loaded. A grin lit up Heller's cherubic features when Grey slapped him on the back.

"Listen, you smart-ass clown, be sure to come back in one piece."

Heller pulled off his watch and slipped it around Grey's wrist to keep for insurance until they met again. Touched by the boyish gesture, Grey removed his own clunky, battered watch and handed it to Heller and said, "Anytime you even think of pulling off one of your goddamned tricks, look at that watch and remember how it almost got you beaten to a pulp. I can still do it, y'know." At that, Heller threw an exaggerated salute, walked to the plane and disappeared through the plane's crew hatch.

Grey knew nothing about the mission but suspected it was to Slovakia because, like Heller, a couple of others on the team he knew were fluent in Slovak or Czech. Watching the fully loaded planes trundle down the runway, he recalled how he and Heller almost came to blows not long before. The incident occurred when Heller, assigned to teach English to Grey, was instructing him on proper conduct for an upcoming meeting with important American military officers who had arrived to be briefed on the Czech underground. Wanting to display some proficiency in English, Grey asked Heller if he should greet them by saying "hullo," or whatever was the proper salutation.[21]

Heller had run a hand through his tawny crew cut in apparent serious thought before he replied and said that "hullo" is low class and only used with buddies. To military brass, you say "Up your ass, sir!" and be sure to lean heavily on the word "sir."

Remembering, Grey relived his chagrin at the results. When the two colonels, two captains, a WAAC, and OSS Major Otto Jakes looked up at the ceiling, obviously trying to repress smiles, he realized he had committed a colossal blunder. Jakes, who spoke German as did Grey, took Grey aside and tactfully asked him if he knew what he'd said and then translated for a red-faced and furious Grey.[22]

As soon as he could break away, Grey raced to the barracks to confront Heller. "You son of a bitch!" he yelled when he caught sight of Heller and prepared to give him the trouncing of his young life. Surrounded by several buddies howling with glee, Heller, with mischievous blue eyes squinted shut, was rolling on the floor with laughter. Someone had called to relay the gaffe. Circling Heller with coiled fists, Grey challenged him to fight like a man. But how can you fight a man so limp from laughter he can't stand up? After profuse apologies from Heller, and within a couple of weeks, their friendship was renewed and now Grey was grateful for the basic English he'd been taught as well as how to be a less rigid military man.[23]

Grey was also well acquainted with Lieutenant Jerry (Jaroslav) Mican, who, at age thirty-seven, was the oldest man on the Dawes team. Born in Prague, where his parents still lived, Mican was a high school teacher from Chicago and fluent in several European languages. The gray-haired agent had undergone varicose vein surgery to qualify for service. Struggling against periodic attacks of asthma, as well as his wife's opposition to his enlistment, Mican volunteered to fight the Nazis who had taken over the country of his birth. Before he left on the mission, he asked Grey to contact his wife and parents if he did not return.[24] Unlike the majority of OSS members who were *young* idealists,[25] Mican was the "old man" of the group.

* * *

The pilots and crew of the B-17s knew little about the purpose of the mission. They volunteered after being informed that a number of downed fellow airmen were in the hands of Slovak insurgents and waiting to be evacuated. The morning of departure they were briefed about the daytime flight into Slovakia during which they would pretend to be a part of the larger bomber squadron accompanying them. Delivering the OSS men and supplies was said to be incidental to the trip that would take them over the Alps and the Hungarian border and through airspace controlled by the Luftwaffe. Forty-one P-51 fighter escorts would stay with them to and from Banksa Bystrica.[26]

American pilots shot down at Tri Duby Airport wait for evacuation to a base in Italy (courtesy of Roy Madsen).

The co-pilot of one of the B-17s was Lt. Col. Howard Dallman. He was to always recall the exhilaration as the loaded planes took off and climbed to an altitude of 14,000 feet. The crew was on constant lookout for Luftwaffe fighters but flak positions had been well plotted and enabled them to pass through the danger zones safely. There were some tense moments south of Budapest when several unidentified craft were sighted but did not attempt to engage them, and the remainder of the flight was uneventful. As they peeled off for their landing, Dallman peered through a hole in the cloud cover and noted that the Tri Duby air base was a only a small dirt strip on which they had to land. Surrounding it on three sides of the field were jagged mountain peaks looming ominously. But he'd flown with Lt. Col. Gilbert Pritchard, a West Point graduate, before and was relaxed as Pritchard put the plane down easily on the rutted runway.[27]

On the ground, men in uniforms unloaded the cargo. The first contingency to greet Green and his team were several Soviet guerrilla officers, followed by a few from the CFI. The airdrome assumed a carnival atmosphere with cars driving up to line the adjoining highway to watch their arrival while partisans and civilians crowded around the planes for a closer look.[28]

2. The OSS Mission Arrives on the Scene

Arrival of needed war materiel for insurgents from air bases in Italy (courtesy the Museum of the Uprising Archives).

A truck full of young men in American Air Force uniforms drove up. One of them, adhering to the traditional rivalry between the Army and Navy, pointed to Green and jokingly asked, "What the hell's the Navy doing here? Isn't this supposed to be an Army outfit?"[29]

Observing the boyish airmen boarding the planes, Pritchard later wrote in his report that the happy expression on the faces of the evacuees who'd parachuted out of crippled planes and been captives in a POW camp was worth the hazardous trip.[30]

During the unloading, the fighter escorts circled the field, their steady drone of engines a reassuring sound. On the ground, the B-17 crews had been ordered to remain on board and keep the engines running. In forty minutes they had finished their task and were ready to take off again. As they bumped their way down the short runway and began to climb and push aside puffy clouds, Dallman kept his eyes on the scene below, watching until Green and his men appeared the size of ants merging into the crowd surging onto the field. Who the hell were these guys who'd volunteered to come to this ratty airstrip surrounded on all sides by enemy might? And what were they here for? Sure, Czechoslovakia was a small country situated between the giant

Plane with evacuees ready to take off to an air base in Italy (courtesy Roy Madsen).

powers of Russia and Germany, but how could it possibly be important at this stage of the war anyway? Well, whoever they were and for whatever reason they were here, he wished them Godspeed. These guys would need a lot of luck to do whatever it was they came to do and then get out of this isolated hole in the mountain ranges.[31]

* * *

Upon arrival, the OSS unit set up operations at Banska Bystrica in a villa hastily vacated by Gestapo officials when insurgents seized control of the town and surrounding area. Lt. John Schwartz was one of two Dawes team members permitted to operate out of uniform. Not wanting to waste a moment, he immediately donned civilian clothing and melded with groups of natives on the street to ferret out information.[32] His radio operator, Charles Heller, was also cleared to wear civilian clothing. Later another agent reported seeing Heller swaggering around town making sure the holster of his pistol was in plain view from beneath his jacket, and he looked like an adolescent Mickey Rooney playing a movie role.[33]

Under the pretext of searching for more stranded airmen, Mican and

Horvath, wearing uniforms, posed as language interpreters while garnering intelligence. In a short time, the unit collected such a volume of information that radio operators Brown and Heller were overwhelmed relaying all of it to OSS headquarters in Bari. The reports gave not only details on day to day development of the uprising, but provided exact locations of possible bombing sites. The precise information enabled the 15th Air Force to bomb the Apollo oil refinery near Bratislava, capitol of Slovakia, a strategic railroad crossing at Gyor, and the Malacky air base just north of Hamburg, Germany, used by the Luftwaffe. Putting these strategic targets out of commission deprived the Wehrmacht of much needed oil, delayed shipments of German military and munitions, and forced the Luftwaffe to rely on more distant airfields in southern Poland and northern Hungary.[34]

These bombings so enraged Hitler that on September 23, 1944, he openly defied Roosevelt's warning to the Axis powers to abide by the Geneva war conventions and reaffirmed the Nazi Commando code he first issued on October 18, 1942:

> All Allied commandos and personnel, whether in uniform or not, whether armed or unarmed, in combat or flight, if surrender is attempted, no quarter is to be given. They are to be executed.[35]

A cursory evaluation of the situation, gleaned by Green's forays about town, revealed that the set-up was different from Yugoslavia. There was little indication of war, and bombings affected mainly airport hangars. The people were friendly and courteous and some paid with their lives by helping airmen. He then radioed Bari asking for another radio operator and additional war supplies for the CFI. Another radioman would enable him to move about more freely to report on outlying areas, but more agents would be a liability.

> This message should be complied with immediately. DO NOT, repeat, DO NOT send in more men, except another radio operator. The enemy is coming closer.[36]

However, political impediments that ruled out aid for CFI insurgents remained in effect. On September 26, 1944, a directive from Colonels Howard Chapin and Walter Ross in Bari notified Green that only permission given by top Air Force command would be effective to further supply the CFI. And in that eventuality, since any such sortie would be a night landing, fighter escorts would not be required, making it a high-risk venture.[37]

Green made frequent forays outside Banska Bystrica to carefully evaluate the military strength and operations of the insurgents. He was soon disillusioned and in a report to Cols. Chapin and Ross, who'd organized the

Lt. James Holt Green, commander of the Dawes Mission, on duty in Banska Bystrica headquarters, September 1944 (courtesy the Museum of the Uprising Archives).

mission, he stated, "I've had a couple of trips to the front and the Slovak people are friendly as are CFI officers. The Russians are a different lot — hard drinking with no control over their undisciplined units. We did not venture near the Dukla Pass where fighting is still heavy but General Golian feels it's only a matter of days before the Red Army breaks through. I'll find out more from the ambassador of liberated Ruthenia who has a reception scheduled next week, but at first evaluation, my impression is that the revolt is too loosely organized to be effective."[38]

Until they arrived, the Americans had no knowledge of Soviets in the area held by the insurgents actively organizing guerrilla bands.[39] One Slovak partisan unit commander noted that the Russians were not pleased to see the Americans or British, and furthermore, they accused anyone who opposed Soviet control of the revolt as being pro-fascist.[40]

When the requested radio operator did not arrive, Green sent another message to notify OSS Bari that they'd collected twenty-eight more airmen for evacuation. Among them was Lt. George Winberg who'd walked forty-one miles on an injured leg to reach Banska Bystrica. Green also alerted Bari

2. The OSS Mission Arrives on the Scene

that the enemy had started offensive drives from three directions and were getting closer every hour. The mission was becoming increasingly tenuous.[41]

Soviet plans for a speedy link-up with the Red Army had been dashed when Gen. Ivan Konev's First Ukrainian Army became trapped at Dukla Pass in early September and was bottled up by German battle seasoned Panzer IV and XI Corps. When the five-week battle ended, there were 120,000 casualties, among the heaviest of the war. It also rendered the position of the Dawes mission even more precarious when the Red Army broke through the pass on October 6, driving hordes of retreating German soldiers through the area held by the insurgents.[42]

Curiously, the OSS in Bari ignored Green's request to send more supplies but no more men, just as they had paid no heed to SOE opposition to any OSS flights. On the afternoon of October 6, while six B-17s were being loaded in Bari for a second flight to Banska Bystrica, a wire sent from London OSS ordering the cancellation of the flight was received at OSS headquarters in Bari. Maj. Otto Jakes, supervising the loading of the planes, stuffed the telegram into his pocket and did not open it until the next day after the planes, carrying a variety of war materials and another fourteen agents and escorted by thirty-two P-51 fighter planes, were on their way to Banska Bystrica.[43] No reason was ever given for the refusal to comply with Green's request of October 1 to send a radio operator, but not more agents, especially in the face of Green's warnings.[44] In addition to Green's opposition to more men, on October 5, Gen. Golian sent a report stating that the situation was critical. Thousands of heavily armed enemy soldiers were advancing on Banska Bystrica from five directions at once.[45]

Co-pilot Howard Dallman volunteered for this second flight, as did Col. Gilbert Pritchard. As with the previous flight, they would pretend to be part of the larger 15th Air Force squadron of bombers, although this time P-51s would accompany them to Tri Duby and then proceed on their own mission. Waiting for the takeoff signal, Dallman glanced around the plane crammed with war weaponry that included 150 bazookas with ammunition, 100 Marlin guns, 100 Bren machine guns with 75,000 rounds of ammunition, as well as plastic and medical supplies and food and warm clothing for airmen still behind enemy lines. He wondered how the mission was progressing.[46]

During the flight, they were again on the lookout for Luftwaffe fighter planes as they passed over the Alps and through Luftwaffe-controlled flight territories. On approach to the Tri Duby airstrip, a heavy pall of clouds obscured the field and they had to search for a spot where they could duck under the blanket-like mist overhead and scan for the landing strip. Remembering the mountain peaks looming on three sides, Dallman was tense during the fifteen minutes before they sighted green flares outlining the airstrip, signifying it was safe to land. They peeled off and began the descent to land with Dallman peering through foggy windows at the curious sight of a large crowd lining the field. As before, crews remained on board and the engines were kept running while CFI partisans unloaded the planes. Dallman watched Green make his way to the aircraft with a number of airmen being evacuated.[47] This time there were no fighter escorts circling overhead like mother hens, leaving the crews anxious.

The distinguished looking Green was a tall man and appeared to tower above most of the flyers, as fighter pilots were often selected because of their shorter height, more wiry builds and quicker reactions.[48] With the twenty-eight Americans were two New Zealander pilots and five Frenchmen, two of them wounded. Some of the pilots had been singled out for humiliation by the Gestapo. They were forced to don peasant clothing before being marched through towns wearing dunce hats while being beaten with sticks. They were elated at being evacuated and upon boarding the planes, they held a hearty thumbs up in appreciation to the rescuing pilots and crews.[49]

Dallman gave a start when he heard Col. Pritchard let out a sharp expletive and said, "Looks like we have a problem!" Dallman peered outside to see the wheels of one B-17 imbedded in mud. Pritchard leaped to the ground and rushed over for closer inspection. Lt. Jack Gorman, piloting the last plane to land, had hit soft ground at the edge of the runway and slid into a deep puddle. Pritchard ordered pilot Fred Ascanti to instruct Gorman to unload the plane and then set flares to it. Instead, Gorman decided to try to put the aircraft back into operation. He held a hasty conference with his crew asking how many would volunteer to stay with him to get the plane airborne. Every hand went up, rendering Ascanti aghast.

"Are you all crazy or have some kind of a death wish? You guys will end up in a POW camp." But Gorman remained adamant.[50]

At this, Pritchard cocked his head upwards and then climbed back aboard his own plane. It would be foolhardy to wait any longer so he gave the take-off signal to the crews on the four other planes. As their plane engine vibrated and they began to climb after takeoff, Dallman kept his eyes riveted on the hapless B-17 whose crew was joined by insurgents pushing and shoving at the mud-splattered plane to loosen it from the prison of ooze. He watched until a cloud bank hid them from view, leaving him wondering about the fate of the crew left behind. An hour later, he and the others were relieved to hear that Gorman's efforts were successful and they were now airborne.

Dallman's thoughts then shifted to the group of new agents who had joined Green. This mission had to be something really big to warrant so many men. This time he felt that these men would need more than mere luck to escape the spider web in which they were enmeshed. His heartfelt farewell salute was accompanied by a prayer. And he was to be left wondering until 1991 when secret documents were declassified and he learned about the objectives and details surrounding his two secret flights into Banska Bystrica.[51]

* * *

Richard Grey was again on the scene during flight preparations. He'd spent many pleasant hours with some of the men during training and gotten to know several of them. From the outset, he was impressed with naval Lt. James Harvey Gaul. Like anyone else, his first impression on meeting the naval officer was to note Gaul's size and bearing. At six feet, five inches with broad shoulders, long legs and arms, Gaul had played basketball at Harvard University. Exuding vigor and confidence, his was a definite no nonsense, take-charge manner, as befitting an officer although this attitude did not prohibit him from organizing outings for the men during training such as the one where Grey joined the group of fifteen who crowded like sardines into a jeep and drove to the coast for a swim in the Adriatic Sea. A few of the more daring dove off cliffs into churning waters, with Gaul, an excellent swimmer, taking the lead. On the way back, he belted out a well-known bawdy soldier barracks song and insisted upon every man adding a verse he knew or making one up. No one meeting Gaul, according to Grey, could take this pre-war archeologist and college professor for anything but a leader.[52] It would not have surprised him to learn that the considerable mission funds of British gold sovereigns, French gold Napoleons, American dollars and Slovak korunas were entrusted solely to Gaul.[53] This money would buy food or information when needed and could mean the difference between surviving or perishing.

For Staff Sergeant Steven Catlos, the two years of OSS training had ended and an objective was finally at hand. Relegated to his personnel file were the endless psychological tests to weed out those not suited for intelligence, exciting demolition classes that included one experiment where he and a colleague unintentionally blew off quite a portion from a Virginia mountaintop. He'd spent hours practicing parachute jumps and endured weeks of language instruction to fine tune his native Hungarian into various dialects and to acquire some Slovak as well. The stocky, sandy-haired, twenty-four-year-old man was another naturalized American selected by Donovan for his fluency in the Hungarian language and familiarity with the culture of his country of origin. Catlos now felt ready to put into practice his knowledge of radio operations, demolition and all the other necessary training the OSS had invested in him.[54]

As the six weighty B-17s trundled down the runway, they were joined by thirty-two B-51 bomber escorts. Interspersed with the excitement of their first mission, a sudden jab of concern and thoughts of his wife, Anne, and almost two-year-old daughter, Barbara, filled him. Would he get back to them safely? He quickly forced the worry aside with an irreverent thought flashing through his mind as they lifted off and were about to meld into white pillowy clouds. He commented to his teammate that the small cemetery now the size of a postage stamp outside Bari was where Saint Nicholas was buried.[55]

"Do you think Santa Claus will remember us as good boys?"

First Lieutenant Tibor Keszthelyi ran a hand through thick, dark hair and his clear-cut features split into a lopsided grin. "I always believed in Santa Claus," he said in a cynical New York drawl. "I hope I still do when this is over."[56]

As the plane labored to higher altitude, the ground beneath faded from view and there was only the drone of the engine, Catlos sat back to ponder on the months spent in Cairo and Algiers risking their rumps on parachute jumps. Now they would land on the runway like the big brass. Made no sense, but after two years in the Army, Catlos had learned that many things in the military seemed to make little sense. As they headed towards their destination, a near heady buoyancy filled him and he cast a glance at his team leader sprawled in a seat next to him dozing. Did the aloof, controlled Keszthelyi feel it, too? His teammate came to with a start when Catlos audibly griped about their method of arrival and uttered an angry retort.

"What the hell did you expect? Kora and Moly to dangle off our chute strings if we came in on a jump?"[57]

Catlos snickered and settled back in his seat for the four-hour flight to Banska Bystrica during which they stood a good chance of running into the Luftwaffe. He flicked a glance across the aisle at their two civilian teammates sitting like robots, stony-faced and staring ahead. Was Francis Moly really a Hungarian Roman Catholic monsignor? And was the dapper Cora with the buffed fingernails gripping a violin case with papers hidden in the false bottom really a skilled radio operator? This pair was the other half of his and Keszthelyi's Bowery mission.[58]

Selected for the mission only ten days before, Catlos and the other men were given no briefing and had little idea of the purpose of the mission or about the country of Slovakia and why it merited such a large mission. The nature of espionage is secrecy, that the less you knew about each other the better, but it led to a constant suspicion of one another. It was fine for security, he felt, but wished he had a better idea of the objectives, a thought he was to later express somewhat bitterly both verbally and in writing.[59] And he would probably have been more bitter had he known that American airmen were briefed on escape routes into Hungary — but not the OSS members.[60]

Slouched in another bucket seat was Sgt. Kenneth Dunlevy, an electronics expert and the extra radio operator Green requested. The boyish looking twenty-four-year-old with the last traces of adolescent acne on a youthful face was the only cryptographer on the mission and had memorized the radio codes of every member of the Dawes unit. He was aware that it was Donovan's creed to obtain information about codes and ciphers of the enemy's operational system when possible. Hitler was equally eager to learn those of the OSS system.[61] Dunlevy had no doubt that as an OSS cryptographer, he would be a prize catch for the German Abwehr Intelligence. This may have added to the suspicion of each other he described later that existed in part among the agents, partially because they had no idea what was going on.[62]

Boarding the plane at the last minute was Associated Press war correspondent and Missouri resident Joseph Morton. Accompanying him was Navy photographer's mate Nelson Paris, assigned to take photos of the landing and uprising for an official record. The photos would highlight stories about the revolt Morton was assigned to write about. He was intrigued with the mutiny in Slovakia and thrilled when *Life* magazine commissioned any material he could produce about the revolt. Morton had written some brilliant pieces about King Michael of Romania before he was deposed and replaced by dictator Ian Antonescu who'd surrendered to the Red Army on August 26. On this flight, Morton and Paris were guests of the 15th Air Force and not any part of the OSS.[63]

Catlos was unable to spot a landing field through the overcast until he sighted green signal flares lighting up the perimeters, and then something less than reassuring. It was a mob of onlookers lining the strip, relegating the mission to tourists rather than a military mission.[64]

It was obvious that Green had not expected, nor welcomed, so many men. Their arrival would require reorganizing operation plans and present billeting and evacuation problems. The newcomers were split into two groups, some to join the earlier arrivals at the villa and the remainder assigned to the Narodne Dom hotel.[65] Hearing artillery and machine gun fire which he estimated to be about ten kilometers away, Catlos wondered what the hell he had let himself in for. All that training to land on a patch of dirt in some provincial town in the hinterland of Europe about which no one outside the place had ever heard! Neither Catlos nor his colleagues could have imagined that all the members of the Dawes team were marching into American, Slovak and Soviet history, a history in which the Soviet and Slovak communists would deny for fifty years that Americans had any part.[66]

Joseph Morton, Associated Press war correspondent covering the Dawes Mission (courtesy the Museum of the Uprising Archives).

2. The OSS Mission Arrives on the Scene

* * *

At the Russian Intelligence headquarters on the third floor of the Infantry Building, it was just another hectic day for Maria. The deluge of incoming communications had grown so voluminous that to save time, she and Soviet shortwave radio operator Maria Radiovna Rudinskaya (code name Tamara) sometimes took turns sleeping on cots set up in a side room. Her attention was piqued when Studensky's aide, Mikhail Gennady Jahovlivic Stalny, dashed in with an exciting report.

"More *Amerikanski* just landed at Tri Duby!"

"What the devil are they doing here?" Studensky asked. "Find out and then have Tamara notify Kiev right away."[67]

Tamara's big green eyes shone with excitement and her soft voice was tremulous when she whispered in Maria's ear that she'd never met any *Amerikanski* and wondered what they were like. At the first landing, Golian hosted a reception to congratulate Green and his men, and Maria had been ordered by Studensky to attend the reception. When she protested that she did not speak English, he ordered her to attend anyway, watch and listen and report back to him.

Donning her good navy wool dress she embellished with a silk paisley shawl, her sole item of finery, Maria had attended the event. There she ran into a CFI partisan commander, Captain Stonek, and broached a question about the purpose for these Americans being there so far from America. Stonek lifted an eyebrow and gave a cryptic response. It was to pick up their downed airmen, a statement he obviously did not totally believe.

Surreptitiously observing the Americans, and drawn repeatedly to Green's chiseled features and dark, perceptive eyes, Maria decided the Americans were more like sportsmen. Even their casual, loose fitting uniforms were similar to sports clothing rather than military attire and their friendly, easy attitude not at all like the formal, haughty military types to which she'd become accustomed. They also bore no resemblance to her adolescent idea of American military men being like the Holy Ghost and larger than life. A curious Tamara interrupted her thoughts by repeating her question,

"What are the *Amerikanski* really like, Maria?"

Maria paused to reflect, then shrugged and said, "Oh, they're nothing special. Besides, our paths will never cross so why bother ourselves about them?"

It was, as she was to often remark later, the most glaring instance of misjudgment she had ever made.[68]

3

AS THE UPRISING COLLAPSES, THE OSS IS TRAPPED

Green's original negative perception and opinion of the CFI partisans and communist guerrillas grew markedly stronger following the October 7 arrival of the additional OSS men. In a report to OSS Bari, he described a "let down feeling overall, noting that Soviet guerrilla officers cooperate with CFI partisan officers only on the surface. Down the line, there is little discipline and no cooperation between the two forces. Guerrilla units are made up of French, Poles, and Russians, with the French being the best of the lot. The country as a whole is not communistically inclined and Soviet assistance is denied for that reason."[1] Another report by a Slovak unit commander on the scene corroborates Green's depiction of Soviet-controlled partisans having units of drunken men, with lurid stories of beatings and rapes and general brutality towards villagers graphically described.[2]

The duplicity of the Russians had a direct impact on OSS agents Lts. William MacGregor and Kenneth Lain when they encountered strong Soviet resistance while complying with their assignment of instructing CFI partisans in the use of American weapons. Both MacGregor and Lain were battle-seasoned veterans of the bloody battle over Anzio Beach in Italy. Recovered from wounds incurred there, they enlisted in the OSS. The Russians would later claim that the United States sent in only a few bazookas and a mere ten rounds of ammunition. The truth is that both OSS deployments arrived with planes loaded with weaponry. On October 7 alone, the OSS brought in 150 bazookas and 2,800 rounds of ammunition in addition to 100 Marlin guns, 10,000 rounds of ammunition, 99 Bren guns, 7,500 rounds of ammunition and other war materiel that totaled 30,920 pounds.[3]

The Russians had told the CFI not to accept American weapons and then sabotaged MacGregor's and Lain's efforts by having local communists convince the partisans that the bazookas would blow up in their faces when fired. So the men refused to even try them out. MacGregor repeatedly demonstrated how safe they were. On one occasion, slyly observing the instructions, Soviet commander General Velichko then challenged MacGregor to a contest. One of his men would fire a bazooka and in turn MacGregor would fire a Russian-made anti–tank gun. However, Velichko did not tell MacGregor that the long barrel of the Soviet gun required two strong men to hold it during firing, and when MacGregor fired, it delivered a powerful kick that sent him sprawling, Velichko and his entourage howled with derision. Noting MacGregor's outrage, his opponent held out his hand.

"It is only a joke, comrade. Come, let us share a drink of vodka."

The fuming MacGregor swallowed his ire and accepted the offer but as he told some of his colleagues later, the only thing he got from the "friendly" exchange was the worst hangover of his life.[4]

All pretense of friendliness vanished when he and Lain persisted in instructing the CFI on weaponry and military tactics. The Russians issued a warning by firing a couple of rounds near them; the message was loud and clear. It was cease and desist or risk having their legs shot. They ignored the threat and continued to carry out their duties but did so with the utmost discretion and secrecy.[5]

It was clear to Slovak partisans under Soviet commanders that the Russians were upset about Americans and Britons showing up on what they already considered Soviet turf. One Slovak unit commander stated in his report that the obvious goal of the Russian mission was to wrest control of the Slovak uprising from their CFI western Allies. One tactic they used was to have Soviet guerrilla commanders refuse any landings at the Tri Duby airstrip for flights from United States air bases carrying war supplies for the CFI, leaving the Slovak partisans desperately in need of weapons to carry on their fight.[6] Although hampered by the Soviet hostility and their lack of co–operation, each man of Dawes proceeded to carry out his particular assignment.

* * *

Agent Lieutenant Daniel Paveltich, a member of the Day team, which was to operate separately from Dawes, had been one of the swimmers who had challenged Gaul to a race while on an outing to the Aegean Sea during training at Bari. Like all previous challengers, he lost. A few days later, Paveltich's team was on the beach practicing throwing hand grenades when a newly commissioned Army lieutenant loped up, intent on turning the informal session into a boot camp by-the-book exercise. The startled Paveltich still had a grenade in his pocket and when he pulled it out, the spoon jumped up. He barely had time to hurl it as far as he could and yell out a warning before his teammates threw themselves to the ground seconds before the grenade exploded. The young shavetail was last seen running from the scene and managed to make himself scarce after that.[7]

Among the newer group deployed to Slovakia was Anthony Fortuni. After the Jews, gypsies were the next group scheduled for extermination by the Nazis.[8] Like Catlos, observer Grey pondered on what dapper Fortuni, a violinist who played gypsy music in finer cafes, could possibly be doing with these OSS men.

Like some of the other Dawes agents, Day team commander Capt. Edward Baranski had ties to Slovakia. The trim, energetic twenty-four-year-old was a serious, no-nonsense leader. An example is that while inspecting the plane being loaded before take-off from Bari, he became irate at discovering crates of toilet paper and blankets as part of the cargo, items he considered to be frivolities. He and his teammates heaved the crates aside and replaced them with others containing bazookas and machine guns. They crammed weapons onto the plane until every inch was filled. Grey later described Baranski as daring but having a short fuse, characteristics that were to work heavily against him later.[9]

Immediately upon landing at Banksa Bystrica on October 7, 1944, the Day team separated from the rest of the Dawes unit to establish their own mission in the village of Svolenska Slatina, twelve kilometers northwest of Banksa Bystrica. Team chief Baranski, with radio operator Daniel Paveltich and S/P agent Emil Tomes, set up operations in a house directly across the street from underground member John Svara, a house painter by trade. Before long, the Americans were eating their meals with the family, while their daughter Vera kept the Baranski and his men apprised of current enemy activities. This allowed the men to move about the area more easily and gather information on insurgents' activities and troop strength and transmit the collected data directly to OSS Bari. Their operation would continue smoothly until mid–October when enemy pressure accelerated.[10]

* * *

For more than a year, OSS interest in Hungary had been vital. In late 1943 they deployed a pair of OSS agents under the code name Sparrow to parachute into Hungary to conduct a mission. Their intent was to foment an anti–Nazi revolt, but the plan proved to be premature due to the lack of reliable information. However, in early October 1944, OSS London learned that Hungarian regent Nicholas Horthy was clandestinely seeking a separate peace

3. As the Uprising Collapses, the OSS Is Trapped   55

plan via the Vatican.[11] With Yugoslavia overrun by the Red Army, forcing German troops retreating from Greece and Yugoslavia to forge north and into Slovakia, with Poland and Romania capitulated, and now Hungary ready to defect, the OSS decided to try again.[12] This operation was the third segment of Dawes, its code name Bowery. The plan was for OSS agents Catlos and Keszthelyi to infiltrate the two Hungarian civilian agents they knew as Monsignor Francis Moly and Stephen Kora across the border into Hungary as close as possible to Budapest. OSS agents Keszthelyi and Catlos would facilitate the move. They would then wait for the radio message with the code words *Piros Rosa* (Crimson Rose), the title of a popular Hungarian folk song, before proceeding to implement the next step. This was to assist their contacts in the Hungarian underground to smuggle Horthy and top political leaders out of the country. Once this trick was accomplished, the OSS would attempt a daring maneuver. They would drop 1,200 Hungarian-speaking paratroopers, on alert in Bari, onto the air base of Margaret Island, located on the Danube River in the center of Budapest, and seize control of the city. However, for this bold project, they needed Russian assistance.[13]

On the night of October 10 Keszthelyi, accompanied by Green and Gaul, appeared at the Soviet compound to request that help. It was midnight and a bone-tired Maria had just fallen asleep on her cot when she felt the touch of a hand on her shoulder. It was Tamara whispering that Major Studensky wanted to see her. A bolt of alarm shot through Maria. "At this hour?" she asked. "What on earth for?"

"Some Americans are here and he needs you to translate."

Maria quickly pulled on her sweater and slipped into her shoes near the cot. Rubbing sleepy eyes, she patted her braids into place and clomped behind Tamara to where Studensky and the Americans waited. The Americans, it seemed, wanted to borrow a car and also needed a detailed map of the Hungarian border and area controlled by insurgents. Gaul's gunmetal gray eyes, even at that late hour, sparkled with vitality. He shoved his officer's cap back, revealing bushy light brown hair and leaned forward to place both hands on Studensky's desk. Gaul's imposing size and boldness inspired Studensky's immediate dislike of this brash American. When Studensky indicated that Maria was to interpret, Gaul turned to her.

"*Parlous vous Français?*"

"No."

"*Sprechen sie deutsche?*"

"Ja."

Gaul had a fair command of the German language and told her that Keszthelyi needed some information. Recognizing Keszthelyi's name as distinctly

Hungarian, Maria took the risk of incurring Studensky's displeasure and addressed him directly. "*Maganak szaksege van felvilogostos?*" ("Do you speak Hungarian?")[14]

Maria was attracted by his easy response and appealing smile and before long the conference quickly developed into a four-ring circus. It was conducted in Russian from Studensky, translated into Hungarian for Keszthelyi, then German for Gaul who then translated it into English for Green. Meanwhile, Studensky scowled, angry that he might be missing some bits of information being passed. Later, as Maria related the incident to a very interested Tamara, she summed it up as resembling one of those comic operas where everyone is talking in different languages while Studensky, as stooge, pretended that he did not understand German.

During the conference Maria had time to size up the Americans at close range. Tall, slender, Green's dark-eyed gaze was steady, but tension marred his aristocratic features and betrayed the calmness and control he evidently wanted to project.[15]

She found Gaul intimidating. He was one of the tallest men she had ever seen and the extraordinary height, big hands, broad shoulders and rugged features, made him seem to grow more imposing by the minute. His deep, resonant baritone telegraphed a take-charge manner and she wondered at first if he were the commander rather than the more formal, soft-spoken Green.[16]

Maria tried to appear unaffected by Keszthelyi's scrutiny. Handsome as a movie star, he was not as tall as Green or Gaul, but his trim physique was capped by lustrous dark, wavy hair and his luminous chocolate brown eyes were captivating.

Studensky was his imperious self and controlled the meeting by not betraying his knowledge of German. This ruse allowed him to carefully scrutinize the Americans while they talked with Maria. However, by the time the Americans left, they had obtained Studensky's grudging promise of the loan of a car and carried with them a blown-up map of the border and area held by the insurgents. As they were leaving, Keszthelyi flashed Maria a smile and she felt her face grow warm. However, it left Studensky grumpy.

"These *Amerikanski* are not soldiers," he snipped with a contemptuous snort. "They're only bourgeois cowboys."[17]

On the night of October 12, Keszthelyi and Catlos successfully infiltrated Moly and Kora across the Hungarian border. Tension mounted while they waited to receive the prearranged coded message from Moly and Kora.[18]

However, when Keszthelyi appeared at the Russian compound a day or two later, it was for a different purpose. It was to invite Maria to join the Americans for dinner at the Narodne Dom hotel. Maria was surprised. The

3. As the Uprising Collapses, the OSS Is Trapped 57

Maria Gulovich is the interpreter for Russian partisans as well as the Dawes commanders lieutenants James Holt and James Gaul in Banska Bystrica (courtesy the Museum of the Uprising Archives).

Russians never asked her to share a meal with them and proper Slovak women did not venture out on their own unescorted, so she gladly accepted. It marked the first of several occasions when she joined the Americans for dinner. She found them to be quite different from European military men. They welcomed her as a desired guest and although their English for a time was mostly unintelligible, she chatted amiably with Keszthelyi and Catlos in Hungarian, Horvath and others in Slovak, and occasionally with Lt. Francis Perry in German. Throughout, she felt a glow of appreciation for these American men risking their lives to help Slovakia.[19]

After that first pleasant occasion, upon returning to her room at the Krutels, Maria glanced out the window to catch a glimpse of dozens of American bombers heading to home base in Italy following a raid. Two were crippled and dropped behind. She fervently prayed for them to make it and was relieved when the two aircraft regained speed and caught up and kept pace with the others.[20]

As enemy troops came closer to the city, the OSS position grew more tenuous and Green ordered some of their heavy equipment moved to Brezno, forty kilometers distant. Gaul supervised the transfer of materials handled by MacGregor, Lain, and Dunlevy.[21]

The need for more weapons was acute and on the morning of October 12, Donovan had personally delivered a memo to officials in Washington, D.C., with Green's request to supply the CFI with 2000 Tommy guns, 5,000 rifles, 300 bazookas, 50 Marlin guns and ammunition for all the weapons. Before action could be taken, though, exiled Czech leaders Jan Masaryk and Edvard Beneš, fearful of offending the Soviets, scotched the idea.[22] And while General Rudof Viest, who arrived on October 4 to replace Golian, awaited the arrival of more weapons, the revolt erupted.[23]

Added to this Czech resistance to more sorties into Slovakia was the refusal of the 15th Air Force to permit further use of their planes to deliver war supplies. They stated they would co-operate in airmen evacuations only. This denial of help did not deter the OSS. Through Supreme Headquarters Allied Expeditionary Force (SHEAF), OSS Bari arranged a third sortie set for the night of October 18. They would use a plane from the Balkan Air Force division to deploy the materials.[24]

On October 13, Hitler's Abwehr army intelligence agency force advised him that Regent Horthy had signed an armistice with the Allies and was preparing to defect to the Russians. Two days later, Nazi SS kidnapped his young son and held him hostage. The next day Horthy resigned under force and German troops seized control of Budapest and replaced Hungarian guards with German occupation troops patrolling the border with trained police dogs. By mid–October, Red Army forces had overrun most of Hungary to Lake Balaton, except for Budapest where twelve German divisions stood in their path.[25] Their heavy enemy reinforcements halted the advance of the Red Army's Second Ukrainian front four miles from the city. The fierce stand-off was to last from October 19 into February 1945, at the cost of 30,000 casualties.[26]

It was also to destroy any hope of Catlos and Keszthelyi implementing the dramatic Bowery plan for American paratroopers to capture Budapest.

From October onwards, after the Russians broke through the Dukla Pass, the German 6th Army would move steadily towards the Carpathian Mountains in northern Slovakia to focus attention on the revolt, the last such uprising that Hitler would have to contend with in the war.[27]

* * *

At the same time, in Zvolenska Slatina, informers had discovered and reported on the presence of the Day unit and its operations. Enemy commanders ordered a diligent search for Baranski and his men. The Day unit

3. As the Uprising Collapses, the OSS Is Trapped

radioed their last messages to OSS Bari on October 12 and 16. With a supply of Pall Mall cigarettes that enabled them to buy needed items, they escaped by secreting their uniforms in the Zvara house and going into hiding, frequently changing disguises.[28] There would be no further contact between Day and the OSS in Bari.

* * *

On October 17, powerful German reinforcements poured over the Slovakian border from northern Hungary, an area poorly protected by CFI partisans. Under the command of ruthless SS chief Heinrich Himmler, specially trained anti–partisan fighters surged in, determined to wipe out partisan units once and for all. The dreaded Direlanger and Kaminski brigades that had decimated the Polish Home Army in Warsaw were joined by the First Tank Army, and, with the notorious Schell Battalion and the 18th Horst Wessel troops, they surrounded the area held by insurgents to launch the final offensive.[29]

The Soviet 38th Army and Czech 1st Army attempted to come to the aid of the insurgents but were halted by the XXIV Panzer Division, leaving the insurgents trapped as Free Slovakia was assaulted from eleven points when tanks moved in and aerial bombing of Banska Bystrica and other towns held by the rebels began in earnest.[30] The ferocious German attack brought the CFI front to total collapse on all sides, opening the way for anti–partisan Nazi Stormtroopers to rampage through the area, killing everyone in their path without pity, including women and children. General Ludvig Svoboda tried to aid the insurgents and suffered 80,000 casualties trying to escape into the hills where they either died in combat or later as captives in concentration camps.[31]

Until the last moment, Keszthelyi and Catlos attempted to contact Moly and Kora by radio but there was no response. Acknowledging the hopeless situation of the mission to make further efforts, Green radioed Bari for help:

> Request aerial supply and evacuation for Americans and two British airmen. Landing site open 3–4 days at most. Urgent.[32]

The situation for the Americans grew increasingly precarious. As more airmen were brought into town by CFI partisans for evacuation, Green frantically sought a way to get them and his men out. He had been angry since October 7 when the additional fourteen men were sent to enlarge the mission despite his specific requests to not send more men. He was also angry at the at the 15th Air Force, which on October 24, acting on information radioed by Dawes, bombed a V-2 Rocket plant near Bratislava. Green had readied his men for evacuation and under MacGregor's leadership, the airmen and most of the OSS agents were transported to Tri Duby. But the Air Force refused to honor Green's urgent plea to evacuate his men. After a day spent waiting and listening to shelling coming ever closer, it was obvious that further waiting was futile and MacGregor escorted the disappointed men back to town.[33]

A desperate Green pursued one last chance. Accompanied by Gaul and Morton, he appealed to Studensky for assistance. This time Gaul was aware that the wily Russian spoke German and directed the request for help in evacuation directly to him. "We have no room," was the stony-faced Studensky's brusque reply. Then pointing a finger at Morton, he said, "Maybe we can take him."

Morton, who had arrived on October 7 with the second deployment, had changed his mind about returning to Bari with the airmen evacuated that day. He'd been impressed with the Slovaks' determination to carry out the uprising and was sympathetic to their cause. A few days earlier he'd told John Trachta, reporter for the Slovak government newspaper *Narodne Obrada*, that he would make it to Zvolen and then get out from there, saying, "I'm out to get the biggest story of my life." Now presented with a chance for evacuation on a Russian plane, he declined, offering his place to wounded airmen.[34] But Studensky refused to consider a switch. It was Morton or no one.

Gaul was incensed. "You've got lots of room on *our* American C-47s," he spat out.

His protest was futile. Studensky coldly dismissed them to prepare for his own departure with the last of the Soviet guerrilla officers and reporters being evacuated. Green, wearing a worried expression, Morton very subdued, and Gaul spouting expletives at Studensky who had never played straight with them, angrily stalked out.[35]

The final bit of irony was that the evacuation sortie planned for October 18 was delayed for a week by bad weather in Italy. By the time the plane at OSS Bari lifted off for Tri Duby on October 25, it was too late. The landing strip had fallen to the enemy. German invasion troops, solidly massed around Banska Bystrica, entrapped the collapsing CFI, along with the Americans, changing what hopes for rescue remained into despair.[36]

For seventy days, with almost no Western or Soviet help, the Slovak CFI rebels had withstood the superior German military might, but they could not last much longer CFI leaders and partisans prepared for one last defensive stand before surrendering the city to enemy forces.[37]

Hour by hour the noose tightened. The belated arrival of a Russian trained Czechoslovak brigade was of little help. With obsolete weapons they were no match for the seasoned, well-armed Wehrmacht. And to no one's surprise, the parachute brigades promised by the Soviets failed to materialize.[38] The crushing end of the revolt was imminent.

That last morning, Studensky approached Maria with a smile. Usually frugal, he handed her a wad of korunas and advised her to buy heavy boots which she would need in the mountains. Tamara whispered to Maria that she would go with her. The two young women were delighted to have a break from the unrelenting work. Maria bought the last pair of leather boots available and Tamara found woolen knit socks and a warm shirt for her wounded soldier husband in a Kiev hospital. For the first time, the colleagues were able to share bits of their backgrounds over a cup of tea and it was a pleasant interlude. "It was hard for me to master the Morse code and then transmit it fast enough to earn a certificate," Tamara confided. "But a friend helped me and I passed the tests. I was working with General Konev's field operations when Studensky recruited me for his intelligence operations in Slovakia. I didn't want to leave Kiev, but..."

At that point Tamara stopped, a sudden unease apparent at perhaps having revealed too much. They both knew she had had no choice. Obedience to a superior's orders was mandatory for all Russians. Maria felt it expedient to say nothing of her experiences as underground courier and ventured only a partial account of her involvement.

"Since I know several languages, I was recruited to help the CFI and then the Soviets with battlefield translations."[39]

The interlude had been all too brief and they reluctantly returned to Soviet headquarters, where they encountered a glowering Studensky and Mikhail. "Where have you been all this time? Who did you talk to?" Studensky thundered.

Aghast at the verbal attack on a cowering Tamara, Maria tried to intervene with an explanation but Studensky stopped her with a belligerent shout. "This matter does not concern you! Return to your work at once!"

When his dressing down of Tamara ended, Studensky and Mikhail set about emptying files into briefcases. Maria and Tamara were ordered to burn remaining documents. They worked frantically to the background roar of mortar shells and exploding artillery. When they finished, Studensky and Mikhail dashed outside to a waiting car while Tamara, lugging the heavy shortwave radio, staggered behind them. Before bolting out the door, Studensky issued one last order to Maria. "Take care of things until we get back!"

To a stunned Maria, the empty rooms and spooky silence were more ominous than the sounds of a city under siege. She ventured to the town square, curious to find out what it was like when there was no government or authority in control. Anarchy abounded. Drunken partisans broke wine and beer kegs open and drank from the spigots, sloshing around ankle deep in froth. Others broke security doors and shattered windows to indulge in looting on a grand scale. Arguments and fights between looters broke out. She likened it to a scene from Dante's *Inferno*.[40]

Shocked and disgusted, Maria ran to the Krutel home only to find another nightmare in progress. Wounded CFI partisans were sprawled throughout the house. Three lay on her bed, turning the covering and sheets bloody. She grabbed what was left of her clothing, consisting of a light raincoat, a pair of slacks and two sweaters and stuffed them into a cloth satchel. A weary Joseph Krutel paused in his ministrations to the wounded men, most of them mere boys.

"Maria, Maria, what are you going to do?"

Taking a last look around the Krutel home that had welcomed her, Maria said, "I have to go back and wait for the Russians to come back."

She reached out to farewell embraces from Anna and Joseph Krutel preparing to minister to another arriving group of the wounded. Hugging Maria closely, Anna sighed and murmured, "Only God can help us now."

Maria ran through streets littered with bodies, stark evidence that the law of gun and gallows had taken over. Near the entrance to the Infantry Building two wild-eyed men raced past. One shoved her aside and shouted, "Death to the traitors!" and fired at the other man, who slumped to the ground. The shooter then whirled to fire at Maria. A bullet ruffled her hair as she hurled herself through the door and locked it. She raced up the three flights of stairs to the Russian quarters, listening for sounds of her pursuer before she slumped into a chair to catch her breath and decide what to do. She would wait an hour, and if the Russians did not return, she would leave and try to find a way out of town on her own. Suddenly, footsteps pounding up the stairs set her heart to racing. She frantically looked around for a place to hide. The shooter had come to kill her![41]

The door burst open but it was not the gunman. It was MacGregor, Keszthelyi and Horvath, who were as startled to see her as she was to see them.

"Why are you still here?" Keszthelyi asked.

"I'm to wait for the Russians to come back."

The men exchanged cynical grins and let out a couple of sharp expletives. "Those Russki bastards are not coming back!" MacGregor told her firmly. "You can't stay here."

Suddenly confused, Maria tried to assess her situation while the men exchanged rapid fire words that Keszthelyi then relayed to Maria in Hungarian: "Forget those Russki bastards, Maria! You don't stand a chance with them."

3. As the Uprising Collapses, the OSS Is Trapped 63

When Maria hesitated, MacGregor fixed her with a stern look. "Your CFI leaders and partisans are abandoning their sinking ship. Your only chance is to come with us." Even with curly brown hair askew, and pant legs stuffed into the top of paratrooper boots, he looked every inch a leader. He ordered them to destroy all communications before bolting down the stairs to find transportation.[42]

Shaken at the callous duplicity of the Russians she'd worked with, Maria was glad that, unlike Gen. Golian, she had refused to reveal names of Slovak anti-communists to Studensky as he'd demanded, saving them from brutal communist reprisals.[43] She set about helping Keszthelyi and Horvath rip out phones and cut all wires, leaving not a single line intact for German use. They were demolishing the main switchboard when MacGregor burst into the room just as a shell exploded right outside.

"We've got to get out now! I'm sure as hell not going to hang around to be captured by any Nazi bastards!"[44]

Maria grabbed her satchel and pelted down the stairs with the Americans to the school bus MacGregor had commandeered. They clambered aboard and he gunned the engine and took off. At the villa he picked up some of the anxious airmen. With artillery shells bombarding the town and Stukas zooming overhead unleashing death and destruction, the bus merged with a long line of evacuees heading for Donavaly, a resort in the mountains twenty kilometers north. Enemy troops were now only four kilometers from the center of town.[45]

Behind them, the scene at OSS headquarters was pandemonium. Machine gun bullets ricocheted off buildings and mortar shells whistled overhead, landing with ominous thuds punctuated by explosions. Frantic to ensure that all the Americans were accounted for, Green ordered Catlos, Perry and Dunlevy to the hotel to make sure all their men were out. The three men darted on a zigzag course through the melee to the entrance to the Narodne Dom hotel at the exact moment a mortar shell landed with a thud nearby. They dove into the nearest brush and covered their ears. When the ground stopped shaking, Catlos leaped to his feet and ran for the door. He knew that the Germans had excellent direction finders and the hotel would be a prime target for destruction. One corner of the roof above the lobby was blown off. From beneath the sturdy oaken bar, a bartender, bits of plaster clinging to his hair and torn shirt crawled out when Catlos banged a fist on the bar and demanded "*Pivo*!" ("Beer!")

The dazed man shook his head in disbelief at the "*Blaznivi Amerikanski!*" ("Crazy Americans!") and pointed with trembling hand to a rack of beer steins on the wall. Catlos grabbed a couple and filled them with the foaming brew which he and Perry quaffed down until an irate Dunlevy yelled, "This is a helluva time for a damned beer bust!"

The trio then raced through the hotel checking rooms and found all their men had left. They pelted back to the villa to do one last thing; it was to notify OSS Bari that their mission was ended and they had to flee for their lives.[46]

On the afternoon of October 26, the following message was transmitted:

> Do not ... Repeat ... Do not send any more supplies. Enemy closing in. Evacuating Banska Bystrica in the morning.[47]

That was the last of the Dawes messages from Banska Bystrica. These had consisted of a thousand cipher groups a day dispensed between September 18 and October 26. The intelligence information they sent was fresh in content, full, accurate, and the only source of information about the revolt for American agencies in the Mediterranean theater of war. It was also the principal source of information for OSS London. The mission had accomplished this feat despite being hampered by having only one receiver, the other one constantly jammed by the Nazis.[48]

The twenty-one airmen now with the Dawes men had been brought into Banska Bystrica by CFI partisans dressed in civilian clothing to confuse the enemy and informers. Rescuers were paid in gold coins. The newly arrived flyers, most in their early twenties and anticipating evacuation, unlike the men in the mission, were not fully cognizant of the precariousness of their situation. Furthermore, they were still in summer uniforms and totally unprepared for the cold mountain climate.[49]

When the enemy offensive accelerated, the Russians had sent in two prominent guerrilla leaders from the general staff of the Partisan Movement in Kiev, although no high ranking Soviets were sent to Banska Bystrica. They were mostly second grade officers and troops. Gen. Asmolov assumed command of the Soviet guerrillas and the Slovak insurgents under their domination, replacing Slovak Gen. Ludvig Svoboda. One opinion is that Asmolov was to form guerrilla bands to counterattack the Slovak National Uprising itself. An underling of Asmolov was Maj. Mikhail Sukayev, who arrived from Ukraine to command the 2,500 members of the S. S. Stalin guerrilla unit, one of the largest of the Soviet guerrilla force.[50] Michael Fedornak, leader of a small Slovak partisan unit, later reported how these two tough, seasoned officers were hostile to the Americans and British and did not even consider co–operation with them, just as they hadn't with the CFI. According to him, it was because the Soviets considered America and England as their enemies and fully expected to end up fighting against the Allies.[51] This belief would play an important part in the fate of the OSS men.

3. As the Uprising Collapses, the OSS Is Trapped

Lieutenants Green (center) and Jerry Mican (left) conferring with Major Sehmer of the British war mission (courtesy the Museum of the Uprising Archives).

The British unit that had arrived in Banska Bystrica first was also the first to leave, vacating Banska Bystrica just before the revolt erupted. On October 27, Fedornak was on patrol with two of his men when they ran into Major Ernest Sehmer and his team in a hunting lodge on the south side of Vrlica Mountain. With them was Margita Koscova, an American Slovak who told him she came to Slovakia to care for her dying grandmother and was trapped when the revolt erupted. She told Fedornak that she knew that the Russians did not like them and asked him if their group could join his partisans. He relayed the request to his superior, Soviet Captain Kudinov, who bristled at the idea.

"What the devil are these spies doing in Slovakia?" he bellowed. "The best thing to do is hand them over to the Germans."[52]

Instead, Fedornak discreetly advised Koscova to make contact with Slovak partisans and set up a base near them. He had one of his men help them relocate, certain that they'd be robbed and killed if they remained in the vicinity of the Russians. He recalled a recent incident where he and his unit had been questioned by communist guerrillas after which he led his unit back to camp by changing directions to avoid being followed and killed to ensure that they did not reveal whereabouts of the guerrilla camps.[53]

This unexpected and galling Soviet hostility that Green noted from the outset was, no doubt, a deciding factor for the commander to throw in his lot with the Slovak CFI. His concern about the disorganization of the large group was outweighed by their ability to obtain food and to have some protection by natives who knew the country. Besides, it would be easier to cross Russian lines under a Czech leader.[54]

Another irritation for Green was Schwartz, who wanted to remain in Banska Bystrica and operate independently. He turned sullen when Green ordered him to stay with Dawes because his expertise in languages and knowledge of the terrain and partisan operations was needed.[55]

By late afternoon of October 26, most of the Americans and Maria were on the road to Donavaly with only Green and a few others tarrying in Banska Bystrica to dispose of equipment. The specially trained Nazi anti-partisan warriors would now turn their venomous attention fully against those in flight: citizens, CFI partisans, Soviet guerrillas, and the Americans. All remaining Jews, presumed to be pro-communist, would be rounded up and deported to death camps. The Jesuits in Rezumborak and others who tried to hide them would have little success. Lastly and sadly, Allied airmen shot down in the mountains would no longer find a safe refuge in Slovakia.[56]

Until the uprising and during the existence of the Slovak state, Tiso had issued no death sentences for political reasons and the death penalty was

3. As the Uprising Collapses, the OSS Is Trapped

abolished. That safeguard changed with a vengeance when he lost control of his government by the revolt and the Germans seized power. The result was the loss of 30,000 Slovak lives to Nazi "justice."[57]

The Germans reserved a particular hatred for partisans and wasted no time building gallows in every village for their hanging. Captives were tortured, first with fingers broken and holes burned in the soles of the feet. Women had breasts amputated before being shot. Anyone under suspicion of giving assistance of any sort to partisans was in danger of a horrible death. Hitler's propaganda view of partisan war was that it served a purpose: "It gives us a chance to exterminate those who oppose us."[58]

The barbarity shown by German occupation troops stunned the Slovaks. Barbed wire curtains came down and two hundred villages were burned, but only after pillaging for all metal on locks, door hinges and machinery. Posters of CFI leaders and known underground agents with a price on their heads were plastered around each town. The crushing financial cost of the occupation would ruin the Slovak economy; however, that paled when compared with the irreparable loss of thousands of lives.[59]

On October 28, 1944, President Roosevelt sent a communiqué to Beneš stating: "We, the Americans, greet our Czechoslovak friends in arms, who have contributed so much to the liberation of their own country and other European countries. This greeting belongs to our friends in war who came to help us from all around the world."[60] The words were of little solace to the beleaguered people.

Ironically, one of Green's early reports now proved to be grimly prophetic. "I think of it as a tragedy that help didn't arrive. The CFI situation looks hopeless. They are left with three options: pull out and defend smaller areas, break into smaller units and operate from the mountains and forests, or try to break through to the Red Army front lines."[61]

For the Americans, though, options had dwindled to one. It was to run and hide in the mountains and keep moving until they met up with the Red Army front. Their enemies would be not only skilled anti-partisan troops in deadly pursuit and informers eager to betray them, but also punishing exposure to blizzards, starvation, exhaustion, illness and unrelenting fear.

4

A Resourceful Maria Joins the Team

The narrow, winding road to Donavaly was lined with ditches and brush that offered some shelter from bombing and strafing, a preview of what was to come. Maria described their headlong flight from Banska Bystrica as similar to the evacuation of Saigon at the end of the Vietnam War as shown on television. Like those hordes of frantic, shoving Vietnamese trying to push their way aboard the last American planes and helicopters, the OSS contingency, CFI partisans, Russian guerrillas, units of the Slovak State Army and terrified civilians made the same kind of mad scramble out of Banska Bystrica.[1]

The road was jammed with buses, cars, trucks, charcoal-powered conversion vehicles and ox-drawn carts. Slogging along on foot were weary CFI partisans, most of whom were ragged and dirty. Trailing behind was a long line of civilians, many of them young parents pulling toddlers on toy wagons loaded with their possessions, or carrying small children on their backs.[2]

At the first sight of the Nazi's diving, screeching bombers, MacGregor let out a bellow. "Out! Hit the ditches!" As they tumbled out and grabbed the first spot they thought provided protection, the Focke-Wulfs and Messerschmitt 109s swooped low overhead to mercilessly riddle the panic-stricken refugees with bullets. Moans of the wounded and dying and whimpering children were mingled with the ear-splitting shrill whine of bomber engines. Maria, with the Americans and other quick-thinking escapees, dove under a concrete abutment off of which reverberated the terrified cries of the hapless trying to evade the steady rain of bullets. Even dusk did not dispel the attack because navigators dropped flares to pinpoint clusters of refugees picked out for further strafing. Only dark clouds overhead finally put an end to the deadly assault.[3]

One of the Dawes men meeting Maria for the first time during the

4. A Resourceful Maria Joins the Team

evacuation from Banska Bystrica was Sgt. Kenneth Dunlevy. He had arrived with the October 7 deployment and remembered taking note of the tall, slender blonde, pretty enough to be a model, and wondering how a looker like that got mixed up in this bedlam. Relating the event years later, Dunlevy said he could never have imagined at the time what a crucial role this extraordinary girl would play in his life, an impact that he would never forget.[4]

The small village of Donavaly was soon overwhelmed with refugees, State Army soldiers and CFI partisans and Soviet guerrillas. The scene was mass confusion. Exhausted men sprawled everywhere, all fire and fight having left them. They watched dully as guerrilla commanders, including Yegerov, ordered documents to be dowsed with gasoline and burned.[5]

At the Sports Hotel where military officers had rooms, Dunlevy caught a glimpse of Green and Gaul huddled at a table with General Viest, whose drawn features reflected deep worry. Dunlevy had reason to be worried himself. As the only cryptographer who had memorized all the Dawes codes he would be a valuable captive for the Germans eager to learn about OSS operations. He had every reason to believe that interrogation and torture would be relentless.[6]

Maria was one of the lucky civilians who obtained shelter when Keszthelyi insisted she take his and MacGregor's room. Commenting on her small satchel and light clothing, Keszthelyi surprised her later by showing up with an armload of U.S. Army winter clothing. The weatherproof parka, woolen pants, underwear, socks and sturdy paratrooper boots would later save her from freezing to death. However, that night she fell into bed and slept like one of the dead she'd seen on the road to Donavaly.[7]

Early next morning, Studensky knocked on the door and ordered Maria to vacate the room and then asked her to cook a chunk of pork someone had given him. She surrendered the room, but refused to cook the meat. She felt a fresh surge of disgust at how callously the Soviets treated anyone when they were no longer of use to them.[8]

The ski resort of Donavaly was green and lush in summer and crusted with ice in winter. Around it were meadows where deer and sheep grazed and children played. But the bucolic ambience was misleading. A short distance away were the Tatra Mountains, a challenge in good weather and forbidding in inclement weather. The Sports Hotel, situated on top of a mountain, presented an ideal target for bombing. Upon arrival, MacGregor and Lain set up a defense by positioning four anti-aircraft guns at strategic points and posted sentries to monitor the progress of the pursuing enemy. A few days earlier, they and Gaul had explored Donavaly as a possible site should evacuation plans from Banska Bystrica fall through. Unfortunately, the four guns were spotted at daybreak the following morning and a flock of J-88s and Messerschmitt 109s swarmed overhead and quickly obliterated them. The attackers then turned their sights on the hotel, sending occupants scurrying outside for cover.[9]

Maria frantically sought a place to hide. From below the hotel, she could hear shouts in German and Slovak from advancing fighters. When a bomber dropped low looking for more victims, she threw herself onto the ground under low-lying brush, recited a prayer and resigned herself to death. Her ears were filled with the sharp ack-ack of crackling machine gun fire that became a steady echo bouncing off the mountains while a film of thick fog, clammy as ghostly ectoplasm, rolled in. When it lifted for a moment, she turned her head to catch a glimpse of black boots of a type worn only by the Gestapo or German soldiers. This sent her burrowing deeper into the brush, shielding her head with her hands. When the blanket of fog lifted again, she peeked through spread out fingers to look for the boots. They and the man wearing them were gone. Rising up slightly and then leaning forward in a low crouch, Maria dashed across the road seeking a better spot to hide. Suddenly, like a mirage, Jan from her courier days, rode up on a horse. He told her Banska Bystrica was occupied and surrounded with barbed wire and buildings were plastered with posters of the most wanted. He also told Maria that her face was on one of them with a reward offered for her capture or information on her whereabouts. Executions for those apprehended had already begun. Telling her that the Americans she asked about were in the forest, he damned the Russians and communists with them to hell and galloped off, like Paul Revere and William Dawes in the Revolutionary War, to warn others.[10]

When the attack abated, Colonel Dobrovsky rounded up the remnants of his Slovak Army units for a final briefing. Victor Frudenfels was one of his officers who was to remember the day and his commander's words vividly:

> Boys, this is it. I have nothing left to feed you, and no arms or ammunition. This is the end of our military mission. You are free to do whatever you choose, to go to your home and family or join the CFI partisans in the Dumbier and Krolova Hola region and fight with them, or wait for the Red Army.

It was clear that the Slovak National Uprising had been defeated and all that remained were mop-up operations. They would attack from mountain passes now that the village was surrounded. Frudenfels refused to take up arms against his own government and remained loyal to the Slovak state. He took off for home, hoping to reach it safely and hide there until the war ended. Instead, on November 1, 1944, he was betrayed by an informer, captured and imprisoned in a German POW camp. When the war ended, he was shipped to Russia from which he escaped and eventually found sanctuary in the United States.[11]

The Slovak armed revolt against the Germans and the Slovak state government that lasted seventy days with almost no Allied help came to an end at Donavaly. The cost of the upheaval in human lives, property and monies remained to be tallied. In Banska Bystrica and nearby towns, enemy troops indulged in a killing spree, shooting on the spot local communists and anyone suspected of aiding partisans. And word had gone out that the Nazis were hellbent on clearing out the Lower Tatra Mountains of partisans' nests once and for all.[12]

Green divided his group of thirty-seven men into four units, led by himself, Perry, Gaul and MacGregor. Their destination was the Klement Gottwald Soviet guerrilla camp in the Prasiva mountain range. Beyond Donavaly, he told them, they would be in territory totally controlled by the enemy and extreme vigilance was crucial. The last message from the area of the uprising to OSS Bari was tapped out on October 28:

> Leaving for the mountains with the CFI. Divided into four groups for faster movement. Enemy coming closer.[13]

Meanwhile, masses of German soldiers were on the move towards the center of Slovakia and the Baruch valley where Fedornak and a large number of partisan units were encamped. It was an ideal spot for Russian pilots to drop bags of supplies with alcohol, medicines and food. From his association with the Russians, Fedornak understood their mentality. A prime example was Colonel Sukayev, commander of three thousand Soviet guerrillas, dispersed throughout the Tatra Mountains. Like other Soviet commanders, Sukayev was suspicious of all civilians, any of whom might inform the Germans of his location to collect the large bounty on his head. He made it clear to Fedornak that neither he nor his guerrillas would provide any comfort or aid to the Anglos.[14]

The Americans set off for the forested mountains with Colonel Vladimir Prykryl's 2,500 partisan Czech Brigade. Before leaving, the CFI abandoned their wounded. Echoes of gunshots resounded in the air, fired by those choosing to die by their own hand rather than be captured, tortured, and then shot by enemy captors. Food and medicine were non-existent. For those helplessly trapped in makeshift medical centers, there was only a spoonful of soup and a sip of vodka to ease their pain and dull the fear. One Slovak partisan commander remembered how Yegerov lounged at a table with a glass of cognac in his hand and plenty of food before him while not far away his wounded, sick, hungry men lay dying.[15]

For Maria, it was a crucial moment. She had to decide her next move. There was little hope of getting back home safely and even if she succeeded, her mere presence would endanger her family because of the bounty on her head. She did not want to be a burden to anyone and she pondered on how and where she could fit in and pull her own weight. Trying to make it on her own would be foolhardy. Constant risk of betrayal from state loyalists or enemy informers ruled out shelter in villages or hamlets because anyone daring to aid her would place his own life and that of his family on the line. And wandering about by herself would invite abuse by hardened, female-starved guerrillas and partisans. The friendlier Americans were her best hope of survival. Making her way towards them, she ran directly into Schwartz.[16]

Schwartz was to leave a definite impression upon some other members of the mission. Dunlevy was one of those who did not like or trust him, describing Schwartz as arrogant and god-like with a chip on his shoulder.[17] Those characteristics were clearly displayed during his confrontation with Maria.

"Tell me the truth, are you a Russian?"

"No, I was only translating for the CFI."

"So you're a communist?"

Maria found his question to be incredible. Every Slovak knew that any person with a clergyman in the family was anathema to the communists. "With my father a priest?" she retorted.

"Then why are you always hanging around us?"

"I guess I like Americans better than Russians."

Noting the charged exchange, Keszthelyi hastened to intervene. Later he would refer to Schwartz as an "arrogant bastard," but at the moment, Keszthelyi only shot him a warning glance which sent the glowering Schwartz stomping off. Keszthelyi then asked Maria if she would be able to get home safely. When she told him she was in the underground too deeply to risk such a chance, he urged her to stay close to the Americans, although their own options were hazy.[18]

The CFI partisans, as Green had stated in an early report, had three options: they could concentrate their forces and defend a smaller area, they could fight through to the Russian front lines, or they could break into small units and retreat into the hills and forests to continue hit-and-run guerrilla style fighting. For the Americans, their best bet was to remain with Prykryl's brigade, at least until they reached Prasiva.[19]

The trail through the woods was narrow, slippery and treacherous, worsened when a thick pea-soup fog rolled over them like a blanket. Ahead lay a challenging pass over the Kozi Chrbat, known as the "Goat's Back" because

4. A Resourceful Maria Joins the Team

of its tight confines, and it was sure to slow progress. Partisan patrols they encountered warned that the pass would be cut off by the enemy and they had only a short time to transverse it.[20]

It was six o'clock in the morning when they started out for Prasiva. Their first scare came at noon when a patrol reported enemy campfires in the Jesenko valley just ahead that they had to cross. Observing his men, but especially the airmen, laboring under heavy loads as they climbed, Green called a brief halt near the village of Norjnica and ordered them to lighten their packs. Paris had hidden his large camera in a barn outside Donavaly and, salvaging only lenses and a small camera, he destroyed some of the unexposed film for his large camera. Others gave away food, which was a grave mistake because they would desperately need every crumb before long. Catlos dropped their only radio and, since it was broken, he discarded it.[21] This act so enraged Keszthelyi that he told Maria he'd have Catlos court-martialed when they got back to their base. His rationale was that he could have dismantled the radio and divided the parts for men to carry to later reassemble.[22]

Associated Press correspondent Joseph Morton clutched his portable typewriter and watched with dismay as naval photographer Nelson Paris disposed of film intended for photos that were to accompany his articles on the uprising and the mission. As it turned out, their concern was needless; the supposed German troops in the valley were actually deserting Slovak State Army soldiers trying to make it home safely and seeking warmth from fires as the murky mist turned into a freezing drizzle.[23]

Maria was outraged to see Mikhail of the Studensky intelligence unit tossing extra winter garments onto the ground and stomping them into the mud. He refused to donate them to others, and hereby cast a cold glance at the wet, chilled airmen who had no warm clothing. Any lingering positive feelings she may still have had for her former Soviet colleagues were shattered forever because of their callous acts.[24]

Sounds of artillery and gunfire receded as they pushed on. The rain turned the valley ground into a sea of mud. After a couple of hours, Green called another halt to confer with Gaul and Prykryl, while the waiting men stood around in miserable clusters. They moved ahead again after Prykryl assigned the Americans a guide familiar with the area to lead them across the slushy valley to another mountain range. The woods were crowded with escapees in flight: CFI partisans, a smattering of Jews and French partisans, and Slovak army soldiers who'd donned peasant clothing hoping to escape detection. The four groups of Americans began the climb up two thousand meters and didn't stop until dusk.[25]

Some of the OSS men whacked off pine boughs to create shelters on the freezing ground to escape from the relentless drizzle, while MacGregor and Horvath coaxed damp twigs and sticks into a sputtering fire. The flyers in dank summer uniforms huddled close to the barely flickering flames trying to dry off their clothing. As the cold, clammy nightfall enveloped them, the attention of Catlos, squatting on his heels with his back against a gnarled tree trunk, was focused on a couple of the youthful airmen who were coughing and appeared ill. Like Dunlevy, Catlos wondered what had happened to the warm winter clothing they had brought into Banska Bystrica on the planes in which they arrived. In his official report he was to describe their grim plight tersely; "it is going to be a long, cold winter with a bad time ahead."[26]

The morning of October 31 was a milestone day for Maria. It dawned on a bleak grayness. She was leaning against a tree, face half immersed in the hood of her U.S. Army parka, when Keszthelyi came to tell her that Green wanted to speak with her. Still uncomfortable with the Americans because she did not speak English, with some trepidation Maria approached the commander standing to one side with a diffident Gaul. Keszthelyi relayed to leave "as is" Green's request to recruit her as guide and interpreter.[27] Seven of the Dawes men were fluent in Slovak, Czech, Hungarian and German, but none among them spoke Russian. Maria's familiarity with Soviet guerrilla operations and their mind-set, and also her linguistic expertise, would be invaluable when they intercepted Russians as they proceeded further east.[28]

Catlos praised the decision both verbally and in his written reports. He stated that Maria was a valuable asset because she was not only familiar with the political and military situation before the Dawes team arrived, but also she was the only one in their group who dared enter Nazi-occupied villages to seek food, shelter, and information. She was also acquainted with most of the Soviet guerrilla leaders and therefore might be able to inveigle whatever co-operation they might be willing to offer.[29]

A hesitant Maria told Green

The captivating Lt. Tibor Keszthelyi, who won Maria's heart in Banska Bystrica.

4. A Resourceful Maria Joins the Team   75

that she was still under orders to Viest, at which Green then informed her that the general was not venturing any further with his CFI, forces; instead, he was rejoining Golian in the village of Bukovec. He urged Maria to ask Viest for a release.[30]

Maria recalled how unfailingly courteous the CFI commander had been on the occasions she encountered him at Soviet headquarters in Banska Bystrica. Like her, Viest had not abandoned the cause of democracy. Now, however, the tatters of his democratic ideals had to be faced realistically. She stood aside for a minute and observed him, grave-faced, with fair hair brushed neatly back, picking his way through the litter of rifles, sub-machine guns, and hundreds of rounds of ammunition strewn along the muddy trail and mountainsides. They'd been discarded by the soldiers of his routed CFI Army. He moved haltingly and appeared to be in a daze.[31]

Viest had assumed command of the CFI insurgents shortly before the Americans arrived on October 7 and probably had little understanding of how precarious the revolt really was, or how untrained, unprepared and ill-equipped was his army. As soon as some of the new soldiers saw that the uprising was essentially a communist-inspired affair, they deserted en masse. Some were adolescent farm boys seeking adventure, others patriotic but naive, and a few were local communists or sympathizers who did not relish actual battle. Now they only wanted to return home and a mere remnant of them remained to fight on.[32]

It was a dark scene of black clouds, chilling rain and the defeat of routed troops that Maria likened to a Greek tragedy. This was Viest's Waterloo and he knew it. She felt she was intruding on a sacred moment and that facing the death of his dream should be between the man and his God alone. With reluctance she interrupted his painful reverie to request permission to leave the CFI. Viest listened quietly, then, hollow-eyed and pale, he spoke to her in a strained voice. "You stay with the Americans, Maria. You know the mountains, the languages, the people and the political situation. Help them in any way you can."

In a near trance, he turned back to confront his own tragic dilemma. Maria never saw Viest again but the memory of the vanquished democratic idealist was to haunt her.

Returning to her resting spot to ponder what her decision to join the Americans would entail, Maria brushed by a couple of the airmen who had found shelter beneath thick, low-hanging pine branches. Staff Sgt. Eugene Yeargin greeted her with, "Hi, Mary," and a smile. She was struck anew with how young and openly appealing these Americans were, but also how unaware of what lay ahead.[33]

In his official post-war report, Yeargin related how he and his crew of five arrived in Banska Bystrica on October 18, expecting to be evacuated. Instead, when the Germans attacked, his crew and the rest of the airmen joined the Dawes unit on their flight to Donavaly and now intent on reaching the Prasiva mountain range and shelter. Yeargin had developed a cold, so the prospect of climbing seven or eight thousand feet to reach the Soviet camp was an ordeal he did not relish.[34]

Fatigue deepened with every foot they climbed until it became a constant, dull ache. They were lashed by merciless winds and icy sleet. Mountain dwellers know that weather can be friend or foe, and that day good fortune smiled on the fleeing refugees when visibility dropped to almost zero, making close pursuit unlikely.[35]

By late afternoon their goal was near. Close to the Klement Gottwald guerrilla camp, Green halted his group. He inspected them and then shook his head with disapproval. "Look at you!" he declared in a stern tone. "You're a disgrace. Stand tall and act like American soldiers! We're on a military mission for the United States, not a bunch of rag tag wanderers!"[36]

A puzzled Maria watched gray-haired Staff Sgt. Jerry Mican, the oldest of the Dawes men, pull a razor out of his pack and scrape at chin stubble. Behind him Schwartz snickered, but then, he was always spruced up. To Maria that order to hungry, dog-tired men seemed ludicrous, just as was Keszthelyi's empty threat to have Catlos court-martialed because he discarded their only radio. Nevertheless, she also complied with Green's order by rubbing her face with snow, tightening her braids, and brushing spots of mud off her parka. Actually, she admired Green's determination to preserve the appearance of an important American military mission with a commander in control, knowing how the image would impress the Russians.[37]

Dunlevy was a native of Illinois and knew all about freezing, damp winters. He also realized that from Donavaly on, it would be "touch and go." Although he had exchanged only a few words with his commander, Dunlevy had formed an impression of Green as a product of the "social Navy," responsible but not as decisive as Dunlevy wished. All the OSS men were specialists but didn't know each other, but his impression was that some, like Mican, Heller, Brown and certainly the boyish airmen, were not equal to the hardships they were facing. He repressed a festering resentment at Green's neglect to brief them, which left him dubious as to how much Green really knew about what was going on.[38]

Second in command, Gaul was a sharp physical contrast to the commander. He had willingly exposed himself to harsh elements in remote archeological digs, played basketball, excelled in swimming, and was accustomed

4. A Resourceful Maria Joins the Team 77

to physical rigors. While not in command of the mission, Dunlevy felt he was a great back-up leader

Maria also had a definite impression of the distinguished appearing Green as somewhat like the Ashley Wilkes character in the novel *Gone with the Wind*. Possibly he was too genteel and because of inexperience perhaps may not have fully grasped the harsh brutalities of war.[39]

The Klement Gottwald camp was the first established by Soviet guerrillas when they parachuted into the mountains anticipating a speedy linkup with Gen. Ivan Konev's First Ukrainian Army. On the camp's outskirts, two sentries leaped from behind large boulders to confront the newcomers. The pair of hard-bitten guerrillas in scruffy clothes ordered them to halt. Hooded eyes staring out of dirt-encrusted faces were hostile and spooky. Lips were raw and cracked from the penetrating winds. Red, calloused hands clutched sub-machine guns while hand grenades and daggers dangled from frayed belts.[40]

The surly guards backed off when MacGregor demanded they summon Velichko. The Russian commander extended a cordial greeting and directed the Americans to a bunker below the top of the mountain. The bunkers were gouged out of the ground and covered with thick foliage so that scouting planes flying overhead could not detect them. Floors were wooden planks on which the men slept. To Catlos' outrage, once out of Velichko's sight, the threatening sentries boldly confiscated the two MC 34s that CFI partisans had painstakingly lugged over the narrow pass from Donavaly.[41]

The camp was well organized and supplied and the Americans were given a meal of a hot stew. Catlos and Dunlevy then cleared out some debris from crowded bunkers to make room for the airmen and Maria, whom Green also ordered to stay in the shelter. The rest of the groups gathered in clusters under pine branches for some protection from the elements.[42]

Inside the bunker the stench of smoke, sweat and filth was overpowering. However, as the blackness of night enveloped the camp and as Maria listened to the drip, drip, drip of the rain, she was thankful for even this primitive dugout. She reached into her backpack to make sure that her rosary and toothbrush, her personal emblems of civilization and security, were still there. She wished she'd had time to grab all the warm clothing Keszthelyi had brought for her in Donavaly and wondered into whose hands they had fallen. But she was grateful for the warm woolen parka. Feeling secure in this remote area, she fell asleep, only to be awakened shortly by an aggravating itch that spread from one spot to another. In the darkness she sensed, rather than saw, the exhausted flyers sprawled out in benumbed slumber thrashing about and scratching. Lice, another indignity of war! Even so, she was grateful that for the moment, at least, they were relatively safe from stealthy attack and certain quick death.[43]

5

Maria's American Serenade

The reprieve proved to be short-lived. Shortly after dawn a CFI reconnaissance patrol returned and reported that the Goat's Back pass over Kozi Chrbat had been cut off by a large formation of German troops. They had captured a large number of CFI partisans and were now on their way to the camp. Immediate action was imperative.

Green readied his group to move out with the Czech Brigade into deeper mountain forests, but first, managed to finagle the purchase of some provisions from brigade commander Colonel Prykryl. The colonel also sold him a horse to transport the heavy bags of food and assigned a partisan guide for the Americans. Gaul issued five twenty-franc Napoleon coins and one hundred Slovak korunas to each of the OSS agents, telling them they would receive that amount every day. In the event they should become separated, these monies might enable them to pay for food or any other available necessities if they were fortunate to come across any.[1]

That same morning, American-Slovak partisan unit commander Fedornak returned from his own spying mission in the vicinity of the village of Poprad to report to his Soviet commander that his reconnaissance unit had not seen any Germans near the Soviet area of operations. He had been relieved to learn that Margita Koscova and the English group had vacated the hunting lodge as he'd secretly advised, and were able to find a better location.[2]

Soviet guerrilla Adam Bukowski privately advised Green not to leave the guerrilla camp, pointing out that they would be entering heavily enemy-infested territory. Green carefully weighed Bukowski's warning, but still opted to leave with the brigade.[3]

In a post-war report by Sgt. Steven Catlos and Sgt. Kenneth Dunlevy, Adam Bukowski stated that Green had told him about his experience with Marshall Tito's well organized and equipped partisans in Yugoslavia, saying that compared to that operation, the Slovak Uprising was merely a "hard luck affair." Green felt that some ill-prepared partisans decided to stage a revolt but ran when the Germans came. The OSS, he purportedly said, had expected a movement like Tito's, bold and well organized and that the Germans had been afraid of the Polish Home Army and feared Tito's partisans, but had little fear of the Slovak insurgents.[4]

It was mid-morning on October 31 when the Americans took leave of the camp with the Czech Brigade. At the last minute, Studensky and his entourage decided to join them since top Soviet guerrilla chief commander A. N. Asmolov had already departed the scene to link up with the Red Army, estimated to be a five-day march. Again, progress was slow and the groups periodically halted for long intervals while patrols forged ahead to scout, leaving the marchers to stand around shivering in the cold for intervals as long as forty-five minutes.[5]

Dunlevy had remained awake during the night before they left the Gottwald camps, and ruminated about their predicament. Crouched near the fire, seeking warmth and some protection from the constant, pelting rain, his thoughts were extremely pessimistic about some of the agents, like Mican, who was older than the other men and with lungs impaired from asthma and legs weakened after surgery to strip away varicose veins. He was not up to the extreme physical and many other hardships they faced. Neither was Heller, the youngest of them all, whom Dunlevy referred to as "a young squirt," capable as a radio operator but very immature in most other aspects. How long would he hold up? Worst of all in this plight were airmen who were no longer in good physical condition but were wearing the same light, tattered summer uniforms they'd worn for weeks. In bitter frustration, Dunlevy again wondered what the hell had happened to the truckload of winter clothing they'd brought in on October 7.[6]

The men of Dawes whom Dunlevy most respected were MacGregor and Lain, combat veterans who were wounded during the savage battle over Anzio Beach in Italy some months before. They were the only commandos of Dawes with actual combat experience and he admired their pluck in trying to help the CFI despite threats from hostile Russian guerrillas and after realizing that the CFI stood no chance of victory. Another fellow agent he thought highly of was Staff Sergeant Joseph Horvath, describing the blond sergeant as a savvy, capable "man's man," and although handsome enough to be a movie star had no conceit in him.[7]

In the report, Bukowski painted a vivid verbal scene of Prasiva after the Americans and the CFI shoved off from the camp. It was one of frenetic activity. Guerrillas frantically dug trenches and threw up extra defense measures at the camp entrance to repel the expected German attack. But the efforts were futile. When the skilled Nazi mountain fighters stormed the fortress at daybreak, the camp was quickly overrun and obliterated with sixty-five guerrillas captured from dugouts. Their fate was certain to be torture and death.[8]

As for Green, initial and subsequent reports had given accurate assessments of Soviet commanders and their guerrilla units. In these accounts, Green expressed his distrust, describing the Russians as "a drunken, unruly bunch." These impressions may have accounted for his unrelenting distrust of the Soviets that led to his decision to cast his and his men's lot with the CFI Brigade.

Green's disapproval, and evident anger, towards the Soviets was not lost on Dunlevy, although he'd not heard those feelings expressed verbally. Rather, he'd deduced from the hostile Soviet reaction to his group's arrival on October 7, and the lack of co-operation from the Slovak communists, that Green had to deal with strong negatives.[9]

Dunlevy's own adverse impressions were corroborated by an incident at the camp when Green asked the Russians to make radio contact with OSS Bari to give information on the mission. The Soviet commander's response was as icy as the winter atmosphere and a strong negative because, he claimed, it was dangerous to reveal their location. This was dubious since the Soviets made regular radio reports to Kiev and the enemy knew exactly where they were. Like Green, Dunlevy realized that it was obvious that the guerrillas had no intention of providing any aid whatsoever to anyone but fellow Russians. The CFI was co-operative, but compared to the well-trained Soviet guerrillas, Dunlevy had little confidence in their abilities as partisans.[10]

Catlos had not relished leaving the relative safety of the camp and experienced a sense of dislocation that one undergoes when leaving a familiar place to wander into a totally unknown, uncharted wilderness. By mid-day, a cold, steady rain turned into snow flurries, further dispelling the flickering flame of hope in his spirits. The arduous mountain trek and lack of food and sleep was already taking its toll on the flyers, who were fledglings at rigorous physical soldiering. He wondered if they could last a five-day march over the rocky, jagged, high mountain terrain to meet up with the Red Army with the probability of blizzards increasing with every foot they climbed. However, despite their grim situation, Catlos felt that in general, spirits within the unit remained hopeful.[11]

Like Dunlevy and Catlos, Maria also felt grave concern for the boyish airmen. As Viest had reminded her, she was familiar with the precarious winter weather in these Tatra Mountains and knew all too well how it could change in seconds. She was especially worried about the flyers, a couple of them exhibiting influenza symptoms with coughing that had worsened from exertion and the thinner mountain air. Their flimsy, damp clothing was an extra hazard. And no one had extra clothing to offer. She remained embittered and disgusted with Mikhail who had wantonly destroyed warm clothing rather than sharing the desperately needed woolen pants and shirts with the Americans.[12]

As they slogged along, Sergeant Nelson Paris had to pause frequently to wipe off his glasses to be able to see the path ahead. At one point, the native of Portland, Oregon, mumbled in near despair, "I've never seen anything like this. Where the hell are we going anyway?"

A brawny man in his mid-twenties, Paris was built like a football linebacker, but his physical appearance was misleading. Actually he was a Navy photographer and had little or no combat training. Furthermore, Paris was not as fit as he appeared to a casual observer. Seeing how hard he had to struggle to keep up, Catlos was glad of the long hours of physical drill he'd been forced to undergo and about which he'd griped, but which were now paying off.[13]

At mid-afternoon, they stopped for a half-hour rest and to gobble the last of their meager rations of bread and marmalade that left stomachs still growling with hunger. Fat, ponderous clouds driven lower by gusty winds indicated that by nightfall they would be depositing snow flurries. Maria's confidence in the CFI Brigade guide, who'd assured them that this particular area was not occupied by the enemy, vanished when it turned out that he did not even have the location of the village they were headed for pinpointed on his sketchy hand-drawn map. Furthermore, she did not trust villagers because she'd learned as a courier that some were of German ancestry and loyal to the Nazi regime. And others were loyal to Tiso's state government and were duty-bound to betray any strangers to the authorities.[14]

Experienced and wily Slovak partisan Fedornak, like Maria, was also knowledgeable about how the Germans operated in towns and villages. They would seek out individuals who had contacts in the underground and pay them to spy and report on partisan movements. This gave them an edge and the result was that too often, before a partisan unit could dig in and set up any kind of defense, a well armed unit of German anti-partisans would sweep in and wipe out the entire unit before they could fire a shot. Also like Maria, Fedornak had no illusions about either the Slovak partisans or Soviet guerrillas whose orders were to kill friend or foe who were unlucky enough to stumble onto their location to prevent the hapless unfortunate from revealing it to anyone else.[15]

From November 2 on, Lomnista Valley harbored the biggest number of Soviet guerrillas or communists commanded by Colonel Mikhail Shukayev, who served as first deputy to chief Asmolov.[16]

The biggest losers of all in this game of seek, hide and destroy were the kind, naive villagers who risked their lives to aid decent partisans. They were often set upon by the thieving ones who returned later and, finding their helpers vulnerable because of their trust, robbed them of everything they had.[17]

Soviet commanders, on the other hand, such as Shukayev, trusted no one, not even his own men. He carefully selected a few to be checked out and tested for reliability before positioning them at locations where the Soviet planes dropped supplies. His distrust was well founded because the parcels were marked with red crosses and contained alcohol, medicine and vitamins which disloyal or renegade guerrillas seized and carted away. They then drank the alcohol after stashing away the drugs and vitamins to sell or use themselves.[18]

Fedornak had been appointed by Shukayev to instruct fresh, incoming Russian guerrillas on how to conduct themselves with the Slovak people. The Russians, he soon learned, had no concept of private property and needed to be warned repeatedly not to steal anything they wanted from the Slovak people. He noted how several of the Russians eagerly breathed in deeply of the freedom they obviously relished. One older man confided to Fedornak, "I do not want to see the communists rule in Slovakia. Once they arrive in a place, no one can drive them out." A few others told him privately that they did not want to see the Soviets rule in Slovakia, because this once free country would change and become like Russia where freedom could be found only in a dictionary. Another Russian guerrilla expressed the wistful hope that "maybe one day God will free Mother Russia from the communists."[19]

The goal of the American group was a village reported to be devoid of enemy occupation. But their partisan guide was vague about the exact location. After fifteen hours of relentless marching during which clothing became stiff and half frozen on the outside, while inside the linings were damp and clammy from perspiration, the Americans and Czech Brigade came to a rocky precipice. It was obvious to the Americans, who stopped for a brief rest, that even the brigade was lost when its leaders walked the weary men around for another two hours searching for an access path to descend an eighty-foot bluff to a plateau that was the site of an abandoned camp. Buffeted by gale-force winds, the brigade plodded like automatons back and forth seeking a way down the boulder strewn, jagged cliff until too exhausted to take another step.[20]

In desperation, Green ordered his group to get down the steep, rocky precipice as best they could. He led the way, with Gaul and Morton following, sliding down the muddy, treacherous slope on the seats of their pants. Halfway down, Green lost his balance and grabbed for something to break

5. Maria's American Serenade

his fall, dislodging boulders that narrowly missed slamming into Gaul and Morton. One pack horse, and then another, lost its footing and tumbled to the bottom of the ravine and others followed, their whinnies of pain and terror pitiful. Miraculously, Maria and all the Americans were able to plunge safely to the bottom. Once there, Green ordered Maria and Keszthelyi to check the men for possible injuries. Fortunately, there were only minor bruises and cuts but no broken bones or sprains.[21]

After everyone had been accounted for, they prepared to spend the night in the woods. Weary to the point of collapse, the men set up camp by laboriously gouging damp twigs and leaves out of the frozen ground to coax into smoky, sputtering flames ignited by another strip of Paris' film. Suddenly, the quiet proceeding was interrupted by an outcry.

"The bags of food and the horse Prykryl sold us are gone! And that bastard of a Dutchman guarding it is also gone!"

The guide and the horse carrying bags of food bought from Prykryl had disappeared. The brigade member who claimed he'd joined after deserting the Nazi SS had now deserted the Americans. All they had left were a couple of boxes of canned soup and crackers. It was three o'clock in the morning before Green, Kesztheyli and Horvath unpacked the boxes and heated up the soup. Maria helped dish it into mess kits and the hungry men gulped it down, looking for something more to fill empty stomachs. But there was nothing more.[22]

Drifting into small groups, the Americans sought protected places on the ground under brush or tree branches on which to spend the long, rainy night. Catlos was to retain a vivid memory of crouching near the sputtering campfire beside Dunlevy and worrying about the pilots with their crews clustered around them like lemmings, abject misery etched on their youthful faces. They reminded Catlos of Boy Scouts lost in the woods without a trusted scoutmaster to lead them to safety. "Poor bastards," he muttered to Dunlevy. "They're going to freeze to death in those flimsy jackets."[23]

Dunlevy's reaction was to spit out a wad of mushy tobacco into the brush and pat the flap of his parka buttoned over his Bible to make sure it was still there. All around them, men coughed and sneezed and Catlos wondered, if like a few of them, the pale and silent Dunlevy was also ill. However, he'd already perceived Dunlevy to be an extremely private man who did not indulge in casual talk and decided not to inquire. It was indeed, as he'd noted earlier, going to be a long, cold winter and a hard time ahead.[24]

On the morning of November 2, Green moved his group to a flimsy wooden hut farther up the mountain. Makeshift sheds such as these were interspersed throughout the mountains and were used by farmers to store hay. Unfortunately, they could be reached only in winter on frozen ground. The trails to them were too muddy to use during the rainy season when wheels of wagons became imbedded in mud a foot deep. But they provided some shelter from the rain and sleet, and were usually out of range of enemy patrols combing the area.[25]

It was clear that some of the flyers could not go on and everyone was relieved when Green tersely told them that they would stay there for a few days to rest. At least two of them, Lieutenant John Drezner and Staff Sergeant Jurgen, were feverish and delirious, and a couple of other airmen were also sick from the flu but not as bad as these two. Furthermore, most of their group was becoming incapacitated from diarrhea, swollen feet and muscle pain from overexertion.[26]

In a welcome shift of arrangements, the brigade moved to a lumber camp some distance away. Dunlevy, for one, was relieved at this development, believing that their smaller group was less likely to be spotted. To remain in contact with Prykryl though, Green assigned Mican, who was fluent in Czech, to accompany the brigade and act as liaison between them and the Americans.[27]

Like MacGregor, Maria was impressed with the determination of Slovak partisans and Russian guerrillas striving to be the masters of their survival and their proficiency in dealing with grim reality. They hacked chunks of flesh off dead horses and dropped them into pots of boiling water slung over campfires. The meat was imbedded with ice, and some of the men were too starved to wait for it to cook completely, and devoured the flesh half raw. Maria refused to eat any because she feared the animals were diseased, and besides, the partially cooked meat was not safe from other contamination. Instead, she wheedled four mess kits of beans from one of the partisans and paid for the bounty with a gold Napoleon that Keszthelyi gave her to secure the deal. Unfortunately, at the high altitude, the stone-hard beans would take hours to cook.[28]

The crude hut was too small for all the Americans; therefore Green designated it only for those who were sick. All others erected shelters out of pine branches. However, as the sleet continued to pepper them with icy slivers, the partisans refused to be shut out and crowded into the hut and forced their way inside the hut, crawling over and stepping on feverish airmen sprawled on the floor until the small space overflowed with bodies. One of the partisans Maria was acquainted with tried to entice her inside, but she refused, knowing that while he may have once had ethics, by now he'd surely changed. Realistically, partisans who retained their humane, softer side suffered a higher mortality rate. Maria didn't reveal that while that same partisan and his unit were away from the camp, she'd stolen a bag of flour from their stash. But she felt no guilt for her act, certain they'd stolen it first from someone else. The whole grain meal was tasteless as wallpaper paste but she concocted a gruel from it which did contain some nourishment for the sick men.[29]

In dire need of more food, early the next morning, Green selected Keszthelyi, Catlos and Horvath to accompany Maria on a sortie to the nearest village. It was a scenario that would be repeated many times in the coming days. While those on raids got rid of some of the tensions, those left behind to wait became edgy and often tempers flew. He admired Morton, who proved to be an excellent diffuser.[30]

It had not been long before Maria's understanding of the German modus operandi was made apparent to Catlos and the other men. Pointing out that patrols usually chose the first or second house on a street or road to check for partisans, she led them to the sixth cottage out of a cluster of a dozen or so in a hamlet in a peaceful meadow setting. The men hid outside behind dense brush while Maria went to the door and knocked. Peering through the branches, Catlos could see the burly man who opened the door and heard Maria address him as "*kraina*" ("one of us"). Something about her must have engendered the stranger's trust because he invited her inside with no hesitation.

Catlos, like his commander Green, had quickly realized the wisdom of recruiting Maria as guide and interpreter. Only a native dared make contact with villagers who were leery of partisans and would certainly be petrified at the sight of men in rumpled American military uniforms. Also, a woman appeared less threatening. These deductions would prove to be accurate.[31]

It also could have been, as Dunlevy surmised, the complete lack of fear in Maria's eyes, unlike the unmistakable fright he'd seen in the eyes of many partisans and natives they encountered. He also felt that her courage inspired and reassured the Americans trapped in a strange land and gave them confidence and hope that they would survive.[32]

For Maria, that first food sortie became a typical first meeting with a villager. Inside the small, plainly furnished house was a young woman with two children. Maria guessed that that her husband was either working in Germany or was in the Army and the older man present was her father. At sight of Maria in an unfamiliar U.S. Army parka and pants, the woman grabbed her two little girls, about three and five years of age, and moved away to hover beside an icon of the Virgin Mary and infant Jesus mounted on the wall.

"*Partizanen?*" she asked tremulously.

The young woman's face, probably pretty not too long before, showed the effects of a hard mountain life. Skin exposed to the elements until it was like sagging, tanned leather, made her look older than she probably was. Lack of enough proper food had turned her once feminine rounded figure into one now too scrawny. But Maria knew that she was the earthy type and a good mother who would die to protect her children.

Maria assured the woman they were not partisans and briefly explained what she had come for.[33]

All this man and his daughter could offer them were two loaves of bread, a half dozen sausages and three large onions, for which Maria paid with a gold Napoleon. The woman's eyes widened in amazement as she turned the gold coin over in her hand, examining it from every angle. The man softened and, losing his wary look, volunteered the information unasked that "the *nemci* gone two, three days now."

However, he warned her not to approach neighbors because one could never tell which ones were loyal to the Slovak state government and would reveal the presence of any stranger to village authorities who would then report it to the large detail of German troops in the nearby village of Solisko.[34]

Catlos noted how Maria and Keszthelyi, obviously greatly attracted to each, had quickly formed an effective team. Returning to camp with their booty, the couple lagged behind the others, walking slowly, holding hands and smiling at each other. In the camp, the two worked smoothly and efficiently, slicing the sausage and bread paper thin to make sandwiches. The sick airmen were served first, wolfing down the meager ration before moving back close to the campfire as possible without getting scorched.[35]

Like many young Slovak women, Maria had completed a six-week Red Cross nursing course which helped her recognize flu symptoms and realize how sick a couple of the airmen were. They needed medicine and extra nourishment, but neither they nor the CFI had medicines and nutritious food supplies were scarce, and what was available was seldom of the high quality needed for quick recovery from an illness. As Maria witnessed the wracking coughing spasms and observed the fever flushed faces of the flyers, a folk remedy came to mind. She wrangled a cup of lard from a partisan and in a skillet sautéed the onions she'd bought earlier. Moving from one sick flyer to another, she coaxed each to swallow a spoonful of the onions and prayed it would help. But all through the night, the deep, barking coughs worried her. Also troubling to Maria was Green, grave-faced and holding his arms tightly against his body, a measure he seemed to resort to when tension apparently rose to nearly unbearable lengths. She felt great sympathy for the soft-spoken, clean-cut commander who would do anything to help his men and knowing there was so little he could actually do.[36]

The next day Green summoned those who had been on the previous day's search to undertake a more stringent attempt to find food. This time he would accompany them. They bypassed the cluster of cottages they had visited the previous day and walked further afield, constantly on the alert for German patrols. A couple of kilometers from the hamlet, they came to a forester's hut nestled in a grove of towering pines. Although it appeared abandoned, they approached cautiously before venturing close enough to see that it had apparently been abandoned in haste.[37]

On top of a small, black iron stove they found a pot of cold, boiled potatoes. The men pounced upon them at once. Maria was touched to observe Green, with his aristocratic bearing still intact, pick up a potato in each hand and with long, tapered fingers, peel off the skins and pop them into his mouth. In the presence of his entire group, he'd borne hunger like the classic officer and gentleman he was. But at that moment, he was merely another half-starved soldier gobbling potatoes.[38]

Finding nothing more edible in the hut, the men went out to inspect a weathered barn, curious about strange sounds emanating from it, while Catlos and Maria made a search around the exterior of the hut. Careful inspection revealed a barely detectable patch of ground beneath one corner of a wall that the others had missed. Using a couple of sharp sticks, they dug aside some dirt and were rewarded with buried treasure — carrots and potatoes and onions layered in beds of straw. They scooped up the bounty into a burlap sack and rejoined the others who were staring in amazement at a bawling calf that Horvath cut loose and was leading out of the barn. Catlos was amused at the reaction of his teammate Keszthelyi, a chemist from New York, who appeared a bit stupefied at seeing a live calf for the first time.

Jubilant at their find, they started back to camp. They had just located the trail when they spotted what looked like a large German patrol coming directly towards them. Tugging and pulling the frightened calf, they scuttled down a hill, barely escaping detection. Green had them switch to another route, this time a rougher and more winding path not amenable to enemy vehicles. It took longer to reach camp but they got there with no further incident. Proudly bearing their booty, they resembled native hunters returning from a successful hunt bringing their day's take and rejoining the waiting men who were half crazed from hunger.[39]

Catlos chuckled at how astounded the partisans were to hear the Americans argue over who would butcher the calf. None of them relished the job. But hunger won out over pity for the calf, lowing for its mother. After the deed was done, Maria and Keszthelyi concocted a stew from veal, carrots, potatoes and onions for thirty-seven famished men standing in line eagerly waiting for them to dish it up. For the first time since they fled Donavaly, everyone not only enjoyed a hot meal, but had enough to satisfy gut-gnawing hunger.

The growing attraction between Maria and Keszthelyi was not lost on the other men, just as it hadn't been on Catlos. He thought they made a fetching pair and wondered why the scowling Schwartz and Gaul, who hadn't been enthusiastic about Maria being recruited by Green to begin with, resented this romantic development that provided a welcome human touch.[40]

"*Cherchez la femme*," he heard Gaul mutter, to which Green replied, "You're making too much out of this, Jim."[41]

Maria was aware of the hostility but found comfort in the fact that Green seemed to appreciate her efforts to be of assistance, never failing to thank her with a warm smile that lightened his serious demeanor. That evening, after they'd consumed the stew, she was gratified to see the commander hunched over the fire near his men with arms relaxed, some of his constant tension obviously lifted, at least for the moment.

Maria realized that males could not understand her unique dilemma as a young female or the precarious situation she was in. She'd never ceased to berate herself for the naiveté of venturing to Soviet guerrilla camps on courier missions with only a youthful male driver as protection and how it led to a near rape she could not forget. Her current plight forced her to analyze a woman's best safeguard when surrounded by a sea of women-hungry young men. She deduced that it was to appear attracted to only one of them and for that purpose, decided that Keszthelyi was her best bet. From the moment they met, she found his urbane manners, shock of glossy dark hair and chocolate brown eyes that reflected intelligence and good humor very appealing. He also spoke excellent Hungarian, making conversation easy. They continued holding hands when the occasion presented itself, but for her as yet, the romantic gesture was primarily to make it clear that personal attention from any of the other men was most unwelcome.[42]

The food plundered from the forester's hut was soon gone. In dire need of more, they had to make another search. On the morning of November 5, airmen Sergeant Eugene Yeargin volunteered to lead them to the village of Klacany near the POW camp where he and his crew had been interred before release by CFI partisans and brought to Banska Bystrica. He and fellow airman Lt. Shafer, Keszthelyi, MacGregor, Lain and Maria walked for several hours on the lookout for the exact location. The ordeal proved to be too much for the two flyers recovering from food poisoning after eating spoiled horsemeat. In addition, they were still weak from being imprisoned and then exposure to the harsh weather since their flight from Donavaly and opted to return to camp. However, Maria persuaded them to continue a bit further until they came upon an isolated farmhouse, almost hidden in a grove of trees.[43]

As before, Maria approached the dwelling while the men stayed under cover. A grizzled male occupant opened the door. It was hard to guess his age, even from that distance one could see his coarse skin, weatherbeaten from the freezing cold, blizzards and winds he was exposed to during long winter months. His gruff attitude matched his outer demeanor. He told her he nothing to spare.

"*Nemci*, they take everything."

"We're starving," Maria pleaded, and held out a gold coin as enticement. "Do you know of any place we can buy something to eat?"

"Oh, you buy?" His tone and expression underwent a sudden change. "I know a man who will sell you something. Come back after dark and I take you."[44]

It was almost midnight before they located the storehouse near Klacany and awakened the proprietor. With more gold coins they were able to purchase four liters of cognac, five kilos of salami, two pounds of creamy Brinza cheese, five loaves of bread, a half dozen jars of tomato conserves, a few dried fish, and small bags of salt and flour. Back at their escort's cottage, he examined the gold coins he'd been paid as though appraising them like an expert, then with a fey smile, waved farewell and closed the door.

On the way back to camp, Maria noted that one of the houses in the hamlet they had visited previously still had a light burning although it was late at night. Hoping to find overnight shelter for the weary men and herself, she knocked at the door hesitantly, all too aware of how frightful was a knock on the door after dark. A careworn woman opened the door a crack and peered out. Half concealed behind her was her teen-aged daughter, who stared unabashedly at Maria who assured her that they were friends and asked if they could stay until daylight to rest.

The woman looked out over Maria's head as far as she could see in the dark before responding. They could stay until daylight to rest. "*Nemci*," she murmured with a meaningfully shrug and beckoned the visitors to come inside. Noting the woman and her daughter's alarmed expressions at the sight of the men in American military uniforms when they entered, Maria smiled and again assured her that they were friends of Slovaks.

In keeping with typical village custom, their benefactor offered Maria the only bed in the house, which Maria politely declined. Instead, she stretched out on a blanket beside the men on the kitchen floor near the stove. The heat felt like heaven's blessing and in mere seconds, they were asleep with their kind householder keeping watch.[45]

The woman awakened her visitors at dawn. The men shaved with water heated in a shallow tin pan on top the stove and slicked back their hair. Maria washed her face, brushed her teeth with salt and warm water and unbraided her hair for a brisk scalp massage before rebraiding. The tall, ungainly girl watched her with fascination. They were devouring a breakfast of ground barley and bread toasted on the red-hot stove lids when suddenly, the peaceful Sunday morning was shattered by a sharp rap at the door followed by an excited boyish voice yelling *"Nemci! Nemci!"* They grabbed the bags of food and ran out the door and into the adjacent woods. In their haste, they missed the trail and had to double back, slowing progress considerably. They walked with a diminished pace until nearly dusk, when they came upon a small band of Slovak partisans occupying a hut. One of the bedraggled men, eyes wary with suspicion, stepped towards them and taking a closer look, broke into a smile and hurried to greet the unexpected arrivals. He was a partisan Maria knew slightly. He insisted that she and the Americans share their bread and cheese and the crowded shelter. It was now almost dusk and too late to continue trying to make it to camp before daylight so they accepted their invitation.[46]

During the night, Maria's hand brushed against Keszthelyi's. His skin burned like fire. In an almost inaudible whisper he told her to leave with the other guys in the morning. He would follow when he felt better.

However, neither she nor the Americans would hear of it and Keszthelyi seemed relieved. The other men lugged his share of the load and they cut their pace to a slow walk on the long trek back so he could keep up. Maria felt ashamed at not sharing their food with the partisans who had generously offered what little they had, but reminded herself that "war is war" and besides, the foreign Americans needed the food they'd obtained more than native partisans.[47]

An anxious Green, fearing they'd been captured, had been watching the trail and hurried to meet them the moment a sentry reported that they were approaching. He asked what had kept them so long. He feared they'd been captured, at which MacGregor retorted, "Not a chance."[48]

Green's welcome and that of the entire hungry, waiting group was as warm as the blazing fire. As before, Maria and Keszthelyi prepared soup from the tomato conserves and slapped together generous sandwiches of salami and cheese. Everyone then bolted down a swig of cognac which lightened moods considerably. Best of all, there was enough food for another day or two if stretched carefully, and the enemy was nowhere near.[49]

As night deepened, from where he was crouched near the campfire burning still brightly from a couple of good sized logs, Catlos overheard Maria conversing with Horvath in the lean-to she shared with him, Keszthelyi, Green, and Gaul. She was commenting on Horvath's wedding ring. At that, Horvath reached into an inside pocket of his shirt and pulled out a small

5. Maria's American Serenade

Lt. Green in a pensive mood after the enemy attack (courtesy the Museum of the Uprising Archives).

leather encased photo of his bride of a year to proudly show off. Catlos poked his head through the opening to take a good look, after which he let out a soft whistle and jokingly said, "If I thought I could find a dish like that in Cleveland, I might be tempted to leave my wife and relocate."[50]

He and Maria gazed with admiration at the green-eyed beauty seductively arrayed in a black negligee, setting off her ivory toned complexion and cascade of auburn waves to a stunning perfection. The depth of love and longing the Teutonic commando bore for his bride was almost palpable leaving them silent. The poignant romantic magic of the moment was broken by the sounds of singing voices coming towards them. Maria, blue eyes wide with wonderment, was puzzled when a half dozen airmen gathered in a half circle around the lean-to, voices lifted in song.

"What are those crazy kids doing and why are they singing about someone named Mary?" she asked Keszthelyi.

He explained that it was a famous American folk song called "Mary Is a Grand Old Name" and that the guys were serenading her.

When the last note sounded, Sergeant Guy Haines stepped forward and spoke up for all the flyers. "Thank you, Maria, for everything you have done for us."[51]

The camp grew quiet and lying awake long after the men were snoring in sleep, by the light of the waning campfire, Maria caught a glimpse of Morton writing in his notebook. She wondered how he could possibly relay to his fellow Americans in the United States, sheltered and secure between two oceans, what it was like for these commandos trapped in a strange land and pursued by superior Nazi warriors whose orders were to take them captive at any cost. However, like Scarlett O'Hara in *Gone with the Wind*, the only American novel she had ever read, Maria decided that such weighty questions were too heavy to deal with at night. She would think about those complex issues tomorrow.

As darkness closed around the camp site like an invisible shield, the fire died to glowing embers, and sentries paced the parameters of camp on the alert for signs of the enemy, stray partisans or spies, Maria dwelled on another of her father's teachings. It was to thank God for daily bread, real or symbolic, both of which she had received in relative abundance that day in the actual food they were able to buy, Green's sincere smile and "thank you," and being appreciated in an unforgettable way by the boyish airmen. God alone knew what the next day would bring, but at that moment, Maria was certain of only one thing: her decision to stay with the Americans was the right one.

Her feelings of gratitude and optimism were not shared by Catlos or Dunlevy, who were still awake and squatting beside the campfire. Dunlevy, for one, was keeping a watchful but surreptitious eye on everything around them. Some of the large group of partisans on the camp fringes seemed to be edgy, an indicator Dunlevy regarded as a possible forewarning of trouble. He decided that he would sleep only for short periods and continue to keep watch as the darkness closed in about them.[52]

6

DIVISION, DEBATE, DEPARTURE

At daybreak the next morning, Dunlevy and Catlos, accompanied by Air Force lieutenant John Brezner and a couple of CFI partisans, volunteered for a reconnaissance patrol. Dunlevy was the first to spot an abandoned truck partially concealed in a thick grove of trees.

"Looks like a set up," he muttered.

But as they drew closer and saw nothing suspicious, Catlos said "There's not a Heinie within a country mile. Let's take a look."

The look yielded a few 12-volt batteries and a charger that they salvaged, as well as some gasoline and two German MG-34 guns. Catlos stashed the battery and starter into his pack to try later in getting their radio working. After reconnoitering further a bit and noting no signs of enemy activity, they returned to camp. They tried the 12-volt batteries but they proved to be too high a voltage for their last radio set and blew out the fuse. But Catlos still held out hope for their usefulness and stashed the starter and the batteries into his pack to try again.[1]

Lieutenant John Schwartz, whose code name was John Krizan, was strong and self-reliant to the point where some of the other men, Dunlevy for one, resented his condescending attitude and arrogance.[2] However, Schwartz had been successful in relying on his instincts during his days in the Slovak underground, the French Resistance and Foreign Legion and even capture by the Germans, which he foiled by escaping from their POW camp. He had made his way to the United States where he joined the Army, receiving coveted citizenship, and was now part of this OSS mission. One official at headquarters in an early report predicted that if any commandos survived this high risk mission it would be Schwartz, whom he described as a clever man.[3]

The anti-communist Schwartz had been angry at Soviet guerrillas since their short stay at the camp near Prasiva. Like Green, much of his resentment was centered around the refusal of the Soviets to radio the position of the Americans to their OSS base in Bari, Italy, in order to give their superior command their current position. He openly exhibited his contempt for their rationale that it would also give away their radio location, which was a lame excuse. Schwartz was not a radio operator but had some radio knowledge. He carried with him the ciphers for the Houseboat mission but not the crystals.[4]

On November 6, 1944, the day following Dunlevy and Catlos' reconnaissance duty, Schwartz, Lieutenant Shaffer, and four of his crew, Gary Haines, Eugene Yeargin, Sgts. Sasewa and Arnett and two CFI partisan guides undertook another patrol to the same vicinity. They followed the trail taken by Catlos and his group the day before and came upon the same truck in the same location. On close inspection, though, the truck appeared to be stripped of everything except its paint. The two partisans passed into the woods five feet ahead of the Americans, unaware that this was a trap with Germans hiding in wait. When the Americans drew abreast of the German patrol, they broke through the grove of trees and ordered the Americans to halt, drop weapons and put their hands up. Reacting swiftly, Schwartz stealthily removed his wallet from a pocket. The wallet contained five hundred dollars and between the bills, a slip of paper with his Houseboat radio code. He tossed the wallet into a clump of brush, certain that the act had escaped detection. But a German soldier unobtrusively picked it up, glanced at the contents, and tucked the wallet in his pocket. Schwartz was relieved, sure that the man would keep the money and discard the wallet. It would be one of the few times he guessed wrong.[5]

When rifle butts prodded them forward, Schwartz deliberately bumped into Shaffer and whispered to him to tell the captors that he was one of the crew. Schaffer agreed, saying he would claim Schwartz was the pilot. Schwartz shook his head and murmured that he wouldn't be able to answer their questions and to tell them he was the navigator.

Overhearing the exchange, the captor leader shouted angrily. *"Stille!"* and backed his order up by aiming his rifle directly at Schwartz' head.[6]

This was the second capture for Staff Sergeant Yeargin and his crew. They had taken off from the Foggia Air Base on October 13 in a B-17 to bomb Blechhammer, Germany. When two engines were knocked out by flack, they took a heading for Yugoslavia. Then the third engine failed, forcing them to bail out near Pucenec, Slovakia. Three days later, partisans brought in pilot Lieutenant Schaffer, radio operator Sergeant Arnett, and waist gunner Sergeant Sesewa. They were taken to the Americans in Banska Bystrica where they were well treated by the natives and partisans.

This time the outcome was different. The captives were first taken to a barn overnight and then imprisoned in Bratislava before being transported to Vienna and Gestapo headquarters where the interrogators took their money, rings, watches, jackets and boots, and gave them their worn boots and clothing in exchange. There, Yeargin was to discover how much the Gestapo knew about him, his history and family, where he was shot down, and other pertinent information. They questioned him repeatedly about radio codes he denied knowing before subjecting him to physical mistreatment, as were all the flyers with him. They were to endure a long, torturous imprisonment.[7]

* * *

When Schwartz and the flyers did not return to camp, a somber mood enveloped the group, especially for Heller, who had volunteered for the mission with Schwartz as his radio operator. Extra sentries were posted to keep watch. During the night, the wind had turned into a lashing force that sliced through flimsy shelters easily as sharp knife blades. Maria was instantly awake with the first crack of dawn when the Russian and Slovak partisans began stoking the fires.

Green was the first to emerge from the shelter. His yawn stopped cold and his expression changed to one of surprise as if awakening from a pleasant dream only to discover that it is not real after all. Moments later, he jarred everyone awake with his unaccustomed shout that someone had stolen their food. It was the food supplies they had bought in Klacany, and also gone were more than eighty CFI Brigade members who had deserted during the night. Even more serious was the theft of Morton's dispatch case, filled with stories of their harrowing experiences and plight with names and locations of kind individuals who had helped them. If these names fell into enemy hands, it would mean death for the compassionate people who had given the Americans or partisans aid of any kind.

Green summoned his people for a briefing and told they were on strict rations. Each man was given some beans cooked in lard and boiled rice, a slice of bread and cheese and warned that rations would get even tighter. And if anyone was able to steal food, they had his permission. Horvath and Miller promptly complied.[8]

Until then Green had reminded Maria of another character in *Gone with the Wind*, the only American novel she had ever read. She compared Green to Ashley Wilkes, gentlemanly in the most improbable circumstances. He had finally accepted the harsh truth that in war, if you wanted to survive, you did anything to that end you could, lie, cheat, connive and steal anything you needed, at gunpoint, if necessary.[9]

6. Division, Debate, Departure 97

Shortly after the discovery of the missing food and brigade, Prykryl sent a messenger to advise Green and his people to move to a safer spot higher up the mountains and that a villager had seen Schwartz and the other Americans with him in captivity. By noon they'd completed the move to Colonel Prykryl's camp where they encountered Studensky with some of his brigade bivouacked in a cold, damp hut with a muddy floor. With him were Tamara and two hard looking, strapping Soviet women. Like Tamara, they were skilled radio operators. One of the women, a heavy set blonde, swaggered importantly about when ordering Green and his people to a barn allocated for the Americans' use.[10]

The move proved to be timely because the next morning, a reconnaissance patrol reported that a large number of German soldiers were rifling through the camp below they'd just vacated. This news ended any hopes for a respite from constant flight. Green reacted by a prompt order to prepare to move on. This time it would require crossing another towering mountain, one called the killer Chebenec. Alarmed at this development, Catlos studied the airmen. Could they make it in their depleted condition and light summer clothing? He and his OSS cohorts had been trained to endure heavy physical punishment, but these boyish flyers had not. Compounding this fact was the toll confinement in POW camps had taken on these young men, as well as the flu-like illness that was worsening. Catlos swore under his breath, wondering again what had happened to the heavy winter clothing brought in on their flight. He feared that dressed as they were in summer uniforms, these airmen would freeze to death.[11]

Before they left, a kind partisan, taking pity on them, gave Maria a leg of raw venison, telling her it was for the pilots and their crews. Like many Slovak citizens, the partisans admired the Allied pilots and crew, and lauded their daring bombing raids on the enemy factories and other strategic locations. Maria hacked the frozen venison into chunks and plunged them into a pot of water heating over the fire. There was enough time to cook the meat, at least a little, lessening cooking time later.[12]

Suddenly, with no warning, a clap of thunder split the air, followed by the crisp crackling of rifles and the rat-a-tat of machine gun fire exploding bullets all around them. Slugs peppering the ground disappeared like icicles dropping into snowdrifts. They were being fired on by the trained and seasoned Nazi Alpine soldiers, whose orders were to exterminate partisans. Wearing white jumpsuits that blended in with the snow, they appeared as vaporous ghosts dealing out death. Like a startled herd of cattle, everyone in the camp leaped up and raced for an escape route while Green shouted to his people to stay together. Led by MacGregor, they tried to form a single line to climb a steep, twisting trail that led to the mountaintop. They were stumbling, skidding on fresh snow layered over ice patches, pushing, shoving in a wild scramble up the slope, and grabbing at bushes to propel themselves upwards. Behind them a small unit of French partisans fired back at the pursuing enemy.[13]

Maria plucked the blobs of venison out of the water and thrust the dripping chunks into her rucksack before joining the melee. She was buffeted from every angle until she lost her footing and tottered. Panic stricken, she tried to steady herself by grasping onto a bush, certain that if she fell to the ground, she would be trampled by the stampeding partisans. The branch snapped and broke into pieces and she stretched out to grasp another and clung to it, breathing in painful gasps. Snow had turned to sleet that peppered them with icy needles. Visibility was only a few feet and she was trying to peer ahead to get her bearings when she heard Keszthelyi call her name.

"Maria, let go!" he commanded, stretching out a hand to her. She let go of the bush and reached to grasp his outstretched hand, sending her feet into a skid until steadied by Keszthelyi's strong grip. Wedged between him and MacGregor, they clawed their way up the crooked, ice-slick trail. Breath became burning gasps and when she felt she could not go another step, they clambered over the crest and coming to a dead stop, sank onto the ground. There was little chance the enemy, encumbered with heavy weapons, could soon follow.[14]

Around them men panting and choking for air also hit the ground, slumped over from fatigue and shock, but mercifully, there were no serious injuries. The wild wind blew with a vengeance through open space with no trees or brush to lessen the velocity of the gusts nearing gale force. Demonic squalls started off with ghastly whines that died out, only to attack again and again. The mountain Chebenec was called a "mountain of death" for good reason. Accounts were legendary of those who became lost or had fallen to their death into deep crevices trying to conquer this mountain. Visibility was about ten feet and a single misstep might send an unlucky victim tumbling to an icy death over an undetected precipice or set off an avalanche that could snap giant pines like matchsticks.[15]

Although safe for the moment from further attack, after a brief respite, Green ordered them to again move ahead. Mingling with the partisans, the Americans, obviously lost, wandered for two hours, aimlessly seeking shelter. Ice formed on the partisans' machine guns, and when the men pulled woolen masks over their faces, the cloth was soon spotted with red blood from nosebleeds. Every breath was a burning flame until finally the sense of cold faded and weakness from deep fatigue and headaches caused by dehydration set in, until there was a dull ache in every bone. Blinded by the white snow, they crept forward and held onto each others' clothing or gun stocks for safety.[16]

At noon they stopped to rest. Maria parsed out the half raw venison and everyone had a small ration. As soon as they'd consumed the small bits, they were ordered to move on again. They had to find their way to the timberline before dark. To keep climbing or merely wandering ahead, they risked freezing because there was not so much as a twig to start a fire. However, to return to a lower altitude meant crossing icy streams they had avoided since leaving Prasiva.[17]

To one side, Green and Gaul conferred on how best to proceed while the airmen stood about in the snow waiting. Two of them were wheezing from uncontrollable coughing from what appeared to be influenza, and a couple of them were delirious. It was clear that they could not endure endless marching. The morale of the flyers plummeted further when segments of the brigade had begun to disperse and leave. This brought the stifled misgivings about the CFI leadership to the forefront.[17]

At this point, the leaders of the dissidents held their own conference. Two of them remembered being in a village close by and had not seen any Germans in the vicinity. The leaders urged breaking off from the OSS, insisting that it was suicide to go one with them. When Green threatened to have them court-martialed if they left, it was met with a total lack of fear. The will of the men to survive evidently was stronger than concern about a future, nebulous court-martial. They finally announced that they were going back. Doing his best to dissuade them by reason rather than arguing like Gaul, Green pointed out that they were only two days away from the Red Army front. One airman said it was still too far and the sick, freezing, starving flyers would not last another day.[18]

The discontent among the OSS members that had been simmering was now in the open. Despite some misgivings, MacGregor had opted for staying with the Russians because of their strong survival motivation. On the other hand, Green's deep distrust of the Soviets persuaded him to stay with the CFI Brigade, now rapidly unraveling. The opposing factions struggled to find a consensus.[19]

Catlos drew to one side to observe and listen to the two groups struggling to reach an agreement. Although Catlos' and Dunlevy's report would officially state that an agreement was reached, it was done only after bitter words were exchanged, if there was an agreement at all.

A worried Maria watched the tableau, disturbed at the angry voices of Gaul and MacGregor in confrontation with opposing opinions, and wondered what they were arguing about. Keszthelyi explained that the airmen could not keep up with the marches and wanted to go back, escorted by MacGregor and Lain, while the CFI Brigade, Soviet guerrillas and the OSS men gathered into separate groups silently listening to and observing the dramatic tableau.[20]

"These Air Force men are free to make their own decision," MacGregor pointed out logically. "And they have chosen this course."

Growing livid at this breach of authority, Gaul shot back with, "But you are not!"

The two tall, dominant men eyed each other and maintaining his cool, MacGregor assumed a reasoning approach and said that he and Lain were borrowed from the Army to train the CFI partisans but were no longer needed in that capacity and wanted to escort these Air Force men to the village where they had hidden before and felt they could do it again. Abruptly MacGregor then broke away from the glowering Gaul to speak to Dunlevy, asking him if he wanted to join him and Lain and the airmen. Dunlevy's response was prompt and sure. He would stay with the mission. His decision was met with a cool response from MacGregor and Lain.[21]

MacGregor then tuned to Keszthelyi. Sensing his inner struggle, Maria held her breath. "Will you come with me?" he asked her in a near whisper. Her response was as quick and firm as Dunlevy's. She knew that all around and in every village and hamlet there were informers who would reveal their whereabouts. She, too, would stay with Green and the mission. With some reluctance, Keszthelyi then told MacGregor that he, too, would remain with the mission.

MacGregor then approached Maria and reached out to take her hands in his. "This is goodbye, Maria. Thank you for everything."

"Where will you go?"

MacGregor gestured towards the airmen, a few of them now appearing anxious and unsure. "With them." Brushing her cheek with his lips, he added, "Go with the Russkies, Maria. Stay with them."

Then dropping his hands to his sides, MacGregor strode back to the defectors and Lain. At the last moment, British agent Kevin Hansen joined them. Anxiety cut through cut through all of them like the howling winds, leaving each one filled with shock and apprehension. Closing ranks with the departing men, MacGregor took command, his king size paratrooper boots plowing a path through the deep drifts for the others to follow as they began to descend the mountain. In moments they were lost from sight in swirling clouds of snow.[22]

Having watched the encounter in stunned silence, Catlos strongly felt that permission for MacGregor and Lain to leave the group was given reluctantly,

6. Division, Debate, Departure   101

if at all. And why hadn't Keszthelyi and Dunlevy joined them? But he pushed those thoughts aside. Dissent, even in one's mind, was destructive for unity of the group, and besides, it had a way of becoming contagious.[23]

A sense of desolation swept over the Americans, as it did to a lesser extent, the CFI Brigade who had benefited from MacGregor's and Lain's expertise in weapons training. The unity of the mission was now fragmented. Walking beside the silent and evidently still troubled Keszthelyi, Maria felt a keen sense of loss. The tight bond that had existed among the Americans was now broken, leaving them adrift.[24]

A tense, angry Green ordered his people to move on and to stay close together. Walking in a single file, they fell into line. Catlos avoided looking at Dunlevy, concerned that what happened could later have severe repercussions.[25]

"Do you think Mac and Lain would have left even if Green didn't give his okay?"

Dunlevy did not answer. He spewed a stream of tobacco juice from the wad of tobacco in his mouth and shrugged. No answer was needed; they both knew that what had happened could have repercussions.

Behind them, Keszthelyi murmured to Maria that Catlos "better watch his ass" or he could get court-martialed for throwing away the radio when they were running from Donavaly. She gave no response, sensing that a breach of American military rules had perhaps been violated, but a lot lay ahead before such talk could be taken seriously. Unlike the flyers, she doubted they would find the help they wanted so badly, so any talk of courts-martial was very premature and meaningless.[26]

As they trudged in silence, each breath became labored, painful knife thrusts forced into lungs tortured from their efforts. Wild, eerie cries of the wind were followed by sobbing-like echoes and sounded like stalking predators or someone in deep torment. The powdery snow sifted down and clung like fine sand to clothing. Slovak mountaineers called it "*biela tmo,*" meaning "white darkness." Freezing hair tendrils melted from body heat only to freeze again while hands and faces were frostbitten from the pounding half-sleet, half-snow. Ice patches hidden under the falling snow made every step precarious. If one marcher fell, he would knock down the others in line like a row of tenpins. Finally, nearing the timberline, the marchers caught hold of low-lying brush on the banks of a stream to prevent sliding into the water. The marchers hesitated before leaping over the swift current dashing against jagged rocks and those unlucky enough to have a foot slip into the water felt it become instantly benumbed.[27]

When the blizzard diminished slightly, they spotted a large number of the CFI Brigade sitting huddled in a grove of stubby pines. They were the members of the CFI who had deserted after stealing their food the night before. Now they were waiting out the storm. Urged to keep moving if they wanted to avoid freezing, they merely laughed at the warning.

Spying several horses tethered to tree branches, Green negotiated to buy a couple of them. The leader, though, would part with only one horse and snaked out a hand to accept the gold Napoleon for payment. Green then ordered Catlos to use the horse to transport the battery and charger he was lugging. Over his shoulder Catlos glanced at the brigade men huddled in brush with jackets pulled up halfway over their faces to escape the cold, noting they already seemed lifeless as statues.[28]

He tied the pouch with battery and charger to the side of the skittish animal, gripping the reins tightly and nudged the horse ahead. It balked at stepping into the cold stream, forcing Catlos to walk the animal along the bank until they came to a wooden bridge with a sign stating "BRIDGE UNSAFE." He hesitated, but then realized that if he hoped to keep pace with his team moving ahead, he had to chance the crossing. He gave a sharp kick to the horse's flank at which the animal pawed a hoof before gingerly setting it down onto the planks while Catlos spoke gently to reassure the animal. All went well until halfway across the bridge, he felt the rotting planks give way. He tried frantically to hold onto the panic-stricken animal as it plunged into the water, struggling to free itself. Standing knee deep in the freezing, swirling stream, Catlos frantically tugged against the horse's strength as it pulled further away, until finally the animal broke free and bolted up the bank and galloped into a cluster of pines. With a sinking heart Catlos watched it disappear before he turned and stumbled ahead, until he began to catch up with his companions.[29]

He was too far away to hear Keszthelyi's acid comment to Maria. "He can't even hold onto a damn horse!"

Maria felt that the derision would have been a blow to Catlos' spirit, who — despite his strong façade of being a loner — had a sensitive side. It was enough to lose the horse with the batteries and charger, which would be a blow to the strongest male.[30]

It was midnight when the weary marchers met up with Colonel Prykryl's brigade. Studensky was still with them, as were Tamara and two of Studensky's aides. Two Jewish partisans lent Horvath, Keszthelyi and Gaul axes to chop branches off trees to erect shelters and start a fire. It was ignited with the last of Paris' film that coaxed twigs and kindling into wavering flames. Huddling close to the fire, the snow on their clothing melted on one side only to become almost instantly refrozen when they turned to warm the other side.[31]

6. Division, Debate, Departure

Maria sat on her backpack and removed her boot to examine her foot, frostbitten from the icy stream. It was swollen and turning white. One of the partisans, who said he was a doctor, inspected the foot and advised her to rub it with snow. He then went down the line checking their freezing feet. Morton's and Paris's feet were also in bad condition and he urged the men to rub snow on them.[32]

In dire need of food, Green tried to haggle with one of Prykyl's officers to buy some supplies, telling him they would pay in gold or Slovak korunas.

"Money?" the man said derisively. "You can't eat money. Besides, my outfit doesn't have enough for ourselves, let alone to sell."

It was a lie, leading the frustrated Green to again order his men to steal food when possible. Horvath and Catlos soon obliged by cadging a slab of bacon and a small sack of flour, while Maria bartered for two rock hard loaves of bread they choked down, leaving them even more ravenous.[33]

After consuming their small ration, they crawled into a tent-like shelter made from pine boughs that provided some protection from the wind and snow. Trying to protect her aching foot, Maria stretched out beside Keszthelyi, worried about not only her disabled foot but also those of Morton, Paris and some of the others. As daylight faded and night crept over the campsite, the temperature plunged downward and all talk ceased until, from a short distance away, a woman voice singing in Russian broke the silence.

> Long ago when my mother rocked me in her arms,
> Long ago when my mother loved me so
> The world was magic, love was everywhere
> Long ago, oh, so long ago.

The singer was Tamara. The pathos in her soft voice gave the simple words a touch of poignant magic. As the last echo of her malady faded into the night, the sojourners retreated into themselves, each surrendering to his or her own personal fears, heartache and loneliness for that one special person so very far away.[34]

In the morning Green and Gaul decided they would stay at their present location until the blizzards diminished. The day was agonizingly long with only another small ration of bacon and a chunk of hard bread to sustain them. The starvation repast was followed by a longer, colder night with the heavy snows unrelenting.

The second morning dawned bright and clear with rays of sunlight creating pink and mauve highlights on the glistening ice-coated drifts beneath a pastel blue sky. The contrast with the previous two or three days was so stark that it was as though the blizzards of the last few days had never happened.[35]

Studensky held a long conference with Prykryl. Then, apparently ready to depart, he approached Maria. He asked first about her foot and then told her they were disbanding and invited her to join them. Every man was free to go his own way but he and his entourage were heading for Poland. Tamara, still lugging the heavy radio and a tight-lipped Mikhail hovered nearby uneasily.

Maria locked glances with Tamara for a second or two and recalled her earlier comment on the unfairness of Tamara doing the most laborious tasks. "Tamara Ivanova," she'd protested, "You do all the heavy work; doesn't Studensky or Mikhail ever help?"

Her question had shocked Tamara. "He's the commander," was all she could say. To her, that explained everything.[36]

Now that they were parting company for good, the bitterness Maria felt towards her former Russian colleagues melted like snowflakes dropping into flames. It no longer mattered. Her only regret was that she would never see Tamara again. When the revolt had collapsed and Banska Bystrica fell to the enemy, Maria had decided to keep moving to avoid suspicion and vengeance. She also promised General Viest that she would stay with the Americans. Most of all, it was Tibor Keszthelyi she could not bear to leave. Furthermore, she had long ago ceased to trust the Russians and now told Studensky she would stay with the Americans.

Fastening her with a long, penetrating look, the officious Studensky had one final word of advice. It was for Maria to get rid of her American clothes, dress as a native, and hide out in some small village. He warned that the Americans walked further into danger with every step they took. At that, he whirled about and stalked off, Tamara plodding in his wake. The rest of his unit broke off into groups of twos and threes and slowly drifted off into varying directions.[37]

The Americans had no other option than to also pull out. The way ahead would be hellish and some of them lightened their packs to ease the journey. Although the temperature had risen a few degrees, it was still bitterly cold and anyway, the pale sunshine and clear skies would not last long. It was only November 12, and the long mountain winter, like the war, showed no signs of diminishing any time soon.[38]

* * *

For MacGregor, Lain, and the flyers, their war had already come to an abrupt end. The men had waded through heavy snows to the outskirts of the village of Zelzno where they came upon a shepherd's hut. It was nearing nightfall and seeing no footsteps in the snow, they concluded the enemy was nowhere near. They decided it was best to stay the night and look for the family they had stayed with previously in the morning. It seemed a most welcome respite.[39]

But the reprieve would be a short one. It ended when an enemy patrol stepped out of the frosty woods, surrounding MacGregor and two of the flyers who had gone ahead to make a quick inspection of the surroundings. At the dreaded shout of "Halt!" they looked up into the circle of sub-machine guns pointed in their direction. MacGregor swore and raised hands above his head. All the Americans followed suit.[40]

Unlike Schwartz before him, the battle-hardened MacGregor had already taken the precaution of instructing the airmen to adhere to the story that they were all flyers. Above all, no one was to ever admit to being a bombardier if he hoped to remain alive. It was a wise precaution because the German patrol commander put a stop to any attempt at conversation. "*Stille!*" he bellowed and motioned for the Americans to drop their weapons and fall into line while his men picked up the discarded guns. For MacGregor and Lain and the Englishman Hansen, this was their first capture and they were now prisoners. For the airmen, it was the second time to be captives of the enemy but this time, their ordeal as German prisoners of war would be decidedly more grim and would last until the end of the war.[41]

7

LOVE BLOSSOMS, EVEN IN HELL

A sense of desolation like a black cloud hung over those remaining in the unit following the departure of MacGregor, Lain and the airmen. The cohesive spirit of unity that had bonded the men together in the mission had been dealt an irrevocable blow. And now that Studensky had disbanded his unit and they had gone their separate way for good, the Americans were on their own.

Maria had no illusions about their precarious situation even before the latest report by a Soviet guerrilla patrol that Brezno had been taken by the enemy, which released a large number of anti-partisan units to be dispersed throughout the mountain area to hunt and kill partisans and anyone with them. The enemy knew that the Americans were with Colonel Prykryl and his brigade but as yet, they did not know exactly where. She felt empathetic with Green over the frustration he must have felt after the fracture of his unit, a blow to his spirit that he could not entirely conceal.[1]

Despite Green's earlier experience observing Marshall Tito's partisans in Yugoslavia, he had not been subjected to the physical and psychological stress on the scale they continued to face. By contrast, Gaul had spent months digging at archeological sites and endured exposure to the elements. Prior to going into the field, he trained at Harvard for hard physical work.[2]

Dunlevy was of the opinion that Green was a product of the "Social Navy" rather than the blood and guts "real" Navy that developed leaders who would know how to cope with the mind-numbing realities in which they were enmeshed. One of the most crucial was the personal decision each agent might have to make in the event of capture.[3]

"I'll chew that pill first to make sure it works," Catlos declared. This was the rubber-coated cyanide L-pill that every agent carried. He was cognizant

7. Love Blossoms, Even in Hell

of the experience of one of the British agents, Jack Wilson, who was to parachute in the vicinity of Vienna. Instead, the pilot was off course and Wilson landed near Bratislava and was captured by CFI partisans. Since he could not reveal his identity and spoke fluent German, he was suspected of being a German spy and they beat him so unmercifully he tried to use the capsule which, when bitten into, kills in thirty seconds. By accident, he swallowed it and therefore lived to tell about it.[4]

Dunlevy raised one eyebrow at Catlos' remark, spat a dribble of tobacco juice from the last shreds dug out of his shirt pocket and patted the Bible in his jacket pocket. Easy enough to say that when capture is not imminent, he thought. But he was a pragmatist and well aware that as the only cryptographer in the unit who knew all their codes, he would be the one most harshly treated in the zeal for information on American intelligence operations. Still, he rationalized, one does not truly know what course he will choose until presented with the actuality facing him, and he prayed that he would never have to decide such a deadly dilemma.[5]

After some deliberation with Gaul, Green ordered his people to press on to where they were told the Russian Red Army front would be. Their first stop was to be the village of Dolnia Lehota. Pushing ahead resolutely, they plodded ahead on frostbitten feet and with stomachs empty. The few spoonfuls of beans they consumed at three o'clock that morning could not sustain them. And as the CFI brigade no longer shared their diminishing supply of food, a bitter point with the Americans, this was to precipitate a final separation from them. When they paused for a brief rest, Green announced that they were splitting from the CFI.[6]

Dunlevy, for one, was relieved at the decision to separate from the CFI. He had felt all along that being part of such a large group made them extra vulnerable, easier to trace and locate as well as slowing progress. He was not surprised when Prykryl insisted on assigning two of his men to act as guide for the Americans. Although they could not have known that at the outset of the revolt, Stalin had placed all resistance units under the NKVD secret police for observation and reports, the Americans had all along suspected them of being more spies than guides.[7] Dunlevy was glad to see Prykryl and what remained of his brigade take their leave and head for Poland.

The guides, Sascha and Pavlo, insisted they had to retrace part of their journey which necessitated a descent into the valley they had just come through and then to ascend to the mountain range and cross it under dark skies turning heavy with snow. After a silent, dreary march of about two kilometers, the marchers stumbled to an abrupt halt. Stunned, they could only gawk at the sight before them. The 83 brigade members who had stolen their food, deserted and then holed up to wait out the blizzard, were now frozen corpses. Their mummy-like faces were almost completely concealed under collars of ragged jackets and woolen helmets. The scene was as shocking as it would have been had they come unexpectedly upon a field of mutilated bodies after a bloody battle. For these men, though, death had not been violent; it had come in stealth under the guise of warmth and sleep. The packhorses were sprawled nearby with legs thrust out like sticks dusted over with snow, the animals resembling wooden carvings.[8]

Catlos murmured a silent prayer and glanced at Morton, mesmerized by the deadly spectacle. He wondered how the war correspondent would describe the stark scene when he wrote this particular story. And the horror shown on the faces of Heller and Brown, the two youngest among them, was to be unforgettable. Averting their eyes after the initial observation, the Americans moved on and before long came across a small a small encampment of partisans. A couple of them were French and able to converse with Gaul and Perry. The rag tag group said they had been released from a POW camp by the CFI during the revolt and were now surviving by their wits and whatever weapons they still had.[9]

The leader told Gaul that although they hadn't spotted enemy patrols for two or three days, which was most unusual, there was a worse problem. It was that villagers were fed up with partisans stealing their food and livestock and complained to the Germans who were combing the surrounding woods searching for stray partisans. The Frenchmen shared their meal of stew concocted from horsemeat and beans and also sold Green some dry beans to take with them. The Americans rested for an hour and then were on the move again.[10]

Progress was painfully slow and they were soon exhausted, cold, and wet from unrelenting snow and sleet. Walking was treacherous. Maria slipped and fell several times and found it harder to get up each time. Curses resounded behind her from men also slipping and falling on snow covered patches of ice. Dunlevy skidded and fell and lay prone until Catlos implored him to get up, then reached down and pulled Dunlevy to his feet. Like wordless robots they shuffled ahead with their unit.

As daylight faded, the temperatures plummeted and the cold turned even more biting and cruel. They did not reach the outskirts of Dolnia Lehota until nine o'clock. Sacha and Pavlos protested Green's decision to stay the night, insisting that the village would be crawling with enemy patrols. Green was adamant, however, and decided they would continue moving in the morning. While the exhausted group flopped where they were, too exhausted to care one way or another, he and Gaul pored over a map.[11]

7. Love Blossoms, Even in Hell

After an hour's rest, Maria decided that trudging around aimlessly was futile. Reports were unreliable and no one had any idea how far away the Red front was. She would seek out a friend who lived in Dolnia Lehota and find out what she could, and with a bit of luck, she might be able to obtain some food. The name of her friend was Terka Pajedova, but Maria called her Zuzka. She was a young woman who had taught school in Hrinova at the same time Maria had. Accompanying Maria was Keszthelyi and the two partisan guides.[12]

Those left behind huddled over campfires, resigned to another night of cold, snow and gnawing hunger. Their ration that night consisted of three tablespoons of beans per man.

Intelligence personnel are trained to be wary of everyone. One never knows who might turn out to be a betrayer. By this time, the men of Dawes had carefully sized each other up and arrived at some semblance of trust with one or two others. That night, Catlos was keenly aware of the misery each one felt and his spirits sank lower than they'd been since they left Banska Bystrica.[13]

Surreptitiously he studied the men around him. Dunlevy, with his eyes closed, was hunched over to preserve his energy, his jaws working over bits of tobacco, barely moving. Horvath sat next to Dunlevy. With his stoic strength and uncommon good looks, the Slovak-American Horvath could have been a movie star playing the role of a brave, adventurous soldier, except that Horvath's solid endurance and efforts to serve the mission were very real.

Lieutenant Lane Miller, the slight, twenty-three-year-old pilot son of a Navy officer, had been sent to Tri Duby to fly a planeload of evacuees back to Bari and became trapped with the rest of the missions. Miller sure didn't have any pull here, Catlos reflected, noting the pilot's fair hair becoming straggly and his abject expression.[14]

Squatting almost on top the fire were the two big guys, Gaul and Paris. Near them was Mican, looking decidedly older than his thirty-eight years. It occurred to Catlos that Green, too, appeared to be older than his thirty-three years despite still bearing himself like an officer and gentleman.

Like Dunlevy, Catlos would have preferred Gaul, a fellow native of Pittsburgh, as commander. The man's features, now much leaner, accentuated his jaw that jutted out like a mountain crag. Amazingly though, Gaul still exuded strength and confidence.

To one side as usual, Morton sat near the fire, straining to see sufficiently to write in his notebook. Catching Catlos' curious gaze, Morton flashed him a smile, his strong white teeth a gleam of friendliness in the near dark. With dismay, Catlos realized that for all of them, morale was at its lowest ebb since they started on this march that appeared to be headed nowhere.[15]

Above and opposite: Jovial OSS agent Joseph Horvath greeting Russian partisans in Italy. Horvath was often teased by agent Steven Catlos because he talked about his beloved wife, Alma, a lot (courtesy Rudy Horvath, brother of Joseph Horvath).

* * *

While the others waited at camp, Maria, Keszthelyi and the two guides set out for Dolnia Lehota. Slithery terrain and the necessity of crossing streams impeded their progress. Sacha and Pavlo were ready to give up until they reached a meadow where walking was easier. It was eleven o'clock and dark as the inside of a cave when they located the edge of the village, where there was only one house with a light still on. They approached it with caution. Pavlo crawled to a spot beneath a window and raised his head to peer inside. His presence alerted a dog inside that barked an alarm. The door flew open and a man stood in the doorway and called out to them. "Come in, come in!"[16]

When Maria stepped forward, Keszthelyi grabbed her arm and gave a negative shake of his head indicating it could be a set up. Maria took a close look and demurred. He was probably a householder who was used to wayfarers stopping by. They entered the house warily while Pavlo and Sascha kept

7. Love Blossoms, Even in Hell

watch outside. Typical of rural areas, the small dwelling had a wooden plank floor with hand braided rugs in the center, featuring one long, single room with a kitchen at the far end. Their host, a sturdy peasant type, gestured at them to sit down at the kitchen table. He hacked off thick chunks of bread and ladled potato soup into earthen bowls from a large pot on the stove. The guides remained outside on the lookout until Maria and Keszthelyi finished eating and then came in and took their turn to eat. As soon as the food was consumed, their host told them they had to leave because the *Nemci* would return early in the morning.[17]

The foursome stepped out into the night and walked further into the village until they spotted another house with a light on. This time, Maria crept to the window and rapped. A startled woman, eyes wide with fear, demanded to know what she wanted. Maria asked where Terka Pajedova lived. The woman opened the door slightly and pointed to a house further on. Again, the men stayed out of sight while Maria investigated.

"Who is it?" Zuska inquired from behind the closed door, at the sound of her knock.

"It's me, Maria."

The door flew open and Zuska hugged Maria but was unable to conceal her shocked expression. "My God, Maria! You're a partisan!"

"No, dear friend, I am not a partisan," Maria assured her. "I'm with some Americans." She beckoned to Keszthelyi to join them while the two guides again kept watch.

Once inside, Keszthelyi and Zuzka's father were soon conversing in Hungarian. The older man was intrigued, but puzzled, by the American presence in Slovakia and candidly asked about their political intent. After hearing Keszthelyi out, the older man leaned back and shook his head angrily.

"You think the Bolsheviks are better than the *Nemci*? I was in Russia in the last war. What I saw and lived through you would not believe. If you knew the Russians like I did, you would never be on their side."

Keszthelyi allayed the man's disapproval by explaining they were not pro-communist, but rather had come to assist the Slovak CFI and to rescue their downed American airmen trapped in the mountains of Slovakia. Now all they cared about was to get back home alive.[18]

Zuzka was avid for details of Maria since she left Hrinova without a word to anyone. Maria replied that no one would believe her story, but one day she would tell her all of it. But right now, she and the men with her were dead tired and desperately needed a rest.

Zuzka's mother sliced sausages and black bread and boiled water for tea. When ready, she set plates before Maria and Keszthelyi. While they ate, Zuzka's father slipped out and returned with his oldest daughter, Mary, who lived several houses away. She would escort them to a store where they might buy food.

It was two o'clock in the morning when they knocked at the door of a shuttered house. The proprietor admitted them only after Mary made herself

7. Love Blossoms, Even in Hell

known. His nervous wife and curious young son filled their rucksacks with bread, bacon, smoked pork and barley. They lugged the bags back to Zuzka's, prepared to say goodbye. However, Zuzka and her parents would not consider allowing Maria and Keszthelyi to wander around at night. They had to stay until morning.[19]

In minutes a bed for them was created from a table that pulled out to the length of a narrow bed and then padded with a feather tick mattress and covered with blankets. Pavlo and Sascha were escorted to the barn where they would sleep on bundles of hay.

The kitchen was warm and cozy from the wood-burning stove. Maria removed her boots and thrust her swollen foot close to the fire. The pulsating ache was a good sign, she decided. It meant that feeling was still present and her foot was healing. Removing any clothing other than heavy jacket was out of the question. Seconds taken to put them on again could mean the difference between life and death.

Like most village houses, there were no doors and rooms were separated by alcoves with little privacy. Keszthelyi stretched out on the soft bed and heaved a contented sigh. By the flickering firelight Maria noted that color was seeping back into his gray, drawn features. But not until Zuzka and her parents retired to their beds did Maria settle down beside Keszthelyi, who reached out to touch her hair, whispering, "I wish I could see it loose and down around your pretty face."[20]

Across Maria's mind flitted the image of green-eyed Tamara whose auburn hair was cropped as closely as the men's. While it was trim, and—like the utilitarian Russian uniforms—easy to care for, the style was hardly attractive. Was that how she appeared to him with her tight braids and military uniform? In any event, in war, women are wise to conceal any attractiveness they possess.

She lay awake for a time, savoring the flying moments. This was nothing like the impassioned love she imagined between a man and woman. Her thoughts swept back to the days just past and realized that she began to fall in love with Keszthelyi when he risked being trampled to rescue her in the stampede when they fled up the mountain. Later, when he refused to leave with MacGregor and Lain but chose to stay with her, she fell completely in love with him. Her closed-off feelings had reopened and added to the growing closeness and trust that was healing the bruised emotions from Velichko's brutality. She had been attracted to other young men and had had a number of marriage proposals, but she had never felt like this. She tried to rationalize that it was the drama and mystery of the adventure, but deep inside she knew that this was different. But what hope was there for them?[21]

Mrs. Pajedova rose at the first ray of daylight to prepare a breakfast of noodles laced with nuts and sugar to be washed down with glasses of scalding tea. When they'd finished, Maria reached for her boots. Forcing the one over her swollen calf felt like pressing burning coals against raw flesh. Catching her grimace of pain, Zuzka exclaimed, "Holy Mother of God!" and rushed off to reappear with a pair of felt boots with leather soles that slipped on Maria's feet easily. All the while, the bubbly Zuzka, whose brown hair framed a round face and sparkling dark eyes, could not refrain from curiosity and once again wondered what she was doing with these partisans and an American. She did not need to mention that her life and those of her parents were also in peril if discovered helping Maria and the American and the partisans.

Rather than explain, Maria diverted Zuska by asking her to get word to her parents that she was all right. But Zuzka could not be put off so easily and wanted to know what sort of future Maria had with the young man she was in love with. Maria shrugged and said the only future they could hope for at the moment was to reach the Red Army front and then, God alone knew.

With a knowing wink, Zuzka slipped into Maria's hand a simple narrow band crafted from silver in local mines. It was suitable for a wedding ring. Maria tucked it in her inner jacket pocket and smiled at Zuska, wishing she could tell her more but it was not prudent.[22]

Before they left, Zuzka's father told them about a farmer who would provide shelter that night for all their group and also information about a large number of partisans bivouacked in deserted barracks near a mining camp about six kilometers into the woods. Two twelve-year-old neighbor boys would show the way for Maria and Keszthelyi to check it out while Pavlo and Sascha carried the food back to their camp.

Keszthelyi was dubious about the boys acting as guides. Could they be trusted? Maria assured him that these boys were not as naive as they might seem. Actually, they could be the safest possible cover because, while they might look and act dumb, they could say "I don't know" to questions asked and be believed. Older boys and adults could not get away with playing that game.[23] Maria had to repress a smile, recalling boys not much older than these two, grown physically into men who flirted with her in class, requiring her to reject them without damaging fragile budding male egos. Nearing the vicinity of the camp, the boys pointed the way ahead and left them to return to their homes.

When they were almost at the camp, Maria and Keszthelyi were confronted by two partisans who materialized out of the pine thicket to block their passage. Bristling with hostility, their eyes narrowed at the sight of a man and woman in American Army uniforms. They brandished rifles at Maria

7. Love Blossoms, Even in Hell

and Keszthelyi's heads and demanded to know who they were and what they wanted.[24]

Maria hastened to explain that she was a guide and interpreter for some Americans who came to help them. And they were told by a friend of this camp where they would find refuge from the enemy. One of the sentries was not convinced and spat out the accusation that they were spies.

"Dressed like this?" Maria came back at him.

Fingering the trigger menacingly, after a long hard look he relented, warning her that they better be telling the truth, and finally let them pass.

The area was under the control of Major Surkov of the Red Army. His eyes were like probing searchlights as he listened to Maria's identify herself and Keszthelyi and explain their plight. However, he agreed to allow the Americans to join them, but he said he could spare only one room. Assuring him they would return with the remainder of their group in a day or two, Maria and Keszthelyi made their way back to the village.[25]

The picturesque trails were an idyllic scene for a painting or postcard. About halfway back to the farmer's house, they paused to rest in a glen surrounded by a sea of tall pines. In the benign setting with soft breezes sifting through the branches, it seemed totally ironic that all around them were German warriors and Soviet soldiers, various partisans, and potential betrayers eager to turn them in as captives. Keszthelyi removed his parka and spread it on the ground and reached out for Maria to sit beside him. She glanced at the towering trees that reached to the sky like a protective blanket and lifted her head to let the soft breeze brush her hair like the tender touch of a mother or lover and drank in the deep stillness that was a balm to her spirit. It was interrupted by Keszthelyi putting his arm around her waist and murmuring, "What a brave girl you are Maria. I have never met a girl like you before."[26]

"Brave? Not really. I am just trying to survive like you and the other men are doing."

Acutely conscious of his touch, Maria's feelings fused into a warm glow, and she leaned against his shoulder. But seconds later, an almost imperceptible sound of a branch dropping to the ground reminded her of their precarious situation. It alerted her sense of warning about partisans or any wayfarers who could come creeping through the woods at any moment and consider them fair game. She arose reluctantly as did Keszthelyi. Hands clasped, they continued their journey.[27]

* * *

When Sascha and Pavlo rejoined the Americans at their camp, the waiting men let out happy whoops when they spied the sacks of food. Equally appreciated was the promise of a warm shelter that night. After a quick snack, Green ordered the unit to move on. They set off and reached the dwelling of the farmer shortly after Maria and Keszthelyi arrived. Green was elated to hear about the barracks where they could stay, although the men were too exhausted to move immediately, and a night in a warm shelter of the farmer's house was most welcome.[28]

The farmer's wife led the men to an alcove used for storage above the floor level rooms of the dwelling. Heat from the kitchen stove seeped through the walls, creating a warm haven. The house was in charming disarray with laundered sheets and pillow cases hanging from ceiling rods to dry and blankets and clothing spilling out of every corner. She warned the men to remain out of sight and disappeared, only to return minutes later bearing a wooden tray with a mound of creamy white Brinza cheese and two loaves of freshly baked bread and hot tea. She was charmed by Horvath, who graciously thanked her.

"You Slovak?" she asked.

He winked. "Once a Slovak, always a Slovak," he replied in their language.

The men hungrily consumed the food and then stretched out on the floor and in seconds were asleep. They were still asleep at dusk when the farmer left the house to check on his livestock in the barn. Catlos cocked an anxious ear towards an unfamiliar sound, then realized it was the creaking of a bucket let down into the well to fill and bring up with fresh water. A minute or two later, their hostess appeared, carrying a bowl of sausages and noodles and more bread and tea. He relaxed. It was going to be a pleasant night for a change.[29]

Maria helped their benefactor clean the kitchen in preparation for a sewing circle that consisted of a couple of neighbor women joining their benefactor for one of the few social occasions farm women enjoyed during the long winter months. Maria was to join the two round, apple-dumpling shaped women whose ages were hard to determine. Almost all adult village women wore long, dark woolen skirts and heavy shirts in winter, and lighter cotton garments in summer. A culture where fashion was important did not exist for them. The visitors accepted glasses of hot tea and plopped into chairs near the stove, baskets of sewing beside them, totally unaware of the fourteen Americans and two Slovak partisans resting in the loft above.

A borrowed shapeless sweater draped over her legs and an old shirt to conceal her American clothing, Maria and the women worked by the light of a kerosene lamp. She was enjoying the familiar play of needle through cloth when there was a sharp rap at the door. The women exchanged warning glances as their hostess rose to open the door. From outside came the sound of a truck engine running and German voices. Maria risked one quick glance at the two German soldiers who appeared to be far beyond combat age. What she saw corroborated rumors of a decline in the quality of enemy troops.[30] Some famous Wehrmacht divisions were said to have been decimated and consisted mainly of phantom troops made up of older men and young boys. Even so, they were still a powerful force to contend with, especially for partisans and guerrillas, whom they feared and detested. One patrol commander described them as appearing like lightning rods out of the darkness to deal out death and then fading back into the shadows like ghosts.[31]

The harsh growl of the soldier at the door reverberated through the small dwelling.

"*Partizanen?*"

The quick response was, "*No Partizanen.*"

The pair glanced over her head to scan the interior of the house but saw only middle aged women whose plain appearances elicited little interest. And all they could see of Maria was the shapeless sweater and afghan over her legs, the kerchief covering her hair, and a sewing basket. Passing inspection, the soldiers said, "*Auf Wiedersehen*," and clumped away, the roar of the truck engine signaling departure.

For a moment their hostess leaned against the closed door, one hand to her chest. "So," she said tremulously, "all is well, for now," and sank back onto her chair, shaking hands barely able to grasp her needle.[32]

Upstairs the Americans shoved firearms back into holsters and relaxed, not speaking until they were sure the visiting women also left, and then only in low voices praising the woman for her courage and coolness under fire.

The noodles and pork sausage had sated appetites and now the warmth of their secret shelter was sleep-inducing. Around him Catlos saw the men drifting into sleep, grateful to the brave couple who would have paid with their lives if discovered offering food and solace to some hunted American commandos thousands of miles from home.[33]

Maria slipped her feet out of the felt boots and stretched out on a blanket and quilt that had been spread out on the floor in front of the stove for her. But she was too shaken from the close call to be able to fall asleep at once. In the soft glow of dying embers she murmured a prayer for these kind natives who extended their blessings of food and shelter to strangers. She said another for the unfortunate men of the brigade whose desire for the warmth they all craved had lured them into a permanent sleep.[34]

Curled up on the floor, Catlos also dwelled on the kindness of their hosts, knowing that the risk of death for these kind people was real. He recalled Green's report to Bari stating he personally knew of such natives who paid with their lives for aiding partisans or American escapees from POW camps.[35]

Catlos would have been gratified to know that his observations about the kindness typically shown by people who loved and worked the land was shared by the father of Mira Mullen, who was one of the planners of the assassination of the infamous SS chief Heinrich Heydrich, whom Hitler referred to as "the man with the iron heart."[36] Mullen's father had observed that there were two kinds of reactions to the horrors of World War II. Those close to the earth knew the value of compassion, whereas the urban bourgeoisie had discarded that saving human trait and it was each person for himself.

Sadly, the assassination of Heydrich resulted in one of the most hideous atrocities of the war. It was the destruction of the Czech village of Lidice where its inhabitants, five hundred innocent men, women and children, were rounded up and shot in collective reparation for Heydrich's life. The Germans relied on collective responsibility to weaken spirits and executed thousands of men, women and children for acts of defiance or resistance.[37]

All the assassins except Mullen's father found refuge in the basement of a monastery until betrayed, tortured and executed. Her father escaped to the United States where he served America, this time against the communist threat. He retired a broken man who spent the rest of his days in repentance and grief over the tragic victims of Lidice whose lives were demanded in retaliation for that of one evil Nazi.[38]

8

A Real Thanksgiving

The weary sleepers were wakened by the crowing of a rooster, bringing harsh reality crashing into any pleasant dreams they might have been enjoying. Faint rays of dawn brought the reminder that the first priority of the new day was to confront and then survive the challenges it presented.

The farmer and his wife were already up. She bustled around the kitchen stoking the fire and preparing breakfast as he tended to the livestock. Warm and cozy beside the fire, Maria was loathe to leave this haven, especially when jagged shoots of pain darted up from the festering sores on her foot. Tugging the felt boots on over the swollen area, she involuntarily let out a soft outcry, bringing the woman thumping over to inspect the foot. She took one look, rolled her eyes and gasped, "Holy Mother of God! You have to see a doctor right away!"

The prospect of finding a trusted doctor was as hopeless as regaining the twenty years of the form of democracy they'd had and for which many, like Maria, were fighting to regain. But to appease the concerned woman, Maria shrugged and said that she would.[1]

With a worried expression, their benefactor summoned the men who clumped down to the kitchen where a large platter of fried sausage and bread and a steaming pot of barley awaited

While the men ate, his wife kept watch at the window. The repast vanished in a few minutes, delicious bites washed down with glasses of hot tea. Outside, her husband drew water from the well while also keeping a watchful eye on roads and surroundings. As the Americans took their leave, he waved a hand in farewell, lips moving perceptively. Catlos and Maria exchanged a quick smile, aware of what he was saying although they could not hear him. He was sending them off with a blessing, whispering, "*Iz Bohom*" ("Go with God"), the customary blessing natives bestowed upon departing visitors.

Before slipping out the door, Green had surreptitiously placed several gold coins under his plate. And just before they moved out of sight of the brave couple, he and his men turned to look back at the humble dwelling, then out of gratitude and respect for their benefactors, bowed their heads slightly and tipped caps in farewell.[2]

It was a seven-kilometer march to the barracks near Kracova. They played it safe by avoiding the roads; this necessitated pushing through clusters of trees with snow-laden branches and heavy brush, which hindered progress considerably. Nearing their destination, Green called a halt and looked them over.

"For God's sake, what a bunch of sad sacks! Straighten up and march like soldiers! We're meeting foreign military officers and its our duty to show them we are American military men with an important mission and not a bunch of rag tag bunch of gypsies roaming around!"

Catlos repressed the acid comment on the tip of his tongue. It was that they did look more like a batch of wet chickens rather than a determined military mission with a purpose. However, like his colleagues, he scraped at chin stubble and sloshed off grime with handfuls of snow and dabbed at spots on his parka, shuddering when the snow numbed his face.[3]

Dunlevy marveled that Maria never needed anything more than a quick pat of snow over cheeks and forehead and to tighten her braids to pass muster. And he marveled at how her neatness and calm composure were a great morale builder for all of the men.[4]

The barracks had been built around abandoned antimony mines and now served as a partisan and guerrilla camp under the command of Major Surkov. It was jammed with several hundred Russian guerrillas and remnants of CFI partisan units. Surkov greeted Green and Gaul cordially. He ordered his guerrillas, who had been inhabiting one hut and were loathe to relinquish it, to surrender it to the Americans. When Pavlo and Sascha also pushed their way into the flimsy structure, the sixteen Americans, Maria, and now their guides, took up every inch of space suitable for a half dozen people at most.[5]

The rudimentary dwelling was a typical shelter used for short periods by shepherds or foresters, but luckily, it was one that had a working stove. In no time, Horvath, Miller and Dunlevy and a couple of the other men gathered enough twigs and small branches to coax into smoldering, smoky flames. Meanwhile, Green rationed what remained of the food and ordered Mican to act as liaison with the remaining CFI and bargain for supplies, even though one officer claimed earlier that they had none to spare. After they settled in the barracks and took a short rest, Maria and Keszthelyi walked back to the

8. A Real Thanksgiving   121

farmer's house to buy a piglet from the couple as agreed upon before they left. They paid for the squealing animal with Slovak korunas and the farmer promised to butcher the animal and deliver it in the morning. He proved to be faithful to his word and the result was that by evening, everyone feasted on roast pork and black bread.[6] Catlos idly wondered if Heller and Perry, both Jewish, had any reservations about eating pork, then realized how silly such a thought had to be. After all, war is war and anyone unlucky enough to be in a war knows that almost any food is acceptable.

They welcomed the bits of news from BBC on the war. But when they tried to contact OSS Bari they failed because the power pack had been rendered unworkable due to exposure to dampness. It was a bitter disappointment.[7]

Gaul remained uneasy at being a part of such a large group and asked Green how long he thought they should remain at the barracks. He pointed a finger at the radio transmitter on top of Surkov's headquarters, their only link to the rest of the world. He commented that the damned thing stuck out like a sore thumb, wondering aloud how long it would be before they would be detected and smoked out.

It was a daily cat and mouse game, with the enemy patrolling the area by day with signal detectors trying to pinpoint their exact location before the Russians finished radioing messages to Kiev and then turned off their radio apparatus. Everyone knew that it was only a matter of time before the Germans located the camp.[8]

As it turned out, the guides assigned by Prykryl did accomplish some good. By snooping around, Pavlo and Sasha came across a larger hut an hour's trek further up the mountain trail from where they were able to survey anyone approaching. And Surkov gave his okay for Green to move his group move to the new location. The flimsy structure was composed of wooden slats and looked as though a good wind would topple it to the ground. But it did have a working stove and a well in the clearing and it had enough space to house the OSS party.[9]

The Americans were allocated three rooms by a dozen French partisans occupying the shack. That evening, Gaul parsed out the remainder of the monies with which he had been charged, with the admonition that the British gold Sterlings and French Napoleons were for the purpose of persuading villagers to sell food or any useful items the men might find of use. Keszthelyi handed his share of the money to Maria for her to keep. She instantly demurred. Keszthelyi was puzzled. "Why not? You've been the one getting food and shelter for us and paying with coins."

Thoughts raced through Maria's mind as to how she would be perceived if found to be in possession of a sizable amount of foreign money. She would be considered just another empty-headed female camp follower deemed to be in the Resistance movement only for money. To make her stance clear, she pushed the bag of coins back to Keszthelyi.[10]

She caught a glimpse of Gaul's frown of disapproval at Keszthelyi's actions and felt a rise of resentment at his coolness towards her. She realized that to this super macho leader-type officer, she was out of her proper place and he could not help resenting her being part of the mission. But it galled her that when he and Green could rely on men such as Prykryl, and now Surkov, Gaul ignored her and displayed his friendlier side only when she was the only person who dared enter occupied villages to seek out food, shelter and information. Fully aware of Gaul's hostility, she decided she had to keep a cool head, even with Tibor who was insisting that she keep the money. Irritated at her refusal to accept it, Keszthelyi stuffed the bag of coins into a pocket inside his parka and angrily strode away.[11]

The next few days were uneventful, providing them with the opportunity to rest and recoup. And the kind farmer on occasion brought eggs, butter, bread and whatever else he could spare. On one trip, he proudly produced some scarce medical items. The pungent ointment he brought was a godsend which alleviated some of the pain of frostbitten feet. Slowly, with shelter, rest and some nourishing food, strength seeped back into exhausted, malnourished bodies and renewed hope into sagging spirits.[12]

The two Slovak nurses at Surkov's camp kindly offered their services to the Americans. Periodically they trudged up to where the Americans were staying to examine their frostbitten feet and do whatever they could to assist in the healing process. The younger woman scrounged up two pairs of rubber boots which she gave to Maria and Morton, because the condition of their feet was the worst. She was of stocky build with broad hips, honey-hued complexion smooth and taut, but round, brown eyes much too sad and brooding for one of her years. The slightly older nurse was rangy and tall. She palpated the swollen, boggy, discolored flesh on Maria's foot and pointed out the suppurating sores to her colleague who concurred that Maria's condition required a doctor's verdict. When Surkov's camp medic showed up to examine the festering oozing spots, one the size of a half dollar, he shook his head gravely and told her she had to get to a hospital if she hoped to keep that foot.

"No, no hospital," Maria said firmly.

"Look, my dear girl, what I am looking at is gangrene, and it is deadly," he said sternly.

Maria refused to consider the ultimatum, and the medic called to the attention of Green and Gaul the frightening condition of her foot. To Maria's surprise, Gaul gently examined the foot and then leaned over and touched her hand and, gently speaking in German, told her they were taking her to a hospital.

"*Nicht! Nicht!*" Maria protested. With her name and photo on wanted posters, her fate if caught by the Gestapo was bound to be a concentration camp, torture and execution. She could not risk even a brief visit to a hospital because hospitals, schools and clinics were checked every day. Besides, with no medicines or means of treatment, she would fare better with the rudimentary treatment provided by the nurses who would not betray her.[13]

One partisan described the stench and pitiful conditions in a schoolroom serving as hospital for partisans in a village near Prasiva. It was a hellish scene of sick and wounded men left to die unattended. There was no medication, nothing to ease pain from infected knife or bullet wounds. Mercifully, pneumonia quickly snuffed out the lives of critically injured young men with many delirious youths calling out for their mothers at the end.[14]

Remembering the stench and lack of sanitation, Maria silently vowed she would die before consenting to risk that same fate befalling her if she went to a hospital. So she continued to let the nurses apply some of the ointment and wrap her foot in clean rags when possible. She wondered, though, if Morton should not take advantage of that offer of hospital care. After all, he was not a military man but a war correspondent assigned to report on the uprising. And now, his frostbitten and infected feet were as bad as hers. In addition to the swollen discolored feet, his plight was compounded by a severe case of dysentery that the camp medic called the "starvation sickness." It was an ugly ailment that caused stomach lesions and rectal bleeding. Were it not for the occasional extra rations of eggs and butter, and once veal from a butchered calf, the very weak and sick Morton would have perished at the camp. Thanks to the additional provisions, he began to improve.[15]

Horvath, and to a lesser extent Catlos, had developed an easy rapport with the younger nurse. For her, Horvath especially seemed to be a hero of sorts, a fellow native-born Slovak who had returned to help their country by fighting the Nazis. For Horvath, chatting with the brave girl brought him closer in spirit to his beloved Alma, a nurse in Cleveland, who at that very moment might be on duty in a hospital. One day, the nurse told him and Catlos how she came to be at this spot. For the cause of democracy, she had joined the CFI and for a time, carried a weapon and went on raids with them. Then she came to her senses and realized that she was of more help as a nurse than soldier. Now she was concerned about the outcome of the uprising since it was obvious that the Soviets had taken control, and she feared the consequences.[16]

Photograph of Joseph Horvath's beloved Alma ("ME") was delivered as he departed for induction into the military (courtesy Rudy Horvath).

8. A Real Thanksgiving

Throughout their ordeal, Dunlevy came to regard Morton as the most tragic of the men of the mission. He felt strongly that the thirty-three-year-old journalist should not have been there, rationalizing that the OSS men, like himself, had volunteered for and received military and psychological training for an intelligence mission. Morton was only there to report on the revolt and he often wondered how the hell the gentle, kind reporter had landed in the middle of this quagmire.[17]

Of course, Dunlevy could not possibly have known how much Morton wanted the assignment and, like any successful reporter, could be quite aggressive in pursuing a story. In August 1944, he'd written about the overthrow of the dictatorship in Romania. His exclusive interview with King Michael was praised by the *New York Times* as one of "glamour, romance, comedy, dramatic suspense and rapid action, like the movie 'The Prisoner of Zenda.'" When offered this "once in a lifetime opportunity" for a journalist, there was no time for even a quick trip home to Missouri to visit his family or see his baby daughter, born while he was in Europe. He seized the chance and at the last minute before take-off, he boarded the plane on October 7 with the men of Dawes embarking on the second deployment of the mission. And now he was trapped with them.[18]

One of Morton's last acts before fleeing Banska Bystrica was to stash a packet of sulpha into the brim of his green woolen knit cap. It could not help his dysentery, but Maria was to credit it and his unselfish sharing of the precious grains of the new sulpha drug with saving her foot when it turned gangrenous.

The morning after the doctor's visit, the boot had to be cut off Maria's foot. But thanks to the grains of sulpha Morton had scrupulously dropped onto the open, festering sores, it was plain to see that they were less pus-laden and the purple splotches of infection area around them lighter and less discolored. Looking relieved, the older nurse gently rubbed ointment over the oozing flesh and then wrapped a rag bandage around it and urged Maria to stay off her feet, no doubt knowing that her advice was futile.[19]

On his next visit, the attentive farmer brought a welcome tidbit of news. It was a tale of propaganda villagers were relating to the German patrols plaguing them. The people were spreading rumors that a large number of well-armed units of partisans were secreted throughout surrounding mountains to seek out and kill Germans and they took no prisoners. Enemy patrols were not eager for encounters with these mysterious warriors who appeared out of the dark to strike without warning and then vanish like ghosts into mountain mist. And since the partisans were always on the move, the Germans could not pin them down.[20] It corroborated a comment made by a young German soldier to a villager.

"*Partizanen* sneak up when the night is black as coal, they kill and then disappear into thin air. They must have a special power from the devil to be able to do that!"

Has they gleaned the truth about these mythical supermen, the Germans would have had little fear of partisans. Their own soldiers were better fed, better armed and would hardly be frightened of these remnants of partisan and guerrilla units who no longer resembled military men. They were more like beggars with straw stuffed in tattered coats to ward off the penetrating cold, and worn out shoes covered with rags to preserve what was left of the soles. Their orders, however, remained in effect. They were to "kill Germans and steal their food and medicine."

Soviet guerrillas used their radios sparingly and the sketchy news from Kiev was consistently negative. Following D-Day on June 6, 1944, there was continuous heavy fighting with heavy casualties in northern France where the Germans had dug in, preparing for a gigantic counteroffensive. By late November, in northeastern France, one of the bloodiest battles was waged and became known as the Battle of the Bulge. And in Italy, the Allied Fifth and Eighth Armies were bogged down north of Rome, slogging through mud and plagued with unprecedented rains as they prepared for a last ditch battle with retreating Germans troops. In the east, the Red Armies were advancing westwards slower than anticipated, held up by the retreating enemy holding onto towns and villages longer than expected. And three hundred thousand German soldiers headed north out of Greece, plowing their way through Macedonia and Yugoslavia towards Slovakia. Determined to protect Austria and Germany, Hitler's orders to his generals to hold Slovakia at all costs, remained very much in effect.[21]

For the moment, the men of Dawes were also dug in, stalled in their efforts to move towards the Russian army front as planned. Still, as Thanksgiving Day approached, there was a lot to be grateful for. They were still alive and uncaptured, although, with the dreaded Alpine anti-partisan troops combing the area for them, who could guess for how long? Dunlevy, for one, speculated on how many more days could they hold out where they were. But in war, he'd learned, one lives a moment at a time as the lessons in the Bible he carried in his pocket had impressed upon him.[22]

* * *

Thanksgiving Day, November 21, 1944, dawned bright and beautiful with a hazy sunshine that transformed fresh snow on pines and mountain peaks into spectacular picture postcard scenes. Inside the hut, with the help of Keszthelyi, Maria prepared a fat goose with a stuffing of bread and onions.

8. A Real Thanksgiving

The fowl was roasted over a bed of hot coals. When almost done, she added sliced potatoes to the pan and chopped cabbage into small pieces and dropped them into a pot of boiling water. The final touch was a head of Brinza cheese and whole grain bread.

When they were gathered around the table, Gaul held a poignant prayer service, beginning by especially asking for God's protection on the missing Schwartz, MacGregor, Lain, and the airmen. The rest of his words were carefully recorded by one man and no doubt remembered by most of them.

> Oh God, we who are gathered here together in thy name and by thy name and thy blessing on this day of Thanksgiving, do offer with deep gratitude and most heartfelt thanks for our deliverance from the blizzards and high winds of the wintry mountains and from the cruel snows fallen upon us and from the perils of the black night in dark valleys.
>
> Gratefully we thank you for preserving our group together and for maintaining our physical health and strength and for buttressing our wavering courage and for providing good even in our darkest days and we ask thy blessing on us and our allies, particularly the Slovak nation, and thy mercy on our comrades who are missing by enemy action and wintry storms. Amen.[23]

When Gaul finished the impromptu service, with his dark gray eyes more solemn than usual, Geen leaned over to whisper to Maria. "I don't know how you managed to produce this feast but every one of us certainly appreciates and thanks you for it." Then the dignified commander dropped his reserve and simply dug into the repast like the rest of his men.[24]

The next morning Maria and Keszthelyi set out to make contact with a youth from Dolnia Lehota, hoping he might be able to provide information on the rate of advance and current location of the Red Army. When he arrived, what he had to say was not encouraging. The Red Army was still four or five days away and German troops were moving in and looked like they planned to stay a while.

Maria repressed a groan. From the day they had fled Donavaly and begun marching towards the Red front, it was always reported to be four or five days distant. The goal had assumed the proportions of reaching the Holy Grail and she was dubious that they would ever get there. She was prepared to leave as soon as the informer slipped away and disappeared into the woods. But Keszthelyi wanted to relax a bit on his cushion of pine needles. He took off his parka and spread it over the soft mound of needles under a tree branch and reached for her, urging her to enjoy this quiet moment in the middle of hell.

They sat in silence for some minutes, caught up in the solitude and whispering of pine branches high above whisked about lightly by the ever-present winter breeze until Keszthelyi broke the silence. "I want to tell you again how brave you are and that you deserve so much better. I keep seeing you walking down Park Avenue in New York, where a bright, beautiful girl like you belongs and not in these godforsaken villages risking your life for us."[25]

Glancing down at her worn American Army pants and scuffed boots, Maria felt grubby and suddenly very tired. "You Americans are the brave ones," she said slowly, "because you volunteered to come here to help this little godforsaken country and the people in these villages. I had no choice."

"There's something about this land," Keszthelyi confided hesitantly. "I've decided to come back after the war and spend some time to get a better perspective as to why the mission was sent here in the first place." He said nothing about relatives not far away in Hungary or his origins there, nor anything about his intentions of seeing her again.

Maria felt a growing unease at the deepening attraction between them, even though relieved that the brutal attempted rape by Velichko had not permanently hardened her to all men. She realized she was falling more and more in love with this man and evidently he with her, even as the pragmatic part of her silently asked, what chance did any of it have?[26]

Evidently encouraged by her silence, Keszthelyi put an arm out to draw her close. To Maria, his strong arms around her created a magic oasis amidst the harsh world in which she'd been engulfed since joining the underground. But acutely aware that this quiet glen was also a dangerous place, after a short time, Maria reluctantly drew aside and arose. Staying in any unguarded spot was foolhardy and with the tide of incoming enemy troops, it was especially risky. Keszthelyi slowly pulled himself to his feet, but before putting on his parka, he embraced Maria and gave her a lingering kiss all but impossible to break away from. Hands clasped tightly, they left their idyll and with regret walked back to camp.[27]

Observing Maria and Keszthelyi approaching holding hands and eyes gazing at each other, Catlos noted the way they looked after each other and felt this was more than a casual attraction. He remarked years later on how these two took care of each other. However, like Maria, he also wondered if there could be a romantic future for her and his Bowery teammate. Or was this merely another whirlwind war love foredoomed to end when they separated?[28]

Their reprieve ended with a surprise visit from the son of a local mining engineer who brought a note for "Captain" Green. The title amused Gaul. "Looks like you've been promoted!" he said to Green. "But how in the hell did Sehmer know where we are?"

Green broke into a broad grin. "Hell, that jacket with 'USA Navy' on the back might as well be a flashing neon sign."

8. A Real Thanksgiving

It seemed that a partisan close to Sehmer's unit remembered seeing a very tall American in Banska Bystrica wearing a jacket with U.S. Navy emblazoned on the back and knew at once that it was Gaul. Accompanied by a guide, Sehmer had come to the barracks to make contact with the Americans and had given the young man a note to take to Green.

The note from Sehmer of the British SOE Windfall team stated he was at Surkov's headquarters and wanted to confer with Green. The commander and Gaul hurried down the trail to the camp headquarters. At the meeting, Green was able to give Sehmer news about one of his men, Keith Robert Hansen, who chose to leave the Dawes mission with MacGregor, Lain and the airmen about which there had been no further word.[29]

The Americans and British agents had not seen each other since the fall of Banska Bystrica. Like Catlos and Keszthelyi's Bowery mission, Sehmer's mission had been to penetrate into Hungary, but action was to be confined to merely reporting on developments of dissident movements. They were ordered to vacate Banska Bystrica when the revolt erupted and had been moving from one place to another until arriving at their current refuge in a hunting lodge called Velky Bok near the village of Polomka.

After conferring with Sehmer, Green decided to return with him to their hideout. He would take Horvath and Brown, his two best radio men, and leave Gaul in charge of those remaining at camp. With some luck, they would get Sehmer's radio working and be able to send a message to the OSS in Bari, giving an update on the mission, their location, and requesting assistance.[30]

Catlos, like Dunlevy, was glad that Sehmer had located them. He had felt badly since he dropped their radio on the flight out of Donavaly in a heavy sleet storm and under a hail of bullets and discarded it because it was broken. Then he'd felt even worse after the charger and batteries they purloined from the Germans, and which he had tied to the horse's back, were lost when he and the skittish animal plunged into an icy stream when the bridge they were crossing collapsed beneath them. Now he felt an upsurge of hope. They would get their radio working and Green could contact their base in Bari. Maybe redemption was near and Gaul's prayer and his silent one added to those of the others asking God for protection and help had been heard.[31]

As darkness descended, those in camp hunkered down for the night. Around the camp several sentries paced about the fringes, peering into the darkness and listening for unusual sounds, any of which sent their adrenaline racing. The informant Maria and Keszthelyi met earlier in the day had warned of an incoming swarm of enemy troops and there could be no let-up on alertness.[32]

What they had temporarily lost sight of was that the enemy was not only Nazi warriors with their crack anti-partisan fighters; they were also the faceless, nameless ones, anywhere and everywhere, who might prove to be the most lethal. It was a pending lesson to be learned, and once perceived, one they would never forget.

9

Maria's Love Is Captured

With Gaul in charge even temporarily, action of some type was inevitable. The very next morning he appointed Keszthelyi, Mican, and Perry to accompany him to the barracks headquarters. Gaul had to replenish their food supply but he also wanted to map out an escape route in case the Germans staged a raid, which was highly predictable considering the amassing of troops near Dolnia Lehota. Upon reaching the camp, Gaul dispatched Perry with a brigade member to scout out the food situation while he and Keszthelyi conferred with Surkov.[1]

Commander Surkov had just finished giving a severe dressing down to a couple of his underlings when the Americans arrived. They had stolen two horses and a wagon from German soldiers in the village. Surkov was irate and ordered them to return them to prevent the Germans from retaliating by burning down their entire village, a usual form of punishment they used to deal with any kind of defiance.[2]

Gaul, Mican and Surkov were poring over a map of the terrain when they heard vehicles grind to a halt in front of the building. At the outcry of "Heinies!" Gaul jumped out the window and bolted for the woods. Mican managed to stumble along behind him on weakened legs but could not run as fast so he dove into some heavy brush to hide. Keszthelyi, who had left momentarily to relieve himself, was still in the toilet a few yards away when he heard the commotion. Keszthelyi had one hand on the door to exit when he detected heavy footsteps approaching and low voices speaking in German. He latched the door and crouched on the floor. The footsteps passed by and stomped into nearby bushes. A shout of "Halt!" was followed by a volley of gunfire. From the direction of the sounds, Keszthelyi judged they were firing on the barracks. Ears to the door straining for further sounds, he heard nothing more, so he opened the door a crack and peered out. A German soldier spotted him and aimed and fired. A bullet struck Keszthelyi in the chest sending him tumbling down two steps to the ground. He leaped up and raced for the woods where he burrowed in a deep pine thicket and listened for pursuers. In the ominous quiet, he felt for the wound in his chest, only to find that a knife in his shirt pocket had deflected the bullet. Heaving a sigh of relief, he remained still and assessed the situation.[3]

Perry was not so fortunate. He was returning to the barracks with the brigade member when the attack began. Impeded by swollen feet and thick brush, he was unable to outrun their captors and both men were captured.

Gaul made it into the woods and pushed through dense growths so thick the Germans could not follow. Mican, unable to run, remained hidden in the bushes. Two soldiers came so close he could hear them talking.

One told the other to keep looking, that the Americans would be a prize to present to Hitler, and that the Fuhrer would exterminate them himself if he could. Mican dug deeper into the snow-covered bushes where he remained unmoving as an animal in hibernation for an hour. Numb with cold, when he felt sure the enemy was gone, he staggered to his feet and began the arduous trek back to the American camp.[4]

The scene they left behind at the barracks was one of total carnage. Resistance was attempted and for several minutes, machine guns barked from both sides. When the attack ended, forty partisans lay dead and the wounded survived only if they made it out of bullet range and managed to reach the woods for cover. Those who could not were burned to death when the barracks was torched. The final shots fired by the enemy attackers were reserved for the two nurses who received "special treatment" meted out to partisans and those helping them. It was a single shot to the back of the head.[5]

At their hut higher in the mountains, Catlos and Maria were checking what was left of the scant food supply when the attack on the barracks below erupted. The barrage of gunfire was followed by the shouts of enemy soldiers charging up the grade.

Yelling for everyone to get out, Catlos and Dunlevy dove out the door with the others on their heels. They churned up the mountain trail and deeper into the cover of trees and brush and snowdrifts as gunfire resounded off the mountain range. Before long, bodies weak from malnutrition and pain from infected feet that had scarcely begun to heal began to slow their progress.[6]

Every step sent jagged knives of pain from Maria's foot to her calf. She turned around at the sound of an agonizing moan behind her. It was Paris. He had slipped and fallen and lay sprawled on the ground, unable to get up. She tugged at the parka of the big man until he was able to raise himself to sitting position. When he leaned on her shoulder, his clutch was that of a drowning swimmer. Paris' size, despite severe weight loss, almost pulled her down with him but she held on and urged him to keep moving. The pupils of his eyes were wide with shock and he didn't seem to comprehend why she was urging him to keep moving and had to stop every few feet to catch his breath.[7]

Catlos glanced back and seeing Paris' plight, halted until he and Maria caught up with him. He grabbed Paris' jacket and held onto it, which helped propel him ahead. As they labored up the mountain grade, others in flight from the attack on the barracks passed them. The Americans learned from some of them that Gaul and Keszthelyi had escaped, but no one knew the fate of Perry or Mican. An hour into the march, Gaul and Keszthelyi caught up with the unit and told them the sad news that Perry was captured but they had no knowledge of Mican's whereabouts. Catlos noted the tears of relief Maria could not conceal when Keszthelyi turned up. The two clasped hands and were inseparable during the march.[8]

The tortuous trail led to the foot of the Dumbier mountain range. Here they all paused to catch their breath and decide the next step. From below, they caught sight of someone struggling up the steep grade towards them. As the figure came closer, they saw that it was Mican, dazed and confused, but determined to reach his unit.

The panoramic Dumbier range was a sea of mountain spruces from which a wall of snow turned the peaks into fantastic views. Drifting down over it all was a fine, powdery snow. It was the dreaded "*biela tmo*," a type of snow so fine and thick it became a "white darkness." As they climbed, vegetation became sparser and soon they were wading through waist-high drifts that sapped what remained of their strength.[9]

Gaul called a halt to evaluate their chances of forging ahead. With the afternoon light fading fast, he evidently realized it would be suicide to go on. They would return to the hut to spend the night. They had progressed about two kilometers down the trail when they came across a half dozen Soviet guerrillas. Gaul and Maria asked if they had seen any Americans. They reported one American and one of the colonel's men captured in the village.

It had to be Perry. He was the sole member of the Day component of the Dawes mission. The quiet man with trim moustache and hair had been scheduled to operate on his own. He spoke excellent German and was to check out the possibility of penetrating Austria — but his chance was dashed when the Germans attacked Banska Bystrica, and he fled to the mountains with the others. He would be forced to reveal their location. Even after considering this, Gaul decided they still had to wait until morning to continue moving higher up. Retracing their previous steps, they came upon a hut a hundred meters from the one they escaped. It appeared undisturbed by the enemy encounter and Gaul told them they would stay there for the night.

The Dumbier mountain range was 8,000 feet high. Mountaineers claimed it was inhabited by demonic spirits who took delight in piling up snowdrifts that made passes impregnable until spring, when the frozen corpses of the foolhardy who tried to cross them were found. Huddled in the hut, Gaul held a conference with all hands. "The Krauts won't look for us in the dark so we'll stay here overnight," he told them. "But we'll leave before daylight to get a head start."[10]

Dunlevy, for one, was pleased at Gaul's command and how he briefed them. Green, who seldom did, would have made a superb diplomat. But he felt Gaul should have been their leader all along.[11]

On December 1, just before daybreak, they left the hut with only a rudimentary map to guide them and set out for Polomka, keeping a lookout for Germans who often made return calls on places they had already raided. They had to bypass the villages of Bystra and Myto and traverse a risky passage across a valley where German patrols could easily sight them. The goal was to make it to the outskirts of Myto by nightfall, stay overnight, then proceed in the morning. In the woods, they came upon a small ragtag group of scruffy Slovak partisans, one of whom claimed he knew the way to Myto. Like many who are eager to help but are not reliable, it turned out he didn't know the way and they wandered aimlessly the entire day and had to stop at last, way short of Myto. But attempting to find their way in the dark would be foolish.[12]

An additional peril was a solitary man they encountered who could be an enemy lookout. Russian guerrillas and Slovak partisans would have shot him on the spot, but Gaul ordered his people to do nothing. Instead, once out of the man's sight, he led them in a circle before veering off onto another course where fresh falling snow wiped out their footsteps. The detour impeded their progress and they did not reach the outskirts of Myto until nine o'clock that night. Fortunately, about two kilometers from the village, they stumbled upon a vacant shepherd's shelter that was more a like barn with a wooden plank floor littered with cornhusks. Gaul's order was for them to "hunker down" while their guide and he slipped into the village to check out the situation.[13]

The night temperature plunged precipitously moment by moment. In the barn, the group huddled on stacks of cornhusks to rest. About two hours later, hearing voices outside speaking in Slovak, they sat up and waited, tense with apprehension. It was a farmer that Gaul and the guide had made contact with and he was bringing them a pail of milk and two loaves of bread. It was all he could offer them.

9. Maria's Love Is Captured

While the farmer was still in the barn, Gaul and the partisan guide returned and Gaul ordered the guide to try to persuade the farmer to provide a place of refuge for the night. The visitor listened to the request, then said hesitantly that he would take two or three, but not more because the *Nemci* came every day to check and it was too risky. After scanning his ragged, exhausted group, Gaul selected Maria, Paris and Miller as being most in need of shelter.[14]

Ordinarily it was a half hour walk to the farmhouse, but impaired with swollen, painful feet, the pace was snail-like and the three needed to rest every few minutes. As they shambled along, Maria studied the two men. Paris had the build of a linebacker but was too thin and depleted of energy. And for the first time, she noted how good looking Miller was. Like many fighter pilots, the twenty-three-year-old Lieutenant Lane Miller was shorter and of a wiry build. Slightly balding blond hair did not detract from his attractiveness. Struggling to survive behind enemy lines, his Navy officer father could not help him and he had lost his former cockiness. Still, he remained plucky and seldom complained.

When they finally reached the farmhouse they were met by the farmer's son. After a brief exchange of words with him, the farmer changed his mind about giving them shelter. German patrols were too close. They could rest an hour and then had to leave.[15]

After the bitter cold they'd endured, entry into the warmth of the small, shabby house was like heaven. At the last moment, the rescuer relented and said Maria could stay, but not Paris and Miller because she could pass for an ordinary native and not endanger the man and his son.

"All of us or none," Maria said firmly, hoping he would relent. With a negative shake of his head, he opened the door, peered out into the night, and then motioned for them to leave. The light inside was snapped off the instant the shivering trio stepped out the door.

It was midnight when they were put out into the bitterly freezing night. The way to the shepherd's hut was colder and darker than before, with their progress slower and faltering. It was six o'clock in the morning before they sighted their destination. Miller pushed ahead gamely to get help and Keszthelyi and Catlos hurried to lend a hand. They assisted Maria and Paris up the last hundred yards to the barn where they collapsed on piles of cornhusks.[16]

Late that afternoon, the farmer returned, contrite about refusing shelter to Maria, Paris and Miller. He extended a burlap sack containing bread and sausages. He also told them of a better hideout, a hunting shack near the village of Myto pod Dumbier. Mican circled the direction to it on Gaul's map, after which Gaul and the guide left to check it out.

Shortly after daylight, the Americans reached the new location, which proved to be roomier and where they could hide for a time. In the shack were three young Jewish partisans. They were cold, dirty and hungry with wild-eyed expressions that left no doubt they'd shoot at anything suspicious. After talking to Gaul and the guide, they agreed to share the building with the Americans and Maria, and then the three men moved out to let Gaul and his people occupy the shack. In turn, the Americans shared what food there was and paid the men with gold coins, which meant that these strays might be able to buy food and not have to steal it.[17]

The shack contained six bunk beds. Maria was allotted one, and the men took turns sleeping on the others with Keszthelyi and Dunlevy sharing the cot above her. Gaul rationed the sausage and bread, although it was not enough to satisfy hunger. But even that scant amount of food proved to be too much for shrunken stomachs and some of the men, as well as Maria, suffered nausea and diarrhea. During the night when she staggered outside to relieve herself, Keszthelyi suddenly appeared beside her and asked where she was going. Embarrassed, she pointed to the woods. Without a word he carried her to a clump of bushes, then walked a short distance away to wait to carry her back. The trip was repeated three more times before the cramps and nausea subsided.[18]

On the second day, Gaul briefed his group. They could stay only a day at most, then he had to find Green. His sharp gaze ranged over the disabled group. He needed one man to accompany him to Polomka. The only possible candidate was Catlos, decidedly leaner, but still hale as most peasants in these parts. Directing the others to remain there, Gaul told them to be sure to stay together. On December 4, Gaul and Catlos departed for Polomka. The two men, natives of Pittsburgh, Pennsylvania, were far apart in education and background and physical size, but were the most physically fit of the group. And they needed to be in good condition because it was a hard twenty-five mile trek to Polomka.[19]

Gaul was from a prominent family, his father a renowned organist in a Pittsburgh cathedral. Although a Harvard graduate and working as a professor while continuing graduate studies, Gaul had undergone rigorous physical hardships in survival training and later exploring archeological digs in primitive regions. He was intrigued with Czechoslovakia and its ancient culture so when the original plan to deploy him to China fell through, he volunteered for the Dawes mission, eager to be part of this country's future.[20]

Catlos was the stocky, only child of sturdy Hungarian immigrants, a brawny specimen able to withstand long hikes and hardships. He was a bit of a loner but also was a take-charge man when the situation called for it.[21]

Disparate in all ways except for commitment to their mission, nevertheless he and Gaul still made a good team.

Near an intersection of two rough trails, they encountered a forester carrying an axe. Gaul told Catlos to check him out by asking the way to Polomka. The forester pointed to railroad tracks a half-kilometer distant and said they were safe to walk on. Although dubious, Catlos and Gaul followed the tracks on the rationale that this was the shortest distance between two points. They made good headway, stopping only to bolt down the last sausage slices and bread. When they resumed walking, Catlos abruptly stopped and leaned over to put an ear to a rail. Gaul dropped to one knee and also listened. The slight rhythmic thrum was unmistakable. A train was pounding its way towards them. Jumping to his feet, Gaul let out a low whistle. The man with the axe had lied.[22]

They jumped off the tracks and raced around a sharp curve and up a slope, Catlos' shorter legs following on the heels of Gaul's long, stork-like lope. Catlos let out a gasp when the train ground to a stop. It was an armor train and they had been spotted.

Several soldiers leaped out of a freight car and ran up the grade firing submachine guns, bullets whipping up snowdrifts around their feet. In a crouch, Gaul skittered through deep snow, Catlos following in the wake of his crane-like glide as freshly falling snow soon obliterated their footprints. They ran until they could no longer hear gunfire. Only then did they stop beneath low hanging pine branches to catch their breath. Daylight was almost gone and they had lost their bearings. They were off course and to continue walking was pointless. But so was staying all night in the forest.

Suddenly, like a flashing beacon, a light appeared in the distance and they made their way towards it. It came from a farmhouse and was as welcome as a lighthouse on a rocky foreign shore beckoning sailors lost at sea to a refuge. Weary to the point of collapse, the two men trudged towards the dwelling. The old wooden exterior was warped but had a high chimney from which smoke was drifting skywards. Detecting no sound or movement inside, Catlos dropped to his belly and crawled to the window to peer inside. A woman's startled eyes met his, then vanished. Seconds later the door was flung open.[23]

"*Partizanen?*"

"No. Americans, lost and starved," Catlos replied in Slovak.

The woman glanced over his head before opening the door wider to let them in. Inside, were three more women of middle age, like their benefactor appeared to be, and they were all spinning flax. The woman of the house led the way to a storage area behind a kitchen wall and motioned for them to sit down. The area was kept warm by chimney heat and light that cast a mellow glow. The woman then thumped to the kitchen and put a pot of water on the stove to boil.

Gaul and Catlos sank onto the floor, listening to the women chatting while they worked. They removed their parkas, leaned back against the wall and began to relax. Before long, they dozed off. But not for long. They were jolted awake by the sound of a vehicle slamming to a stop outside and the sound of dreaded German voices. The two drew their guns as the woman unbolted the door latch.

"*Hier sind Partizanen?*" ("Any partisans here?")

"*Partizanen?* No."

"Americans?"

"*Americanski?* No." The tone of the woman's voice indicated that the very idea was preposterous. "No men here ... all in Austria, working."

It was probably true because most Slovak men and boys over fifteen either volunteered to work for wages in German factories or were drafted for heavy labor. Others were in the Slovak State Army or CFI members in roving bands of partisans. Not more than a dozen feet from where the stolid-faced women were spinning flax, Catlos and Gaul were poised with guns drawn, waiting. The relief was indescribable when they heard the words "*Auf Wiedersehen*" followed by the sound of the door closing, bolts slamming into place and heavy footsteps retreating. They sat back, drained of energy, until their benefactress appeared with a home-crafted tray holding two glasses of steaming tea and plates with mounds of smoked pork smothered in a deep layer of mashed potatoes. She assured them there would be no more patrols that night.[24]

The ravenous men gobbled the food and gulped down the tea. The let down after their adrenaline-pumping close call took a while to ebb and be replaced by drowsiness. Spreading parkas on the floor, they plopped down on top of them and were asleep in seconds, the chatter of the women a few hand-breadths away reassuring as a soothing lullaby.

They were awakened at dawn by the rustling of their benefactress stirring about. They got up, donned their parkas and joined her in the kitchen. With a welcoming smile, she set bowls of porridge on the table with more glasses of hot tea that the men hastily consumed. When they arose to leave, the woman handed Catlos a cloth bundle in which she had wrapped some bread and cheese. Her eyes widened in disbelief at the two gold coins he proffered in exchange. They watched her turn the coins over in her palm, studying them with keen interest.

"*Angliski?*" she asked.

"Yes, American gold."

Flashing the men a wide smile revealing a gap where a couple of teeth were missing, she murmured *"Dyakumen"* ("Thank you"), then opened the door a crack to peer out before motioning to them that all was clear. When Gaul and Catlos stepped outside, the woman said softly, *"Iz bohom"* ("Go with God") before closing the door.

The two men retraced their steps, avoiding the railroad tracks. Before the turn that would take them out of sight of the farmhouse, they paused to look back. Gaul lifted the tip of his cap in gallant gesture of salute to the unseen angel of mercy. Catlos followed suit and added a silent prayer of gratitude and viewed the spiral of chimney smoke drifting upwards like incense offered up to heaven, still in awe at the courage of the women.[25]

The last rays of daylight were fading when they reached Polomka, having made the 25 miles in a day and a half. They went directly to the notar, the town official who recorded the names and addresses of every person in his territory. The man knew of Sehmer and Green's location and assigned a youth to escort them to the cabin where they were in hiding. It was a two-kilometer hike to the three-room cabin nestled in a grove of stately evergreens. When Gaul and Catlos arrived, Green had been overseeing Horvath and Brown working on the radio with the help of Sehmer's team. He was as dumbfounded at their appearance as he was to hear Gaul's report, to which he listened intently, his serious features a study of concern.[26]

Major Ernest Sehmer's flame-hued hair was topped with a black beret and he exhibited a cheerful countenance but his keen eyes missed nothing. The other members of his team were Lieutenants Arthur Zenopian and Jack Wanderfer (code name Wilson), Sergeants Guilliam Davis and James Willis. Also with the Britons was Slovak-American Margita Kascova. The short, dark-haired woman, who appeared to be in her mid-thirties, wore thick glasses and an unsmiling countenance. The Cleveland resident had come to Slovakia to care for an ailing grandmother until she died, and then was trapped when the revolt broke out. Fluent in German and Slovak, she'd joined the British in Banska Bystrica to serve as interpreter.[27]

Sehmer, Green and Gaul held a brief consultation and decided that Catlos would stay in Polomka to help with the radio. In turn, Willis would return with Gaul to Myto in the morning to help escort the others to their hideout. After non-stop efforts to get the radio working, early in the morning of December 6, 1944, the following words were tapped through to London OSS. It was the last message that the Dawes mission would send.

> Thirty in our group in estate near Dolnia Lehota. Southeast of Brezno. No news Baranski, Novak, Paveltich. Schwartz. MacGregor, Lain with flyers. Whereabouts

unknown since November 10th. All equipment lost. Majority in bad condition from exposure, bad feet, exhaustion from long marches and starvation diet. Make drop soonest to Sehmer ... complete heavy....

A few minutes later, they managed a follow up message:

Enemy cutting us down ... we're still holding out. Request drop ... we'll keep four signal fires burning for five nights. Need guns, food and medical supplies for thirty ... Repeat....[28]

Catlos heard an anxious Green ask Private Robert Brown if he had gotten it all. "Sure as I ever was," Brown replied, his smooth, unlined face encased in its first grin in days.[29]

Gaul and Willis returned to Myto on December 10. Plans were laid out for the Americans to move on to Polomka in two groups, one to start out on the 14th, the other on the 15th. Gaul also brought back a letter from Koscova addressed to a Lutheran minister who might arrange for the sale of a couple of horses to transport the most disabled.[30]

Morale of all those at the barn was heightened by the prospect of finding sanctuary in Polomka. Not wanting to waste time while they prepared to depart, Gaul directed Keszthelyi to make contact with the minister and arrange to buy the horses. Mican would act as interpreter. The order was clear, they were not to remain overnight but return immediately.

Gaul had met the minister, as well as his wife, on his first cursory check with their guide and discovered that the couple spoke excellent German. They had served him a delicious meal and he'd enjoyed a hot bath. But now there was no time for Keszthelyi and Mican to partake of any pleasantries. They had to get in and out of the village as soon as possible.[31]

During the night, Maria awakened with a bad dream about Keszthelyi being captured. When they had not returned by late morning, a worried Gaul, accompanied by Dunlevy and Willis, went to the village to search for them. They learned nothing. When they came back, a distraught Maria prevailed upon Gaul to make another search.

They sought out the minister who professed to know nothing. But watching the minister's wife, Maria detected a furtive look in the woman's eyes and told her they were lying and demanded they tell the truth. Finally, she admitted that her husband had lied. The men had stayed because the older one was sick and could hardly breathe and had to rest. The younger one took a bath but they left before dawn. The couple later heard later that the Americans were surprised by an enemy patrol and captured. The patrol then started back towards the shack but had to turn back in the face of deep drifts and a sudden blizzard.[32]

9. Maria's Love Is Captured

It was about ten P.M. when Gaul and Maria returned but Gaul ordered them to prepare to move on at once. The patrol would be back at any time.[33]

Maria was numb with shock from the discovery that Keszthelyi had fallen into the hands of the enemy. Huddled on her bunk bed, her mind went over those last moments with Keszthekyi. It was after Gaul and Catlos left for Polomka when she, Keszthelyi and Micam made a sortie to try to obtain more food. That day the peasant sold them milk and two loaves of hardened bread and a pint of honey. It was all he could offer. But he told them to wait for another two hours and he might have something more. Mican offered to carry the bread and honey back to the barn while Maria and Keszthelyi waited for the peasant to return with more food.[34]

They had sat in a secluded spot and let the spirit of tranquility and the solitude seep into their weary bodies and discouraged souls. After a few minutes, Keszthelyi reached out to take one of Maria's hands in his. "You know we are all grateful to you, Maria," he said softly, "especially for dealing with the Russians. We're damn sure that some of them are as eager to knock us off as the Nazis."

"Not all of them, but some would," she agreed. "But you are the brave ones, volunteering to come here to help our poor country caught like a tiny mouse between two big tigers."

He confided that he kept visualizing New York, which he missed very much and he wished she could see it with him. Maria confided that she always dreamed of travel and seeing America but now, who could even think of such plans?

The gentle stirring of branches high above lulled her into the hope that there could be a future for them after the war. That fleeting hope was crushed when the peasant returned to tell them that he was unable to find more food and the stark reality of their plight obliterated any hazy dreams. Disappointed and clinging close to each other for comfort, hand in hand they had walked back to the hut.[35]

As she relived those recent moments, in the background she could hear Gaul's angry tirade concerning the capture. Lost in deep reflection, she failed to take note of Gaul's stormy expression until his large head suddenly loomed over her bunk. In a loud stern voice, he demanded, "Where's the money?"

"Money?" Maria repeated in confusion and then said she did not know.

"Keszthelyi gave it to you."

"I did not take it."

"Well, we'll see! That's American property and has to be returned."[36]

In shock and wounded disbelief at his orders, Maria emptied her pockets. Gaul's big hands then overturned the mattress and dragged it outside to search the lining. His efforts yielded only lint and dust. When he grabbed her rucksack, it was too much to bear. She fled to the woods and stumbled to a bed of needles and collapsed on it to let the tears flow at the humiliation and to try to think her way out of this nightmare that was happening. She simply could not take any more of Gaul's hostility. In a little while, a plan of sorts was formed. She would contact her aunts Tatiana and Elena when she reached Polomka, then stay with them in nearby Sumiac where they lived. Now that Tibor was gone, it was time she was on her own anyway, as it was obvious that she was no longer wanted.[37]

Keszthelyi's last words to Maria were that he wanted her to have the money in case he did not return from Myto. Those words kept coming back to her. Out of superstitious fear, she had refused to accept the money because if she *had* accepted the money, it meant he really would not make it back. Furthermore, she did not want the other men to misconstrue acceptance of the money as perhaps payment for favors, or that she was motivated by money. A ray of comfort penetrated her grief and despair when she realized that Tibor had left her something far more precious than gold coins. It was his diary, tucked safely inside her jacket next to her heart. He'd entrusted it to her before he left on his last mission to buy the horses. Feeling a resurgence of hope, she reached up to gently caress the bulge that was the diary and was convinced that as long as she had the diary, she would know that Tibor was alive. And she would not let anyone else know about the diary, lest they reveal it to Gaul.

Her heart heavy and lost in thought, Maria barely felt the warm hand until it grasped hers. She looked up into Morton's blue eyes, lit with understanding and concern.

"I'm sorry Maria," he said gently and added that while it was not an excuse for what Gaul had done, he asked her to understand that the guy was pretty shook up about losing two men. She shrugged and said that he had never wanted her in the first place, to which Morton said, "Well, the rest of us did and still do."

Maria believed that his sympathy and caring was sincere. She also felt that this Associated Press war correspondent, whom one of his colleagues described as "an ever smiling gentleman," was the best of the lot next to Tibor. She allowed Morton to help her to her feet, then drying her eyes with a sleeve, she rejoined the group. After all, since she would not be with the Americans for long, she could endure what had to be endured and bide her time until the right moment to break away became clear.[38]

10

Waiting in Vain for Help

On December 6, 1944, the same day that Green and Sehmer were able to reach OSS Bari by radio, officials at the base were puzzled to also hear some faint signals from Houseboat, Schwartz's code. Schwartz had carried his cipher and signal plan but not his crystals and without them, contact was weak and not fully established. However, it also raised questions about Lt. Baranski's Day team since Green had reported no knowledge of them or their whereabouts since they separated from the Dawes team in Banska Bystrica on October 7, 1944. Ironically, however, the fate of three members of the mission had already been decided by the enemy at the time the Houseboat was code was heard.

After Captain Edward Baranski, Lieutenant Daniel Paveltich, Anton Novak and Emil Tomes, the members of the Day component of Dawes, had departed for their assignment base in northeast Slovakia, there had been no further contact with Dawes. Reports on their activities were made by the Day team directly to Bari.[1]

Team commander Baranski was fluent in Slovak and had volunteered for the mission for personal reasons. The mother of this graduate of the University of Illinois had emigrated from Vrhace, Slovakia, and like some other members of the Dawes unit, Baranski had close ties to Slovakia. He wanted to do what he could to help its people. The tall, masculine commando left behind a wife and pre-school age daughter.[2]

Daniel Paveltich was of Yugoslavian origin and became a legend for his experience of almost misfiring a hand grenade at a fresh Army lieutenant while in training in Bari. Fortunately, he had a couple of seconds to toss it far away and the only casualty was the scared shavetail who ran like the wind to seek safety and was never seen by the Dawes unit again.

Anton Novak was a major part of the team, chasing down leads of information and active in disseminating information to the Slovak people by way of leaflets, etc. He was clever and quick-witted and dependable. The fourth member of Day was Special Agent Emil Tomes, whose function it was to help set up operations at their post near the town of Zalenka Slatina in the northeastern corner of Slovakia. His assignment was to recruit local agents for penetration behind enemy lines into Moravia, although the explicit order to the Day team was to confine their operations to Slovakia and not cross over the border into adjacent Moravia, occupied by the Germans.[3]

They established contact with John Zvara, house painter by trade, secret agent for the underground by choice. His wife and daughter Vera were also active in the underground. Wearing civilian clothing, the Day team members wasted no time setting about collecting information on military movements, locations of factories producing war materials, and other important data. They then radioed all information to Bari with some excellent results. Their precise details enabled the 15th Air Force to hit more targets with precision. All went well and for a few weeks they were able to carry on with their operations until October 23, when commander Baranski sent Novak to Banska Bystrica to obtain information on the latest developments in the revolt. When he returned, it was to find his teammates gone and Zalenska Slatina in the possession of a German division. He learned from Vera that Baranski, Paveltich and Tomes had escaped with the intention of joining the CFI partisans at Polana, where there was a large unit of three thousand men under the command of Major Dubsky. On November 1, Novak was able to locate Baranski and rejoin him and the rest of their unit in Polana.[4]

Baranski then decided to move his men to Detvaskae Lazy. At that time, he was still in possession of the W/T radio set and he and his men were wearing American military uniforms. On November 5, Baranski again deployed Novak to determine the precise position of the German troops. Vera informed him that the 3rd Battalion of the Palezi Division had left the area with orders to search and clean out partisans from their nests surrounding Polana where Baranski, Paveltich and Tomes were hiding.[5]

Novak hid in the Zvara house for three days until November 9, when German soldiers returned from hunting and killing partisans with carloads of American military equipment that the sergeant in charge was selling as souvenirs. Among the booty was an American W/T radio set and Novak wondered if it could be Baranski's. He was relieved to learn that Baranski, Paveltich and Tomes had escaped, but he was unable to locate them for several days. During that time he helped resistance fighters write and mimeograph leaflets to drop in the main streets and business buildings of Zalenska Slatina. The leaflets urged the natives not to denounce members of the resistance forces. A local priest and a principal of the municipal school helped Novak and Vera

10. Waiting in Vain for Help

produce five thousand leaflets which were distributed as planned and he was trying to obtain new identity cards for the group from a notary.

On November 17, a stranger delivered a note to the Zvara house informing the family that Baranski was in hiding in Piest pri Detve in the house of John Vrto. Upon hearing this news, Mrs. Zvara hurried to the location to confirm the accuracy of the message. Baranski told her that at Polana he had lost his W/T radio set but managed to destroy the cipher. Paveltich was still with him but Tomes had fled in a different direction and might have been captured.[6]

On his last visit to Baranski, Novak was asked to buy batteries for Baranski's new W/T radio set he was constructing. When Novak reached Zalenska Slatina to comply with the request, he met Vera at the railroad station where she was waiting with dreadful news. Her parents had been detained by the police for interrogation. Under torture, they were forced to reveal the location of Baranski and Paveltich. Shortly thereafter, a contingency of Alpine antipartisan forces arrived at Piest pri Detva. But before Novak could reach his teammates with a warning, they were taken prisoner on December 9. Unfortunately, they were again wearing civilian clothing which would definitely seal their fate as spies, for whom torture and execution was certain. Their uniforms were found in the house where they had been hiding as well as Baranski's memo book with information obtained from the Zvaras, an activist priest and school principal. The whereabouts of Tomes remained unknown.[7]

The Zvaras and Vrtos had been betrayed by Frederick Fiola, an acquaintance, and Jan Ryzek, a local watchman by trade. Novak was able to give this information to a local Protestant minister before he managed to escape to Lieskovce.

Novak avoided detection by dyeing his hair red and traveling under a new name. In Liesvokce, he joined a partisan group heading for the Red front. Along the way, they blew up a bridge and warehouse, killing German guards in the process. This sent the enemy into a frenzy, determined to capture the rest of the Americans and anyone else with them. The Germans were adept at using propaganda to entice natives to turn in the Americans and partisans. They whipped up anti-partisan feelings and fears by claiming that the partisans and Americans were raping their young women and shooting innocent people. The disinformation helped fuel the interest in finding Americans still on the loose.[8]

* * *

While Gaul was still fuming over the capture of Mican and Keszthelyi, and not sure whether to wait until morning to take off for Polomka, two stray partisans waded through high snowdrifts up to the hideout.

"*Nemci*," one of them said. "They look for you." He pointed to the high drifts. "They come close, but too much snow and dark. But they come back in the morning," he warned.

Faced with this development Gaul moved fast. He told his people that they were leaving immediately. It would be a long, hard two days' march with pursuers on their tails. They had to force themselves to exert their physical resources above and beyond what they had so far given if they were to make it safely to Polomka.[9]

The marchers proceeded single file, heads bent against buffeting winds that lifted tree branches to slap against faces and bodies with near stunning force. Gaul trudged alongside Morton, his craggy features dour. When Morton moved aside, Dunlevy perceived that the open rebuff was probably because Morton was angry at Gaul's shabby treatment of Maria over the missing money. Again Dunlevy pondered about Morton, guessing that he did not realize how terrible was their plight. The Associated Press war correspondent with no military training whatsoever was a diplomat and diffuser, with nothing false about him. He had simply landed in the wrong place at the wrong time and into the middle of a king size mess.[10]

Walking at any time on rugged mountain trails was difficult; at night, it was treacherous. With no adequate guide, Gaul had to rely on his compass and maps. He ordered them to stay in the middle of the road and remain alert to spotters who would reveal their location. To deter easy pursuit, he used his skill with maps and changed courses intermittently, further slowing their progress. Groves of trees and clusters of thickets became sparser, creating open spaces that added to their chances of detection. They'd walked about seven kilometers when, in the distance, they caught a glimpse of an enemy patrol careening down the road towards them. Gaul let out a soft but stern order. "Get down!" he hissed. It sent everyone sprawling on stomachs to burrow under what cover they could find. Fortunately, the patrol passed by without detecting them.

It was five o'clock in the morning when Gaul called a brief halt. Rations were a chunk of hard bread and two thin slices of sausage. They sat on the cold ground to eat, shivering and waiting for the order to resume marching. Before they took off again, Gaul issued firm orders. There was to be no talking, not even a whisper! And no smoking! The sound of a voice or light of a match or smell of smoke was enough to give them away. The strength of his leadership was evident as he led them through some dangerous areas, and he proved to be a first-class officer for such a trip.[11]

Two kilometers along the rutted trail they came upon an isolated farmhouse. Maria offered to investigate and Gaul reluctantly gave his permission.

10. Waiting in Vain for Help

A woman answered Maria's knock and studied her with curiosity but also suspicion. She seemed to be alone but Maria knew that any children would be hidden, and the men were either away working in Germany or Austria, or were partisans unless too old for either occupation.

Maria told her she'd lost her way and was very cold and asked if she could come in and get warm. The face of the middle-aged woman was inscrutable. She looked Maria over unabashedly, then glanced over her head to scan the area surrounding the house before she finally bade Maria to come in.

Upon questioning, she told Maria that German patrols had formerly dropped by once a day but for the last few days they came more than once and seemed to be searching for someone. Although Maria said nothing, the woman had evidently already sized up the situation and told her to take another route where she would be unseen. Her son would show Maria a little-known shortcut that would avoid patrols, she added, before slipping out to the barn to fetch her thirteen-year-old son Josef, who would be their guide.[12]

Maria and Josef walked openly along a pitted road that was seldom used while the men stayed on the fringes, ready to dart for cover. As she and the boy approached a fork in the road which would take them to the short cut to Polomka, an enemy patrol truck suddenly rounded a curve and headed their way. It was too late to hide.

"If they ask you who we are, tell them I'm your aunt Luba and we are looking for a stray cow," Maria told him. "We'll just keep walking and acting like everything is just fine." Fortunately, the soldiers merely slowed down, looked them over, and went on their way without stopping. To Maria's surprise, the boy remained cool, not so much as a hint of concern showing on his freckle-faced countenance.

The shortcut veered off into dense woods and onto a path rutted with holes hidden under snow. Falling or tripping could mean a broken bone or severe sprain. Tangled growth coated with caked snow sprang back when pushed aside, an icy reminder of nature's power to humble the hardiest human being. As dusk began to fall, Josef told them he had to return home but that another guide would meet up with them in the morning to lead them the rest of the way. Shyly, he turned to Maria and told her that when he grew up, he wanted to come to America and see the men who were here to help them. Maria managed to relay his desire to Gaul who seemed touched. He told Josef that he was a brave young man and he hoped to see him again one day. The praise and appreciation seemed make Josef grown another inch or two while his boyish face wore a big grin. At that he turned and disappeared into the woods, turning once before he was out of sight to flash the admired Americans one last wave.[13]

The marchers were exhausted and resigned to another freezing night of waiting for daylight before moving ahead the rest of the way. Maria sat on the ground near Heller and noted that despite their ordeal, his round cherubic face looked almost absurdly adolescent. He had also seemed to grow close to Miller since Schwartz's capture. Across from them, Morton was trying to boost Paris' spirits. The broad-shouldered Navy photographer, who had been assigned to photograph the landing in Banska Bystrica, was of a gentle nature like Morton. But he seemed to have a weaker physical and emotional constitution that needed bolstering. Nearby was the usually silent Dunlevy, still a puzzle to Maria who had decided that with his blue eyes and ruddy skin, he typified the "average" young American male. Around them others in the unit were interspersed. A little to one side was British agent Willis who had returned from Polomka with Gaul. All of the group appeared lost in their own thoughts as night deepened and the cold grew more penetrating.[14]

With the first rays of daylight, what remained of the bread and sausage was consumed, leaving them all still hungry and exhausted. When they finished, Gaul ordered them to move on, not waiting for the promised guide the boy Josef mentioned. However, sometime in the early afternoon their new escort caught up with them. He presented a startling image of a guide in his sheepskin jacket, white felt pants and white felt boots, hardly mountain attire. His appearance left Morton transfixed with curiosity and eager to jot down his story. The man spoke good German, which enabled him to converse with Gaul.

When their escort told him it was another six or seven kilometers to Polomka the reaction on Paris was unnerving. His face paled and eyes rolled back in his head before he toppled to the ground. The new guide calmly reached down and grabbed a handful of snow and rubbed it over Paris' face, then lifted him to sitting position. The "treatment" revived Paris somewhat and by sheer force of will, he got to his feet, and plodded along with his unit.[15]

It was dusk on the night of December 16, 1944, when they staggered the last steps to the cabin near Polomka. Green and Sehmer had been on the lookout for them. The new arrivals found the bluff, hearty Sehmer to be a decided contrast to the tall, slender and reserved Green, physically and psychologically. The British commander of his Windproof team was of medium height, stocky, and exuded energy and a buoyant spirit. His ruddy face was peppered with freckles and he wore his black beret tilted at a rakish angle over thick, curly red hair. He spoke excellent German and greeted the new arrivals warmly, particularly Maria, saying, "It's a bloody good time you women had someone else besides us blokes to talk with."[16]

Margita gave only a polite nod of acknowledgment while Maria stared at her with a cool countenance. It was plain that a mutual dislike and distrust had spring up on sight.

It did not help matters that Maria's arrival was of keen interest to the partisans in the cabin. A half dozen lounging against the walls of the cabin brazenly looked her over. And the cold reaction to the introduction to Margita was noted by some of the Dawes men, especially Catlos. Like Gaul, he viewed this mutual antipathy as a potentially combustible situation requiring diplomatic handling on the men's part. But Sehmer, if any of them, was up to it, Catlos decided, watching the Briton assume the role of genial host by rubbing his hands together and then setting about brewing tea. A devilish glint in his green eyes seemed to denote that he relished this arrival of the newcomers who would help eradicate the boredom of their days.[17]

The antipathy between the two women was almost palpable. Maria had been the sole woman with the Americans until now and was possibly jealous of having a rival. She also held Margita responsible for sending the note to the minister that resulted in Keszthelyi's capture. Margita, on the other hand, no doubt resented the much more attractive Maria. She had been with the British men since they landed in Banska Bystrica in September resented Maria's encroachment on what had been her domain.[18]

Horvath, particularly, was glad to see Maria. He told her that she had arrived just in time. His uncle Antolik, who had been providing food supplies for the men, had informed him that some villagers were eyeing him with suspicion and it was risky to be seen anywhere near Polomka, so they had to find another way to obtain supplies. Maria welcomed the opportunity to visit the village because she could give Antolik a note to her aunts in nearby Sumiac.

Ignoring Margita's watchful, disapproving eyes, Maria washed her hair and sponged some of the grime off her parka. She then changed into her spare pair of slacks and sweater, feeling renewed.

Horvath escorted her part of the way to the village where a man named Paulo took her to Antolik, who was relieved to see Maria. He told her that a large number of German and Hungarian soldiers retreating from the Red Army were amassing around Polomka. They were confiscating all available food to feed the hundreds of soldiers expected to arrive. While this would be the last day he could provide supplies for the Americans and British, he would try to arrange a food chain from nearby Telgart, although he could not promise much. He would also smuggle Maria's note to her aunts in Sumiac.[19]

The closer they got to the Red Army front, the bolder and more insolent the Russian guerrillas behaved. They were often a rowdy bunch, committing theft and raping any young females they came across. Sadly, there was no treatment available for the venereal diseases their victims contracted.

Soon after the arrival of the Dawes people, British agent Sergeant Guilliam Davis, who spoke excellent German, accompanied Maria to the well when she went to draw water. He warned her to never wander around by herself but always be in the company of American or British men. He shot a malevolent look at the guerrilla who had sauntered behind them, amorous intentions telegraphed by his lascivious stares at Maria. He backed away when Davis flashed a silent warning from blazing blue eyes that hinted at a ready temper.

Davis' reaction sent a fresh wave of pain through Maria. She realized how much she had come to depend on Keszthelyi and his protection, as well as his understanding and engaging persona, which had enhanced the efforts she made to be of use to the mission.[20]

The group in the cabin numbered more than thirty-five: fourteen Americans, five British as well as Margita, and about fifteen partisans. A two-hour hike above the cabin was a hunting lodge called Velky Bok, where a hundred or more Soviet guerrillas under the commands of Colonels Shukayev and Dymko were encamped. Some of the Anglos and Americans were billeted there. Green, Brown, Horvath and Catlos usually joined them at the lodge. It made the nightly conferences with Dymko and Shukayev more convenient for Green and Sehmer.[21]

The next few days were an interlude of peace. They had enough to eat and with shelter, sufficient food and rest allowing the Americans to recuperate from exhaustion, infected feet began to heal. One afternoon Antolik's son brought a package and note for Maria from her aunts begging her to come stay with them because she was not safe in her present location. In the parcel were two gifts wrapped in colorful Christmas wrapping. One contained a white blouse with crocheted collar and a sweater, the other a box of cookies she shared.[22]

Sehmer was a dynamo of energy and movement. Every morning he strode to the nearby stream outside and splashed his face with icy water and scraped off his beard. Behind him marched Davis, usually belting out a Welsh folk song in resonant baritone. The Americans had grown scruffy but before long, they followed Sehmer's example of sprucing up and everyone's morale was thereby raised. Following ablutions, Sehmer brewed tea for all, which they drank with whatever was available for breakfast. Once this was out of the way, Sehmer's adventurous spirit could not be suppressed. Nor would he permit any defeatist talk in his determination to raise morale. Eyes twinkling, he would say, "Let's go see what we can find out." This always sparked an interest in Green and Gaul after which the trio would ferry forth on a searching expedition.[23]

10. Waiting in Vain for Help

Once the commanders were out of sight, those left behind felt free to vent their frustrations. British Lt. Arthur Zenopian was one who openly expressed resentment at the presence of women. On one occasion, after Margita and Maria clashed verbally over how a particular task was to be performed, his insulting comments (in German) were loud and clear enough for everyone present to hear, particularly Maria and Margita. "Who in the hell needs these women? They are only trouble."

He ceased only when Davis shook a beefy fist under Zenopian's nose and told him to shut up. Davis knew his way around partisans and had punched a couple of them. He was protective of Maria and this, too, annoyed Zenopian.

Zenopian reminded him that he held superior rank and Davis could not talk to him that way. When Davis retorted, "I just did!" Zenopian's response was a glare followed by slamming out of the cabin.[24]

Zenopian was regarded by all the others as the strangest among the agents. He was of Armenian origin and was fluent in German and English. In his late thirties, the swarthy, wizened, sullen British national was a chronic complainer about various ailments. Like Maria, however, Dunlevy silently suspected that some of this was an act and that perhaps he was the best spy of all because he appeared so unlikely a prospect for an intelligence mission.[25]

The SOE was able to reach Bari by radio on December 16. It sent a garbled message of their location and the bad condition of the men and the need for supplies. The response from Bari was a message that on December 18, on the first night of good weather, they would deploy three planes to drop supplies. On December 20, the plan to implement retrieving the plane drops of supplies began. Three- or four-man crews rotated stoking signal fires on top the mountain, keeping watch over the designated drop zone where the parachutes with supplies were to be dropped by planes of the 15th Air Force. Unfortunately, the eager anticipants had no way of knowing that day after day, heavy snows and bad weather in Italy delayed the drops.[26]

Adding to the frustration was the fact that the road from Polomka had been cut off by deep drifts. They were rapidly running out of food but the faithful Antolik was determined to provide something for Christmas. He sent word that a wagonload of supplies secreted under a load of wood would be brought to a designated spot. Catlos, Dunlevy and Morton were selected to help the two Slovak boys carry the supplies to the cabin. The wagon made it to the edge of a clearing, where the burlap bags overflowing with food were unloaded. The two local youths who had volunteered to help Catlos, Dunlevy and Morton carry them to the cabin sat on logs to wait. As the Americans plodded through the snow towards them, Dunlevy deposited splotches of tobacco juice beside the path, courtesy of the scarce pipe tobacco Sehmer had shared with him.

The path to the clearing was dotted with deep ruts crusted over with fresh snow that slowed their advance. Halfway to the clearing, the Americans spotted a half dozen partisans who looked them over with stony-eyed suspicion. Catlos greeted them in Slovak which elicited no reply. Dunlevy expressed his own suspicion of the scruffy, flint-eyed band, with a large deposit from a stream of tobacco juice in the white snow that clearly indicated his opinion of them. But Catlos felt the men were only on a hunting expedition and not a threat — a good thing because Catlos and Dunlevy had left their weapons in the cabin to allow easier movement for carrying the bags of food. The two boys waiting at the meeting place jumped off the logs and hurried to help the Americans. They divided the food into smaller packs easier to manage and hoisted the bulging bags to their backs. With Dunlevy in the lead, they were toiling up the steep trail when the youths abruptly stopped. "*Nemci. Nemci!*" one cried out at sight of an enemy patrol about fifty yards above and blocking their path. The youths dropped their packs and raced for the woods, staccato echoes of machine gun fire muffled by thick foliage and falling snow in their wake.[27]

"Halt!" The shouted command reverberated off the snow-encrusted slopes. The three Americans froze for an instant before dropping packs and, like the boys, darted towards the woods. Dunlevy's efforts to run were impeded by his heavy pack from which the straps would not come loose. Glancing over his shoulder, Morton saw his struggle and slowed long enough to pull out a small Beretta and fire at the patrol. The light popping sounded like a toy gun, but Morton's return fire momentarily slowed the rush of the patrol.[28]

"Roll, man, roll!" Catlos shouted at the frustrated Dunlevy. He made it a short distance up a grade and tumbled over a log to the ground while bullets peppered the snowdrifts near him. When the pack dropped off, he crawled to his feet and leaped over a shallow creek and disappeared into a dense pine thicket. The three Americans ran for their lives until the sounds of gunshots died away. They continued until the thin mountain air that hampered breathing compelled them to stop.

The youths had disappeared, leaving the supplies behind. This was the first venture of these Americans into strange territory and it soon became clear that they were lost. With the afternoon waning and the temperature dropping, they would freeze to death if they ceased moving. They wandered around for an hour trying to retrace their earlier steps, pausing only to search for clues of their whereabouts and for Morton to catch his breath. But fresh falling snow had erased all footprints. Becoming more anxious by the moment, they paused for a rest and to take their bearings. Morton leaned over to take a close look at the ground, groaned and pointed to disappearing prints made by his wooden shoe. They'd been walking around in circles.[29]

Clammy and numb with cold, they plodded on, combing the area for a landmark. But every clump of trees and clearing looked the same and led nowhere. Just when they feared they would perish in the woods, Catlos' keen eyes caught a glint of dark patches in the snow. He bent over for a closer look, then looked up at his companions with a big grin.

"Either of you know some asshole who chews tobacco?" He pointed to the spots which were nickel-sized brown splotches now frozen on hard crusts of snow left by Dunlevy's tobacco juice along the path they had descended earlier. They were like beacon lights leading them home.

It was almost dark when they reached the cabin. They reported their near capture and the incident with the guerrillas encountered on the trail. These same culprits were now lounging on the floor in a corner. Their story to Green and Sehmer was that they fought off the enemy patrol. Instead, they'd actually watched the Americans get ambushed without firing a shot at the Germans. Secreted behind one of them were two of the food packs, retrieved after the patrol left.[30]

Realizing how close they had come to capture, Dunlevy's concern over the poor security deepened. From the outset he had been troubled about Green, Gaul and Sehmer relying too much on self-serving Soviets for security rather than having their own men patrol the area. He decided that when possible, he would assist in acting as sentry. The lax security had become a sore point with him but he dared not question the decisions of superior officers. It was a touchy situation that would later trouble Dunlevy.[31]

11

A Christmas of Hope

By mid–December 1944, it was clear that the Red Army was slower than expected in reaching eastern Slovakia and, like the rest of the war, seemed to have come to a stalemate. Harsh winter weather, added to an unanticipated ferocious enemy defense, had the campaign all but stalled.

General Mark Clark's 5th and 8th Armies were still bogged down in Italy on craggy mountain peaks with fast flowing rivers threatening danger at every turn. The Germans continued to hold Budapest under siege with massive casualties mounting as they tried to stem the approach of General Malinovsky's 2nd Ukrainian front. The Battle of the Bulge still raged with masses of troops on both sides engaged in a determined effort to prevail, fighting savagely in Belgium's Ardennes Forest through the bitterest cold winter in years.[1]

Before it ended, the Battle of the Bulge would go down as one of the most costly battles for both sides. The Germans would count 130,000 casualties wounded and killed; the Americans, 10,000 dead, 20,000 missing in action and 20,000 captured.[2]

On the home front, popular band leader Glenn Miller was reported missing since his flight from London to Paris on December 15, 1944. They had taken off in bad weather and were not heard from since, nor were any traces of him or pilot Jack Morgan ever found. His disappearance was a mystery that has never been resolved.[3]

A lighter media story was a report that on December 21, two officers of Panzer divisions were sent to Bastogne with a white flag to tell the Americans they were in a trap and if they did not surrender, they would be chewed to pieces. General Anthony McAuliffe replied in a one-word well-known American expression: "Nuts!" It had to be explained to the English speaking Germans that in translation it meant "Go to hell!"[4]

And in Polomka, the Americans and British were also in a holding

11. A Christmas of Hope

position and growing restless. On the day following the near capture of Catlos, Dunlevy and Morton, a commander of a Soviet guerrilla unit at Velky Bok sent their master twin snoops, Hans and Fritz, on a scouting expedition. On their return, they reported that an estimated three thousand German soldiers and a full Hungarian brigade were pouring into the area surrounding Polomka. A number of these soldiers were in a special Abwehr anti-partisan unit bent on revenge against partisans and guerrillas and assisted by Slovak Hlinka collaborators who would know where to find them.[5]

Hans and Fritz were former Wehrmacht soldiers who had defected and joined the Soviet guerrillas. Being fraternal twins, they did not resemble each other. Brown-eyed, swarthy Hans was shorter and had the amiable temperament of a good waiter. Fritz had hazel eyes and chestnut hair and was of a serious nature. Commanders of Soviet guerrillas, and what remained of Slovak partisan units, relied on the canny Nazi-hating twins, admiring their daring and knowledge of enemy battle tactics.[6]

On a particular evening, as dusk descended over the mountains, Green, Gaul and Sehmer made another of their nocturnal sorties to check out the situation for themselves. At the last moment, the Soviet guerrilla commanders Lieutenants Dymko and Shukayev joined them. Some action, any effort that would slow the hordes crowding in and preparing for battle, was called for. But what could their puny numbers do that would affect the mass of trained combat soldiers opposing them?

Sehmer, for one, had vowed that they would not "bloody well sit on our asses and brood." They would do something. The men set out on their mission, looking tense and determined, and returned at midnight wearing expressions of satisfaction. It was Gaul who let it out that they had blown up a railroad tunnel leading to four hundred miles of railroad and highway the Germans needed to move men, munitions and supplies. It had been targeted by CFI partisans and Soviet guerrillas but the Americans and Brits had gotten there first and now a strategic key tunnel was destroyed. Morton eagerly recorded the story, evidently relishing the idea of how a handful of men, armed only with a few explosives, were successful in thwarting the still powerful Wehrmacht. But that triumph was to be short lived, merely a Pyrrhic victory, because the resultant fury of the enemy whipped up their drive to "destroy the partisans."[7]

The mountain area surrounding Polomka was divided into two major Soviet guerrilla camps. Dymko commanded one and Shukayev the other. Their men were bivouacked in the 50-room hotel at Velky Bok from where they operated. Prior to the arrival to the masses of enemy troops, there had been a tacit operational agreement existing between leaders of German and guerrilla and partisan patrols. To avoid unnecessary confrontations, Germans patrolled in the morning, guerrillas and partisans in the afternoon, with the adversaries mostly staying out of the way of each other. But the tenuous peaceful co-existence was about to change.[8]

For the Americans and Maria, the days settled into a more positive mode, waiting for the Red Army front to reach them. Finding a dependable source of food and recuperating from frostbitten feet were the major concerns. Moods mellowed considerably as physical conditions improved and hopes for rescue looked better every day. The afternoon when Sehmer brewed tea was the high point of the day for most of the men. For Maria it was the lowest. During the day, keeping the cabin in order and preparing meals and interpreting for both Russians and Americans kept her mind occupied. It was when the afternoon waned that she most missed Keszthelyi and her family. As twilight slipped over the high mountain peaks, her spirit was savaged at times by melancholy. Seeking solace, she drew closer to kindred souls Horvath and Morton, each battling his own private despondency but empathetic to her loss.[9]

Horvath could no longer slip into Polomka to see his relatives, which doubtless made the longing for his wife of one year more piercing than ever. Time and again Maria caught him gazing over the horizon, apparently not really seeing the staggering beauty of mountain vistas and a sea of snow-topped pines. His wife, Alma, was a nurse and on one occasion, he confided to Catlos and Maria that she had taken on extra duties to fill in the time until he returned home.

Maria was impressed with the unabashed adoration the fantastic-looking Horvath held for his wife. Both men were intelligent, and strong, but Horvath had the street smarts learned in extra military experience and was outstanding in every way.[10]

Dunlevy was one of those who admired what he termed this "man's man" and felt that Horvath was possibly the most tragic of the unit. He had volunteered for this mission to aid the people in the country of his birth, leaving behind the promise of his adopted country and being with his beloved, gorgeous wife with whom he had spent only a few short months. The mission had hoped to be out of Slovakia by Christmas, but it was not to be, making this the loneliest and most troubling Christmas of their lives, as well as for millions of fighting men and their families the world over.[11]

The Soviets received depressing news via shortwave radio just before Christmas, adding to the heavy burdens felt by all. The Allies were still trying to fight their way through the Brenner Pass between Italy and Austria with the Germans battling fiercely to hold them back from Slovakia and Austria.

11. A Christmas of Hope

A small group of airmen and two OSS agents splitting away from Green's command are captured at a similar shepherd's hut near the village of Zelzno (courtesy the Museum of the Uprising Archives).

The Red Army had an additional adversary when Ukrainian General Vlasov threw in his forces with the Germans waging a fierce offensive against the Red Armies.[12] While an uneasy world waited, holding its collective breath, like the countless millions whose fate depended on the outcome of the war, the men of Dawes and the SOE were also bottled up in a holding pattern except, possibly, Major Sehmer.

Two days before Christmas he was struck with another of his daring notions. Deviltry lurking in his bright blue eyes, he rubbed his palms together, declaring, "We have to find something nice as Christmas gifts for the ladies, don't we now? They are doing a splendid job of taking care of us blokes."

His strategy was already mapped out. On previous sorties, he and his cohorts had noted that the Hungarians were scavengers, grabbing every single item they could get their hands on. A raid to relieve them of some of their stolen booty could pay off. Joined by Green and Gaul, they set off on their own special scavenger hunt.[13]

Those who remained in the cabin got busy. Horvath chopped down a pine tree which he and Miller dragged into the cabin and set up in a corner while Maria searched for something she might use to make decorations. The bright wrapping paper on her aunt' gifts would do. She and Horvath snipped and cut out a Santa Claus to suspend from the ceiling and red hearts and blue and white stars to hang on the branches. As a final touch, Horvath divided a large candle into two segments, one that he placed on top of the tree and the other on the table to be lit after dark.[14]

A festive cabin welcomed Sehmer and his crew when they returned, lugging two burlap bags and a large battered valise. Sehmer, with a devilish twinkle in his eyes, handed over the booty to Maria and Margita that they had stolen from a couple of absent Hungarian officers. The men watched the two women dig into the bags and pull out shapeless dresses, queen-size cotton stockings, and dowdy underwear, all several sizes too large for either woman, but creating a lot of hilarity. To cap off the presentations, Sehmer then ceremoniously presented Margita with a blue sweater and knit socks, and a brown angora sweater to Maria. Green gave her a pair of black slippers and Margita a bright head kerchief.[15]

The dynamic Major Sehmer of the British war mission meets with the Americans (courtesy the Museum of the Uprising Archives).

With a mischievous glance, Sehmer dangled one last item from his hand, pretending not to know what the enormous whale-boned corset trimmed with white ribbons really was. Laughingly, the men tossed the garment around like a football until Morton caught it on a high pass and slipped it over his hips to sashay around the room in Mae West style. The men hooted and howled and Maria laughed until her sides ached. Only Margita did not seem to find it funny, muttering that the antics were in poor taste.

Entering into the celebration spirit, Green plucked an American flag out of his backpack and mounted the stars and stripes to one wall. Not to be outdone, Sehmer pinned up the Union Jack beside it. Viewing the transformation

11. A Christmas of Hope

of the humble cabin, and declaring it fine work, Sehmer rubbed hands together and announced, "Now this calls for a party! And I'll take care of the drinks."[16]

Like an alchemist, he concocted a mixture from bottles of liquor he'd brought back in a separate bag, Before long, he was presiding over a brew bubbling in a pot, adding more dollops from the bottles they'd purloined until a nostril stinging, pungent odor permeated the cabin.

"What in hell's name is that stuff?" Gaul wanted to know. "If it tastes like it smells, it has to be lethal."

"Not at all, m'lad," Sehmer said with a broad wink. "It's called Shunagainsky chai. A good medicine, as you'll see."

It was hot tea spiked with slivovitz, vodka and cognac that Sehmer claimed he had learned to make from General Mihailovich's partisans in Yugoslavia. After tossing off a portion of the drink, the men waxed merry. Even Margita, accorded attention, gifts and a glass of the chai, thawed out.[17]

The two slightly tipsy women prepared a stew from venison, barley, carrots and potatoes. In the relaxed, genial mood, they were cordial to each other. While the stew was simmering, Maria changed into the feminine blouse her aunts had sent her and topped it with the sweater from Sehmer. They sparked up the navy blue slacks she had washed and dried. Stepping into the slippers Green had given her, she impulsively snipped a ribbon off the corset to pin on her braids. Dunlevy was always to remember a lesson he learned that day. It was how powerful the effect of a feminine woman conducting herself in a proper manner has on men. One such woman can civilize a room full of otherwise unruly, rowdy men.[18]

When night fell, the soft glow of the candle on the table and flickering firelight ushered in a near mystical camaraderie that dropped like a gentle mantle over all in the cabin and seemed to enfold them within it. Dymko, the iconoclast whose derring-do even surpassed that of Sehmer's, had joined the party while it was in full swing. He was known to play tricks on enemy morning patrols, ordering his men to throw rocks in such a way that the patrol thought they came from behind. The thud of unseen rocks spooked the horses, causing them to rear up and throw unwary riders and then bolt away out of their reach. But that evening, Cossak hat tipped over one dark eye, and black eyes pensive, Dymko seemed to be subdued and reflective.[19]

Lt. Shukayev, who had arrived earlier, was lounging across the room taking in the scene. His hazel eyes glistened beneath tawny hair brushed back and he sat ramrod straight but when Maria glanced his glanced his way, he flashed her a perceptive wink.[20]

Both Symko and Shukayev, the Russian who had earlier commanded

The rustic cabin hideout at Polomka, preparing for a poignant Christmas (courtesy the Museum of the Uprising Archives).

1,500 men, now broken into smaller units, were tough military officers who had escaped German POW camps. They were cynical, astute and fearless.[21] But on Christmas Eve 1944, these two hardy, capable guerrilla commanders, the stranded Americans and British men, with Maria and Margita, let down barriers to eat and drink together. Christians, Jews, and atheists were bonded in a united spirit for the moment. In keeping with the spirit flowing among them, Gaul borrowed Dunlevy's Bible to conduct an impromptu religious service. He began by calling for two minutes of silent prayer for their missing teammates, and then, his deep baritone sounding like a benediction in the quiet room, went on with the service. Catlos lifted his gaze for a second during his prayer to see that Zenopian, as well as Morton, was writing down the words.[22]

"Oh, God, we who are here gathered in Thy name and by Thy name, and by Thy blessing, on this day we offer with deep gratitude our most heartfelt thanks for our deliverance from the blizzards and high winds of the wintry mountains and from cruel snows fallen on us and from the perils of the black night and dark valley. Gratefully we thank thee for preserving our group together and for the buttressing of our wavering course and for providing food,

11. A Christmas of Hope 161

even in our darkest days. We ask Thy blessing on us and on our Allies, particularly the Slovak nation, and Thy mercy upon our comrades Jerry Mican, Tibor Keszthelyi, Kenneth Lain, William MacGregor and John Schwartz, these who are missing in enemy action and wintry storms. Amen."

When he finished, Gaul unthinkingly tucked the Bible in his pocket rather than returning it to Dunlevy, who hesitated to ask for it. He would never see it again.[23]

A tide of Christmas memories swept over Maria, of preparations during past Christmases shared with her parents and sisters. The Midnight Christmas Eve Mass was conducted by her father in an unheated church, with only the glowing spirits of worship to provide warmth. Before returning to their homes, parishioners hugged and kissed each other and exchanged fervent wishes for a blessed, joyous Nativity.[24]

Sitting to one side near the firelight, Morton had stopped writing, his genial countenance now reflective and sad. In his eyes was a longing so profound, that those nearest to him were taken aback. His wife had given birth to a baby girl while he was gone and his daughter was eleven months old. This was her first Christmas and he obviously yearned to be with her and his wife. Putting his notebook into a pocket, he rose and moved to the window where Horvath lingered, gazing into the dark night, and gently patted his shoulder without saying a word. None was needed. The poignant tableau touched all who witnessed it, setting off deeper feelings of homesickness for their loved ones and the always present but repressed dark fears that they would never see them again.[25]

Gaul, apparently finding the unexpected somber mood not to his liking, sparked it up. He composed a poem with everyone's name in it, which soon rekindled the earlier light hearted mood. Entering into the ambience, Zenopian and Davis created entertainment by thumping hands together while Zenopian belted out a popular American song of the day, titled "Pistol Packin' Mama."

The lyrics ended with the pleas that the jealous "pistol packin' mama" lay her pistol down. The others picked up the tune and joined in, Catlos singing in Hungarian, Gaul roaring in German, and Davis resonating in Welsh, with the partisans and Soviet guerrillas creating their own rowdy version that only they and possibly Maria understood. A couple of them clapped hands and danced, one man with the corset dangling from his ragged uniform, still keeping time to the beat. Even the usually somber Margita laughed when Hans and Fritz took turns donning the corset and demonstrating their version of a sexy woman's walk. After Sehmer produced another gallon of slivovitz, a potent plum brandy, the party grew increasingly boisterous. The only men missing from it were Brown, Willis and Dunlevy, who were on duty tending the signal fires and keeping watch for the expected plane drop.[26]

After a time, the candles and fire burned down, the elation subsided and a tide of nostalgia engulfed the group that could no longer be suppressed. Catlos was overcome with the desire to be with his family, the longing so keen that it felt like a physical ache. His parents and wife and little daughter would be attending Midnight Mass at Saint Ann's church in Hazelwood, a working class section of Pittsburgh. When Mass ended, the congregation usually remained sitting, loathe to depart the sacred church, until someone would begin singing. One by one, all others would join in, singing the old, beloved Christmas carols. Later, he could not recall who it was in the cabin who began the singing, but suddenly the words of the old hymn were being sung in hushed voices.

> Silent night, holy night
> All is calm, all is bright...[27]

A hush fell over the cabin as the last remnants of revelry faded. As the firelight faded, one by one, hesitant voices were lifted up in song, words of the old carols sung as they had never been sung before by any of them. When the last one ended, Davis concluded with a solo, "Rose of Tralee." The heartfelt singing seemed to create a sense of peace that passes understanding and brought an ephemeral spirit of community that was almost palpable among those in the cabin.[28]

It did not, however, extend to the sentries pacing the ground outside. The falling snows drifted higher and the wind picked up after a lull. Dunlevy whom Maria called "little bear" because of his seriousness and diffidence, had not joined the festivities because he feared that the drinking and lax atmosphere was a threat to their security. Furthermore, he did not relish the fact that sentry duty had been entrusted solely to the guerrillas. The apparent lack of concern over increasing enemy action in the area of Polomka also worried him as it did Horvath. He refused to entrust their safety to partisans or guerrillas and had voluntarily joined Hans and Fritz to keep watch outside. The three men paced back and forth in the cold, blowing on hands to warm them, keen eyes and ears watching and listening. Hans noted how quiet it was and felt this meant trouble. His brother, Fritz, agreed that it was too quiet and decided that they would go out early in the morning to see what was happening.[29]

The holiday atmosphere of Christmas Eve was re-ignited on Christmas Day. Antolik had smuggled in a generous supply of food and Maria and Margita prepared a banquet of pork, potatoes, carrots, onions and rich, black bread. Gaul and Sehmer trudged up to the "big house" as they called the ski lodge at Velky Bok, to bring back more slivovitz. Dunlevy, Brown and Willis, absent the night before, were present at the Christmas dinner.[30]

The scenery outside was as benign as a picture postcard, but even so, Dunlevy viewed it as deceptive; and he remained worried about the massing of troops around Polomka. Surely, their presence in the cabin had to be known.[31] As the day waned, the holiday spirits ebbed. They came to a crashing end when a guerrilla eyed the women suggestively, which brought a threatening shake of a fist from Davis. This universal hand gesture resulted in a punch by the guerrilla, answered with a stronger punch from Davis, requiring Gaul and Sehmer to pull the men apart. An irate Dymko then shoved the offender outside and issued the recalcitrant man a stern dressing down. He was last seen lurching down the trail, angrily kicking up tufts of snow in his wake.[32]

The animosity between Maria and Margita flared up again. The "jealousy" exhibited by the two women ignited into bitter words. Maria had been with the OSS for a long time and evidently resented Margita's intrusion into her domain.[33] Catlos also felt that her nose was out of joint over the competition from Margita.[34] Added to Maria's irritation with her rival was Gaul's and Zenopian's obvious disapproval of her presence. "What did I tell you?" Zenopian said to the men nearby. "When there's trouble in the ranks, you can chalk it up to *'cherchez la femme.'*"

Hearing this, Maria decided she'd had enough. She would leave the next day to stay with her aunts. All she needed was the right opportunity to break away. It presented itself when Catlos, Zenopian and Davis prepared to take their turn at tending the signal fires on top of the mountain. Worried about the lax security in the cabin, Dunlevy joined them. At that, Maria grabbed her parka and rucksack and followed them out into the night. Impulsively, Morton came along to walk with them part way to the lodge and to ask about Maria's foot. In her scant English, she told him it was better thanks to the sulfa he had so kindly provided.[35]

The sulfa he'd shared from his vanishing tiny cache had helped immensely. And although improved, the deep pocket of infection had not had time to completely heal and walking any distance was still an ordeal. Morton's large blue eyes shone with concern for her. "Be careful, Maria. You are brave but you have to take better care of yourself."

"I will," she assured him.

Like Dunlevy who had profound respect for Morton and was sorry this war correspondent had been plunged into this mess and didn't realize the gravity of their plight, Maria appreciated his unique qualities. He always tried to bring peace and hope to replace the fear.[36]

When Morton asked Dunlevy to stay with the group in the cabin earlier, Dunlevy had declined. He left primarily because of the drinking and lack of adequate patrols. He never talked to Morton again.[37]

That Christmas night, they paused on a plateau of the steep climb to the lodge. After saying goodbye to them, Morton turned and descended a few yards and then abruptly stopped, wheeled around and labored back up to where Maria was still standing. Taking her hands in his, he gave her a penetrating look of concern before leaning down to land a tentative kiss on her cheek with lips stiff and cold, and again uttered words of caution.

"Maria, please be careful."

"Yes, I will."

She then watched him skid back down the trail until he disappeared around a bend. His caring, unlike that of Keszthelyi or some of the other men, had no suggestion of sexual context. It was more the caring of one good friend for another. His wife was a most fortunate woman, Maria decided, and she would tell him that when she saw him again.

It was almost dark when they reached the lodge. Maria changed into her heavy Army clothing, leaving the warm sweater that Sehmer had given her on under her parka. She laced up the paratrooper boots over her throbbing foot and set out with the four men to tend the fires. The conflagrations had been kept burning for five nights, from December 20 and the next night would be the last. The smoke drifting towards heaven was accompanied by prayers and hopes that the desperately needed parcels of medicine, food and weapons would fall like manna from heaven at their feet any moment.[38]

The subdued team on duty dragged logs and cuttings to toss onto the blazing flames. On the mountaintop, the wind swooped down in whistling gusts before dying out with lonely, tormenting whines, only to return with stronger force. Periodically they searched the skies hoping to spot a plane, but none would arrive that night. They had no way of knowing that at the Brindisi airfield in Italy, an impenetrable overcast had grounded all planes for days. As the first streaks of dawn lit the sky, the disappointed team stacked up logs for the next group and wearily trudged back to the lodge. The fires would burn one more night and they hoped the help they prayed for would finally arrive in time.[39]

12

BETRAYAL: ATTACK AND CAPTURE

After tending the fires, as soon as they reached the lodge on Homolka Mountain, Maria went into the kitchen to concoct breakfast out of whatever food was available. Lt. Dymko was already at the table. A prankster, Maria never knew for certain when he was jesting and when he was serious, as in this instance.

"You better tell your people to get ready," he said, his expression dour.

"Ready for what?"

His answer was a shrug and a few terse words. "Maybe the devil is coming."

Maria studied him and tried to guess if he was merely joking. His black eyes were almost hidden under his cap, but that morning they were not mischievous. Instead they were unusually somber and brooding. As it turned out, it was too late to warn anyone about anything. Seconds later, the rattle of distant gunfire echoed throughout the entire mountain range, shattering the quiet morning. Leaping to his feet, Dymko grabbed his sub-machine gun and shouted, "Everybody out!"[1]

It brought his guerrillas as well as Catlos, Dunlevy, Davis and Zenopian on the run. Outside, they scrambled for cover, eyes focused on the trail to the cabin below, which seemed to be the origin of the shots. The rat-a-tat of gunfire continued sporadically for about two hours. When it stopped, they saw black smoke drifting skywards. It had to be from the burning cabin.[2]

Dymko's penetrating eyes darted this way and that, trying to determine the next best step to take, and he ordered his restless men to wait. He had to figure out what was going to happen next before he acted. It wasn't long in coming. About two hundred and fifty men, many in black Vlasov uniforms, some in civilian clothing, were moving up the trail towards the lodge. The dark line of marchers resembled a funeral cortege, except for sunlight glinting off rifles and submachine gun barrels. As they drew within shouting distance, one of the men was shoved forward. He was carrying a white flag.[3]

Sprawled in the snow near Dymko, Hans let out a gasp. "Look, its Fritz! Those bastards got Fritz!"

"Lt. Dymko, we want to negotiate!" one of the leaders directly behind Fritz called out when he was in hearing distance.

"Send three of your men forward!" Dymko shouted.

"No, we will talk only with Hans."

"I'll go," Hans quickly offered.

Dymko considered for a few seconds then gave his okay. Eyes squinting in the sunlight, the tense Dymko, finger on the trigger, waited for the next development while Hans, rifle on his shoulder, skidded down the steep path. When he had descended, the leader issued a command for Dymko and his men to drop their weapons.

"What have you done with the people in the cabin?" was Dymko's reply.

"The English and Americans are safe with us. They have voluntarily surrendered."

As those near the lodge watched, they could see a column of men creeping towards Hans and Fritz, the brothers completely unaware of being slowly encircled. Seeing their predicament, Dymko issued an order to his men. "Fire three shots over their heads. If they are friends, they will not fire back."[4]

The immediate answer was a volley of gunfire from the attackers and cannon and mortar shells from the village thudding around them. While Dymko readied his men for a counterattack, the firing from below ceased. Puzzled by the sudden quietude, Maria lifted her head to see what was happening. Davis pushed it down and growled at her to keep it down and to follow him. Slowly they crawled out of the line of fire as Dymko ordered his men to counterattack.[5]

"Lieutenant Dymko, we're friends," the spokesman for the attackers called out. "You might as well surrender like the Americans and English did."

At this, Fritz threw down the white flag and yelled, "Don't surrender! The Americans and the British did not surrender!"

This had to have hit a raw nerve with Dymko. Like his fellow Ukrainians, with nationalistic longings, they had been betrayed by both fascists and communists and he hated them both. Each in turn forcibly rounded up their young men and women to serve as slave labor, motivating other young men like Dymko to form partisan units and operate from forest and mountains, determined never to surrender. Out of 1,920 partisans in one Ukrainian group killed by Germans, 90 percent had no guns.[6]

Dymko scrutinized the scene before making his next move. When the leader again demanded that Dymko surrender, his response was a curse followed by a burst of gunfire, after which all hell broke loose. Mortars and cannon from the village thudded against the mountainsides, barely out of range of the lodge. Above the din they heard Hans shout, "Never in hell surrender!"[7]

"Fire back!" Dymko ordered his men. The intense and unexpected resistance from the guerrillas evidently stunned and confused the attackers. They drew back, but only momentarily. However, it gave those near the lodge the chance to get away. When Maria raised her head to see what was happening, Davis pushed it down and growled. "Stay down and follow me!"[8]

They rolled towards heavy brush as the guerrillas, greatly outnumbered, fired another volley at the enemy attackers, now regrouped and advancing. After judging their chances of succeeding, Dymko evidently realized further fighting would be suicide. He ordered his men to fire one last volley and then run like the devil into the woods and keep going.

As bullets flew in every direction, Dymko and his men, with the Americans and British, loped like deer to higher ground and denser woods. Once out of bullet range, they paused to look back at the scene behind them. Heading upwards from the cabin were about two hundred fifty men, many of them Vlassovites in black, others in Hlinka guard uniforms and some in civilian clothing, and a smattering of Germans in Slovak army uniform. Outside the cabin they caught a glimpse of Green, evidently wounded and holding his shoulder, with Gaul and Sehmer and the others behind them being prodded towards Polomka. "Jeezus! They got them all!" Catlos heard someone say.[9]

Shocked and silent, Catlos, Dunlevy, Maria, Davis and Zenopian joined those in flight and pushed deeper into the woods. An hour later, they stumbled across Dymko and a contingency of his men. At this point, Dymko ordered his men to form small groups and disperse, while he and the remainder of his unit would stay with the Americans and British. Shukayev with his unit of Soviet guerrillas was nowhere to be seen.[10]

They tramped for an hour through snow as fine as sand that soaked feet to their ankles until they came to a forester's hut. Opinion on what to do next was divided. Zenopian told Davis they had to stay with the Russians as he could not make it much farther without rest. Dymko agreed to let them stay with his group. He assigned them space in the hut and then delegated one of his men and Davis as sentries.[11]

An hour later, the keen ears of the pair caught a cracking sound emanating from surrounding brush. Someone was approaching. Diving for cover and fingers clamped on gun triggers, they waited. Suddenly, like a ghost, a white-faced Pavlo emerged, eyes wide with shock and wearing only his breeches, boots and a woolen undershirt. All he was able to escape with was a tale of horror.

He and Horvath had been at the stove preparing breakfast. Miller was

Joseph Horvath and a Slovak partisan prepared breakfast on an old stove — possibly this stove, in the rebuilt cabin — the morning after Christmas when the enemy attacked. All except Maria, Catlos and Dunlevy were captured (courtesy Rudy Horvath).

already up and outside washing in the stream. The others were just getting up. At about eight A.M., with no warning, slugs began flying through the windows and roof and around the cabin, wounding him and Major Stonek. Shivering with cold, Pavlo described how everyone in the cabin was taken by surprise by the attack. Pavlo grabbed his automatic machine gun and dashed through the door opposite the side of the cabin being fired upon. Unfortunately, he had to abandon his weapon to force his way through the thick camouflage of pine branches stacked against the cabin. He fled a hundred meters into the woods from where he watched the attack.

The enemy, some in peasant clothes and others in enemy uniforms, descended a narrow path above the cabin, guns poised for action. He saw Miller at the stream raise his hands in surrender when the firing began and be taken prisoner. A moment later, a skirmish broke out with partisan resistance. An hour or so later it ended, after which the fourteen people were taken out of the cabin and marched towards Polomka. When the soldiers started for the lodge, Pavlo set off on the run to where the British and Americans were, managing to hide from the enemy returning from the lodge. At about

12. Betrayal

three P.M., the enemy passed by without seeing him. He wandered through snowdrifts and reached the lodge, which, like the cabin below, had been torched, incinerating any wounded unable to escape. He followed footsteps in the snow until he came upon a unit of Slovak partisans on patrol. The commander gave him the direction taken by the British and Americans.[12]

Fedornak, the unit commander, later revealed that the men in the cabin and lodge had been betrayed by a Slovak partisan, who tipped off an Edelweiss anti-partisan troop of the German Revenge unit. Fedornak and his men had been three kilometers away when the attack occurred. They saw the smoke and went to investigate. Reaching the lodge about eleven P.M., they found only the foundation left. They stopped to make hot tea and then moved on.[13]

The captors confiscated all documents and items in the cabin — a camera, American and British flags, and a shortwave radio and several pistols. There was more than enough to give away their real purpose for being in Slovakia.

A short time after Pavlo reported on the fate of Green and Sehmer and their people, Shukayev and thirty of his men arrived. Always competitive, he and Dymko differed over a route to take towards the Red Army front lines. After a private discussion, Maria and the Americans and British decided to remain with Dymko, which they did until December 31. At that juncture, with the enemy surrounding the area, the situation had become intolerable. An uneasy Catlos forced the issue, pointing out that it was better to keep moving their small group towards the Red front on their own than remain in one spot with the large number of partisans and guerrillas.[14]

His proposal was not well received by Zenopian, who dreaded the cold, hunger and hardships they would endure on another march and preferred to take their chances remaining in some kind of shelter. Although his rank superseded that of Davis, when told that Davis was staying with Catlos, Dunlevy and Maria, Zenopian had no choice but to remain with them as he could not survive alone among the hostile Russians. And like Fedornak, Dunlevy also was convinced they were safer by staying on the move.[15]

Zenopian's resentment was to fester, a major factor apparently being that in essence, Maria had become very much the leader since the capture of Green and the men of Dawes. He refused to acknowledge that since she knew the land, the people, the resistance leaders, both Russian and Ukrainian as well as Slovak, and since she was the only one able to communicate with the Soviets in Russian, their fate depended on how well she performed. For him, as it had been for Gaul, this was no doubt hard to accept.[16]

Before moving on, Dymko assigned a guide named Sascha to assist them, which was a charade. He was actually a spy as was assigned to every person involved in the resistance movement by the NKVD (Russian secret police), and under orders to observe and then report on their activities. By this time, though, the Americans and British, as well as Maria, had caught on to this game and realized that the best they could hope for was a genial spy.[17]

It was January 1, 1945, when the two Americans and two British, Pavlo, Maria and guide Sascha (whom they called "Sha Sha") again set out for the Russian front. Fresh snowfall limited visibility but was good for passing undetected through mountain passages. Every step was painful and it became difficult for Pavlo to keep up. The wound on his thigh in which a bullet was still imbedded, had developed a puffy, angry looking, mottled circle of infection around it. It was early evening when they limped to a deserted farmhouse where they stayed for the night. Outside, guards took turns patrolling the roads and edges of wooded areas while inside, Maria and the two Americans and two British men and some of the Russian guerrillas crowded onto the floor to sleep. Others not lucky enough to squeeze into the tight confines had to crouch under the trees outside. Dymko was one of them.[18]

At eleven P.M., the sound of airplanes overhead shattered the stillness of the night. It was the long awaited airdrop of supplies arriving too late. The desperately needed food, medicine, weapons and winter clothing, as well as personal mail to the OSS agents, would fall into hostile hands. Actually, a couple of the parachutes were located by one of Shukayev's men, who refused to share the bounty.[19]

Maria had found Dymko to be a man of mercurial moods. One day he would be tough, suspicious and brusque, the next he could exhibit a lighter mood where he was joking and friendly. That night it was a melancholy one. Hovering near a campfire, he began to sing. Davis asked Maria about the lyrics and why the melody sounded like a funeral dirge. She listened and then translated his poignant song.

> You're safe but very far away, my love
> Between us lie mountains, fields and forests,
> But for me, death is always four steps away.

The fire died down, the wind whistled through cracks in the hut and each of them drew deeper into their most inner selves. There would be little sleep that night.[20]

Early the next morning a patrol reported that the enemy knew about them and had orders to clear the mountains of guerrillas and partisans and to find the remaining Americans and British. Post-war reports later stated that at one point, there were ten thousand well-trained enemy troops hunting them down. There was no other option than to keep moving if they wanted to stay ahead of their pursuers.[21]

12. Betrayal

The tragic news the partisans gave left Maria, Catlos, Dunlevy, Davis and Zenopian shaken. Horvath had been singled out of the captives and taken to the center square of Polomka and with hands bound and a dunce cap forced over his head, marched around while being beaten by sticks as villagers were forced to watch. Among them were his cousins and uncle. When the Gestapo had enough of their cruel and sadistic sport, they loaded all the captives in trucks and drove them away to a destination unknown.[22]

This revelation intensified the question of what to do about Pavlo, who could not continue marching on a journey with no end in sight. Maria and Davis scouted around and found a kindly forester who would care for Pavlo until he recovered enough to make it home. They pooled gold coins out of what was left of funds to pay the rescuer. As they departed, Pavlo's woeful expression was somewhat like that of a child being abandoned by parents.[23]

Their party had dwindled to Maria, Dunlevy, Catlos, Davis, Zenopian and their guide, Sha Sha. The road ahead would be an especially hellish one. They had to cross the Hron Valley before slipping across a bridge over the river and then through a ring of enemy soldiers guarding barricades at each location. Sha Sha had devised a detour that might circumvent enemy posts, but it was over killing terrain and an unmarked path with more rocks and more barricades. The only advantage was that visibility continued to be so poor that it made them harder to detect.[24]

At four A.M. on the morning of January 3, with Sha Sha still their scout, they started on the rigorous trek to get through the valley where vegetation that could shield them was sparse, and then cross the river. Tree branches laden with ice slapped against faces and bodies while they waded through deep drifts. Soles of boots imbedded with slick clumps of snow could skid and cause a bone-breaking fall. They crept past the heavily guarded main road and railroad successfully, but the worst hurdle lay just ahead. It was to make it across the bridge over the river Hron. They negotiated the planks by crawling on hands and knees, heads almost skimming the ground and inching by under the noses of the enemy. Fortunately their luck held and they slipped through the ring of enemy soldiers and reached the other side safely.[25]

For some time, Catlos had been aware that all was not well with him. He had been suffering bouts of dizziness, but now, they were compounded by episodes of intense nausea and stomach cramps. How much farther could he make it, he wondered?

They continued heading southwest, just missing a German patrol of twenty-five men combing the woods for them and stray partisans. They stopped at a forester's house to try to buy some food and as usual, the men stayed under cover while Maria made the contact. An elderly man opened the door. Taking one look at her, he mumbled, "*Nemci* come, they look in every house for *Partizanen*," and then closed the door. They left and walked another kilometer. The afternoon visibility diminished and the temperature began dropping. Catlos felt he had reached the end of his strength and he prevailed upon his colleagues to return to the forester who might change his mind about giving them shelter. He rationalized that the Germans rarely made nocturnal visits and the forester might take pity on their plight. It proved to be a wise move. Although the man still refused shelter, he sold them a bag of apples and two loaves of bread and gave what proved to be the best possible advice. It was to proceed to Rejdova where, he assured them, there were no enemy soldiers in that village.[26]

It was late afternoon when they reached the top of a mountain on their route to Rejdova and came upon a primitive shack, or more accurately, a lean-to with walls. But it provided some protection from the elements. They flopped down on the floor and hungrily bit into the apples and broke off chunks of bread to devour. At midnight, they heard the murmur of lowered voices outside. They sat up in panic, expecting the worst. But the wayfarers turned out to be two dozen partisans on leave, on their way home to Poland. Several crammed inside the lean-to with Maria and the men, and those who could not edge a way in took shelter under trees.[27]

It was a wretched night for Catlos. His body felt so hot from a raging fever that he welcomed the cold wind hissing through the cracks. He'd also developed a pounding headache. While those near him slept like the dead, he lay awake wondering if he could even make it the short distance to Rejdova.[28]

Sha Sha's opinion of himself as guide turned out to be fanciful. Setting off at four A.M., he led them in circles to the background echoes of steady gunfire. When they stopped for a brief rest, there was the sudden thrum of planes overhead. Every gaze was turned towards the blue sky above, trained on a large formation of American bombers — hundreds of them — flying towards Germany. The thunderous roar of their engines was like music to a jubilant Dunlevy who clasped Catlos on the shoulder and pointed at the roaring flotilla. Thumbs jerked skyward, Davis cheered them on with a "Go get 'em, Yanks!"

Fresh hope was reborn at the stirring sight. It symbolized hope to all of them for an especially beneficial new year of 1945. They'd be all right. They'd make it out okay.[29]

They reached Rejdova just before darkness set in. Maria ventured to an outlying house to spy out the situation while the men waited. The woman who answered her knock on the door greeted her warmly and invited her

12. Betrayal 173

inside. The attractive dark-haired woman, who appeared to be about forty years of age, flashed a secretive smile. "*Nemci* gone. We tell them many here are sick with the typhus."

The villagers spread the rumor that sent the Germans scurrying because they had little immunity to the disease. It was safe to invite the waiting men inside, too. They were warming themselves at the stove when there was a sharp rap at the door. Before the visitors had a chance to hide, the door was thrust open and in trooped several villagers, all bearing food. Word of the arrival of the Americans had been relayed like some mystic telegraph system and they came out of curiosity to see and to welcome the foreigners.[30]

One young woman brought a slab of bacon and her mother a large jar of blackberry jam. While their hostess was slicing the bread and slathering the slices with gobs of jam, more visitors arrived bringing pork and potatoes, and one man a gallon of delicious red wine. Most unexpected, every donor refused payment for the food. This was the first time anyone who had helped them refused money.

After they'd eaten, the British, Americans, and Maria held a conference. The town was a main throughway to the east, and while presently troops had vacated the town, that would not last and they could expect an influx of fresh troops bound for Germany at any time. And the Red front, they were told, was still thirty kilometers distant. Also, Catlos insisted that he was too sick to go any further. When Jan Kristak, a Hungarian-speaking villager, offered him refuge, he decided to take it. His rationale was that if he did not make it out, Dunlevy would still try to get back to Italy to report on the Dawes mission. He would go on with Maria, Davis and Zenopian and take refuge in a nearby abandoned mine until the Red Front passed through. Dunlevy, Maria and Davis did not completely buy Catlos' story, but he was adamant about staying and they had no choice.[31]

At midnight, they were still reviewing their options when the town notary arrived. The officious, middle-aged man sized up the situation and urged Maria to stay in the village. She was crazy to think she could pass through the front lines safely. When Maria said they had to try, he turned cynical.

"Do you know what happens to young females when those Siberian wolves catch sight of them? Stay here, I can give you a job and you'll be safe." He then regaled Maria with stories of rape and then death for hapless women who wandered across the path of the Siberian Army. She could be his secretary and would be protected.

"I have a price on my head," Maria told him. "Will you still protect me?"

In the village of Rejdava, agent Steven Catlos becomes ill and is given shelter at the Kristak family house (courtesy Jan Kristak, son and grandson of the elder Kristaks).

At her rejoinder, he turned aside, obviously not believing her. "Which one of these men is your lover?"

Maria was glad that Davis did not get the gist of his statement or a war would erupt then and there. Maintaining her composure, she replied, "You insult me and make me glad I am with these Anglo men."[32]

She also was sure that if she abandoned them, they could not survive. Dunlevy would not make it through, he was too boyish looking and spoke only English and, while brave and shrewd, would be robbed and then shot by Soviets who detested Americans. Davis was battle and street-wise but his German would be suspect so close to Russian lines. Furthermore, his Welsh temper would bring a bullet in the back from some edgy, brutal Soviet guerrilla before they went much farther. Arrogant, complaining Zenopian would be sure to rub a guerrilla the wrong way before the day passed and it would be either a bullet or knife in his ribs. Only Catlos, with his foxy peasant persona might make it. His attitude of "if anyone was going to survive, it might as well be me" would an effective cover. With her language ability and her close contacts with Studensky, chief of the Russian Kiev office for guerrillas, as well Generals Viest, Golian, Jegerov and other guerrilla and partisan commanders, she was a buffer for these men and their only chance to deal with the Russians and live.[33]

When the notary was convinced that she was adamant about staying with her companions, he dispatched a guide to escort them to the next village. Before they departed, leaving Catlos behind, Maria removed Keszthelyi's diary she had been carrying under her parka and gave it to the notary for safekeeping and to be turned over to the Americans when they arrived. Giving it up was like parting with a piece of her heart. As they took off for the mine where she, Davis, Dunlevy and Zenopian would find shelter, Sha Sha and another guerrilla, wearing mufti, slipped away to try to make it to their homes. Maria and the two men were on their own.[34]

The break in the unit was not without rancor. Davis muttered that Catlos was "not all that sick." Zenopian's envy was unmistakable, as he would prefer to stay in Rejdova. And Dunlevy felt desolate at being the last American of the mission still on the run. It had been eight weeks of wandering over murderous terrain on badly infected feet, half starved and under constant siege and their ordeal was far from being over. He could not even find solace in the pocket-sized Bible he always carried. It was in Gaul's possession since Thanksgiving when he used it for the brief service he conducted, and only God knew where their captors had taken him and all the other Dawes men.[35]

Maria's pronounced limp indicated unremitting pain. Observing her day after day, Dunlevy marveled at her stoic endurance and courage and was to remember how he never saw fear in her eyes, nor did she allow her physical appearance to deteriorate, as did the men. She was always tidy and willing to risk her life by entering villages infested with informers to try to obtain food and shelter for them. If he made it back to Italy, he would inform his superiors about all Maria had done for the Americans. But pragmatic Dunlevy knew that making it back to his base in Italy remained a very iffy proposition and would require a major miracle at least.[36]

13

Unlikely Shelter from the Storm

Catlos was stung by the undisguised disapproval of his companions for deciding to remain in hiding at the home of Jan Kristak. Only Dunlevy agreed that it was an adequate plan. But Catlos refused to dwell on it, feeling too miserable. All he wanted was to lie down and sleep. His head reeling with dizziness and abdomen besieged with sharp, gripping pains, he pulled himself up to the hayloft of Kristak's barn, flopped down and lay prone on a clump of hay.

Kristak pointed to the chamber pot in a corner he could use, told Catlos to settle down, said he would be back soon and left. He returned an hour later carrying a coarse woolen blanket draped over a steaming pot of cabbage soup. He urged Catlos to eat some. But even a couple of spoonfuls of the cabbage swimming in a salty liquid and sour cream made him retch. He lay down again, welcoming the oncoming darkness and finally fell into a fitful sleep, only to be awakened by the drone of airplane engines overhead. He sat up, listened, and let out a groan. It was the planes dropping the supplies they had waited for, arriving too late. The parcels would only fall into enemy hands now.[1]

The night passed, then a day, and another night. Periodically Kristak brought hot tea and food his wife and daughter had prepared. By the third night, Kristak grew alarmed at Catlos' condition. If he died in the hayloft, it would be a problem for them to dispose of his body. They would have to smuggle it to a disguised hideout outside the village clandestinely created to shelter partisans. As they argued about what to do with the American, Catlos overheard Kristak's daughter, Anna, pointing out that he needed medicine and warmth and insisted that he be invited to come into the house to recuperate. Kristak finally relented, and gave Catlos an oversized woolen shirt

13. Unlikely Shelter from the Storm

and pants to cover his uniform. If questioned, he was to claim he was a Hungarian soldier too sick for active duty.[2]

The young German medic who dropped by periodically for something to eat made an unexpected visit a day later. There was no time to hide, so Catlos got into bed and covered up with blankets to his chin. The young medic looked Catlos over from the foot of the bed and decided Catlos had the flu. He gave Catlos two opium pills and left. The opiate soothed his dysentery and reduced his fever. Two days later, the improvement was noticeable. The reassured Kristak invited Catlos to join the family for regular evening meals and afterwards to listen to the nightly radio broadcast.[3]

A routine developed in which the days were spent in the hayloft, then joining the family for a simple meal in the evening followed by avidly listening to news on the radio. The reports depressed Catlos. The Battle of the Bulge had finally ended with heavy casualties on both sides. The Allies were forging ahead towards Germany. The Germans were retreating north through Italy towards Hungary and Slovakia, while General Zhukov's First White Army and General Ivan Konev's 4th Ukrainian Army were moving slowly but steadily west, and they were closing in on the Germans. But the war was far from over.[4]

As the evenings passed quietly without event, Catlos grew more at ease with the Kristak family. He enjoyed the lighter moments when daughter Anna sang Hungarian songs to him and tried to elicit his identity. But he would say only that his name was famous and often heard on their radio. He meant, of course, Slovak general Fernand Catlos, who deserted the Slovak State Army to become a leader of the revolt. But the family never caught on. And as the days crept by, little by little, both Catlos and Kristak became complacent.[5]

One evening after they had finished a meal of potato soup and dark bread and were listening to the radio, the door burst open and a stranger entered. He wore a tattered Hungarian army uniform and stared hard at Catlos, then Kristak, who greeted him coolly although he did not introduce Catlos. The man sat down uninvited at the kitchen table and continued to eye Catlos suspiciously. Finally he declared, "You're an American!"

Neither Kristak nor Catlos responded. The visitor then said he wanted to go home but his Hungarian uniform mean he'd be shot on sight by the Russians. He demanded Catlos' give him his American uniform. When Catlos continued to ignore him, the man's eyes hardened, the slight smile faded, and he leaped to his feet. "Good luck, Yankee!" he sneered and slammed out the front door.[6]

Kristak jumped up and locked the front door as Catlos hurtled out the back door out into the night. The Hungarian would surely turn him in.

Where could he hide now? The barn was too obvious and besides, he had left his gun hidden under the hay. Running directionless into the night in freezing darkness was suicide, and while Kristak had told him of the hidden shelter in the woods, he had no idea how to get to it, especially in the dark. While pondering his next move, he jostled against the sheep pen, setting off a frantic baaing of sheep, but also a light in his mind. There had to be a door. He felt about for it and pushed through the small aperture, squeezing past the frightened sheep. Then he groped around the ceiling and found an opening to the loft above. He eased his now thin body through it and stretched out flat, filling up every square inch of space. The overpowering stench revived his queasiness, now compounded by bowel cramps sweeping over him in sickening waves. The unaccustomed exertion left him breathless. Lying inert and unmoving on the wooden planks trying to muffle his wheezing, he detected soft, padded footsteps creeping around the pen, setting off another clamor from the alarmed animals. Only when he heard one of the pursuers say that the American could not have gone far and they'd get him in the morning, was he able to resume normal breathing. Shivering with cold, exhausted and heart pounding in dread, he finally drifted into a fitful sleep. He was awakened at daybreak by a knock on the floor beneath. He had carved a small knothole in the wooden floor and peered through. It was Anna. Hunger had replaced nausea and he hoped she was bringing food. But when he saw the young woman crouched in the pen below, his heart sank. All she carried were two pails of slop for the sheep. She called up to Catlos to slide the opening to one side. Lifting her long black woolen skirt, she untied a rope from around her waist that was balancing twin pots suspended from a thick leather belt. She handed the containers of food up to him, saying she'd return later for the pots, then turned and sashayed saucily back to the house.[7]

The ritual was repeated for a week. Then one evening a worried Kristak came to tell Catlos he had to leave the next morning. German soldiers were sweeping into their village in large numbers and searching every house and barn for partisans and some Americans on the loose. Worse yet, officers had commandeered his house for occupation. Before the ordeal ended, 5,000 German soldiers were bottled up in Reydova by Romanian troops. He did not have to remind Catlos what the consequences would be for him and his entire family if Catlos were found.[8]

At daybreak, Catlos was startled by orders shouted in German followed by ricocheting gunfire. Through a peephole he saw that a German medical unit had moved in. That meant heavy fighting and casualties were expected. He had to get out undetected, but how? Trying to devise a plan, Kristak suddenly appeared with a parcel of food wrapped in newspaper and a moth-eaten

13. Unlikely Shelter from the Storm   179

The Kristaks 23-year-old daughter Anna boldly slipped past occupational enemy forces to bring Steven Catlos food. Photograph of Anna and her husband in later years — both now deceased (courtesy Jan Kristak).

coat and woolen cap he'd dug out of a trunk. The coat covered Catlos to his ankles and the cap hid his unkempt hair. His legs, weakened from the confinement, buckled when he followed Kristak into the house where he hastily ate a slice of bread, washed down by a glass of hot tea and was ready to leave. Kristak refused the gold coins offered and told Catlos that the only reward any of his family wanted was a return of the democracy Americans had helped them obtain.

Stepping into the yard, Catlos kept a surreptitious eye on the German sentries he would have to pass. He picked up a bale of hay and walked slowly across the yard. Truckloads of enemy soldiers whizzed by and when one slowed to look him over, he realized he had to do something else. A ragged farmer carrying hay into the woods defied common sense. Glancing about, he spied a woodcutter's axe imbedded in a stack of logs in the yard next door. No one was visible so Catlos casually strolled over, yanked the axe out of the log and slung it across his shoulder and then strolled boldly past two sentries stamping feet and blowing on hands to warm them. The German soldiers still wore a type of shoe called dice boxes that did not protect them from the cold whereas Russians wore a felt boot that kept feet warm.[9]

One young sentry flashed Catlos a friendly smile as he walked across the road and then into the woods where he continued walking until breaths were painful rasps. Before long, the exhilaration he felt at deceiving the German soldiers and escaping under their noses vanished. He had to find the shelter that Kristak told him was hidden in the woods, camouflaged by tree branches and hard to detect. Finally, remembering a couple of clues Kristak had given, a search revealed the shelter. He crept into it and leaned against one side, suddenly feeling hopeless. Dimly he wondered where Dunlevy, Maria and the two Brits were now. Had they, too, been captured like Green and Gaul and the others, or were they lucky enough to have found the mine they planned to hide in? And were any of the Red Armies near?[10]

* * *

After Catlos decided to stay with Kristak, his companions proceeded towards the village of Hankova where a guide was to escort them to the mine. From under the cover of trees, they observed enemy soldiers searching Rejdova for them house by house and guards patrolling the perimeters of the village. They had escaped just in time.[11]

When Gregor, the new guide, arrived, they set off once more. The path was treacherous and Maria skidded on a hidden ice patch and tumbled to the ground, her knee colliding with a hard object. Pain shot up to her groin and the knee joint began to swell. Zenopian's face contorted as he went into a rage, yelling that they were on the front lines and by damn, he would not put up with any more of Maria's female tricks. At this, Davis shook a fist under his nose and told him to shut up. Zenopian did not back down and dared Davis to hit him. Davis growled that if he did anything to Zenopian, it would not be to hit him, it would be to shoot him. Zenopian then informed Davis that he had superior rank and that Davis would have to obey his orders. Davis retorted by saying Zenopian wasn't even English, and furthermore was a coward and lazy as hell. The two angry men pushed and shoved at each other as Maria, Dunlevy and Gregor watched in dismay. Finally the outmatched Zenopian moved aside, his countenance a mottled study in fury.[12]

Earlier that morning, their contact had traveled to the village of Bystra to determine the best possibilities of crossing to the front lines. When he returned, he advised them it was too hazardous to attempt a crossing because the low mountain ranges had only sparse woods, leaving them with little or no cover. Also, enemy troops were rapidly retreating and sometimes taking a shortcut through the woods. The front was expected to reach their present position in a couple of days and he recommended that they hide out in a nearby mine that had been abandoned for over a hundred years to wait it out.[13]

Fed up with Zenopian's unrelenting hostility, Maria insisted that the men go ahead without her and she would catch up as soon as she could. The gesture was futile because she could not walk.

"None of that!" Davis growled and hoisted her onto his back. In the dark, their movements were slow as tortoises. Minutes into their trek, they were startled by the sound of ringing church bells. It brought them to an abrupt stop. "What the devil is that?" Davis wondered out loud.

Maria explained that it was January 6, the Eastern Orthodox Christmas Eve celebrated by Orthodox Church members all over the world. The next day, January 7, would be their Christmas. Her own heart was heavy, remembering that this was the first Christmas she'd spent without her family, and she grew morose wondering whether she would live to see another.[14]

The mine corridor was cold, narrow, damp, and moldy as a grave. It was so crowded that occupants were lined up like logs. Davis set Maria down and, for her protection, positioned himself on one side, and Dunlevy on the other. Zenopian edged as far away as the narrow confines permitted, still irate and brooding at having left the Soviets in their camp.[15]

Huddled like moles in the mine, one day passed and then another, and with the tight confines, darkness and cold, it felt like being buried alive. On a couple of occasions, a villager brought food—the second time, a bottle of rum with the food. Declaring him an angel, they consumed chunks of bacon, black bread and marmalade, and finished off the repast with a shot of the liquor. Later, Maria was to credit the rum from keeping the men from going stir crazy from boredom and confinement in their self-imposed prison. The angel's name was Pasternak, and he was the town registrar from Hrbaky, an adjacent village.[16]

The only diversion to alleviate the tedium was a game they invented. It was picking lice out of crevices in their clothing and dropping them over the flames of the candle Pasternak brought. The one with the highest count for the day was rewarded with a second shot of rum.[17]

When several days passed and Maria's foot and knee had improved somewhat, she felt she could no longer endure the cramped space, darkness, or fetid air. On his next visit she told Pasternak that she would go with him to the village, hoping to make contact with a certain man who might have current, reliable information on the location of the Red Army front lines. At Pasternak's house, she borrowed peasant's clothing to wear over her uniform and parka, after which he introduced Maria to his eighteen-year-old nephew who would accompany her to the front. Arrayed in a heavy loose blouse, long skirt and a man's topcoat, she set out with Alexei to walk the four kilometers to Bystra to try to find a spot where they could slip through the front lines to safety. In Bystra, Alexei took Maria to the home of a man he called Urban who would help her. Nearing the dwelling, he gave Maria a description of the man and then slipped away to return home.[18]

Shock eddied down Maria's spine when the man who opened the door did not fit the description given. Furthermore, he was as startled to see Maria as she was to see him. Glancing beyond him, she a saw a half dozen German soldiers seated at the table, relaxed and smoking. One of them lounged against his host's sheepskin coat slung over the back of a chair leaned back to rake her over with a piercing stare. She estimated she had mere seconds to act. Flinging her arms around the peasant's neck, she exclaimed, "Yanna! I'm so glad I found you home and well!"

The startled man gave a sigh of relief and managed to stammer, "Sister-in-law, have you found your husband yet?"

"Maybe these gentlemen can help me."

The soldiers, cracking ribald jokes, suggested to their commander that maybe she'd sleep with him and he tendered the invitation to Maria. Deciding to keep it light, she replied that she dared not comply as her brother-in-law would tell on her. At that, the soldiers laughed and got up to leave. In passing, the commander whispered to Maria that he would be back later and he would make sure that no one would tell on her.[19]

As soon as they left, with a sigh of relief, Urban told Maria of a bigger mine closer to the front lines where her group could hide. The front was still six kilometers distant but the fighting had come to a standstill and every inch of ground was under tight guard. It would be fatal if they tried to cross. While Urban was stuffing a burlap bag with bread and bacon, a truck filled with German soldiers slammed to a stop in front of the house. They climbed out and walked to the edge of the woods to relieve themselves. Grabbing a small hose, Urban slipped out the door and removed the cap from their gas tank. In seconds he was back with a quart of gasoline he'd siphoned into a bottle. He instructed Maria to mix it with the salt he would give her and they'd have a light for the interior of the mine.

He accompanied Maria part way to the nearby mine and then left her to proceed alone, promising to return that afternoon with another guide to show them the way to the larger mine. Maria was making her way slowly along the road when a horse drawn cart pulled up alongside, occupied by two German soldiers.

"Fraulein, that bag looks heavy," one called out. "We will give you a lift."

At first glance, they looked harmless and she climbed into the cart. Suddenly smiles turned to leers. Close up, although young, they were coarse and hardened. To deter them from any physical attack, she quickly told them her husband was digging trenches for the Germans, and she had gone to find food to feed him when he returned home that evening. Evidently her good German was convincing because when they reached the outskirts of the village and she pointed to a house claiming that it was where she and her husband lived, they stopped the cart to let her out.[20]

The stout older woman who answered her knock looked alarmed and admitted Maria very reluctantly. She seemed to be alone but Maria suspected she had hidden any young daughters or other children in a secret cellar or some other concealed spot. The woman was visibly relieved when Maria left after a few minutes.

By then, it was almost dusk and Maria deemed it too risky to proceed any further alone and decided to return to Urban's house rather than wander to the mine in the dark. Although her reappearance was an alarming aggravation, Urban instructed her to sit down and act as though she lived there. Germans soldiers who had arrived after she left were staying in the house overnight and would return any minute from a patrol.

Maria kicked off her boots and shoved them under the chair and put on her felt slippers seconds before one of the soldiers entered. The soldier, who appeared to be about twenty years old, plopped down beside her and asked what a beautiful girl was doing in such a godforsaken place. Maria smiled and maintained steady eye contact to distract him from looking down and catching sight of the paratrooper boots. Fortunately, Urban had tucked the burlap bag of food out of sight. The soldier leaned over and took her hand, his breath acrid with alcohol, and asked if she lived there. When Maria replied that she had come to visit her uncle, he pressed his knee against hers and said he wanted to give her some presents. Maria forced herself to smile as a hint that she was not averse to his proposal. He hurried to the rear of the house and returned with a half dozen cigars, a pack of cigarettes and two decorative candles. He dropped them into her lap and moved closer, brushing her cheek with his lips just as a strident male voice outside called out, "Hans?"

He squeezed Maria's hand and told her he had to obey orders but would be back soon. The instant he was out of sight, Maria divided the food into two parcels, slapped on her paratrooper boots and set off on the trek to the mine. On the way, another German patrol passing called out, "Now there's a partisan!"

Maria answered gaily, "If you think so, then you're my comrade." Her excellent German and buoyant attitude brought a laugh and they drove off, waving until out of sight.[21]

Reaching the mine safely, where the worried men greeted her heartily, Maria presented the cigars to Dunlevy and the cigarettes to Davis. When they asked where she had gotten them, she said only that, like the Trojans, Germans, too, came bearing gifts. Dunlevy bit off an end of the cigar to chew. Davis and Zenopian divided the cigarettes and they all had a drink to celebrate Maria's safe return.[22]

The next day, true to his promise, Urban arrived to escort them to the back entrance of a larger antimony mine, known as the Petramanovce mine, undetectable to a casual observer. The front entrance was guarded by German soldiers in camouflage. Urban had once worked in the mine and knew the corridors as well as he knew the interior of his house. He led them through a gloomy passage, half crawling over men stretched out over almost every inch of space. At the far end, he stopped and hammered on an exposed pipe with a coded signal of two taps, pause, again two taps, pause, and two more taps. A ladder dropped down and they climbed to a higher level and emerged into a larger space occupied by four deserting Hungarian soldiers. They had been sleeping on pieces of boards arranged together and using a carbide lamp for illumination.[23]

Before he left, Urban told Maria that the Germans were confiscating most of their food and the Russians would take what was left. It was up to her to help him find food for their group if they were to eat at all. The next day, still wearing the borrowed clothing, Maria accompanied Urban across the Hungarian border to the farm of a friend. In addition to the usual bacon and bread, the farmer sold her a dozen apples, a rare treat.[24]

13. Unlikely Shelter from the Storm

Day by day, the corridors of the mine became increasingly crowded with hundreds of refugees, deserting Slovak soldiers, CFI partisans, boys fleeing military conscription, a smattering of Russian guerrillas, and a few Jews who had managed to escape the final clutches of the Gestapo. One far end of the corridor was used as a latrine and the stench was numbing. Communication was limited to whispers and kept to barest necessities.

Then one night Urban did not show up as promised. It was a bad omen. At dawn, they were jolted awake by the thudding of mortar shells, and the crackling echo of machine gun fire reverberating off the walls of the mine. The explosive sounds were accompanied by shouts, curses, and anguished screams from the wounded, interspersed with pleas for help in Russian and German. The ear-splitting cacophony was compounded by the floor quaking beneath them until they shook like reeds. Above the din, the pitiful screams of agony and the raw terror overshadowing everything like a black shroud epitomized a scene from hell.

During the melee, the occupants heard an exchange in German voices at the entrance, wondering if there was anyone inside. When a flash of light swept the interior, Dunlevy was sure it was a flame thrower and tried to brace for the conflagration. Had those soldiers investigated the mine inside even a yard or two, those therein would have been as good as dead. The voices faded away as the clamor and roar of battle climbed to an ever-deafening din, and those huddled on the floor of the mine burrowed down like hunted prey. Dunlevy, and no doubt each of the others, feared that their lives were doomed to come to a violent end at any second.[25]

14

ULTIMATE HORROR AT THE HANDS OF THE NAZIS

For a week Maria and the three men were entombed in the Petramanovce mine. Despite the unrelenting din of battle that reverberated off the walls, the ear splitting noise could not completely shut out the cries of the wounded and dying. In the clammy darkness of the mine, there was scant distinguishing between day and night and conversation all but ceased except for necessary exchanges.[1]

On the ninth day, they awakened to something strange. It was a near absence of deafening sounds that seemed to have receded into the distance. The battlefront had passed them by. In near disbelief, Maria and the three men descended the ladder and crept to the entrance of the mine. Like moles, they peered out into the early morning light and blinked repeatedly at the unaccustomed brightness. As far as they could see, the atmosphere was gray from smoke and dust, silent as death, and the land ravished with deep gouges, rubble and debris. What had been houses and barns was wreckage with trees and brush devoid of so much as a leaf, and the area equally empty of animal or human life. Men, women and children had gathered their livestock and fled to the hills, mines and caves and other secret places they had staked out and remained in hiding. In a daze, the four began walking towards the village of Bystra.[2]

Suddenly, a military vehicle loaded with soldiers rounded a sharp turn, careening around craters and headed directly towards them. There was no time or place to hide. They stood frozen with apprehension as the American-made jeep slammed to a stop. It was filled with Romanian soldiers.

"Good God!" the commander exclaimed after sizing up the ragged, gaunt foursome. "Who the devil are you?"

Maria addressed him in Russian and related their story, adding that one

American soldier was still in hiding at Rejdova. She did not betray those still in the mine who might be construed as enemies. The officer ordered them to climb into the jeep and drove them to headquarters at Sitnik. Along the way, the vehicle passed Soviet soldiers breaking into homes and stores, stealing everything in sight. It was shocking to see uniformed men openly lugging pots and pans, clothing, dishes and shoes, anything they could grab. But it was only a hint of what was to come.[3]

* * *

After roaming about until he stumbled onto the hideout, Catlos spent two nights in it. He was weak, half frozen and near hallucinating when he was rescued by a Romanian patrol combing the woods for stray German soldiers. One of them lit a match to thaw out Catlos' frostbitten fingers and hands, chapped and raw from exposure. When they reached their command post and heard his incredible story, he was given a pair of shoes to replace the boots left in Kristak's sheep pen. With hope renewed, he asked "Is the war over?"

It was January 23, 1945, and the war was far from over, they told him. He asked about Dunlevy, Maria, and the two Brits but was told it would be weeks before they finished sorting out refugees. As Catlos was handed his dog tags they'd taken from him for inspection, some of Green's words came back to him. "Don't forget who we are!" Green had admonished. "We're Americans on a military mission, by damn, and not some rag tag group of wanderers!"[4]

Comparing his dirty, frayed uniform under the moth-eaten coat and Cossack cap borrowed from Kristak with the comparatively dapper Romanian soldiers, he felt more like a gypsy than a self-reliant American soldier. Where in heaven's name were Dunlevy, Davis, Zenopian, Maria, and all the others, he wondered? Had they been captured, too?[5]

* * *

Dealing with the sea of refugees arriving in waves was a daunting task for the authorities. No one knew what to do with Maria and the Americans and British. After several hours of waiting, Maria asked to speak to the commander on behalf of their group and requested from him a transfer to the Russian Division. The beleaguered commander was glad to be rid of them, and the five set out to walk the seven kilometers to the next camp at Stitnik. At noon, they paused to listen to church bells and take note of peasants on their way to work the fields carrying hoes and rakes stopping to make the sign of the cross reverently and then continuing on their way. The sight of Christians observing their faith was reassuring.

As enemy troops invaded Rejdova, Catlos evaded capture and hid in a bunker (marked at the extreme right with an x) until, freezing and sick, he was rescued by Romanian soldiers (courtesy Jan Kristak).

On arrival at the Soviet camp, they were again shuffled about because they had no identification. The camp was in total disorder and chaos. Refugees of myriad nationalities were trucked in and there was no workable procedure to handle them. An orderly finally talked to them and said they were to go to another camp in Rozyno. However, it was sixty kilometers distant, much too far to walk and there was no transportation. Maria asked to speak to the officer in command and, surprisingly, he agreed to see her.[6]

The general had Maria tell her official story several times before agreeing to have them trucked to Rozyno. It had been rehearsed a number of times with Catlos and Dunlevy and she knew what to say and what not to — such as mentioning any involvement in espionage. Evidently she was convincing, and once they reached Rozyno, an aide found them some clean clothing and a place to sleep. The next morning they were assigned a room in the adjutant's quarters and given a hot meal of potato soup and halushki, a dish made of steaming noodles sautéed with onions and cabbage. A bit later the aide doled out some clean underwear and the last garments from the unit's allotment. That night they slept on cots with wooden slats covered with coarse,

14. Ultimate Horror at the Hands of the Nazis

thin mattresses. But after sleeping on wooden planks on a cold mine floor, these cots felt like resting on goose down feathers.[7]

The next morning they were transferred to Rimski Sobata. On the way they again encountered vestiges of war as the truck bounced around deep craters gouged out by mortar shells and wreckage piled in every direction as far as they could see. Dunlevy was disgusted and repelled at the sight of soldiers from General Konev's Ukrainian Army seizing every item they could get their hands on. Cutlery, clothing, musical instruments, toys, carpets, and china were carted off. As they proceeded on their way to Berlin, the Russians continued to engage in "lootin,' shootin' and rapin'" as one critic was to describe the pillage.[8]

It was night when they crossed the Hungarian border and arrived at their destination. The very first interrogation they were subjected to was a good indication of what being under Soviet jurisdiction was like.[9] Davis, for instance, was irate and could hardly restrain his fiery temper. "Bloody fools accused me of being a Slovak army deserter!" he groused.

"Join the club," Zenopian snapped. "They think I'm a German deserter. Me, a British Army officer! He demanded to know the name of my Nazi commander!"

Dunlevy, for unknown reasons, was issued a pair of American Navy officer's patent leather shoes. "American lend-lease," he told them, pointing at the items. His remark met with blank stares.[10]

Maria's first interrogation was a degrading experience. With leering smirks and eyes raking her over boldly, she was asked if she had sex with all the men in their group. Seething, she managed to remain outwardly calm as she rattled off the names of Studensky, Yegerov, Surkov, Dymko. Shukayev and other Soviet guerrilla commanders she knew and assured the inquisitors that any one of them would vouch for her work with Russian military intelligence. It changed the tone of the session somewhat. Although Maria realized they did not believe her, they did provide better food and a place to stay. The meal of pirogi, a meat filled dumpling, was cold but delicious. The unoccupied house they were assigned had no furniture left in it other than two narrow cots. Zenopian and Davis shared one, while Dunlevy insisted Maria take the other and he would sleep on the floor.

On the morning of January 29, 1945, she had just fallen asleep when she was awakened and summoned for further questioning. When she stepped into the interrogation waiting room, she was astounded to encounter Catlos, emaciated and pale as a ghost, but very much alive. She called out his name in Hungarian. "Istvan!" Catlos, equally amazed, leaped up and swept her into a warm embrace.[11]

As they awaited questioning, Catlos told her how he had been found and murmured that the Romanians were decent men, but he could not figure out these Russians. Maria then told their story again to another set of interrogators before she was permitted to return to their assigned room.

Dunlevy and Davis were pleased to see Catlos, and even Zenopian, who had made it clear all along that he did not like Catlos much, welcomed him warmly. After comparing stories of what had transpired after they separated in Rejdova, Catlos dared raise the question always on their minds but never openly referred to. Was there any word of Green and Gaul regarding the other guys taken prisoner on January 26? The only responses were negative shakes of heads, doleful expressions and silent prayers of hope for their survival.[12]

But even as they pondered and prayed, the fate of the men captured on December 26 at Polomka had already been decided and was soon to be carried out. Green, who had fulfilled all given tasks except the evacuation of 21 airmen and his Dawes unit of 19 men, was doubly betrayed: by the 15th Air Force which refused to pick up his people after a bombing raid in Berlin and then by a vengeful partisan who had been at the Christmas celebrations in Polomka.

*　*　*

Green and his unit as well as Sehmer and his men, with Margita Koscova, were first taken to Banska Bystrica for preliminary questioning. It was also where Keszthelyi and Mican had been imprisoned since their capture on December 12. Then on December 29, all the Anglo Americans were shipped off to Bratislava for more intensive interrogations. The information in the reports sent to Heinrich Himmler, head of the SS, led to his decision to have them transferred to the Mauthausen concentration camp, a hundred miles from Linz, Austria. It was rightly known as the "death camp," a place where sadistic and brutal-beyond-belief interrogators were free to unleash their pathological instincts and hatred upon prisoners. The captives' journey into hell was about to begin, since both Himmler and Ernst Kaltenbrunner, head of the Reichssicherheitshauptamt (RSHA, the Reich Security Head Office), had a special hatred for Anglos involved in intelligence work.[13]

On January 17, they were transferred to the Bunker, known as the Death House. The square building set apart from the rest was painted a metallic gray inside and out, lending it a forbidding, cold, institution-like atmosphere. Security was elaborate and there were no escapees. Here, Green and his men were to learn how skilled was the Abwehr, the German intelligence organization. Unlike the relatively new OSS, the Nazi spy system had been in effect for thirty years and the Gestapo and RSHA had developed most effective methods of interrogation. For instance, the enemy had complete

14. Ultimate Horror at the Hands of the Nazis

dossiers on all of them. How much more could any of them reveal to appease them and how much could they keep secret? This was not to be a cat and mouse game.

In his reports, Wilhelm Muller, summoned from Berlin to act as interpreter, stated that he felt out of his element with the interrogation teams. But then, he'd felt as displaced as any refugee in Germany since his return from his travels and hotel concierge position in London when the war started in 1939. Things were not destined to get any better, and on arrival at Mauthausen, he sensed that everything would go from terrible to worse.

Standartenführer Franz Ziereis, head of Mauthausen concentration camp, lived with his family in Linz. In his mid–forties, the beefy SS officer was balding and his blue eyes set in a large, round face exhibited a foreboding iciness. He could hardly disguise his excitement when five special interrogator specialists arrived from RSHA headquarters in Berlin to question the Americans and British. One of them, SS criminal commissar Walter Habecker, immediately formed a formidable duo with Ziereis.

Habecker was a large man, well over six feet tall. A completely shaved head gave the 53-year-old officer a brutally ghoulish appearance. Flaunting a burning cigar, he removed a heavy gold ring from his finger and twirled a thick wooden stick. He glanced at his supervisor, Sturmbannführer Schoenseneiffen, who had come with him from Berlin to oversee this important task. The supervisor nodded, signaling that the business of extracting information from these prisoners was to begin.

The interrogators formed two teams. Muller, the civilian interpreter, was elected to work alternatively with both teams. He had lived in England and traveled and was familiar with Anglos. The scholarly 30-year-old was of slight build and wore heavy spectacles. He had been discharged from the Wehrmacht for health reasons and was not suited for the type of brutality he was to witness. When Green was led in and motioned to a chair, he struggled to hide his pity for what he suspected lay ahead for the Anglo prisoners at the camp. Both of Green's hands were bound beneath his knees, forcing him to bend over double to ease the strain. It was an effort to talk.

"Ask him about the Jew who says his name is Wilson."

Green replied haltingly. "I know nothing about him except that he's an American flyer like the rest of us."

Habecker was annoyed at the response and hustled around the table between them. Wielding his stick, he landed heavy blows on Green's shoulders, back, and side of his neck. Schoenseneiffen nodded approval. He moved closer for a look at Green and frowned. "Isn't this the one who signed under protest in Bratislava before he would say anything?"

When told he was the one, Schoenseneiffen said, "Well, let us show him just what we can do. We will hang him."

Habecker, with a malicious glint, interjected. "Wait!" He turned to Muller. "Ask him what those distinctions on his jacket are. A gangster like him doesn't merit decorations. Tell him to take them off and put them on the table."

Green removed his jacket and hesitantly placed his naval lieutenant's bars on the table. Habecker examined the jacket and tossed it back to Green. "Tell him to put this rag on now that we've degraded him."

Muller reached over to help Green, who was painfully trying to maneuver his sleeve over a plaster cast on his arm. "What are you doing?" Ziereis demanded.

"Just helping him."

"Are you married?"

Muller hesitated and finally stammered, "No."

"I should have guessed. Otherwise you'd know how to treat these people killing our women and children!" Ziereis took a few paces around the table until he was an inch or two from Green's face, staring malevolently at him while directing orders to Muller. "We want to know about their spy operations from their headquarters in Bari until now. The Führer wants to know everything about the OSS."

Green stuck to his story of rescuing downed flyers, so Habecker switched to another tactic. "Bring in that Jew."

For several hours, British agent Jack Vandorfer, with the code name of Wilson, had been quizzed, first by Habecker, and then SS Untersturmführer Arndt, also from Berlin. Wilson was the first to be subjected to the Tibetan prayer mill, a device Habecker had brought with him. Three or four sticks the size and shape of pencils were lodged between Wilson's fingers and the hand tightly squeezed, causing such excruciating pain that tears streamed from his eyes. But he refused to inform on the others.

"So! We'll hang this Jew!"

Wilson was dragged to the gallows set up in a corner and tied to it by his wrists. The apparatus and he were lifted about a foot or two off the floor. The pain shooting through his arms was intolerable. After fifteen minutes, he was let down, babbling almost incoherently.

"This Jew from Vienna speaks German very well," Ziereis said with an evil grin as Wilson answered questions in perfect German. He admitted to being a Jewish émigré and parachuting into Slovakia, but maintained he was Scottish, not English.

When they brought Wilson in to confront Green, his head hung down in shame at having been broken. Only Muller caught the almost imperceptive nod of understanding Green gave the suffering man before he turned to Habecker. "I admit I was not telling the entire truth. This man is a Briton and I did not think I was entitled to talk about him."

The Germans, evidently satisfied for the moment, permitted Green and Wilson to be returned to their cells. The next day, Gaul demanded medical care for Green, whose face and neck were swollen and discolored on the left side. A half hour later, a medic arrived to dab a foul smelling ointment on the wounds and treat him with a heat lamp.

"Thank you, I feel much better" said the grateful Green.

When Willis was summoned for questioning, Habecker was delighted. "Another Jew," he said scathingly and began to beat the Briton even before preliminary questioning. Muller felt the blood drain from his face at the merciless act.

"Why do you strike him? Can't you see that he is ready to speak?"

Habecker wheeled about, raising the stick threateningly at Muller and glowered. "Get out of my way or I'll hit you instead!"

"Maybe a stay at this place might do you some good," Schoenseneiffen told Muller, sternly disapproving of any sympathy shown prisoners.

The torture of Willis was futile. They had him confused with Wilson, whose real name was Vandorfer, and he'd already given explicit information.

For eight days, the unshaven captives, weak from insufficient food and the ordeal of imprisonment, were subjected to slaps, beatings by fist, various other tortures and unrelenting questioning. One of the worst was Arndt, who enjoyed wielding a bull whip. Unlike the other SS officers, he was not fair-haired and his black hair and yellow tinged features had a distinct Mongolian cast. Every time he lashed a prisoner, he glanced at Schoenseneiffen for approval. The supervisor of the operation was the youngest of the lot, probably 30 years old at most. He was a tall, well built man with thick brown hair and blue-gray eyes and calm mannerisms. He laughed when Habecker yanked at Sehmer's red beard to force him into a chair.

"Hang this one for sure! Hang this English dog!" Ziereis urged, and struck Sehmer on the back of the head.

"Where did you learn such good German?" Habecker barked.

"In Berlin, before the war," Sehmer mumbled through swollen lips. He glanced with apprehension at the gallows, obviously hoping he would be spared.

"This is the one who was with that communist, Tito," said Habecker.

At this, Ziereis clamored, "Why do you wait? Hang him! Hang him!"

However, even after twenty minutes of the excruciating torture, Sehmer revealed only a fraction of what he might have. But for the time being, they suspended further questioning of him.

"Bring in the big one."

Evidently Gaul tried but could not completely conceal his inward rage and the contempt he felt for the SS. His terse responses were in brusque German. That and apparently something else about Gaul — his bearing or his size — spared him the gallows but not the stick, bull whip, or beatings by hand.

"Too bad," Habecker grinned when they released Gaul to his cell. "That one would make a good German, eh Muller?" The interpreter did not reply.

The most barbaric of the tortures were reserved for Baranski. Until Malthausen, he, Paveltich and Tomes had given false names and claimed to be American airmen. But when pilot Lane Miller told Muller he had the same last name as his, it had inadvertently revealed their true identities. Habecker and Schoenseneiffen were irate at the successful duplicity Baranski had achieved until that point. Their wrath was further inflamed because of Baranski's successful spying out and then revealing the location of the irreplaceable rocket plant that led to it being bombed to rubble.

"This fellow thinks he is so clever!" Schoenseneiffen sneered. "He deserves special consideration. This one we must hang!"

Extra beams were brought in and erected on one side of the room. There were two beams high on one wall, and one across them beneath the ceiling. Beneath the beams was a wooden table. Baranski, despite being subjected to beatings by hand and the Tibetan prayer mill, had revealed nothing. Now he stood to one side watching. He stiffened when shoved into the chair.

A gloating Ziereis gave the order. "Let this saboteur know that he better tell us the truth or something really bad will happen to him, not just a beating."

Baranski, noting the chain being prepared, cast Muller an uneasy smile. "Now I know what they want to do. Tell them I'll talk."

Schoenseneiffen scowled. "Ha! Now the swine wants to talk! No! First he must hang so he'll know he can't tell any more lies!"

Baranski was forced onto the table. His hands were tied behind his back and wrists attached to the chain that was then drawn upwards.

"Now tell him to start talking!"

Baranski closed his eyes and bit his lips until they bled but said nothing. Habecker kicked the table from beneath him and Baranski's face, contorted with pain, his body swaying, still said nothing.

"The lying saboteur is still enjoying himself too much!" Schoenseneiffen said. "Pull his legs down!"

14. Ultimate Horror at the Hands of the Nazis

When his legs were yanked straight down, this forced Baranski's arms to pivot backwards with full weight upon them. The agony was unendurable and he gasped for breath.

"For God's sake! Let me down!" he pleaded.

Ziereis sneered until he saw Baranski's eyes bulge and his face change rapidly from deep red to deadly white. He was murmuring something over and over, barely audible, as he hung onto the chain.

"What is the American dog babbling?"

Muller listened for a moment, hoping his face did not reveal his feelings. "I think he is praying," he said reluctantly.

Schoenseneiffen and the other SS officers laughed. "So, let's be nice and let him down."

Baranski slumped to the floor but stood on his feet. His hands were cramped with blood and wrists criss-crossed with deep cuts. He was prodded into the next room and into a chair in front of a table, the only two furnishings in the airless, gray room. His head fell forward. He was a broken man.

"Give the saboteur a drink!" But when Baranski tried to hold the bottle of water, it dropped out of deadened hands. "Then give him a cigarette. We need to revive him so he can talk."

Baranski recovered enough to take a few puffs and smiled in gratitude at Muller before the questioning resumed. It was interrupted when Arndt broke in to hand a telegram to Schoenseneiffen. After he read it, he seemed to lose interest in further questioning and was in a hurry to leave.

"Send the report to Berlin," he told Muller. "They will know what to do with these spies."

Later that morning, Muller was ordered to talk to the other prisoners again, this time in their cells. He went from cell to cell. Forming a special liking for Keszthelyi and Horvath, he talked to them at length. Horvath asked him to mail a letter to his wife, pointing out that it was merely personal. Muller scanned the message of Horvath's eternal love to his adored Alma and tucked it in his jacket pocket. Horvath gave a smile of thanks.

Keszthelyi, too, wanted him to mail a letter. It was to his parents and merely said that they were not to worry about him; he was all right and would see them before long.

Outside Ziereis was waiting. He knew prisoners and their desperate wishes all too well. "What did they ask you to do?"

"Mail letters."

"Give them to me."

Reluctantly, Muller removed the two envelopes and handed them to the commander who tore them up without opening them. "Fine work, Muller."

It was early the next morning when Muller was called again to interpret. An agitated Gaul was sitting in the chair, waiting to talk to him. "What is going to happen to us?" Gaul asked.

Muller hesitated. He'd been instructed to tell the prisoners that they were to be transferred to a prisoner-of-war camp. But he could not bring himself to say it, knowing the other alternative was a more likely possibility, so he said he didn't know.

When Green was brought in, he appeared conciliatory. "On behalf of my men, I want to say we are passing the time well," he told Muller. "But do you have any books we could have to read?"

This surprised Muller and he replied that he was reading the book *Oliver Wiswell* and enjoying it. During the exchanges, Muller was puzzled. Was it his imagination that the questioning was strangely subdued?

"Bring that Morton fellow," Schoenseneiffen ordered.

Morton, too, obviously feared the worst and asked what was going to happen to them and mentioned that they had been imprisoned for a month.

"Tell him he's to be sent to a prisoner-of-war camp," Ziereis warned and Muller repeated the words.

Morton again insisted, as he had previously, that he was a reporter and had nothing to do with the mission. Furthermore, by now serious inquiries by important people were being made.

"So?" Ziereis muttered when this was repeated to him.

Morton did not give up easily. "He asks to send a telegram to the Associated Press," Muller related to the officers watching. "He believes that the power of the press might help negotiations."

Ziereis looked at Schoenseneiffen. The supervisor, standing ramrod straight, raised an eyebrow and gave a contemptuous shrug. "The American press has no power here." He glanced at his watch. "It's time for lunch. We can finish with these swine afterwards."

Muller was still eating his lunch when a guard came running and told him to come quickly. Muller followed and encountered Arndt and Habecker standing in the hall talking excitedly and ordered him to go right in. Inside the room, Schoenseneiffen, Ziereis and two other SS officers were waiting. One of the officers had a stethoscope dangling from his neck and was hovering over Gaul. Another was writing down his comments. Muller was puzzled. Neither of these were medical men. In front of the table were Schoenseneiffen and Ziereis, observing. When Ziereis looked at Muller, something unusually blank and dead in his expression caused a chill to race through Muller's veins.

"Tell him they are being sent to the prisoner-of-war camp today and that

14. Ultimate Horror at the Hands of the Nazis

guards will use their weapons if any try to escape," Schoenseneiffen said very calmly.

Muller was puzzled and said, "Kommandant, this man speaks good German."

The SS officer did not turn a hair. "I told him in German and now I want to make sure he hears it in English as well."

Muller did as ordered. He looked down and noted that the bottom sheet was half covered on top with another sheet. Gaul was leery and hesitated and Muller was ordered to tell him that Green and the English major had already signed. The paper shoved under Gaul's nose showed Sehmer's signature at the bottom of the sheet. Most hesitantly, Gaul scratched his name to the bottom of the sheet and added his date of birth and military serial number. When he left the room, Schoenseneiffen with a sly grin peeled off the top sheet and showed the bottom one to Muller. It was blank.

Green did not easily capitulate. Muller felt a twinge of sympathy when he detected fear in Green's eyes as he underwent the phony physical exam. It was obvious that Green suspected that this was a trick. Finally, seeing that the Sehmer and Gaul had signed papers, Green scratched his name in his large sloping handwriting to the bottom of the sheet and added a few words.

"What is that?" Schoenseneiffen demanded to know.

Muller read the words slowly. "I am signing under extreme duress."

Ziereis became enraged. He opened the door and shouted at Arndt in the hall to come in and give Green the works. Arndt swung his bull whip, the first lash landing on Green's buttocks. The second was higher. Hands bound, Green was unable to protect his forehead as the whip slashed across it. A large blood red circle immediately formed on Green's pale brow. Zeireis laughed and pointed at it. "Look! The halo of Jesus!"

Finally Green was led out, pale and trembling, to the amusement of his tormentors and Muller was ordered to bring the other in quickly. One by one the prisoners were led in and without being given a chance to ask a single question, were coerced into signing blank sheets. Margita's golden earrings were torn off and tossed beside the paper with her signature. Muller was vexed. Why was everyone in such a hurry? As the last prisoner was hustled out, he was unable to restrain his puzzlement and asked Arndt what was going on.

Whip still in hand, the SS officer gazed out the window as the line of prisoners marching single file towards the stairs to the basement passed out of his vision. When they were out of sight, Arndt, with malicious grin, said, "They are on their way to hell."

When Muller asked what he meant, Arndt said they were going to be shot.

"When?" the astonished Muller asked him.

"Right now." He was amused at the distress Muller displayed. "Don't worry, they will have an easy death."

Muller glanced up at the bright, cerulean-blue sky. What a beautiful, sunny morning. What an awful day to die! Was this really happening? Feeling dizzy, he glanced down at the table where a telegram lay. It was an execution order from SS chief Ernst Kaltenbrunner. Beneath his signature was that of the SS supreme commander, Heinrich Himmler.

Each prisoner by turn was stripped and led into the execution room, told they were to be photographed and then would be given prison garb. Margita was the first to be taken into a bare room alone and ordered to stand with her face to a dummy camera. Behind her was SS Hauptsturmführer George Pachmayer, executioner posing as photographer. He pressed the barrel of the revolver into the back of her neck and squeezed the trigger. The room was soundproof and the shot could not be heard outside it.

Gaul refused to face the wall and glared at Ziereis. "I am an American prisoner of war. Why am I to be shot?"

This infuriated Ziereis. "*Fotografieren!*" he shouted, waving his hands in Gaul's face, trying to convince him that he was being photographed.

"I am an American officer; why should I be shot?" Gaul repeated, the exchange between them lasting five minutes.

Finally, Schoenseneiffen snarled. "What are you waiting for? Is he so special?"

Ziereis, enraged at losing face, ordered the two SS guards witnessing the executions to force Gaul's face to the wall. He pulled out his own gun and shot Gaul.

Green was the last to be executed. But the first shot did not kill him. When he was dragged to the cold storage room to await cremation, his movements indicated that he wavered in and out of consciousness before the last flicker of life winked out.

The killings were efficient. The entire massacre took twenty minutes, an average of an execution a minute after which, Schoenseneiffen told Muller casually when they returned upstairs to make a protocol with all the witnesses' names.

Ziereis turned and smiled. "I'm glad to be rid of them. They were here too long. I can use some of their things for my men, especially the shoes." Almost out of the room, he turned to his cohorts. "This fellow Green, he was suspecting something. Did you notice how scared he was being examined by the 'doctor'? No wonder he was so slow to die." The SS officers grinned in appreciation of the trick.

Still sitting in a chair, Muller turned to study the uniform jackets of the

14. Ultimate Horror at the Hands of the Nazis

Mauthausen Prison, where the 14 members of the Dawes Mission were transferred and eventually executed on January 24, 1945. The prison was aptly referred to as the death camp (courtesy Rudy Horvath).

prisoners, hanging near the door to the basement, shoes lined beneath. He'd been at Malthausen two weeks and had gotten to know the men well. And now, their lives had been snuffed out.

"And that fellow Gaul," he heard Ziereis say, "Hauptsturmführer Roth said he'd have to break the American's legs to stuff him into the furnace."[14]

SS Obersturmführer Heinz Esenhoffer pawed through the personal effects of the prisoners. Among them were some silver identification bracelets and dog tags. Surely these would be worth a good many marks as souvenirs. When he ordered a Polish prisoner named Wilheim Ornstein to help carry the corpses from the execution room to the refrigeration room, Ornstein furtively removed the bloody tags from Paris' neck and secreted them in a pocket. Given a chance, he wanted to prove that these were Americans who had been executed without a trial.

"These Americans and English," he said to Roth. "How could they kill such men?"

The response of Hauptscharführer Martin Ross, in charge of the crematorium and gas chamber "shooting gallery," was a growl. "They were spies! Just do as you're told!"

In the room above, where he had not heard a single shot fired, Muller prepared to take his final leave. He walked slowly out into the sunlit afternoon. His duties had ended. It was just a job, he kept reminding himself. And after all, as Habecker and Ziereis had told him over and over, these dead prisoners were the enemy. And in war, wasn't the goal to kill as many of the enemy as possible? Then why, he asked himself, did he feel so sad?

Behind him, Hauptsturmführer Adolf Zutter, adjutant at Malthausen, was efficiently carrying out orders to destroy all top secret documents concerning these prisoners. First to be burned was the telegram from Kaltenbrunner and Himmler.

"Nobody will know," Schoenseneiffen assured Zutter before he and the SS delegation departed for Berlin. "The Führer will be pleased to hear that we carried out his orders of death to all spies," he said with an expansive smile. "Yes, the Führer will be very pleased indeed."[15]

15

MARIA AND COMPANY: CAUGHT IN THE CROSSHAIRS

Following the exciting reunion with Catlos, Maria emptied her rucksack on the floor to examine her remaining items of clothing. To her dismay, lice had infested her few garments, except for the brown angora sweater, a Christmas gift from Green and Sehmer. She set it aside for safekeeping. In the morning when she returned from another interrogation session, the sweater was gone. Outrage overrode her normal caution and she returned to the interrogator's headquarters and demanded to see the officer in charge. She told him that someone had stolen her only sweater and she needed it.[1]

To her surprise, the official did not denigrate or berate her. Instead he barked a question to his aide, asking who was watching the Anglos. Informed that it was Private Gregor, he ordered the aide to have his bag searched and, if he had the sweater, to return it to Maria. Then he curtly dismissed her, saying, "Now don't bother me with any more of your trivial affairs!"

An hour later the sweater mysteriously reappeared in front of their door. Maria asked no questions but grabbed the sweater and tucked it away beneath the thin pillow and would sleep on it to keep it safe. And she would not let it out of her sight again.[2]

On January 30, 1945, they were moved to Lucenec. They were allotted one tiny room in a decrepit house with no heat, and two rickety cots were the only items of furniture remaining. For warmth, the Russians had chopped and burned every other bit of the owner's furniture in the small iron stove. Maria shared one cot with Dunlevy while Davis, Catlos and Zenopian squeezed onto the other. Quarters were tight but it was too cold to sleep on the floor. The worst aggravation, though, was that a guard was assigned to keep watch over them. The message was clear: they were not refugees, they were Soviet prisoners.

The next morning, they were all ordered to strip off their clothes to be sent to the boiler room for delousing and then to take baths. Catlos relished the order until he saw the bath facilities. The "bathtubs" were outside and consisted of rows of round metal drums filled with tepid water, and surrounded by guards. They eyed Maria with keen interest as she approached.

"*Yah, panya*!" ("a person of royal status") one of the hard-eyed toughs said to the other, who snorted in derision.[3]

Davis and Dunlevy did not like the looks of "those bloody bastards!" and decided to take turns escorting Maria to and from the bath area. The Russian guards did not budge from their spot while Davis and Dunlevy took turns with a quick, hit-or-miss kind of bathing before wrapping themselves in coarse homespun sheets for towels to return to their room where they spent the entire day waiting for their clothes to be returned.

When their clothing finally arrived, they were aghast. Every item had shrunk to child sized garments. Holding up his parka for inspection, Davis then tossed it aside saying, "I guess this could fit an eight-year-old kid, but that's about it."[4]

The damage was complete: not one item of clothing was usable. And the ill-fitting mish mash of Russian military clothing given as replacements were shabby and patched. Soured by their plight, Zenopian began to complain loudly about his various ailments and requested medical attention. Older by far than Catlos, Dunlevy or Davis, Maria felt that perhaps Zenopian did have some real medical problems and offered to speak to the camp commandant on his behalf. One glance at the sallow, haggard face was enough to convince the medic that Zenopian was ill. It led to their being moved to a hotel room, but again with a Russian guard at the door. The room had four beds and Maria had one to herself, but the feeling of luxury did not last long. That evening a pregnant, very sick girl was brought in, along with a two Slovak partisans. The girl, pale and weak, was obviously in distress and moaned all night long.[5]

Pushed beyond measure at what he deemed an indignity, Zenopian loudly protested that he was a military officer and a man of his rank should not have to put up with this annoyance. He demanded to be placed elsewhere. In the morning, Zenopian was re-examined by the camp doctor. The doctor checked out a bad case of scabies and general wasted demeanor, then looked at the gaunt Catlos, Dunlevy and Davis as well as Maria and issued hospital orders for all of them. This time, the men were billeted in a separate room from the women. But it still did not suit Zenopian, who continued to complain. To everyone's surprise, the next day he was whisked off to another camp, reserved for officers of higher military command. However, he left only when assured that he would receive medical treatment worthy of an officer of his rank. Davis's parting shot was that he was a pompous son of a bitch and they were well rid of him.

Catlos found the entire matter ironic. While he, Dunlevy, Davis and Maria were in reasonably good health, they were detained in the hospital, whereas Zenopian, who was either sick or at least looked as though he was sick, had been sent off to another camp.[6]

At night Maria was kept awake by Stella's moans. The young woman writhed in pain and told Maria she'd been raped and to terminate the resultant pregnancy, a medic had given her quinine pills, assuring her that that the medication would relieve her of all problems. However, the abortion was incomplete and the girl suffered excruciating spasms of agony. Maria was frightened but hesitated to ask for medical help. No telling what else these butchers would do to her. All she could do was bathe Stella's forehead with a cool cloth and hold her hand. At daybreak, Stella sat up with a sharp outcry as a torrent of blood gushed from between her legs. She then fell back on the bed, drenched in perspiration. Maria grabbed a woolen shirt and wrapped the gore-drenched tiny fetus in it and assured Stella that she would now be all right. When she asked who had done this to her, sadly Stella admitted it was the partisan commander who had recruited her. She had trusted him completely, only to be raped many times. Maria prayed that Stella had not contracted a venereal disease that would end hopes for a decent life, wherever that might be in the chaotic post-war world.[7]

The next day they were transported to another hospital. This Red Army facility bore little resemblance to any modern hospital; it was more akin to a backwoods medical treatment clinic. The wounded lay in open wagons in the freezing outdoors and the interior reeked with a sickening stench of rotting flesh. Reverberating through the rooms day and night were agonizing screams from Russian soldiers being operated on with no anesthetic or antiseptic other than a shot of vodka and raw garlic rubbed on the wound. They were interspersed with groans and pleas for help from the hopelessly injured and dying. Many were mere adolescent boys who'd suffered fatal head wounds because they had no helmets and often wore no socks. And all were malnourished. Dunlevy learned from one officer that for breakfast, their ration was a slice of raw bacon and a shot of vodka.[8]

The third day Maria developed severe dysentery. Billeted on the sixth floor of a building with no elevator, it was an ordeal to walk up and down the stairs and then have to pass Soviet guards posted outside the toilets. Davis, also afflicted with what he bitterly termed the "Russian Revenge," escorted her down the stairs and back. However, his presence only provoked the guards more, who taunted Maria and referred to her as *"Panya"* ("the royal one"). But the menacing glares from Davis's fiery blue eyes kept them at bay.

Their stay in the hospital lasted from February 1st to the 10th. During this time they were subjected to repeated questioning, restricted from moving about and kept under constant guard. The disorder in the camp never improved. Fed up with the confusion, Dunlevy groused that he'd thought the Russians would be more organized.

At this Davis bellowed, "Organized! These bloody Russkies couldn't organize a Christmas Club."

Repeated requests that Dunlevy and Catlos posed about the Russians attempting to verify their identities went unanswered, and they grew increasing anxious about their fate.

On February 10, they were taken to Yasziser, Hungary, the Soviet headquarters for counterespionage. Catlos and Dunlevy had concocted an airtight story and briefed Maria many times until she knew their story as well as they. This time the questioning was more intense and the interrogators openly hostile and dubious about answers given. Catlos and Dunlevy chafed at the rudeness they were subjected to, as did Maria, and the constant surveillance that grew more and more oppressive and intimidating.[9]

At the beginning of one interrogation session, Dunlevy's watch was stripped from his wrist and the new patent leather shoes the Romanians had given him removed and disappeared into a back room. When he protested that he could not walk around barefoot, he was handed a pair of worn, scuffed boots a size too large. Dunlevy seethed with anger but dared not protest further. These Russians were as cold and merciless as the Carpathian mountain winter they had endured and meant business, deadly business. During questioning, Dunlevy repeated his name, rank and serial number, battling the constant fear that he might inadvertently slip up and somehow they'd find out he was the mission cryptographer. But his story held tight.[10]

In another room, the firearm the Romanians had given Catlos to replace his left in Kristak's sheep pen, was confiscated. As had Dunlevy, he rattled off his name, rank, and serial number. When he pointed to the dog tags around his neck as corroboration, the interrogator only sneered and asked who he had stolen it from. He was accused of being a Slovak army deserter, and his repeated requests for them to contact OSS, Bari, to verify their identities, were ignored. Finally, he decided to pretend to be dumb and was very careful to conceal the fact that he spoke Hungarian fluently. Bored with his seeming stupidity, the inquisitors finally dismissed him, leaving Catlos with the conclusion that the dumber anyone talking to Russians appeared to be, the better off he or she was.[11]

15. Maria and Company

The game took a nastier turn when they discovered that Maria was the only one in their group who spoke Russian and she was repeatedly questioned. They summoned her at all hours, with no regard for inconvenience or that she had to pass by female-starved Soviet guards who gawked and made lewd remarks, and were especially intimidating at night. Allusions by the team of interrogators were made to her "spying," and her protests that she had not been a spy but a courier and interpreter were disregarded. And then one of her worst of fears became reality. A sheet of paper was shoved under her nose with the stern order to "Sign here."[12]

The brief declaration was as binding as chains and she felt a cold chill as she carefully read the words. They stated that she was volunteering to work for the NKVD, the Soviet Secret Police, thereby placing herself under their jurisdiction. Knowing it was foolhardy to protest, Maria stalled for time by keeping her eyes riveted upon the paper. She tried to think of an escape, but there was none until her eyes strayed to the ring on her left hand and an idea occurred. When guards earlier appeared openly lascivious and threatening, Davis had urged Maria to use his last name and claim they were married as it might offer some protection. Having no other option, she scrawled the name Maria Davis on the sheet. But the interrogators were not convinced and pointed out that on her other papers her last name was Gulovich. She told them it was her maiden name before marriage. When he asked which of the Anglos was her husband, she replied, "The English man." When he demanded to know where her records of marriage were, she was momentarily stymied. A regular and official marriage required a certificate from church and state. So she had to quickly come up with yet another plausible story.

This version was that Major Ernest Sehmer, Davis' army commander, had performed the ceremony in Polomka. In England and America, she attested, his role as captain of a military unit is similar to being captain of a ship and he had authority to perform a marriage ceremony. She nonchalantly placed her left hand over the paper to casually display the silver wedding band Zuzka had given her. Only later did Maria realize how remarkable it was that her interrogators accepted her story. It may have been because their minds were on more important business, such as the Polish couple she was ordered to spy and report on.[13]

The Polish wife was a woebegone forty-year-old, her emaciated husband wearing ragged clothing and a haunted expression that made him appear a decade older than his forty-two years. They were devastated to learn the Russians were sending them back to Poland. Their plans had been to join a nephew in London who begged them to come live with him. In Warsaw, the woman told Maria tearfully, everyone they had known was dead. Maria discerned that they were Jews, but decided not to ask, rationalizing that she would not be compelled to report what she did not know. Her report stated that the couple wanted to stay in London only long enough to recover their health. But Maria knew that there was virtually no chance for their request to be granted.

During the next two nights Maria was summoned several times between midnight and one o'clock to interview arriving refugees and was never escorted back to her room. Furthermore, there was no lock on her door, leaving her lying awake and in constant fear of attack. On the third day, her relief was boundless when told she would move into the room Davis, Catlos and Dunlevy shared. Stepping inside, she flopped wearily onto a cot in the corner and slept the next night through for the first time since their arrival.

The following day, a new commandant, who was a youthful colonel, quizzed Maria about their complaints. She explained that no one was trying to verify their identities and that they were starving from the scant rations. Food was scarce and needed for the vast Red armies rolling in. Cattle and all other animals were slaughtered and every particle of hoarded grain forced at gunpoint to be turned over to them. The plunder was complete, leaving civilians to starve.

The colonel, however, did heed their complaints and gave her a small amount of money, about three thousand Hungarian pengoes, and told her to buy something to eat. She was escorted to the bakery designated only for Russians and bought several round bagel size buns. The whole grain breads were doughy but nourishing. However, by now, neither she nor her three companions held any illusions of there being any benefits to being under Russian care.[14]

As February 1945 drew to a close, Marshal Zhukov's troops rampaged through Slovakia, their goal Bratislava, Berlin and then Prague. Malinovksy's troops had taken Budapest after one of the costliest battles of the war. More than 50,000 Germans and Hungarian soldiers were killed, and 138,000 taken prisoner.[15] The Russians were now proceeding towards Vienna, while the rest of the Allied armies were prohibited by orders from General Eisenhower from getting there first. It was to be the Soviets' victory. And Czechoslovakia was a prize: there was little war damage, its economy divided between agriculture and industry and its fourteen million people famed for their technical knowledge.[16]

The only change for the four in their group was relocation to Hatvan, Hungary. This refugee center was specifically for people liberated by Russians or Americans rather than those who had escaped or were released from POW camps. Wearing an array of cast-off Russian military clothing, and with their identities still in doubt, Catlos, Dunlevy, Davis and Maria may as well have been from insignificant Third World countries.

Incoming refugees were divided into separate national groups. French and Dutch were in one section, English and American in another, and the hapless majority from Eastern Europe not even labeled. This commission was supposed to arrange for evacuation of all Allied people back to their countries of origin. But the usual disorder and chaos prevailed with Davis bitterly stating that the Russians could not even organize a 2-car funeral procession.[17]

On March 6, Dunlevy, Catlos and Davis, along with an assortment of diverse refugees, were issued deportation orders to Odessa. Maria was told that she would remain and work with the NKVD. Panic-stricken, she appealed to the camp commandant, saying that her orders were to stay with the Americans and English to their final destination.

"By whose orders?" the dubious commandant snapped.

"By General Rudof Viest." Then noting that his name did not seem to register with the official, Maria quickly added, "and Major Ivan Studensky."

Furthermore, she did not want to be separated from her husband. At this, the doubting interrogator challenged her to prove she was married to Davis. She held out her hand to display her silver wedding band and said that Sehmer, her husband's military commander, had a record of the marriage. She caressed the ring, not out of sentiment, but as though it might become a magic talisman. And it did indeed. Surprisingly, the commandant finally agreed to let her go with the Anglos to Odessa, but with the stipulation that she would then return and fulfill her assignments with the NKVD for an unspecified length of time.[18]

In the hotel where they were billeted while awaiting to be transported to the train for Odessa, the scene was mass pandemonium. Frantic people of every conceivable nationality and babbling in a multiplicity of languages, milled about, sharing rumors and trying to extract some vestige of assurance from each other. Maria had to evade a drunken Russian soldier, a crude specimen whose Asian features branded him as one of General Malinovsky's Siberian troops, the cruelest and most brutal of the Soviet Armies who raped and pillaged at will. Accounts were rife of women and little girls as young as eight years of age, after "liberation" by the Soviets, being dealt out like cards from a deck for sexual abuse. Some young women killed themselves rather than submit to repeated mass rape, and many fathers shot their wives and daughters to spare them that horror. And any symbol of Nazism doomed an entire family to instant death.[19]

To elude her pursuer, Maria popped into the room of a young woman who seemed friendly. She was a member of an internationally known prominent family whose immense business holdings were based in Holland. The attractive woman, wearing a fur coat and silk blouse, said her name was Andrea, that she was married to a Hungarian ambassador and they managed to leave Budapest just before the Red Army overran the city in late January. Maria's would-be paramour, clutching a bottle of vodka, would not be dissuaded and pushed his way inside.

"She's with us," Davis snarled and shoved him out the door. The soldier was too drunk to be intimidated and tried to re-enter the room until Nikolai, the Russian guard assigned to make sure they reached Odessa, took charge. Ordering the pest in strong Russian terms to leave, and bolstered by another shove from Davis, the would-be paramour was propelled out of the room and into the hall. Still holding tight to the bottle of vodka, the renegade staggered down the hallway, no doubt looking for another female victim.

A new arrival uncorked a bottle of cognac and passed it around. Toasts were offered; "To the Americans!" "To the British!" and "To the French!" until the bottle was empty.[20]

Maria felt sympathy for Andrea, who appeared ill and despondent. She had been raped by a Russian soldier and confided tearfully to Maria that she now had a raging case of syphilis. Her husband, who hovered nearby, was devastated and humiliated by the rough-shod treatment they were subjected to because of their economic and social status, and he was powerless to resist.[21]

As the bottles were emptied, the talk soon waned, and under the vigilant guard of Nikolai and surrounded by raucous Russian military men, the realty of their precarious situation struck each captive in a personal way, and one by one, each retreated into his or her inner self, wondering what their fate was to be. Certainly, Maria, Catlos, Dunlevy and Davis suspected, even if the other refugees and prisoners did not, that once they reached passed over the Russian border and into Odessa, their fates would be sealed and it would require a major miracle to change it for the better. But, as they were about to understand, miracles don't just happen. Sometimes they have to be invented.

16

DESPERATE "HAIL MARY" ESCAPE PLAN WORKS

Arrayed in an odd assortment of Russian military garb, Maria, Catlos, Dunlevy and Davis were crammed into a truck with a number of other refugees that included Andrea, her husband and sister and transported to the train station. The scene was one of wild confusion with hordes of people babbling in countless languages and milling around the cars, trying to shove and push their way into already overflowing cars. Their group sprinted along the tracks trying to find a car that wasn't already jammed to the limit but finally had to settle for one with standing room only.

The train carried no food or water for the two-way trip and the single toilet was at the far end of the car. The adjacent car was marked "First Class" and reserved for Russian military officers. A dozen or more were lounging in the upholstered seats, drinking and enjoying a riotous time.[1]

"*Zhenie*" ("Women"), one murmured when he caught sight of Maria, Andrea and her sister. Overhearing the comment, Maria smiled at the speaker and when he smiled at her in return, she asked if her group could sit on the floor of their car. Travelers resorted to this primitive act routinely as it prevented stagnant circulation in legs caused by standing on them for long periods. Because of Maria's good Russian, and her being the only woman wearing a Russian military uniform of sorts as well as lovely Andrea in her fur coat, they were bound to pique curiosity and underwent a probing scrutiny by the Russians.

"Come in," the officer finally invited. None of the men offered the women a seat as it was unheard of for a Russian military officer, or most Russian men for that matter, to condescend to a woman in any way. When the train gave a sharp jolt and began moving, Maria and her party sprawled on the floor. The officer who had invited them into the car snapped his suitcase open and produced bottles of cognac confiscated from the Germans.[2]

He held up a bottle and asked, "Will you join us in a drink?" He first downed a generous portion of the liquor before passing the bottle to Maria. She took a sip and felt the powerful brew burn its way down her throat but managed to refrain from coughing. Andrea eyed the bottle with distaste and muttered that she would not partake of their liquor. Maria, speaking softly in German so only Andrea could hear, urged her to take a tiny sip as this was customary politeness. To refuse would be considered a grave insult to their hosts. Andrea finally relented and managed to choke down a few drops of the potent liquor. When chunks of bread and cheese were passed around, it made the drinking a bit easier. And it was a good thing because as soon as the cognac was gone, bottles of vodka were produced.[3]

Dunlevy was absorbed in watching freight cars being loaded with furniture, new automobiles, farm implements, mattresses, and sundry items stolen at gunpoint from Slovak and Hungarian businesses and homes. The plunder was heartless. Natives unable to hide belongings in caves or bury them before the Red Armies forged through were stripped of all possessions by wave after wave of Red Army liberators.

Dunlevy abstained from alcohol and intended to avoid the bottle of vodka pressed upon him until a mean-looking Soviet officer, noting his refusal, deemed it a personal affront. The ruddy-faced, half drunken Russian took a long swig from his bottle and then deliberately passed the bottle over heads of those in the car directly to Dunlevy.

"To President Roosevelt!" the officer toasted with a taunting edge.

The Russian was mollified when Dunlevy pretended to down some of the despised alcohol, and added another toast. "To Batuishka (Little Father) Josef Vissarionvich Stalin!"[4]

"To Churchill!" another drinker called out.

"To the toilet," Maria murmured, her churning stomach in an uproar from the liquor, commotion and anxiety.

She grabbed Andrea's hand and they squeezed a path to the toilet through bodies packed in the car as tightly as sardines in a can. The toilet was a square closet-sized cubicle containing a round, wooden bucket imbedded in a hole in the wooden floor which had to be emptied at every stop. It was already overflowing and the foul stench rendered them breathless. Andrea was first to enter the cubicle and when she emerged, complained of feeling very hot, dizzy and nauseous. Emptying her bladder, she told Maria, was as painful as passing ground glass. Her face contorted with hatred for the Russians as she confided that her husband would kill every one of the "black-hearted beasts" he could.

As they pressed their way back to the car, Maria reflected on her own

16. Desperate "Hail Mary" Escape Plan Works

near rape horror and a resurgence of fear arose, not only for herself, but for all the women who were now at the mercy of unregenerate female-denigrating Russian communists giving new meaning to the age-old boon of the grabbing the spoils of war. She advised Andrea to lean against her husband and avoid any eye contact with the Russian soldiers. And she also made a point of remaining close to Davis to create the image of a happily married couple.[5]

From the moment they boarded the train, Catlos and Dunlevy racked their brains trying to devise a means of escape. It was now or never. An opportunity presented itself when a Romanian soldier wandering through cars searching for an empty seat spotted Catlos. He greeted Catlos as *"Amerikanski"* in a friendly manner, pointing at the tiny patch of a U.S. flag that a nurse in the hospital had sewed onto Catlos' sleeve. He then asked Catlos if he was joining the American Army in Bucharest. Catlos gave a casual affirmative nod to indicate he knew about the American post in Romania, but this was the first he heard of one and his heart beat wildly with eagerness. There was hope after all. "America good, strong," the soldier said in a parting comment before edging his way back out of the car.[6]

As the train wound its way through the picturesque Romanian countryside, it stopped at way stations to let clusters of Russian and Romanian soldiers disembark. Those leaving mingled with peasants dressed in patched, worn clothing, and made way for new passengers. To Catlos the scene was reminiscent of a set of giant bellows expanding and then contracting, but rather than air, these bellows inhaled people and then exhaled them, repeating the process. Revved up by the exciting news of an American command post in Bucharest, Catlos was unable to close his eyes all night. During the sleepless hours, an idea was hatched in his mind. He then divulged it to Dunlevy, Maria and Davis in hasty half-whispered bits and pieces when Nikolai was not watching.

On his next trip to the toilet, Catlos inspected the window above the bucket, now propped open for air. It just might be possible for him, thirty pounds lighter than he'd been when the mission started, to pry his way through the opening. As the train slowed to a stop in Bucharest the next morning, the hastily devised plan would be set into motion. As soon as the train stopped, Maria would get off with the two other women and distract Nikolai by doing anything she had to in order to delay re-boarding. This would allow Dunlevy, Davis and Catlos to carry out their part of the action.[7]

In spite of their caution, Nikolai noticed their whispered verbal exchanges and demanded to know what they were talking about. Maria told him that the Americans were not well and unable to drink the stronger Russian liquor but were afraid to offend the Russians. A sarcastic Nikolai retorted that in

Odessa they'd have to learn to drink like Russians because everyone drank vodka night and day.

When the train slowed, the women prepared to exit the car, but the ever alert and suspicious Nikolai barred their path to the women's lavatory. Maria persuaded him that there was plenty of time for the women to wash their faces and hands in the station lavatory and get back on the train. To make sure they did, Nikolai followed the women and posted himself outside the lavatory to wait, too engrossed in keeping watch on the women to notice when Davis, Dunlevy, and Andrea exited the car.[8]

As soon as the train slowed and passengers began to gather belongings to disembark, Catlos shoved his way through the melee to the toilet. He pushed his way inside and held the door shut with one foot while perching precariously on the rim of the bucket with the other foot. Balancing himself like a gymnast, he hoisted his body up to the small opening. Now a rather emaciated version of his former stocky self, Catlos could just barely wriggle through the window. Still undetected, when the train ground to a stop, he jumped to the platform just as someone pushed open the toilet door. He made his way to the lobby, moving neither too fast nor too slow in order to avoid drawing unnecessary attention to himself. As it was, everyone was intent on his or her own business, even the Russian soldiers spilling out of cars in profusion entering the station, Catlos grabbed the phone on an unoccupied desk and barked into the receiver. "American Post?" At the other end, a voice responded with, "General Schuyler's quarters."

"Listen carefully," a nervous Catlos said quickly. "I don't have time to talk. I'm Sgt. Steven Catlos of the OSS. Agent Kenneth Dunlevy, a British agent and a Slovakian young woman are with me. We're captives and being sent under guard to Odessa by the Russians."

He heard a gasp, followed by a crisp order: "Put Ross on the other line."

Colonel Walter Ross was later said to almost drop the phone when he heard Catlos' excited words. "Good God! We'd given you up!" he bellowed. "Where the hell are you?"

Catlos quickly told him they were at the train station, being sent to Odessa by Russian orders and were under guard to make sure they got there.

"Listen to me, Catlos!" Ross commanded. "Whatever you do, don't get back on that train! It'll take about twenty minutes for us to get to you. Sit down, lay down, do whatever you have to do in order to delay until we get there. But *do not* get back on that train! There will be no help for anyone who does!"

Catlos hung up and bolted back to Davis and Dunlevy waiting anxiously in the station. They told him that Maria, Andrea, and her sister were still in the lavatory, stalling the "Russki bastard of a guard" who was chewing his nails in frustration.[9]

Catlos had instructed Maria to wait for the prearranged all clear signal before they came out of the lavatory. She had been playing for time while Nikolai pounded on the door of the lavatory every few minutes, demanding to know the reasons for the holdup. Maria whispered to Andrea and her sister to make noises as though they were suffering. When they complied with agonizing groans, she called out to Nikolai through the closed door, "The girls are sick! Can't you wait a few more minutes?"

Their groaning came to an end with the first note of Catlos whistling "Yankee Doodle Dandy." It was the signal to come out of the lavatory. When Maria gingerly opened the door, it was just in time to catch sight of a contingency of American G.I.s storming into the station.[10] With Davis holding onto one of Maria's arms and flanked by Dunlevy and Catlos, they were hustled outside, Andrea and her husband and sister in their wake like baby chicks seeking protection from the mother hen. In the station, the Americans and Russians geared up for a confrontation. The showdown was a drama fit for a western film. The frightened stationmaster stood by wringing his hands while the commander of the Russian soldiers ordered all refugees to return to the train. His order was interpreted for the Americans by a Russian-speaking American soldier. Instead of complying, the commander of the American soldiers ordered Catlos and the others in their group to "make tracks" while he and his men faced down the Russians.[11]

Nikolai trembled with fear at failing in his duty. The Russians soldiers, too, were fearful of reprisals. But when face to face with the better armed and determined American military men, in the confusion they backed off long enough for the well-ordered contingency of G.I.s to brush past the stationmaster and curious onlookers with the people they were rescuing and escort them at gunpoint to a couple of military cars at the curb waiting with motors running.

Stunned at the swift action, Maria hesitated. Davis grabbed her arm and snapped, "*Schnell! Schnell!*" ("Hurry!") and pushed her out the door into one of the cars and leaped in himself. As it began to pull away from the curb, Nikolai grabbed a door handle and hurled his body inside. "My orders are to stay with you," he told Maria tremulously. "So I'm staying."

When a shocked Maria asked him if he knew what desertion of his post would mean, he turned ashen. "I know, but it's death for failure to perform my duties if I stay. I have no choice."[12]

In contrast, a jubilant Catlos looked at the G.I.s and exclaimed "You're the best damned good looking people I've ever seen in my life!"

Dunlevy and Catlos were dropped off at the hotel assigned to the Americans. When Maria tried to follow, the driver said, "Not you, miss." Catlos and Dunlevy jumped out of the car and without a farewell, dashed into the hotel, leaving Maria feeling crushed. She watched her two companions, with whom she had stared death in the face for five months, disappear as the car sped off again leaving her wondering if she would ever see them again.

Minutes later Davis was dropped off at British headquarters and the car continued to a villa where Maria, Andrea and her husband and sister would stay. Rather than sharing in the jubilation they and the others were feeling, Maria felt a sense of desolation at the sudden departure of the men for whom she had come to feel an affection akin to that of a brother.

* * *

The villa at 33 Ste. Batiste had been the residence of Minister Antonescue of the Romanian Parliament before the Allies assumed control. Maria and her companions were assigned commodious rooms by the wife of Colonel Harry Carter. When the genial host tactfully inquired what he might get for them to make them more comfortable, as one, the women rattled off "lipstick, face cream, toothbrushes and toothpaste, and mascara."

The colonel, taken aback, promised to do what he could, knowing that the Russians had done a thorough job of looting. "You'd think that these women would want something more practical," he muttered to his young aide as they walked away.

"Maybe you've been in the military too long, sir," the grinning private said with a chuckle.[13]

The only decent garment Maria had left was the angora sweater Green had given her and she was delighted when Andrea lent her a pair of pajamas. She undressed and ran a bath with hot water and then stepped into the steaming tub to lie back and luxuriate. It was the first hot bath she had had in five months. Afterwards she curled up on the bed to relax. But she could not rest. The bed was too soft. She folded blankets and a sheet and spread them on the floor to stretch out on. When the young daughter of the housekeeper burst into the room to clean it and found Maria naked and dozing on the floor, the astonished girl backed out into the hall and Maria heard her say to her mother, "These women are barbarians. They don't even know what a bed is for!"

The incident jolted Maria back to reality. All sense of peace and rest vanished and worry took its place. Her perilous days with the Dawes men, and finally only Dunlevy, Catlos and Davis, had come to an end. These Anglos had the protection of powerful governments, whereas she was a powerless

16. Desperate "Hail Mary" Escape Plan Works 215

non-entity from the now non-existent Slovakia, with its fate up for grabs, and she wondered what was to become of her.[14]

* * *

As it turned out, Catlos and Dunlevy were premature in celebrating their escape. They were kept incommunicado while cables flew back and forth between Washington, D.C., Moscow and Bucharest. The irate Soviets demanded their return as well as that of Nikolai, who had applied for political asylum. Washington's explanations were rejected. In the meantime, they were admitted to a hospital for physical examinations. The hospital was operated by nuns and was a vast improvement over the Soviet hospitals they had seen earlier. The first step was to remove their clothing for delousing. Concealed behind the door, they dropped their disheveled clothing into the hands of a twinkling-eyed nun, who in turn handed them sheets to wrap themselves in and then told the two men to follow her. Feeling foolish, they padded behind her to the huge bathroom where a king sized tub filled with hot water awaited. The nun motioned for them to bathe and then left.[15]

The pair sloshed and lathered and shampooed in the soapy water with great zest and scrubbed away at the barbarity acquired during their long ordeal of being hunted like animal prey. But while that ordeal had ended, another began. It was the effort to clear any doubts about how they came to be the only ones in the nineteen-man Dawes mission to escape capture.

It was apparent from the first debriefing questions that there was mistrust about them and questions arose as to why they had not been captured as the others were. The inference of possible malfeasance embittered Dunlevy with a sense of rancor that was to last. Not only was his good name tarnished, but he and Catlos were prohibited from mingling with other soldiers on the base who cast questioning looks as they passed by. He found it corrosive to his spirit to be under suspicion of any neglect or wrongdoing. What would it take to end the suspicions? Or would they end?[16]

* * *

At the villa, Maria and the other women were prohibited from venturing away from the villa by themselves. Colonel Carter lent Maria some money to buy a few items of clothing and with a great sense of relief, she discarded the Russian uniform and purchased a tailored dark blue dress from Andrea, a pair of stockings, and colored yarn to embroider the plain white collar of the dress. After donning the garments, she inspected herself in the mirror and decided she again looked like the respectable school teacher she had been when her adventure into espionage and her subsequent ordeal began.[17]

In a surprise visit the next morning, Catlos, Dunlevy and Davis appeared at the villa and told Maria to get ready for a shopping trip. The trio then escorted her to a couple of shops where fine clothing, a bit out of fashion from being long in hiding, was available. The men pooled a sum of Romanian ilkeis together and added to what little American currency they had left, it amounted to about fifty dollars, a estimable sum in that era and place. Maria was able to purchase a fine-cut gray tailored suit, red mohair sleeveless sweater, white blouse, pale blue dress, a navy blue handbag with matching pumps, a pair of sturdy walking shoes and a smattering of lingerie. There was even some money left over. During the wait while Maria selected and tried on the clothes, the men had located a beauty parlor and escorted Maria to it. The set-up was primitive, actually only a chair and sink, but the beautician was an expert. She snipped the uneven lengths of Maria's hair and shaped the tresses into a soft frame that accentuated her delicate features. The men drank beer during the cut, shampoo, towel drying and final brushing. When Maria emerged, it was to a chorus of wolf whistles.[18]

The pragmatic Catlos, always a hearty eater, declared he was hungry and why not find the best place in town to take this gorgeous girl to and show her off? Food and wine, like most items of value, had been squirreled away by the canny Romanians to whom wars were not a novelty, and had remained hidden until the marauding Red Armies passed through. At the dining room of a fine hotel, they were amazed to find roast pork, potatoes and cabbage being served. Washed down with fine wine, it made a delicious and robust meal. When they had their fill, the waiter rolled up a dessert cart.

"Forget pastries, I want whipped cream," Catlos said to a chorus of assents from his companions.

Even after the uncomprehending waiter finally understood this strange request, he remained perplexed. Minutes later he emerged from the kitchen, accompanied by the equally baffled chef, bearing large bowls of whipped cream. While the four, like greedy children, spooned down the rich fluff until they were gorged, the waiter and chef stood by to watch as did other diners.[19]

Fully sated with the rich meal, they exited the hotel and strolled down the wide boulevard back to the villa. The magic of the moment slipped away when Davis asked Maria what she was going to do now and she had to tell him she didn't know. His frank question was disturbing because she was fully aware that she was a bother because no one knew what to do with her. She had managed to submerge in her unconscious the fact that she'd been coerced into signing the paper stating she would work for the NKVD, but Davis' query brought it to the surface. That was a burning secret she dared not reveal to anyone, even to these men she trusted as much as she could trust anyone.

16. Desperate "Hail Mary" Escape Plan Works 217

After all, it was possible that any of the three, like Schwartz and possibly Gaul, might suspect her of being a double agent. Instead, she told them that like most European students, she had dreamed of one day studying in the United States and maybe even teaching. Now her utmost concern was how to get out of Bucharest and avoid being returned to Russian jurisdiction.[20]

It had been spring the year before when Maria sheltered Hannah and Zolton and ended up in the Slovak underground and finally with the American OSS and British SOE. Remembering, even the scent of fragrant blossoms and, in the sky above, a rising moon could not revive her *joie de vivre* of the day they had just spent together. The men, too, seemed to be lost in reflective moods. Catlos, however — normally rather constrained — was in a rare expansive frame of mind and wanted to eradicate any remaining melancholy feelings and celebrate their rescue. This was relatively rare for this serious man, but he did not want to suppress the relief and gratitude he felt at simply being alive and well. Impulsively, he launched into a popular song of the day he kept hearing on the radio:

"Oh give me land lots of land..."

He stopped abruptly in mid–verse, declaring that he did not like to drink alone or sing alone and prodded the others to join him. Side by side, arm in arm, the bonded buddies who had survived a brutal battle for survival strolled towards the bright lights of the city reaching out in welcome. Soft breezes carried their words forward, filling the fresh spring air with incandescent hope.[21]

17

Freedom's High Price

For Catlos and Dunlevy, the euphoria of celebrating their survival and reunion with Maria faded in the next few days. Both were increasingly troubled by the cold and calculating timbre of the questioning they underwent. Repeatedly they gave individual and joint accounts of the Dawes mission, from the time they landed in Banska Bystrica to entrapment and their struggle to reach the Russian front lines and then, how one by one, and two by two, and finally all in the cabin at Polomka were captured, whittling their numbers down to just the two of them. They gave a detailed account of their struggles to survive in hostile Russian-appropriated territory. Especially irksome were the loaded questions about Maria and subtle insinuations that she may have merely been an opportunist. Why was she involved with the Dawes mission? What exactly was her role in the Slovak revolt? What were her motivations? And why was she with the communists?[1]

Catlos reiterated that to his knowledge, she neither expected nor received any monetary compensation from the men of Dawes. In fact, she had refused payment for daring forays she made into dangerous areas to search for food and shelter. And Dunlevy emphasized how easy it would have been for her to accept invitations to go into hiding with natives where she would easily blend in, and later with relatives in Polomka, but she refused to abandon her commitment to the Americans. It was because of her courage, fearlessness and resourcefulness that they managed to obtain the little cooperation they did from frightened Slovak natives and distrustful CFI partisans, and would have gotten nothing from the hostile Soviets guerrillas without her adroit persuasiveness and expertise in speaking the Russian language.

They provided details about the many occasions when Maria entered enemy-occupied villages, which none of the Americans could have done. They would have starved, frozen to death, or been shot by suspicious Russian guerrillas without her skilled intervention.[2]

17. Freedom's High Price

Dunlevy especially was stung by the thinly veiled suspicions as to how he and Catlos evaded escape in Polomka while Green, Gaul and the others did not. Why were they away from the cabin when it was attacked? There was a subtle inference that they may have paid someone to be able to get away. Did they ever reveal their radio codes to anyone else? As interrogations went on, Dunlevy found it hard to suppress the gorge of anger welling up which he found more painful than undergoing the amputation of a small toe because of frostbite that never healed. He also suspected that Headquarters knew what had happened to Green and the others but wasn't telling. Dunlevy was further wounded to learn that his father had died in December while he and his mission colleagues were fleeing pursuit over rugged mountain terrain in raging blizzards.

When agitation at not being returned to Bari grew to an intolerable level, Dunlevy gave in to an impulse, an act he rarely committed. He boldly addressed Colonel Walter Ross one morning on the street outside their hotel and revealed how he had just learned his father died and he wanted to get home and be with his mother and brother to provide what consolation he could. The understanding Ross told Dunlevy that he and his father had been classmates in college and he remembered him well. He would see what he could do.[3]

Ross proved to be as good as his word. The next day Dunlevy and Catlos were appointed to act as special aides to General Schulyer. This was a slick way of circumventing Soviet restrictions over Allied jurisdiction in Bucharest without securing Russian approval. Aides were permitted to accompany their general wherever he traveled. Two days later, Catlos and Dunlevy were on a plane with the general bound for Bari.[4] Their only regret was not having the opportunity to say goodbye to Maria.

As they flew over the Aegean Sea on approach to the Brindisi air base, Catlos peered down at the cemetery where Saint Nicholas was buried, remembering how he had pointed it out to Keszthelyi on their flight to Banska Bystrica. He wondered again about his teammate Keszthelyi and the other men of Dawes still missing and speculated whether news of them was being deliberately withheld from him and Dunlevy.[5]

More briefings in Bari rankled Dunlevy. Being kept in isolation and not permitted to speak with anyone but interrogators was an ordeal. It finally affected Catlos and he had difficulty keeping a damper on his resentment. He finally exploded to Dunlevy one day, asking "Does the Big Brass actually suspect us of disloyalty? Us? After all we went through?"

Finally, on the morning they were cleared for deportation to Washington, D.C., Ross summoned them into his office. His demeanor and tone were somber. He began by saying that what he had to tell them had not been completely verified as yet, and it was strictly confidential. However, a Berlin Transradio broadcast on January 25, 1945, gave the names of Green and Sehmer as being among the eighteen of an Anglo-American party which had been executed as spies the day before. But until they could sift out fact from rumor, the names of all those captured would remain listed as missing in action.[6]

The news left Catlos stunned, as it did Dunlevy, both trying to absorb the horror of this reality. Later in Washington, D.C., there would be the Bronze Star, Legion of Merit medal, Purple Heart and Associated Press and hometown headlines, but at none of it would matter much. The only thing Catlos felt sure of was that he and Dunlevy had flown into Banska Bystrica confident young OSS agents on a daring mission and were returning to their country as saddened old veterans with the knowledge that fourteen of their nineteen-man Dawes unit had not been so fortunate.[7]

* * *

For Maria, loneliness stalked every moment after she heard that Catlos and Dunlevy had left Bucharest even though Colonel Carter and his wife were kind to Maria and the other women. He invited them to join him on short drives through the lovely Romanian countryside with its prolific agricultural fields, where — far from the ravages of battles and revolts — war seemed an absurdity. At times, Maria wished that she, like Morton, could record her experiences in a journal. But she was not a writer. And furthermore, the underground had left the indelible impression that it was wise to reveal as little as possible to anyone else by word or in writing. Silently, she pondered about Keszthelyi's diary and whose hands it was in now. Was it friend or foe? And what had he written in it anyway?

News of the war filtered into the villa. They heard that on April 1, Slovak president Tiso and his cabinet had fled to a monastery cloister in Vienna seeking asylum where they surrendered to American Army officials. Instead of asylum, they were turned over by the Allies to the Czech government-in-exile back in power with Edvard Beneš as president. One of his first acts was to ensure his revenge on ex–President Tiso, who would later undergo a trial by a coalition government and be sentenced to death by hanging. And only a few in the United States or the media expressed anything but ire for the monsignor. An exception was Edward DeLaney, whose writings contrasted how Tiso had shielded and saved American flyers from the enemy but was repaid by execution with the tacit agreement of the United States.[8]

The Red Army now occupied most of Slovakia, financially bankrupt from the German occupation. The new coalition government, interspersed with Slovak communists and based in Kosice, was now in power. Rumors of

17. Freedom's High Price

Hitler's capture were rife but no one knew for sure. And people openly wondered why the Germans fought on when their defeat was imminent.

For several days in early May they heard frantic pleas over the BBC saying, "Prague is asking for help! Prague is asking for help!" The Czechs eagerly awaited the arrival of General Patton's Third Army just ten kilometers from Prague. Neither he nor General Mark Clark could figure out why General Eisenhower held back the Western Allies and allowed the Soviets to take the city.[9] Nor were the Czech people aware that Beneš had sold them out by his agreement with Stalin in December 1943 for Czechoslovakia to become a Soviet satellite, and that Czechoslovakia was doomed as a democracy and was to become part of the Soviet communist bloc.

On May 2, 1945, the suicide of Hitler, burrowed in his bunker beneath the Reich Chancellery since early January, was broadcast from Radio Hamburg. It passed almost unnoticed, his death overwhelmed by the tragedy of the powerful nation whose destruction he had wrought.

Then on the morning of May 8, Colonel Carter bolted into the Reception Room and shouted, "The war is over!" Everyone in the villa crowded around the radio to listen to the announcement by Moscow News, which only Carter and Maria understood since it was in Russian. It proclaimed that the Germans had signed a treaty of surrender now that Berlin, the final holdout, had been taken by the Red Army. The version they heard was that the noble, invincible Russians had achieved victory alone; there was no mention of the other Allies. Finally, they managed to reach the BBC where a newscaster with a pronounced British accent announced, "Germany surrendered today … the terms of the surrender are…" before the words faded in and out. And then the final addition that took no one by surprise. It had been confirmed that on April 30, 1945, Hitler and some of his top officials had committed suicide in their Berlin bunkers. But it no longer mattered because no one was listening.[10]

General Vlasov and his troops, trying to surrender to the Allies, were to be turned over to Moscow's liberators by Soviet demand. Instead of sharing the victory, the fate of the Vlassovites would be a deadly one.[11]

Andrea, head in her hands, sobbed uncontrollably as her husband, face creased with tears, held her close and patted her soothingly as though she were a child, while her sister hovered nearby anxiously.

Maria and Evelyn, the English girl in love with a Hungarian officer, laughed and cried at the same time. The dignified Colonel Carter danced around the room with his wife and then every other woman present. He finally stopped only long enough to announce that they were going out on the town to celebrate and ordered them to don their finest apparel.

Maria dashed to her room to change into the new pale blue dress and Navy pumps that Davis, Dunlevy and Catlos had bought her. She splashed cologne on her wrists, dabbed on lipstick and ran a comb through her hair before running back downstairs to join the others. It was just in time to see Davis bolt through the door. He grabbed Maria and swung her around crazily, and kissed her cheeks repeatedly, saying, "We made it, luv! It's really over and we made it!"

They all jumped into the waiting limousine as Carter and his party, with car horn blasting, drove triumphantly to the Black Hotel in downtown Bucharest. Once a five-star international hotel, it was still a fine place and every inch jammed with celebrants. Precious jars of caviar long hidden were opened and champagne corks popped, sounding like rifle shots, as the precious liquid gushed like fountains into crystal glasses. Drunken Romanian, Russian and Yugoslavian soldiers surged around the room, pausing to toast the Americans and British.[12]

As groups of them arrived and departed, the party grew more raucous. Russian soldiers leaped onto tables and danced, totally oblivious to the fact that the bottles of vodka they twirled overhead were spilling contents over other revelers. Strangers, some former adversaries, embraced joyfully, dodging waiters staggering in and out of the kitchen balancing heavy trays laden from the cache of wine, whiskey, vodka and schnapps that had been kept safe from the reach of marauding Nazi and then Russian soldiers.

It was dawn before the celebration wound down. When the still exhilarated Colonel Carter gathered his people together and announced that they would walk back to the villa, his suggestion was met with enthusiasm as everyone felt in need of fresh air. Linking arms, the colonel and his wife, Maria and Davis, Andrea and her husband, her sister and a new male acquaintance weaved down the boulevard, followed by a straggling group of Russian soldiers. They paused periodically for the Americans and Russians to exchange weapons to fire into the air. Then a couple of the Russian revelers began singing at the top of their lungs. It was a sentimental Russian folk song:

> Apple trees were aflower
> River mist all around
> Young Katiusha sang a love song
> of her lover in a distant land.[13]

Not to be outdone, Davis raised his baritone that rang out above other voices with the words of a well-known British naval chanty. Evidently Davis, out of respect for the women and the occasion, adhered to the less bawdy version with a single exception:

17. Freedom's High Price

> Bless them all
> Bless the long and the short and the tall...
> Bless all the corporals and W.O. ones
> Bless all the sergeants and their bloody sons
> For I'm sayin' goodbye to them all
> As back to their billets they crawl,
> I'll get no promotion this side of the ocean
> So cheer up m'lads, fuck 'em all![14]

For Maria, the sense of fun and lightness that had blessed a similar rejoicing event just days before when she had strolled down this same boulevard with Dunlevy, Catlos and Davis, was missing. Now the Americans were gone and Davis was leaving any day. In the midst of all the revelry, she felt a shiver and was swept with the chilling realization that the party was really over.

The party was also over for Slovakia. The Red Armies rampaged through their land, the people not able to understand why the West accommodated the USSR, which they deemed to be the devil incarnate.[15] And Slovakians wondered why, after getting rid of a lesser evil, they didn't free the world from the greatest evil of them all, the Soviet Union.

Like everyone in the villa, Maria slept late the next day, her head throbbing from a headache and her emotions dull and gray. Her pensive mood was lifted when Davis made an unexpected appearance in the afternoon. Still in a mellow mood, he greeted her with, "C'mon, luv. What you need is bit of fresh air. A lovely day it is. How about a row on the lake?"

Davis rented a canoe and rowed towards the far bank of the small lake in the middle of a park. Maria began to relax and enjoy the play of sunlight on waves rippling in the wake of the canoe. She dipped her hand into the lake and watched Davis' strong arms ply oars through the water as easily as if they were chopsticks. Impulsively, addressing him as Guilliam, she asked when he was leaving. He shrugged and said any time, as soon as official things were cleared up.

In the tranquil silence that followed, Maria studied him surreptitiously. His neatly trimmed dusky hair glistened in the sunlight and as he turned for a moment to let his gaze flicker out over the shore, she was racked with a sudden stab of pain that almost took her breath away. For a mere second, he looked like Tibor Keszthelyi. But it was not Tibor. It was another terrific man who had lent her his name that saved her life. At that, she suppressed a smile, remembering Evelyn, an English girl at the villa who urged her to marry Davis. "You're so right together. And remember, being married to an American or Englishman will give you a ready made ticket out of this place."

When Davis dropped her off at the villa, Evelyn rushed to meet them and handed Davis a stack of mail, explaining she had just returned from British headquarters and the packet of letters had arrived for him. The top letter slipped to the floor and the return address caught Maria's eyes. It was that of Mrs. Guilliam Davis. He'd had never mentioned a wife so it was probably his mother. But when he bent over to pick it up, his gaze met Maria's and in that instant, she knew. His expression of bewilderment was touching. As was his explanation.

"I married a week before I shipped out. Now, I'm not sure. I hardly know her...."

Maria reached out to grasp his hand. "Give it a chance," she urged, "Do give it a good chance. You both deserve that." She had a deep surety of knowing that her advice was right. Any romance deserved a chance and she fervently wished that hers with Tibor Keszthelyi, wherever he was at that moment, stood a fighting chance.[16]

* * *

The excitement and jubilation that flamed at the war's end soon fizzled out. Gigantic problems of resettling millions of displaced persons brought a different kind of challenge. Settling of old scores brought more deaths, such as General Vlasov and his renegade Ukrainian Army who tried to surrender to the Allies in Prague. Instead, the Allies turned them over to the Soviets, who sentenced the top officials to death and consigned his soldiers to slave labor in Siberia or slaughtered them.

Maria's fate remained tenuous as did that of countless other refugees. Every means was tried by desperate refugees to be retained under Allied jurisdiction. One such desperate victim, a Polish pilot who had flown on numerous missions for the Royal Air Force, asked Maria to marry him. He had applied for permission to remain under British jurisdiction and was refused. As a married man, however, his chances for acceptance were better. His plight, along with those of thousands of defecting Russian soldiers, or those released from POW camps in Germany, was bleak. Many committed suicide rather than fall under the Soviet brand of justice. The knowledge of these tragedies heightened Maria's desperate need to get out of Bucharest and the outstretched tentacles of the NKVD. There was no loophole to evade; Stalin had put all resistance groups under NKVD control.

Colonel Carter and she spun plots and strategies to smuggle her out, with or without an exit visa. None proved feasible and by the end of May, she was no longer able to sleep because of anxiety. They had reached a dead end. It opened up a trifle when a casual acquaintance offered her sound advice. The savvy Slovak-American young woman, married to a Romanian petroleum

17. Freedom's High Price

firm engineer, urged Maria to keep pestering the Americans for help. That was the only avenue of possibility, because once they pulled out, she was a dead duck. She'd be sent back to Slovakia and face charges.

Maria intensified her appeals to Carter. Eager to be free of her problems, in turn he pressed Colonel Ross for a solution. Cables flew back and forth between Washington, D.C., and Bucharest. One highly placed American officer felt she was an opportunist trying to elevate herself above her class.[17] Another stated she had used the Americans and was trying to continue doing so.[18] And, with the Russians refusing to release her, Maria's case seemed hopeless until she met with a newly arrived Czechoslovakian consul general. When she related to him her precarious situation, he said he would see what he could do, but was frank in telling her that he could promise nothing. When Maria was summoned again a few days later, she braced herself for the worst. But this time, he viewed her in a new light and greeted her heartily.

"Good God, girl! What did you do that made the Russkies so mad at you?" he asked.

"Nothing, except refuse to spy for them."[19]

Maria had no idea that she and her family were regarded as anti-communist. She had not joined the uprising against the Slovak state home regime but primarily against the German control and out of concern for the postwar Slovakia.[20]

When the consul general said they had denied her an exit visa, Maria felt crushed. Evidently taking pity on her, after a thoughtful moment, he relented and said that since his own position as consul was only temporary, he certainly wouldn't be getting any promotion. So what did he have to lose? He would personally release her, but it was on one condition. She was never to go back to Czechoslovakia. Her spirits soaring, Maria was prepared to agree to almost anything.

On June 20, 1945, her benefactor handed Maria a valid exit visa and the next day she was on a U.S. plane bound for the OSS base in Bari. To her surprise and delight, in the adjacent seat was Davis, also going to Bari and then home to England. Maria had never flown before and the Welshman laughed at her gasps of fear at the sudden rises and drops of the plane. He patted her hand in assurance and explained that they were merely air pockets and reminded her that they had endured far worse.

Davis' final papers were soon cleared and on the evening before he left, Maria joined him for a farewell dinner of pasta and wine at a homey ocean front restaurant. He would be leaving in the morning and he asked about her situation.

Saying she felt like the last leaf on a tree with Dunlevy and Catlos gone and now him leaving, she admitted that she remained in limbo because the Americans refused to give her the documents she needed to emigrate to the United States.

Declaring them bloody fools, Davis insisted that she deserved the best from "those blasted Yanks." Then turning reflective, he reminded her that they had gone through bloody hell, and there were times he was sure they never make it out. Turning to her, he said, "You saved my skin more than once." With deep feeling he asked, "Did I ever thank you?"

"No need to. You also saved my skin more than once, you know."

Talk turned to their Dawes and Windproof companions, primarily Sehmer. "Crazy redhead!" Davis said of his commander. "I was always afraid he would get us killed playing those jokes on the Germans and Hungarians. But the bloke was like that, had some kind of fire in his belly."[21]

In turn, Maria spoke highly of Green and how hard he tried to save his men and never lost that fine sense of grace even when the going was hardest. Neither brought into the open what they had to be thinking and wondering about the others and what had happened to them. After a spell, the talk gradually dwindled; too much could never be said, and too much would never be known.

Maria gazed out at the Adriatic Sea as the sun dipped lower over the horizon, turning the turquoise waters to a deep indigo blue. Deepening shadows crept closer as they prepared to leave. The final moment of parting had arrived.

Just inside the front door of her hotel, they lingered for a moment. "Guess this is really it," Davis said, his voice a bit hoarse. "It's bloody awful to say goodbye to you, Maria. But I will never forget you."

"And I will never forget you, Guilliam," Maria responded, thinking how trite her words and wondering why people get tongue tied when saying goodbye.

He held her hands tightly for a moment before he bent down to brush her lips with his and murmured, "Be happy, Maria."

He smiled, tipped his hat and, giving her a smart salute, walked jauntily out the door. As his rapid steps carried him beyond her view, Maria sent forth a silent wish and prayer for this gallant, brave Welshman and the real Mrs. Guilliam Davis he would soon be joining.

18

Maria Departs for the United States

When the OSS operation in Bari was relocated to Caserta, Italy, Maria was transferred with the staff. They were housed in the luxurious former palace of King Victor Emmanuel and Maria was billeted with twenty-five American girls performing office work with the OSS. Although her English had improved, she still felt awkward amid the chattering young women. In addition, exaggerated stories about Maria were circulating which brought a steady stream of military officers and secretaries parading past her work area to give her the once-over, as she labored to complete the report on her assignment with the Dawes mission. The curiosity bemused and puzzled Maria until the day she looked up at the young woman standing in the doorway openly gaping at her with intensity.[1]

"You must be the girl," the other woman blurted.

"What girl?"

"The one who was with all those OSS men who were executed."

Maria felt the pen drop from her hand and some force she had managed to hold coiled up inside suddenly shattered. She stared back at the woman, unable to speak.

"Are you all right?" the woman asked anxiously.

Maria could not respond. She grabbed the edge of the desk to steady herself and tried to stand up but could not. Suddenly, a man loomed over her and, with concern, asked, "Are you all right?"

It was Colonel Chapin who helped Maria to her feet and led her past gawking co-workers into his office where he settled her in a chair and closed the door. He filled a glass of water and handed it to her. "We thought you knew," he said gently.

"No. I never gave up hope."

Chapin then told Maria to sit tight and hurried to summon someone who had been in Mauthausen with the OSS men. He returned with Lieutenant Jack Taylor, who took one look at Maria, who appeared ready to faint, grabbed her hand and lifted her to her feet. "We're getting out of here," he announced brusquely.[2]

He propelled Maria past curious co-workers out to the street and into a Jeep. The afternoon was stifling hot as he whipped the vehicle along narrow, cobblestoned streets and out into the countryside. After a half hour drive, during which neither Taylor nor Maria said a word, he pulled the Jeep to a stop in a shaded area and turned off the ignition. Speaking softly in German, he told Maria that he knew how hard this news had to be on her. For the first time, she really looked at her companion, a handsome, gray-haired man with shadows so dark in deep-set blue eyes that for moments the pupils seemed to turn black.

When her shock subsided a little, she was able to ask Taylor the questions burning in her heart as well as her mind. Had he seen Tibor Keszthelyi? How did he look? What did he say?

Speaking hesitantly, Taylor said that Keszthelyi, like all the men in the death camp, appeared emaciated and very tired looking. He had not had an opportunity to really talk with most of the men of the Dawes mission. However, he had spoken once or twice to Green and Gaul, but what was there to say? They obviously feared and guessed their fate as commandos and dreaded what lay ahead.[3]

Taylor did not reveal what he knew about the torture perpetrated on the men of the Dawes and Day missions to wring information from them about their operations before executing them. Nor that he had experienced torture himself. Although the tall, gangly man had gained some weight since the Red Cross evacuated Mauthausen a day before the SS pulled out and he was released — weighing 112 pounds, weak and suffering from a chronic fever with sores over his entire body — the grim effects were plain to see.[4]

Taylor and two other volunteers in his mission had been dropped south of Vienna, but their equipment was never recovered. After hiding out for two months, he was betrayed to the Gestapo by one of the volunteers. His signal and cipher pads had been buried and were given to the Gestapo by the betrayer. He had hoped to reach Green and get word to Bari to drop another radio for his mission. A friend named Margit Buchleiter had carried the message to her friend in Vienna, but the girl who was to contact Dawes about the radio was found dead. At Mauthausen, he was given a pad with drawings that showed the Germans had fairly complete knowledge of the Houseboat and Dawes plans, much of it wrung from torture of the Dawes men.[5]

When Maria's composure crumpled and she broke into sobs, Taylor put

18. Maria Departs for the United States

an arm around her shoulders, and let her wail in grief, releasing some of the shock and pain. She repeatedly condemned herself, saying that if Tibor had not listened to her and left the mission with Mac and Lain and the airmen, he would still be alive. It was all her fault.

"Let it all out," Taylor urged. When her weeping let up, he shook her shoulder gently but in a stern tone told her to stop blaming herself; Keszthelyi was a mature man who made up his own mind. They all were, or they would not have been in this murky intelligence business. Feeling completely drained, Maria leaned back in her seat on the drive back to the OSS offices. Escorting her inside the building, Taylor suggested that they take a little drive every afternoon for a few days to talk, if she wanted to. And even if she didn't, getting away for a short time from the questioning gaze of intrusive onlookers would help.[6]

With gratitude, Maria leaned on Taylor's support until she finished her report, although she perceived that he had his own demons to combat. At times, his blue eyes turned dark as night with remembered nightmares too horrible to talk about, and during these episodes he drove in silence, hands clutching the wheel so tightly they turned pale to the point that they appeared bloodless. But he never revealed a word of his own experiences other than that he had gotten out of Mauthausen only because a prison guard had misplaced his file — purposely, it seemed because he mistook Taylor for someone else.[7] Why didn't any of the men of Dawes get such a break? she had to ask.

"Those guys were hot property. A real catch," he said bitterly "A big honor for the one responsible for snaring them."

"Like the hunter with the biggest kill," Maria added.

"Exactly. That's what war is, hunt and kill," Taylor snapped and then clammed up. He did not tell her that knowledge of OSS operations in Bari was wrung by torture from members of the Dawes, Houseboat and Day teams before execution. Or that among American items on Mauthausen commandant Frenz Ziereis' desk was a pair of U.S. Navy insignias that belonged to Green. Only the knowledge that Ziereis had been killed in a shootout with one of Patton's soldiers on May 9 alleviated the bitterness at all.[8]

And now, Taylor had his own official agenda. It was to investigate and collect data from Mauthausen on brutal SS officers who participated in the torture and abuse of prisoners and compile evidence to prosecute them for their war crimes. The only easy part was locating data; the Nazis kept meticulous records and little was left hidden. He procured for the OSS the death registration of Mauthausen of all who died from January 1939 to April 1945. His painstaking efforts would lead to enough evidence for guilty verdicts and execution by hanging of 61 sadistic SS torturers.[9]

The drives ended when Maria's report was complete and submitted through proper channels. To Maria's surprise, the editor was critical about some of her personal observations which he felt were not within regular military guidelines, after which he applied his own heavy editing hand to the report until it became, in her opinion, a rather pallid account of the mission. However, she was rewarded with a trip to Rome for rest and recreation where she opted to go alone, unable to bear the carefree attitude of the giggling girls from whom she felt alienated.[10]

In the Eternal City, she meandered along the busy streets with their hordes of people until she was tired enough to sleep at night. But even then, slumber often eluded her as bits and pieces of the recent past reached out to plague her. One by one, in dreams or a half-awake state, flashes of memory of the men of Dawes coursed through her mind's eye. Soft spoken and gentlemanly Green, who had done his utmost to be a wise, effective commander; Gaul with his imperious ways but the one most of the other men most respected as leader; Horvath of the Aryan-blond good looks and an unabashed passionate love for his beautiful wife, and yet one of the manliest men she ever met; flame-haired Sehmer whose matching fire in his eyes that lit up every room he was in; tousle-haired Heller just out of his teens, and Morton, the kind, smiling, peace-making reporter who did not live to see his baby girl. Then, of course, there was Catlos, with a steely drive to survive, who kept to himself mostly except for the late developing friendship with Dunlevy, the quiet, determined young man who kept his own counsel. One by one they paraded past her mind's eye, but always, at the beginning and at the end, there was Tibor Keszthelyi, of the film star good looks, a complex man of subtle wit and warm caring and the first man with whom she was destined to fall in love.

In Rome there were many men who were eager to assuage her loneliness. She accepted the invitation of Major Charles Hoestler for an afternoon sail and then a drive to Naples where they had drinks in the Red Cross Club that had once been part of Emperor Hadrian's castle. She found comfort in the sea and its eternal tide of waves advancing and receding, a steady reminder that they had endured through eons of life and death and would always be there, providing the balm that lost souls needed.[11]

In August 1945, the OSS office was transferred to Salzburg, Germany. There, Barbara Podolski, a Czech girl married to an American Army officer and who wore the same size clothing as Maria, gave her one of her WAAC uniforms, enabling Maria to blend in with the surrounding military personnel better. Years later Barbara remembered Maria as a frail looking blonde, and that her own efforts for the Allies were minimal compared to Maria who "went through hell."[12]

18. Maria Departs for the United States

Glancing in the mirror with her new mode of dress, Maria felt strange. For moments, she felt she didn't know who she was or who she was supposed to be. But whoever that was, she could not forget that the NKVD was searching for her and would do so relentlessly with the intent to force her to fulfill spying assignments they had planned. And since she, like everyone in the underground had been placed under the auspices of the NKVD, they had the authority to enforce their own rules.[13]

When Maria was allotted two hundred dollars by the Post Exchange, she felt as elated as a child let loose in a candy store. She swooped up cigarettes, candy, personal items and fabric for clothing that she stuffed into a duffle bag to stash under her bed in the dorm shared with some of the other girls.

In the days that followed during what seemed an eternal wait, the news they had been longing to hear became reality. On August 12, 1945, the radio blared out the announcement that "Japan Surrendered!" It was followed with a sparse mention about something called an atom bomb that had been unleashed on the Asian enemy. Everyone present in the villa crowded around the radio to listen intently to scant details of the terms of surrender. The message was unmistakable. World War II was finally over. The treaty was signed on the USS *Missouri* on Sept. 2, 1945.

Major Vratislav Hruby, intent on celebrating, invited Maria and several others to ride with him to town where the partying proved to be long and riotous. Driving back hours later, the slightly tipsy major launched into song. At the top of his voice, he belted out the lyrics of the popular melody titled "Besame Mucho." Maria tried to join in the celebration as she had when the war in Europe ended. But that was before she knew that Tibor, Micvan, Green, Gaul, Morton, Horvath, and all of the men captured in Polomka the day after Christmas were dead. And there was still no news about MacGregor, Lain and the airmen. This time she could not join in any singing for the end of a war that came far too late for the man she loved and his military colleagues of the Dawes mission.[14]

The finality of the war's end brought a let down feeling to the military people around Maria. But to her and millions of refugees or released POWs, it ushered in a new worry that began when the Allies started repatriating most of them to their countries of origin whether they wanted to return or not. Among them were many Russians trying to desert, and their fate would be grim. A year earlier, on May 31, 1944, the Soviets demanded that any Soviet nationals who fell into Allied hands during the liberation of Europe must be returned to Russia. Especially targeted were soldiers from east and central Europe whose goal was emigration to the United States, although they didn't have a chance because all immigration had been halted.[15]

One morning Maria overheard an American officer comment to his aide. "Another Ukrainian and a Russian ended it today." He referred to the soldiers from these two countries who had committed suicide rather than succumb to being returned to their country of origin only to be executed or doomed to slave labor in Siberian work camps until they died.

Maria's desire to emigrate to America was unwavering and she also knew it required nothing short of a miracle to bring her hope and desire to fruition. It came in the form of Major Hruby who, after wracking his brain, advised her to apply for a scholarship in the United States. As an experienced teacher, she stood a chance of getting a prized visa. But for that, she needed more identification than her dog-eared railroad passport issued by the now-defunct Slovak state, and all other necessary documents were stored at her family home.

Major Hruby arranged for Maria to visit her family by transporting her with several other passengers to the U.S. Embassy in Prague. There, she waited for the next step, which came in an unlikely way and via the most unlikely man. It was a gray, rainy day in September when the base commander approached her with another man in tow. She was as astonished as Lt. John Schwartz when he appeared. All he had been told was that he was to drive into Slovakia on a special OSS mission with another person, and it turned out to be Maria![16]

While they waited for their orders to be processed, in cryptic sentences he described how he managed to escape execution. One of the airmen had been tortured until he revealed Schwartz's identity. When an SS chief confronted Schwartz with the slip of paper he had thrown away with his code written on it, he felt it was all over. But he was indeed as quick-witted and clever as he was reputed to be. When asked what a bomber crewman was doing with gold coins and radio signals, he quickly told them that the paper and money belonged to a British SOE officer who had given it to him to pass on to his major with his unit in the mountains. Not wanting to be caught with these items, he'd thrown the paper away. While he was fabricating this excuse for having the code in his wallet, Schwartz figured he'd have time before they checked on Sehmer to think of something else if need be.[17]

He then made it a point to talk to an Austrian doctor who had let it be known that he was eager to be released from prison duty. Schwartz informed the doctor that he would sign an affidavit testifying that he and others had been well treated in prison if the doctor released him and any other airmen he could. The ploy worked. That very day he, Yeargin, and Haines were released and holed up in Vienna in an NKVD jail for a time until they were released to the Americans. Now he was trying to track down Nazi SS to stand

18. Maria Departs for the United States

trial for war crimes. And most happily, he shared the wonderful news that MacGregor and Lain had been released from POW camps and were back in the Air Force.

It was General Donovan who was later to testify that in some prisoner of war camps, chiefly Mauthausen, horrible methods of torture were common. One was to spray water on prisoners and then shove them outside to freeze to death under a sheet of ice. Mauthausen was run by men who had been thugs before the war, and the Dawes leaders and men were educated and from another world.[18]

Later Maria was to learn directly from MacGregor how he and Lain had been stripped and doused with cold water and shoved out the door into the cold to freeze. But they never admitted to being OSS spies, and two days before their slated execution, a Ukrainian patrol stormed the prison and rather than the prisoners being executed, it was the camp guards and officials who were shot in their stead.[19]

In turn, Maria filled Schwartz in on what happened with her in the six months following his capture and during the weeks when she and the other uncaptured British and OSS men were on the run. Now though, what both Maria and Schwartz wanted most was to see their families in Slovakia. But how could this be accomplished?

The canny fellow Slovak did not let Maria down. He took her to see Frank Weizner and Allen Dulles, chief of OSS Europe and currently in Prague. They cut through red tape and requisitioned a jeep and gas coupons. In no time Schwartz and Maria were on their way. The first stop was in the hamlet where Schwartz's grandparents lived. There, his grandmother hobbled out of a humble dwelling to throw herself into Schwartz's arms, while his grandfather was more restrained. Then the couple wept and clung to their grandson like a life raft. Arms wrapped around the smiling young man, they led him and Maria inside their home where they would not let him stop talking. Finally they bade him and Maria to rest and the pair were soon fast asleep on cots in the kitchen until sunup the next morning. It was hard to leave the elderly couple, and they would let Schwartz go only after he promised to visit them again soon. Then it was on to Maria's family.[20]

"The road ends in Jukabiany," Maria always laughingly warned visitors about her home village, because it was the last stop before the Polish border. At first, Father Edmund, his former erect carriage slightly bent, could not believe it was his eldest daughter. He was so overcome with emotion he could not utter a word while a river of tears flowed down ashen cheeks. In contrast, Anastasia could not stop talking and praising God who had answered their prayers, it saddened Maria to note that her mother's chestnut hair, without a strand of gray one year ago, was now almost white and her lovely face lined and drawn.

A bottle of brandy that had been hidden under the barn was produced and uncorked and poured. Sipping the powerful brew, Maria and her parents talked. They had not received any of Maria's letters from Bari or Prague and feared she was dead. Father Edmund related how he had been summoned to an adjacent village to identify the remains of a young woman who had been declared a traitor and executed. He forced himself to look at the body sprawled on the ground and then, for the only time in his life, he fainted from shock, even though it was not that of Maria. The sight of what had been a young woman so recently alive and full of vitality now a bloody corpse was too much for him to bear.[21]

In turn, her father listened intently to Maria's account of the men of Dawes. When she finished, he buried his face in his hands and wept for them and their families. "My God! My God! What a burden to have brave sons!"

"And daughters," his wife, Anastasia, murmured sadly, dabbing at tear stained eyes. "Does not war claim daughters, too?"

Maria tried to stay out of sight of other villagers but even so, her presence was known and duly investigated by Igor, one of her rejected suitors, now the communist leader in the village. He dropped by unannounced to inquire as to how long Maria planned to be in Jakubiany. When she told him she was home to stay, he merely smiled. He was not deceived and Maria knew it would not take him long to put the pieces together. She had to get away before he did.

After the gifts of candy, cosmetics and cloth for new dresses were presented to her excited younger sisters Eva, Tanya, Magda and Anne, and some special items reserved for her parents, the talk began to wind down. Tension again set in as the time for Maria's departure loomed. That last evening together she and her father talked until two o'clock in the morning. The thought of leaving him and the rest of her family was unbearable, but neither could she stay.

Maria confided to her father that was she planned to try gaining entry to graduate school in the United States and, after completion, to return to Slovakia to teach in a university. His blue eyes, reflecting extreme suffering, brimmed over and he hardly seemed to hear her words as he murmured, "You'll be gone again, just like Marta."

The poignancy of his tone cut through Maria like a sharp knife blade. Marta, two years younger than Maria, had with Julius been the instigators in her decision to help his sister Hannah and her child. That seemingly innocent act then thrust her into the underground movement organizing the uprising, working with the CFI and Russians, and finally the Anglo-Americans.

18. Maria Departs for the United States

And now it was forcing her to become an émigré, if possible, to escape the consequences which would be dire indeed.[22]

When the first wave of rampaging Soviet armies swept through their land, her father had prudently hidden his wife and daughters until the Armies moved on. The hounds of hell had a field day, forcing children to watch their mothers being raped. Young women and girls were repeatedly sexually ravaged, and husbands or fathers who tried to protect them were shot.[23] One young woman sobbed her story of being raped by 50 half-drunken Russians. Waves of executions followed, some merely of those accused and without a trial.

Everyone loyal to Tiso, especially church leaders, was turned over to the NKVD. The only ones exempt from a quick death sentence were physicists and scientists who helped make the V-2 rockets; they were exiled to Russia to be used as technical experts in developing weapons.[24]

It was during this period of chaotic upheaval when Marta disappeared and her parents did not know where she was other than a brief word from her saying that she was involved in some new cause which was bound to be dangerous.

Feeling her father's anguish, Maria begged him to come to America with her. His bishop could provide the necessary papers. As a young priest, he had turned down offers from parishes in the United States because his wife would not leave Jakubiany. In his eyes was a faraway look of longing, possibly of the long-ago dream of emigrating to the United States he once had. Finally, he sighed and, in a resigned tone, said, "I won't abandon my parish or my people."

His sense of sacrifice embittered Maria. "You're too idealistic, Father! Your people, or many of them, will abandon you."

"A common fate of pastors," he replied quietly.

Maria had already gleaned what was happening in Slovakia even before her father filled her in on the current status. There was a race to purchase Communist membership cards stamped with a pre–1939 date. This prized document entitled the holder to become eligible for food parcels that UNNRA, the American relief agency, was distributing. Without that card, Slovak natives received nothing.[25]

The card had yet another value. It provided some protection from the arrests and mock trials set up by the People's Tribunal, a frontier-type justice system composed of local communists. Spies had come out of hiding to make accusations against neighbors, friends, and anyone against whom they held a grudge. And the resultant justice was brutal. Father Edmund finished his description of what he saw occurring with a prediction of a new reign of terror to come and ended with a sorrowful summation. "One tyrant was thrown down and another, a worse one, is in his place."[26]

On her last day in Jakubiany, Maria's own eyes viewed sights she could never have imagined she would see in her tranquil village. Hunger was rampant and the begging eyes of small children scavenging for food would forever haunt her. The Russians had slaughtered all livestock and seized every possible particle of food to feed their huge armies. Even seeds were confiscated; however, Father Edmund assured Maria that Anastasia had hidden some and they would be able to plant them soon and with God's grace, there would be a fall harvest. All Maria was able to do was make a silent vow to help financially in any way she could.[27]

The final parting was one of wrenching agony amid a torrent of emotions. Before the final goodbye, Maria's parents had one last urgent request. It was that she would search for Marta and persuade her to return home. Maybe the Americans could help, Father Edmund said in a plaintive tone. Maria promised she would try her best to locate her sister.

With the first rays of dawn, Schwartz drove up in the jeep, jumped out, and after a few brief words with her parents and sisters, got back into the jeep and gunned the motor to hurry Maria along. No use prolonging the pain, he later explained. As they drove away, Maria turned to look back at her family, hands waving and eyes overflowing with tears, until the last bend in the road that took them out of Jakubiany. The anguish on the faces of her parents and sisters was wrenching, as was the view of the picturesque village that would be forever imprinted on her mind and in her heart.

They departed just in time. Her mother was to write later that two days after Maria and Schwartz left, two men in civilian clothing and speaking Ukrainian came to ask her parents where she had gone. They said they did not know and fervently prayed that the pursuers would never guess that Maria was on her way to join the Americans and then, God willing, on to America and freedom.[28]

Schwartz did not try to offer futile comfort because there was none. What had to be, had to be, as they had learned so well. Fortunately for Maria, she could not have even imagined that it would be another twenty-five years before she would see her parents and sisters again.

19

A Bronze Medal for Maria

The OSS assignment for Schwartz and Maria was to investigate rumors that some renegade units of General Vlasov's army were still waging battle against the Soviets in the area of the Dukla Pass and to check what was happening in rural areas near the pass. The rumors proved to be just that: empty tales of those who hoped to eradicate local communists in control, just as they had the Nazis who had been vanquished. Sadly, any hope of being rid of communist control was to remain an empty dream for the next five decades.[1]

After they completed their reports, Schwartz then drove Maria to Bratislava and dropped her off at a hotel where a room had been reserved for her. For Schwartz, it was to be a week of rest, he said, and then unfinished business, which was to track down Nazis who had worked in concentration camps and help bring those guilty of war crimes to justice. Already she sensed that invisible armor of granite hardness slipping around him again, the shield that she once found impossible to penetrate and very irritating. The camaraderie they shared on the brief visit to the country they loved was ebbing as they parted to go their separate ways.

He climbed out of the jeep and lifted her bag to the ground. Giving her an impulsive hug he said, "We misjudged each other, Maria, didn't we? We both love this little bit of a country, and our people and we want the best for them." His eyes grew dark as he added, "Some damned fine men paid a high price for it." When his words ended, the stony faced commando she had know earlier was back in control.[2]

There would be other investigations, ferreting out the truth, such as the one initiated by the Associated Press to learn the fate of war correspondent Joseph Morton. The early, sketchy news of the execution of Green and the captives taken on December 26, 1944, impelled them to search out the facts. Lynn Niezerling, a friend and colleague of Morton's, accompanied by Lieutenant Kelly O'Neill, USNR, first went to Paris to talk with Werner Muller and then to Mauthausen. Morton had always carried his war correspondent I.D. and was in American uniform, so there was no reason to doubt his identity and classify him as a spy. Even so, the two investigators could not detect the slightest evidence of any trial for Morton and the men of Dawes between their arrival at Mauthausen on January 7 until their execution on January 24, 1945. This was a blatant violation of the Geneva Convention regarding treatment of prisoners of war.[3]

The signatures of the Dawes men had been burned by the SS as American armies approached the prison, making a search difficult. The long and torturous silence since October 7, 1944, when Morton and the other men landed in Slovakia, remained in effect and not until May 30, 1945, was there a breakthrough. That occurred when Werner Muller, German interpreter at Mauthausen during the Americans' imprisonment, and Wilheim Ornstein, a Polish prisoner assigned to the crematory, were captured by chance. They held the keys to the fate of the men of Dawes and were to testify later that the men were shot and killed by SS executioner Georg Bachmeyer in the presence of Franz Ziereis and camp chief Adolph Zutter on orders from Ernst Kaltenbrunner.[4]

Mauthausen, on the banks of the Danube, was a cold, dreary prison and for Niezerling, just knowing that her friend Morton had been imprisoned in one of its gray, high-walled cells was very painful. Morton had had a burning desire to be a war correspondent and had been in Rome in 1943 and later also witnessed the arrival of the Red Army in Bucharest. He had been nominated for the Pulitzer Prize for his brilliant, colorful stories about the events he witnessed in Romania that were said to rival *The Prisoner of Zenda*. The very thought of gentle Joe, full of confidence and helping to keep up the morale of his group, only to die in this hellhole, was a blood-chilling shock.[5]

Among the many tributes attesting to the appealing personality of Morton was one made by fellow Associated Press correspondent William McDermott in his story published in the Cleveland *Plain Dealer* on July 16, 1945. He described Morton as good company, exceptionally alert and an adventurous correspondent who did not mind danger when incurred by necessity in getting a good story. He brought imagination and resourcefulness into the profession for which he had a boy's romantic delight. However, ironically, Morton's final story on their brief landing in Banska Bystrica had been sent but censored and was never published.[6]

One of the more gruesome details they learned was that on his deathbed after being fatally wounded in a shoot-out with General Patton's soldiers, sadistic Nazi Mauthausen interrogator Franz Ziereis confessed that some of the Dawes men had been beaten, glass slivers had been shoved under their fingernails to make them talk, and that they were submitted to other tortures. And when Wilheim Ornstein, a Polish prisoner who had witnessed the bodies after the execution, turned over to them dog tags from two of the Dawes men that he had kept hidden, it put a final cap on any hopes that Morton had survived.[7]

Her OSS duties fulfilled, Maria checked into the hotel and then set out on the mission her parents had asked her to undertake. They knew how to get in touch with Marta but didn't dare write. Maria made a phone call to the number they gave her to reach her sister and then went to the park nearby on the banks of the Danube to meet a contact. With every passing hour her stay in Bratislava grew more precarious. And she knew that trying to connect with a loose knit underground with many leaks and breaks in its operations was like trying to sift water through a sieve. After waiting most of the day and getting more anxious by the minute, finally an ordinary-appearing and acting young man approached Maria and asked if she was looking for her sister. When she said she was, he led her to Marta's current hideout she shared with the man with whom she was enamored.

Although still a beauty, Maria was shocked at her sister's overall physical appearance. The once-envied burnished auburn curls were faded, and the much admired ivory complexion that admiring swains wrote poetry about had turned dull. More startling was the leaner figure replacing former lush curves, giving her a slightly hard cast. Still present though, was the gleam of purpose that shone in Marta's green eyes. This time it was for the cause of organizing resistance against communists in control who were proving to be even more oppressive than the Germans.[8]

The freedom gained and treasured by Czechoslovakians at the end of World War I was lost in World War II. Democracy was crushed and the law of the jungle prevailed with the strong seizing anything of value. It was no secret that Stalin had had his eyes for a long time on the silver and gold waiting to be harvested from Slovakia's mines, and he was not about to relinquish these or any other of the spoils of war he had seized. Chief among them was the measure of freedom Slovaks had enjoyed, only to have it snatched away and her people consigned to oppression and spoliation far more ghastly than anything in its history.[9]

Maria stayed overnight with her sister, during which she tried to convince Marta to relinquish her incentive to take up battle against the local Slovak communists and their Soviet leaders who had replaced the Nazi oppressors. This far more powerful enemy had the support of Western Allies and would be invincible. Maria pleaded with Marta to come with her and seek asylum in the American jurisdiction. She had fought a good fight, and any new battle opposing communists at this point was hopeless for a long time to come.

It was a pyrrhic victory for Slovaks who were now worse off than they'd been under the Nazis they defeated. Maria had just seen with her own eyes the rapid changes, such as preparations in progress for seizing all private property, with strict communist rules imposed on water, gas, fuel, housing and food. Even the mildest dissidence could result in arrest on flimsy charges and from which there were no appeals. Villagers said of the incoming Soviets, "They broke into homes and killed, stole and raped on a large order." Reports would describe the brutal shooting of husbands and fathers who tried to protect their women and children from Russian soldiers indoctrinated by General Marshal Zhukov to "remember, only the unborn are innocent."[10] The Orthodox churches were plundered, and priests and bishops were murdered or sent to Siberia. The NKVD routinely raided towns and villages and rounded up young women and girls for sex orgies where they were violated and infected with sexually-transmitted diseases.[11]

And although Father Edmund was well known and an opposer of fascism, still, he was a priest and therefore an enemy of communism. There was always the chance that some false accusation would be made against him with the usual tragic results. False charges could be brought against him at any time, leaving his wife and four daughters among those most vulnerable. As she tried to persuade Marta to change her mind, Maria saw the zeal burning ever brighter in her sister's eyes and realized it was futile to try to reason with a zealot, especially one who had resisted fascists and was now centering her sights on communists. Furthermore, Marta declared that the red devils would make every Slovak pay for Tiso's alliance with Hitler and no one would be spared. So she preferred to continue her fight rather than passively await retaliation.

Marta's assessment was on point. There was already a drive against any reaction to the communist takeover in Eastern Europe, with Slovakia the main target. Local communists had already launched investigations into Slovak citizens' political and church activities, with large scale arrests being made. The reign of terror was to be good practice for them.[12]

When the discussion failed to deter Marta in any way, Maria had to give up. Sadly bidding her sister farewell, she made her way back to the hotel, heart laden with concern for both her sister and parents hoping and praying for Marta's return. For Maria, though, the immediate challenge was to pick up her suitcase and belongings and then board the next train out of Slovakia without being detected by the experienced spies of the NKVD.

That organization had numerous ways of tracking down wanted individuals. One method, a very intimidating one, was using the public radio to broadcast announcements. As Maria was walking across the hotel lobby, a musical program was interrupted with an announcement.

"Gita!" the command issued used her code name and was crisp and authoritative. "Report to headquarters at once!" They had traced her and knew exactly where she was, proof that Stalin's orders to place everyone in resistance groups under surveillance remained very much in effect.[13]

Every word on that NKVD agreement Maria had been forced under duress to sign stood out in her memory in huge and ominous black letters. They stated that if she failed to live up to her assignments, she would voluntarily submit to discipline. Maria had witnessed Soviet-type discipline where the barest concept of justice was totally alien, and she would have none of it. She would grab her satchel with its few belongings and run.

The desk clerk, a young woman about Maria's age, glanced furtively around the lobby, and seeing no one else but Maria, beckoned to her. She whispered that two men had inquired about Maria and were waiting in her hotel room.

Murmuring a word of thanks, Maria turned and hurried out into the street and jumped into a passing cab. At the train station, she tried to lose herself in the crowd. But she still elicited curious glances and half expected at any moment to feel a tap on her shoulder. The cars were packed, with standing room only left. She pushed her way into one where she stood in a packed aisle and managed to be concealed from any suspicious onlookers outside by positioning herself behind a large man blocking the window view with heavy arms holding the overhead strap. Only when the train pulled out of the station and picked up speed did she relax a little. She was reasonably hopeful that with the necessary documents she had obtained at home, she would reach Pilsen safely and rejoin the Americans. The city was under Soviet jurisdiction; however, the constant supervision was not yet as rigid as in some other areas.[14]

Maria submitted the report on her mission with Schwartz at the Dukla Pass area to OSS chief Allen Dulles and his deputy, Frank Weisner. Then with trepidation she related the incident with Igor in Jakubiany. The men nodded and did not have to put into words what they all knew: Maria had to be removed from the long tentacles of the NKVD, which was possible only in a totally American jurisdiction. Dulles assured Maria that they would help, which he did quickly by adding her name to the list of people for the next convoy to Salzburg, which was beyond Soviet control. Then, evidently in an effort to cheer her, he wished Maria a happy birthday.

She had forgotten the date. It was November 21 and her 23rd birthday. With a ceremonial touch, Dulles produced a bottle of champagne from a desk drawer and poured the bubbly liquid into three crystal goblets. They toasted her with good wishes and the bottle was emptied in short order.

That night, Maria secreted the fresh document she was given with the name of Maria Davis safely beneath the lining of her purse. She then sewed her birth certificate and school credentials into the sleeves of her WAAC uniform, recalling her father's teachings about heaven and how hard it was to get there. The devil, he warned, tried until the last minute to trip up believers. The Soviets, she was convinced, had apparently taken a course in the devil's tactics, because they, too, remained determined until the last moment to bar her, and any other refugee who might be useful to them, from the promised land of America.[15]

In this instance, rather than crossing the mystical river Styx, Maria had gleaned through a literary course, her goal was to safely cross the barricade erected between Soviet and American areas of jurisdictions, guarded by well armed, flinty-eyed Russian soldiers. When the truck, overflowing with passengers, ground to a stop at the barrier, one officious Slovak soldier sauntered over to accept the manifest with its list of passengers the driver held out. With what seemed to be deliberate snail-like delay, one by one he examined the names before he returned to his post and picked up a phone. He then announced each name to the listener on the other end, after which he carefully inspected the passenger whose name was called out. When Maria began to quake with fear, the driver warned, "Don't show any concern. One wrong look or action and they'll know something is wrong." Surreptitiously he reached over and held her hands tightly together in his to keep them still. Finally, the last name on the list was called out: "Maria Davis."

A long delay followed during which she could not control her trembling. "For God's sake, don't screw it up now!" the driver hissed, squeezing her hands together until they were numb. Maria glanced around with apparent unconcern, but was actually trying to determine which was the better course of action if denied passage. Should she make a run for it now and be shot in the back, or wait to be hauled away to be tortured and then shot? When she felt she could not endure another second of uncertainty, she heard the miraculous words. "All is in order." To Maria, those few simple words in Russian, and then repeated in English, never sounded so beautiful!

The heavy wooden barricade was lifted and the driver, with a jubilant "Let's go, Baby," gunned the engine and whipped the jeep across the strip of

19. A Bronze Medal for Maria   243

no man's land and onto American held territory. He slammed the vehicle to a halt and helped Maria out, at which she collapsed on his shoulder and sobbed with relief. She stopped abruptly when she felt that dreaded tap on the shoulder. But it was not the NKVD; it was an American Army officer wearing a big grin and greeting her with, "We've been expecting you. Welcome to the free world."[16]

* * *

Much of the euphoria that followed her narrow escape faded in the next few weeks. November slowly passed and then December while she waited for the required immigration papers to be processed. It was not until January 7, 1945, that Maria received the necessary documents and climbed aboard a troop ship overflowing with 4,000 service men and 120 women, in LeHavre, France, bound for New York. Two weeks later she stood with other windblown passengers on the deck of the ship for her first glimpse of the Statue of Liberty.

Maria arrived at Vassar College with a letter of acceptance from the college and fifty dollars in her purse. Housing was at a premium in the post war era and she was given a room at the YWCA. Several years older than most of the students, Maria was also light years older in life experiences which created a gulf between her and the other students. She earned her board and meals by waiting on tables in the dining room, which further distanced her. Feeling like a carp out of water, the fish her mother traditionally served at Christmas, she plunged into her studies, especially the English courses. Life became a whirl of classes, waiting tables, study and keeping up with class assignments. One sunny morning months later she lifted her weary head to glance out the library window and was surprised to discover that it was spring. She set aside her work momentarily to gaze out the window and mused on how spring was an annual magical rebirth of the earth. But instead of the feeling of expectancy with which she had always greeted spring, it was merely feeling older with the road before her unclear, but on which she had to keep plodding.[17]

There were more hurdles to overcome. Maria did not fit into any typical bureaucratic peg; therefore, no one knew what to do with her. In her request for more funds to see her through her college stint, a letter from the U.S. Army was sent to Dr. Henry Noble McCracken at Vassar. It stated that the Army had fed and clothed Maria since 1945, obtained a scholarship for her and brought her to the United States, all with their funds. She was never officially employed by the U.S. Army and all this was done in gratitude for her efforts. Perhaps she would like to be a ward of the Army indefinitely and had been told that this was not to be. It concluded with the statement that any further support would have to come from private sources.¹⁸

But that day, her thoughts still somber, she turned back to her books and the assignment only to be interrupted by another student who had come to tell her that the dean wanted to see her immediately. The summons left Maria shaking. It had to be bad news from home or that she was not doing well in her studies. Instead, the dean greeted her with a broad smile.

"Congratulations," she said. "You are asked to be present at a ceremony at West Point Academy to receive an award for heroism. What an honor for Vassar!"

A week later, arrayed in a new pale blue dress and still in somewhat of a daze, on the bright morning of May 25, 1946, Maria and a gathering of viewers stood poised near the parade grounds at West Point Academy waiting for the ceremony to begin. The crowd milled about, watching companies of cadets forming to await the arrival of Generals William Donovan and Maxwell Taylor, and other dignitaries. The crowd grew quiet when General Donovan stepped to a microphone to read a letter of commendation from President Harry Truman over the loudspeaker.

"The President of the United States of America, authorized by special Executive Order, has awarded the Bronze Star medal to Maria Gulovich, Czechoslovak partisan, for meritorious achievement in ground operations against the enemy." He continued:

> Maria Gulovich served as guide and interpreter for members of a special unit organized by the United States and sent with a specific mission to operate in the heart of enemy-held territory in Czechoslovakia from October, 1944 to January, 1945. After the capture and subsequently reported execution of most of the mission's members, she began a trek through enemy-held lines to the Russian forces with a group including two American enlisted men. Scorning the dangers of capture, and surmounting the most severe hardships of exposure to bitter winter weather in the mountainous country, she never weakened and remained a constant source of encouragement and aid to other members of the group. Her knowledge of the terrain and languages, together with her constant willingness to undertake hazardous reconnaissance trips into enemy-infested villages seeking food, shelter and information, made her a priceless asset to the group, which finally reached safety in Russian hands. The mission with which she served contributed intelligence of distinct value to the war effort and, before detection by the Germans, rescued a considerable number of Allied flyers forced down in enemy territory. Maria Gulovich, through her gallant disregard for danger and her faithful, effective performance, was instrumental in making those contributions possible.¹⁹

At its conclusion, Donovan stepped forward to pin the bronze medal on Maria's dress and said, "The dangers you courageously braved and terrible hardships endured bespeak an ardent spirit devoted to freedom and justice. Your cool and determined behavior under enemy fire is matched by skill in negotiating for sustenance in enemy infested areas. I commend you for your exemplary heroism in serving the Dawes mission and the United States of America."

As General Taylor and other dignitaries stepped forward to shake her hand and murmur tributes, the words were half drowned out by the band playing "Stars and Stripes Forever" while cadets in full dress uniform paraded by and a flag fluttered in the breeze high above.[20]

That evening, Maria was feted at a ball where she whirled the evening away with a plethora of cadets curious to find out who this girl was to merit such attention. One of the other girls asked, with some envy, "Do you know who you just danced with?" When Maria professed that she did not know one cadet from another and was told it was Glenn Davis, a famous football star from West Point and who was engaged to the film star Elizabeth Taylor, she remained puzzled, never having heard of either famous American.[21]

A few weeks later Maria was an invited guest to Hyde Park and a tea hosted by Eleanor Roosevelt who greeted her with a handshake, saying, "So you're the heroine of the underground."

Maria felt herself caught up in the special glow surrounding Mrs. Roosevelt and sensed a pervasive power of spirit emanating from the former first lady. When she left the luxurious home of her hostess, her feet barely touched the ground. These honors had been bestowed upon a girl from a remote Slovakian village who had dared to dream of a world of freedom for all but could not have imagined one of such possibilities. Whatever the future held, she was sure it could hardly compare to these honors.[22]

* * *

At the conclusion of the ceremony at West Point, Donovan had instructed Maria to contact him when she graduated and he would find a suitable position for her. It was another sun-filled morning when Maria, Vassar graduation degree tucked in her purse, took a bus to New York City and stopped in at the OSS office, only to be told the general was out of town.

"But he asked to see me," Maria said.

The disinterested young receptionist, gazing at her from under an arched eyebrow, airily replied, "Oh, the general says that to everyone. But no one really knows how to reach him. He just breezes in and out."

Her blithe comments on the general's manner of operations fitted a description of Donovan by one critic as being hyperactive, mercurial and assertive. Some also thought him erratic and unpredictable, albeit charming.[23]

So much for promises, Maria thought as she left the building. The cool reception and rejection was symbolic of words someone once said, "The wise spymaster does not receive or expect a reward." The message was clear; she was now completely on her own.

In her purse was one hundred dollars and an address where she could rent a room from a Czechoslovakian expatriate. But first, she impulsively decided, she would take a side trip to Fifth Avenue about which she had heard so much from Tibor Keszthelyi. She ambled down the street with its fashionable shops and stately buildings, pausing under the awning of a building for a moment to assess her whereabouts. Two young women exiting the front door looked her over before one said with a disdainful sniff, "Another would-be fashion model."

Maria glanced up at the sign on the building that identified it as a John Robert Powers model agency. The very idea of her having any ambition to be a model was too much to even imagine and she almost laughed out loud.

As she made her way to the bus stop, she almost collided with a naval officer who had slowed down to give her a careful and inviting scrutiny. For a moment, her heart stood still. His dark brown hair and smiling brown eyes were so very much like Tibor's. A keen sense of grief, something she had been able to suppress during the long months of study and work, now cut through her armored emotions like a sharp knife. This was the area he'd enjoyed so much, and now he was gone and she was here in his place. The realization ushered in a flood of feelings and memories of the short time they shared together and the twisted reality of their world that had spun so rapidly and mysteriously that it left her for moments feeling disoriented. Now she had to adjust to a new world, one in which Tibor was not present to render help for her as she had for him in that former world.

Nearing the bus stop, words of Keszthelyi's seemed to float back, borne on a breeze that ruffled her hair. "You are the bravest girl I ever met, Maria," he said and crowned his words with a kiss. The remembrance was followed by that of her father, whose parting words were always "*Iz Bohom*" (Go with God). It was a benediction that was accompanied with the sign of the cross and a gentle kiss on the forehead that left the heart mellow and serene. These two extraordinary men had exerted a powerful effect on her and had believed in her as had Lt. Green, the commander of the mission and some other members. Now she must continue to believe in herself, despite being in a strange land far from Czechoslovakia.

19. A Bronze Medal for Maria   247

Walking tall and straight, she paused a moment to look up into the bright blue sky and from some inner source, felt a surge of strength rising. She had gotten this far and prevailed and by the grace of God and the love of her fater and Tibor and the memory of the brave men of the Dawes mission to draw on, she would make it the rest of the way.

Epilogue

As the war in Europe ground towards an agonizing finale, the families of the Dawes men waited anxiously for news about them. On April 8, 1945, the OSS sent letters reporting the men listed as missing in action, giving the families false hope. On May 8, when the war in Europe ended, and the need for secrecy on the mission also ended, Mrs. Harriet Gaul, mother of Lt. Harvey J. Gaul, wrote a letter to General William B. Donovan appealing for more information.[1]

"My mind has been racing all over what you call Central Europe sifting all newspaper articles and weighing all radio news, unable to focus on the one spot of vital interest to us and where Jim went. I have lost ten pounds and my hair turned gray watching every mail for another letter from you — dreading a boy on a bicycle bearing bad news in a telegram. In human kindness, must this suspense continue?"[2]

On May 3, 1945, an early Associated Press news release on the fate of Morton was lost in the deluge of news reports on the impending end of the war. And not until May 30, 1945, did OSS acting director Charles Cheston send a reply to Mrs. Gaul stating that Gaul and his colleagues had been taken to Mauthausen prison, "but beyond that nothing on which we can base a definite statement concerning kin can be made."

He mentioned the Christmas party and Gaul's prayer and sent her a copy. But details on next of kin were limited to capture with no reference made to possible mistreatment or execution.[3] Nor was anything mentioned about the citizens in Polomka being forced to go to the main square and watch the American men being put into trucks. Among them were relatives of Horvath who had warned him to leave the cabin and move on because of the danger of betrayal, but Horvath assured them they were expecting a plane to rescue them. Instead, he would be especially singled out for severe punishment because of his local origins.[4]

To Cheston's letter regarding the capture, Mrs. Gaul wrote back: "In my darkest premonition I did not imagine anything so disheartening as that ambush right after their Christmas party. Someone must have betrayed them. Perhaps it was their footsteps in the snow."[5]

The investigation of Lt. O'Neill and the Associated Press' Lynn Neizerling, a colleague of Morton's, was completed June 4, 1945. It was reviewed by various OSS officials and finally sent by Director Cheston to Brigadier General John Weir. By July 26, there was enough evidence available to report the men as having been murdered. But the facts remained so fuzzy that as late as October 30, 1945, Congressman Sol Bloom was trying at the behest of a friend of Green's to obtain information about Green's fate.[6]

After contacting other families of the Dawes men and a relentless, frustrating pursuit to learn the true story, Mrs. Gaul wrote a poignant letter to Cheston. "The whole thing seems to be a history of narrow margins where things went wrong instead of right. So many 'ifs.' The only thing I am glad about is that if Jim had to die for some other country, it was Czechoslovakia, for that is where his heart was. He was called there — a fate — and because we sold them down the river in Neville Chamberlain's day, it wipes out our shame — our best and finest did try to do Something!"[7]

Her statement concurs with that of others who had noted Gaul's special regard for Czechoslovakia and how eager he was to be involved in its development.[8]

* * *

The small country which Gaul so admired lies in the heart of Central Europe and existed in an uneasy state in the immediate post-war period. It was too small for independence and too important to be left alone — an ethnic node between Germany and Russia — destined for sovereignty or subjection.[9]

But Czechoslovakia remained a prize. Its fourteen million people enjoyed an economy well balanced between agriculture and industry and its workmen were the finest in Europe. There was little war damage and technical know-how was advanced.[10]

However, it was the fate of Slovakia to bear the brunt of retaliation from vengeful Soviets. Formerly the most balanced economic unit in Europe, the Slovak National Uprising reduced it to beggary — the cost astronomical for trains, planes, tanks, weapons, food, ammunition, railroad cars, etc. Rebels murdered four to five thousand Slovaks and buried them in mass graves. The Jews, who until August 1, 1944, found relative safety in Slovakia, were pursued and dragged off to concentration camps. The uprising cost 20,000 lives and debt escalated when the state of Slovakia, on May 8, 1945, ceased to exist.[11]

With the end of Slovakia as a separate republic, it was open to local communists to take control of Bratislava, the capitol city. Party members who had done nothing during the war and holed up all those years to save their hides for the day of victory intended to rule the city and were successful in doing so.[12]

In a drive to stamp out any adverse reaction to the communist takeover, the main targets of the communist regime were those involved in political or church activities. Large scale arrests and a reign of terror began as Marta had warned Maria.[13] Because of his position as supervisor of ten parishes, the communist government wanted Greek Catholic priest Father Edmund to use his influence to convert his priests to Orthodoxy. When he refused, he was kidnapped; a bag was put over his head and he was driven to a camp in West Slovakia where the Nazis held their prisoners and was forced to labor as a stoker of a furnace. For weeks his family did not know where he was until someone they knew saw him in jail and told his wife.

Anastasia was given eight days to vacate their home of 23 years and, not being in the work force, was not assigned housing. A friend found housing for them in Presiva. She and Father Edmund were declared "enemies of the people" and from 1949 until 1953, they remained on internal exile. They were never allowed to return to Jakubiany.[14]

But the worst for Slovakia was yet to come. It began in 1948 when the coalition government headed by Edvard Beneš, who had returned from exile in London, was dissolved. Local communists staged a coup and marched on Hrdcany castle where Beneš was staying. He died on September 3, 1948, and Jan Masyrk also perished with questions about his demise never completely resolved. Czechoslovakia then fell under complete control of communist leaders in Moscow.[15]

Slovak citizens who had helped or collaborated with Americans were still being sought and labeled as traitors. One of the Americans rescued by Slovak natives was Roy Madden, among the twenty-eight airmen evacuated from Banska Bystrica on October 7, 1944. He and his crew were shot down in September 1944 near the German-Czech border en route to bomb Bleckheimer, Germany. The pilot was killed and one man captured, but Madden and the rest of the ten-man crew had gotten out of the plane alive when a boy suddenly appeared. He spoke no English and they no Czech. He gestured for them to follow him to a barn where they would stay the night. Later an older boy appeared with bread and some food. The next night he took them to another barn where they were to hide. Slowly, some underground partisans, led by Slovak partisan Pavel Harustiak, gathered their crew and additional airmen together and transported about thirty of them by truck and ferry boat to Banska Bystrica and turned them over to Green. He immediately radioed Bari and arranged for their evacuation on October 7. The quick, capable way he ferreted them out was something that co-pilot Robert Newburgh never forgot. And he would always remember the courtesy of the people in Banska Bystrica and how safe the Americans felt with them.[16]

Roy Madden also never forgot partisan Pavel Harustiak, who later escaped to Vienna. Newly married, he risked returning to Slovakia to get his wife. Instead, he was captured and shot. His wife was stripped of all benefits and had to live in penury. She never remarried.

In 1948, the two boys who had helped Madden and his crew were working on their farm one day when two Gestapo-like men drove up. Their younger brother was in the field but out of sight. Warning him to hide, they continued working until they were mowed down in a blaze of gunfire.[17]

Honored posthumously are Pavel Harustiak and his group of partisans who rescued many downed Allied airmen at risk of their own lives and those of their families. Among the Americans saved was Roy Madsen and the crew of 10 that Harustiak and his fellow partisans rescued. Later, trying to rescue his wife, Harustiak was captured and shot (courtesy of the Harustiak family).

Madden was so taken with the courage and kindness of the Slovak people he met that he was determined to return to Slovakia. After learning the Slovak language in six months, in 1947, as part of a Mormon missionary team, he volunteered to work with the Slovak people for two years, but had to leave when the communists seized control a year later. He went back once more in 1994 to look up the boys who had helped him and his plane's crewmates and learned of their tragic fate. Sadly, the younger brother who survived the killings had since died. Madden was given the pilot's parachute, helmet and goggles that had been buried, and he sent them to the pilot's family.[18]

The fate of Generals Viest and Golian remained a mystery with many rumors and various accounts of their end circulating for years until an article appeared in a Slovak newspaper with bits of information on what happened in their final days. As that story reported, on November 2, 1944, seeing the cause of the revolt hopeless, the two generals tried to flee to Russia. They had arrived in the village of Bukovec with a small contingency of Slovak partisans, mostly young student supporters, and intended to continue their journey the next day. They would find a safe crossing of the Hron River and continue to the village of Ondrey (St. Andrew) and then proceed east to meet up with the oncoming arrival of the Red Army.[19]

One of their key men, Captain Steiner, posed as a beggar by wearing a tattered old coat over his uniform. He was greeted warmly by a group of German soldiers and offered something to eat. He ate with them and then continued to an empty house where he intended to hide. Believing he was safe, he removed the top coat, revealing his uniform. German guards who had followed him burst into the house and tortured him until he revealed the location of Viest and Golian.[20]

German soldiers then surrounded the village, raided several houses and threatened to shoot those held at gunpoint and burn the village. At that point, the two generals, hiding in the home of Josephina Rypakova, came forward and surrendered to save the lives and property of the villagers. Viest and Golian were said to have been taken to Germany and executed. Captain Steiner was also reported as executed in a prisoner of war camp in Flossenburg, Germany, in 1945.[21]

The father of Mira Mullen was one of the ten men who plotted the assassination of SS chief Reinhard Heydrich, whom Hitler called "the man with the iron heart." A group of six called the Anthropoids was given the assignment. Heydrich was ambushed near the Hrdcany castle, and lingered between life and death for three days. This high-ranking Nazi who had eliminated two million people in Poland in six months, had just arrived in Slovakia to oversee the genocide of remaining Jews in Slovakia. The assassination sent Hitler into such a frenzy that when three of the Anthropoids were traced to the village of Lidice, Hitler ordered the entire village to be destroyed. Five hundred men, women and children were rounded up and died in fusillades of bullets and then the entire village burned. The Anthropoids escaped and hid in crypts in the Karol Barromeaus Greek Orthodox Church until betrayed for a reward. Trapped inside the basement, the men shot each other rather than waiting to be tortured and then executed by the Nazis.[22]

Mullen had been a famous Czech athlete and was in charge of the International Bank where he associated with heads of states. On his own, he had created secret compartments in the attic and basement of their family home in which American escapees were hidden. Mira's sister was ten years old when the Gestapo came to question him. They drank out of his unique World Fair crystal goblets given as an award, then tossed them in the fireplace, and proceeded to tear up rare books and search the entire house for an American pilot suspected of being in the vicinity. They hung Mira's ten-year-old sister by the heels until her mother became hysterical, but neither she nor the child knew of the compartments and could not tell the brutes anything. Fortunately, the American pilot secreted in the basement that day was not discovered.[23]

Mullen came to the United States in 1946 and Mira was born in 1954. She was eight years old during the Cuban Missile Crisis and her father taught her to drive in the event he was wounded and could not save her. He did work for the Central Intelligence Agency and in 1975, posing as a businessman, was imprisoned by communists who knocked out all his teeth. A friend in the CIA managed to get him released but he was a broken man whose wife had divorced him. On his deathbed he wept over the murdered innocent victims of Lidice while Mira comforted him by pointing out that the death of the monster Heydrich saved the lives of thousands. Her father had told her many times that the people in villages and close to the land have compassion, and he especially grieved for those who perished in Lidice. Mira assured him that they were exactly the kind of people saved by Heydrich's death.[24]

The fate of Tiso was considered another tragedy for many. His aim had been to avoid bloodshed and the German occupation of Slovakia. He planned to have the Slovak Army take over the government at an opportune time — with the fall of Cracow in the north, Miskovec in the South — and allow a new political party to be established temporarily until the United Nations was formed and then turn it over to them. General Augustine Molor revealed the plan to Soviet military staff in Ukraine and asked for political independence for Slovakia. The Soviets were willing to reorganize the kind of independence the Slovaks had in 1939 — but insisted that the Red Army join the Slovak Army in the deal, which then never materialized.[25]

The Jewish question had been a heavy load for Tiso with such continual pressure from Germany that it threatened to sink the Slovak ship of state. However, Jews who remained in Slovakia seem to have been comparatively safe until August 1944 when the revolt erupted. Tiso had saved 35,000 to 40,000 Jews from deportation, but when the revolt failed and Slovakia was occupied by the Germans, those who did not flee to the mountains were turned over to the Nazis to be pursued.[26]

Tiso was captured with members of his cabinet while seeking asylum in a monastery near Bratislava. He surrendered to the Allies and was put on trial in Germany, his destiny decided by a jury that included several local communists. The jury sentenced him to death and he was hanged on April 1, 1947. His death caused few media ripples, the main one from Congressman

Alvin O. Konski in his speech to the House of Representatives protesting the murder of Tiso who had given aid and comfort to Allied men trapped behind enemy lines in Slovakia.[27] Journalist Edward Delaney, who had become acquainted with Tiso while visiting Slovakia, wrote that his execution was a grave injustice.

* * *

The life story of General Andrej Andreevich Vlasov contains enough drama for several classic films. The son of a village tailor, he graduated from an Orthodox seminary but opposed his father's wishes for him to become a priest. He was early impressed with Lenin's promises to the people and was motivated to take a military training course, after which he was sent to the front. He served brilliantly in China, and received the Order of Lenin award, and he quickly rose in the military ranks. Summoned to Moscow to meet with General Zhukov and Stalin, he was given the almost impossible task of saving Moscow from the Nazis battering the city. Accorded only fifteen planes and scarce weaponry, he nevertheless succeeded and then went on to save beleaguered Leningrad and received the Red Banner award.[28]

There, Vlasov's eyes were opened. His men were starving and the people did not want to fight for Stalin and Bolshevism. On March 19, 1942, they surrendered en masse to the Germans. His army was encircled and Vlasov was captured and sent to a POW camp in Ukraine. While there he learned in a coded letter from his wife, sneaked to him in prison by a friend, that the NKVD had searched his home in his absence. Disillusioned, he realized at that point that no one was safe from the communist vise he was finding to be most cumbersome. He had his fill of Bolshevism.

He was debriefed by the Germans and when offered a chance to fight the Bolsheviks, he thought it was possible with German help. He co-operated with them on the condition that this was a liberation and not a conquest. However, he received little actual assistance from the Wehrmacht in his service as commander of the Russian Liberation Army (ROA) he was permitted to establish. One of his first acts was to compose a document titled the *Smolensk Manifesto* and disseminated copies. It called for abolition of forced labor camps, collective farms, termination of the reign of terror and demanded justice. This was a revolutionary bombshell and he was hailed as a messiah as thousands rushed to join his army. Since his army never accepted the Nazi doctrines, he was initially welcomed by the West in 1943 and 1944. That changed when he made it clear he wanted to fight Stalinism, thereby receiving the condemnation of the West, which was allied with Stalin.[29]

On January 28, 1945, Hitler entrusted Vlasov to the position of high command over his military forces of the Committee for Liberation of the Peoples of Russia, which became operational in March 1945. In a surprise turn, Vlasov then proceeded, without German approval, to move towards Czechoslovakia. On May 5, 1945, his army liberated Prague and was hailed as heroes and welcomed with gifts and flowers. An account of this feat appeared in the *Saturday Evening Post*, saying, "Prague was really liberated by foreign troops after all, not by the Allies, who did not arrive until the shooting was all over, but by 22,000 Russian outlaws wearing German uniforms. The leader of the renegades is General Andrei Vlasov, a former hero of the Red Army."[30]

However, when the Czechs set up a provisional government, Vlasov was rejected in favor of General Ivan Konev's army, which was chosen to march into Prague as liberators. So on May 8, 1945, Vlasov and his army marched south to Pilsen to negotiate with the Americans while an impatient General Patton remained poised on the sidelines, also prepared to march triumphantly into Prague. Over the radio, the Czechs implored him, "Prague is asking for help ... Prague is asking for help."[31] But no help arrived. General Eisenhower stopped Patton from proceeding as conqueror to favor Stalin's wish to have Gen. Zhukov take the city.[32]

Vlasov looked for a way out of the trap closing around his men, and on May 10, 1945, met with an American general who was sympathetic but told him he could not guarantee them non-repatriation to the Soviets. On May 11, 1945, he learned his division had surrendered their arms and were now prisoners of war, with the area scheduled to be turned over to the Soviets the next day. The general offered Vlasov the chance to save himself by fleeing to the British zone, but instead, he rejoined his division. He pointed out to the American general that the men in his division were not volunteers for German service; rather they were a political organization which should be treated according to accepted laws of war. But the American commander-in-chief refused to accept him or his men as prisoners of war and Vlasov's deputy gave his last order to the division: dismissed.[33]

Panic ensued. Shots were heard in nearby forests fired by men preferring death to repatriation to Russia. Celebrated by the Czechs only days before, they were now hunted and turned over to the Soviets. Leaving the castle where he had stayed pending negotiations, Vlasov was betrayed by an ROA captain to save himself. Their car was stopped and a Soviet commissar aimed his pistol at Vlasov who opened his jacket and said, "Fire!" To which the commissar replied, "Not I — Comrade Stalin will judge you."

Before he was led away, Vlasov's representative was accorded a meeting with General Alexander Patch, commander of the U.S. 7th Army. Vlasov did not ask for his own safety but that of the million men who joined his liberation movement to free Russia from communism. He requested political asylum and appealed to the American people who believe in the idea of freedom. Patch was ready to accept them under the same conditions as German war prisoners but American higher command declared Vlasov as no longer possessing the status as bearer of a flag of truce and was now a prisoner of war.[34]

U.S. General Kennedy, on his own, was ready to accept him and his men and promised not to repatriate them. On April 27, 1945, members of Vlasov's air force marched into Muensinger, near Stuttgart, and laid down their arms. But Kennedy's pledge to Vlasov and his men was not to be honored. In an operation devised at Yalta known as "Operation Keelhaul," most of Vlasov's 900,000 soldiers were forcibly repatriated to Russia.[35]

The move began in February 1946 when one of the refugee camps inhabited by 3,000 veterans of the ROA was encircled by American troops. At 5:00 A.M., searchlights were turned on and trucks arrived. All those in the Russian barracks were ordered outside to form ranks. They were searched, their possessions confiscated and tossed into the mud: watches, bread and a last pencil. A list of names was read, and they were prodded onto trucks and ordered to lie down. American soldiers with billy clubs and machine guns climbed into the trucks beside them and forbade the prisoners to move. They were driven to cattle car trains and forced into them. The only escapees were those who had sewed razor blades into their coats and slashed their wrists. This was repeated in almost every camp and there was no reason given, or mercy, or hope. The U.S. Third Army soldiers had orders to shoot and kill those unwilling to return.[36]

Vlasov and eight of his leaders were indicted for treason, espionage and terrorist activities against the Soviet Union and in providing service to the German intelligence service. On April 19, 1946, they were condemned to death by hanging. On August 2, 1946, the Russian periodical *Izvestia* reported that the sentence had been carried out and that Vlasov's severed head was placed on exhibition in Moscow's Red Square.[37]

* * *

The unique story about the participation of American men in the Slovak National Uprising quickly passed into post-war oblivion with the survivors of the Dawes mission, like millions of ex–military men, picking up the threads of their lives. Then in August of 1964, the five men were summoned by the State Department to return to Slovakia to participate in a 20th anniversary celebration of the Slovak National Uprising event planned by the Soviets. Lain, Schwartz, MacGregor and Catlos accepted but Dunlevy refused to attend.[38]

A smiling Kenneth Dunlevy receives a citation in Washington, D.C., for his service in the Dawes Mission (courtesy Maria Gulovich Liu).

Like his colleagues, the State Department speedily propelled Catlos through the normally time consuming process of obtaining passport photos, a passport and other travel documents. He was flown to New York where he joined MacGregor, Lain and Schwartz waiting to embark on their flight to Europe.

At the disembarkations in Paris, Stuttgart and Vienna, there were treated royally. On August 28, which was the 20th anniversary of the onset of the Slovak National Uprising, the American Consulate in Vienna provided them with money and they were briefed on the current situation in Czechoslovakia. A newspaper front page story with their photos was placed on the table and Catlos read it, surprised to see how much was known about them. He decided against keeping the paper or even taking it into Czechoslovakia and left it on the table.

In Bratislava, a translator was waiting and escorted them to a nice hotel where they enjoyed a sumptuous meal, courtesy of communist officials. They even displayed a small American flag in the center of the table, the first time an American flag had been publicly displayed in Bratislava in twenty years.

The four men rented a car and on their drive to Banska Bystrica, they stopped at various villages and encountered locals in pubs and beer halls who could not do enough for the visiting Americans. Nearing Banska Bystrica, where people were being bused in for the anniversary event, traffic was gridlock. They took a side trip to the lodge at Donavaly, where they had stopped in 1944 before taking flight into the mountains, and they met Hungarian, Czech, French and other partisans who welcomed them cordially. They were given rooms on the second floor and stayed overnight. Catlos looked around the village with keen interest to see that nothing much had changed. Bullet holes were still in the walls and the surrounding land was parched and neglected, a notable contrast to the crisp, green, well-tended lawns in Austria.

They arrived in Banska Bystrica on August 30, but Catlos' luggage did not. He had to purchase some clothing and was amazed to discover that he could have his new pants altered within the hour. They were finished just in time for them to meet with Russian premier Nikita Kruschchev, who arrived with a military escort and was to present them with medals of honor. The crowd of a hundred thousand or more was so dense and disorderly that even the guards assigned to get the Americans to the podium could not force their way through. The Americans became separated with Lain and Catlos ending up in a building that housed the NKVD. They were offered drinks and watched the program from there, after which they were escorted to the banquet. By then, the speeches had ended but the crowd was able to acknowledge the Americans publicly. A couple of Hun-

At the State Department reunion in 1964, Steven Catlos receives the Medal of Honor by a Slovak official for his contributions to the mission. Kenneth Dunlevy declined to attend, and Maria Gulovich was not invited (courtesy the Catlos family).

A sightseeing tour of Banska Bystrica before the reunion: left to right, John Schwartz, Kenneth Lain, Slovak hostess, William MacGregor, Slovak official, and Steven Catlos (courtesy the Catlos family).

garian generals tried to persuade Catlos to go into Hungary but he refused, pointing out that his passport was for Czechoslovakia only. Besides, from what he had already seen, he placed little merit in their assurances of safety.

The four former OSS agents did not receive medals from Kruschchev. In fact, they got several letters threatening them if they accepted any Russian medals. At one point, Catlos began to hand out President John F. Kennedy's half dollars, which were a huge hit. He later laughingly said that he had never been kissed on the cheeks so much in his life and there was no doubt that the natives loved President Kennedy and wanted the Russians out.

When the crowd dispersed somewhat, MacGregor, spotting General Velichko, pushed his way towards the Russian and held out a hand to greet him. He was met with a stony glance and the statement, "I do not recognize you," as Velichko brushed by him. This time the icy atmosphere was totally different than the acceptance, albeit lukewarm, he had given MacGregor and the mission when they arrived in Slovakia twenty years earlier.[39]

Catlos could hardly wait until the event ended. He had his own agenda, which was to get away in time to return to the United States and attend his son's graduation from a U.S. Army boot camp. He was driven to Bratislava and reached the border at 11:00 P.M. Since no vehicles were permitted on the road after dark, Catlos had to walk the half mile to the crossing alone on a dark cobble-stoned road in the middle of mined areas where a misstep could be his last.

At the guard station, the officials would not release him because he had signed to rent a car and the car had to be delivered before he could leave. Catlos' explanation that his three fellow Americans would do so fell on deaf ears until he was allowed to make a phone call and a higher official accepted his credentials and ordered his release. At that, the thwarted captain of the guards sneeringly asked him how he would get to Vienna without transportation if they did let him cross. Catlos gestured toward the lone car marked with a Consulate General sign plainly visible, parked outside the border gates with lights on and engine running. Obviously it could be for no one but Catlos. He dashed to the waiting car that whisked him back into the land of freedom but not before further questioning, this time on friendlier grounds. On the way home he pondered on the fact that getting out of Slovakia the second time was easier, but it still was risky business. Sadly, he noted how much freer Czechoslovakia had been in 1944 than it was in 1994.

He spent the next day trying to reserve a seat on a plane to New York, all of them fully booked. Again he produced credentials that impressed the necessary officials enough to hold up a plane ready to take off after bumping a passenger to make room for Catlos. He arrived in Pittsburgh near midnight and was besieged by newspaper and television reporters waiting to interview him. After a day of rest, he proceeded to the Great Lakes area to see his son graduate.[40]

Catlos and Dunlevy remained friends but neither ever saw or spoke to Maria again. Ironically, Dunlevy was on a field trip in 1962 for his employer to the small California town where she lived, but since Maria had been told to keep a low profile, he had no way of knowing her whereabouts and thus, like ships that pass in the night, they were in close proximity to each other geographically but kept far apart by circumstances.[41]

Maria had been sought out by Mrs. Harriet Gaul and did meet with her and her daughter to talk of Lieutenant Harvey Gaul. They were avid for every detail she could muster. On one occasion she met with the family of Lieutenant James Holt Green and on another, with the uncle of Tibor Keszthelyi, who was eager to hear the story of their time together and about the tragic mission. Finding the repeated telling painful, Maria welcomed her retreat into a private life as wife of a former naval lieutenant in a small California town where fellow residents and neighbors had no idea she was the first woman awarded the Bronze star for heroism and honored by a full dress parade at West Point.[42]

Lain returned to Illinois, MacGregor to Florida, and Schwartz to New York and neither Catlos nor Dunlevy ever saw them again.[43]

Watching the uprising anniversary events on a television set was young Jan Kristak, who had heard about the Hungarian-speaking American soldier that his mother and grandparents hid in the barn and the house and was sure Catlos was the one. Kristak wished he could be at the event to meet the American in person and hear his story, but he had to be content with the knowledge that the tales told him by his mother, Anna, about close calls she and his grandparents encountered in hiding Catlos in their house are real. He hoped that one day Catlos would return and he could meet the American hero face to face, but Catlos never returned to Slovakia.[44]

Maria, an American citizen and married with two children, remained on the NKVD Most Wanted list and was not invited to the event nor mentioned in any of the media reports.

* * *

A number of postmortems on the Slovak National Uprising have been expressed in writing and discussed with various conjectures given as to why the revolt failed.

One view was that morale was low, the revolt unorganized, and many Slovak citizens refused to destroy the state. There was little assistance from Beneš or anyone else, the partisans did not have enough weapons, planes, food or other supplies to fight, and thousands deserted after Donavaly when the revolt crumbled.[45]

In their OSS report and in interviews, Catlos and Dunlevy described being selected for the mission only ten days before take-off with no briefing on CFI operations, topography, weather, political or economic conditions in the area and little idea of the purpose of the mission. It was good for security, but bad for morale.[46]

In a letter to the author, one Slovak researcher pointed out that the uprising was not well prepared and there was no real help from any side. It was lost from the beginning, but was a political success because Slovaks had identified with the Allies and did eventually succeed in obtaining a measure of democracy on the basis of equality with the Czechs.[47]

Others point out that it was naive to think that Germany would respect rules of the Geneva Convention regarding American prisoners suspected of being spies simply because they were in uniform. Also there was little knowledge of the terrain, and hiding and evading became an urgent logistics problem. It was possible to hide six or seven men, but not thirty-seven as it turned out.[48]

Fingers were pointed and questions raised as to why war correspondent Morton and Paris, a naval photographer, who were not part of the mission, were permitted to board a 15th Air Force plane and for Morton to change his mind about returning on October 7 as planned. His decision to stay in Banska Bystrica sealed his fate. And why was Morton, with no training for a military intelligence mission, allowed to join the high level of a mission such as Dawes anyway?[49]

Others stated that the OSS foray into Czechoslovakia was a mission ill conceived and planned and that those who returned were lucky — they survived the revolt that failed.[50]

Perhaps the most realistic summation is that "the mission was a needless loss of lives with the men ill prepared to take on an operation of the magnitude of the Dawes mission with ancillary Day and Houseboat thrown in for good measure."[51]

By 1948, Donovan, who had early on volunteered to share OSS agents' identities with the Russians, apparently had a change of opinion about the Soviets and was to say in a warning regarding Czechoslovakia "that the USSR was now their and our enemy where there were no rules and no mercy."[52]

World War II is now fading into history and the current situation in this still new century shows considerable changes in Czechoslovakia. Heretofore, the Czech Republic, always in the forefront of any progress in central and eastern Europe, is again enjoying a renaissance of the arts and literature with Prague a prime choice for writers and artists to vacation or live. However, for the first time, the formerly neglected area of the Slovak Republic, with its spectacular mountains and rich agricultural plains, is eagerly sought out by foreign interests for development into resort areas and industry and the Slovak Republic is also flourishing.[53]

Perhaps, the words of hope from CFI partisan commander Vavro Rysovy, who had been active in the Slovak National Uprising, wrote in his book *Zilina* should be considered by Slovak leaders: "One day when Czechoslovakia is free, the names of Green, Gaul, Horvath, Mican, Perry, Heller, Keszthelyi, Miller, MacGregor, Lain, Schwartz, Baranski, Novak, Paveltich, Catlos, Heller, Dunlevy, Morton and Paris, would be emblazoned in Czech and Slovak history as a gallant force who paid a heavy toll for volunteering to help a small country in their struggle for freedom."[54]

That may require more than gratitude or good wishes to achieve if the reports from friends who returned to live in Slovakia after residing in the United States for decades are to be noted as a general prevailing attitude. "Neither the older or younger generation alike show an interest in the Slovak National Uprising and the reality of its cost."[55]

In contrast, accounts of the uprising in American books state boldly that "it was a high, terrible price to pay for a bold operation — but such a price was paid by the Dawes mission."[56]

One can only hope that the words of tribute spoken by President Dwight D. Eisenhower to a gathering of Slovak Americans celebrating the anniversary of the Slovak National Uprising in 1950, will become familiar to every Czech and Slovak: "I am proud of the fact that members of the United States Armed Forces did take part in this Uprising. Thanks to that fact, the friendship between the United States and Czechoslovakia has been sealed by the blood shed for a common cause."[57]

May the memory of those courageous heroes of the Dawes mission who paid the supreme sacrifice for the cause of freedom be eternal.

* * *

Chapter Notes

Prologue

1. Brown, *Wild Bill Donovan*, 48.
2. Ibid.
3. Churchill, *Closing the Ring*, 43.
4. Goldston, *Sinister Touches*, 86.
5. Brown, *Wild Bill Donovan*, 6.
6. Mikus, *Slovakia and the Slovaks*, 165.
7. Snyder, *The War: A Concise History*, 84.
8. Halaf and Tacka, *We Were Not Alone*, 48.
9. Rysovy, *Zilina and the Slovak National Uprising*, 131.
10. Jelenick, *The Parish Republic*, 5.
11. Snyder, *The War: A Concise History*, 84–95.
12. *Last Secrets of the Axis*, The History Channel, November 11, 2003.
13. *Slovakia at the Crossroads*, 192.
14. Korec, "The Cross in the Snares of Power," *Slovakia Quarterly*, September-December 1954: 94.
15. Durica, *Slovakia During World War II*, 184.
16. *Slovakia at the Crossroads*, 192.
17. Rysovy, *Zilina and the Slovak National Uprising*, 131.
18. Durica, *Slovakia During World War II*, 171.
19. Brown, *Wild Bill Donovan*, 621.
20. Ibid.
21. Brown, *Bodyguard of Lies*, 277.

Chapter 1

1. Hymoff, *OSS in World War II*, 83.
2. Brown, *Bodyguard of Lies*, 277.
3. Jelenick, *The Parish Republic*, 94.
4. Korec, "The Cross in the Snares of Power," *Slovakia Quarterly*, September-December 1954: 105.
5. Brown, *Bodyguard of Lies*, 112.
6. Zlamal, *The Partisan Captain*, 100.
7. Delaney, "I Met President Tito," *Slovakia Annual* 22, no. 40: 22.
8. Maria Gulovich, interview, April 11, 1990.
9. *U.S. Stars and Stripes*, September 11, 1992.
10. Maria Gulovich, interview, April 25, 1990.
11. Brown, *Bodyguard of Lies*, 107.
12. Maria Gulovich, interview, April 25, 1990.
13. Ibid.
14. Ibid.
15. Ibid.
16. Ibid.
17. Marion Cizarik, interview, April 25, 1990.
18. Jelenick, *The Parish Republic*, 100.
19. Maria Gulovich, interview, April 25, 1990.
20. Goldston, *Sinister Touches*, 81.
21. Ibid.
22. Maria Gulovich, interview, May 5, 1990.
23. Kelley and Mini, *Memories of the National Slovak Uprising*, 63.
24. Maria Gulovich, interview, May 5, 1990.
25. Ibid.
26. Jelenick, *The Parish Republic*, 69.
27. Maria Gulovich, interview, May 17, 1990
28. Rysovy, *Zilina and the Slovak National Uprising*, 129.
29. Ed Gray, *Los Angeles Herald-Examiner*, September 9, 1992.
30. Keegan, *The Second World War*, 506.
31. Maria Gulovich, interview, May 17, 1990.
32. Alcorn, *No Bugles for Spies*, 46.
33. Maria Gulovich, interview, May 17, 1990.
34. DeLaney, *Five Decades Before Dawn*, 112.
35. Kirschbaum, *The Anniversary of the Slovak National Uprising of 1944*, 192.
36. Maria Gulovich, interview, May 19, 1990.
37. Ibid.
38. Brown, *Wild Bill Donovan*, 527.
39. Hrabak, "Slovak National Uprising of 1944," 11–12.
40. Korec, "The Cross in the Snares of Power," *Slovakia Quarterly*, September-December 1954: 94.
41. Brown, *Wild Bill Donovan*, 209.
42. Baldwin, *Battles Lost and Won*, 75.
43. Keegan, *The Second World War*, 484.
44. Ibid.
45. Victor Frudenfels, letter, August 5, 1992.
46. Maria Gulovich, interview, May 19, 1990.
47. Zlamal, *The Partisan Captain*, 38.
48. Hrabak, "Slovak National Uprising of 1944," 12–13.
49. Maria Gulovich, interview, May 19, 1990.

50. Ibid.
51. Zlamal, *The Partisan Captain*, 37.
52. Maria Gulovich, interview, May 28, 1990.
53. Zlamal, *The Partisan Captain*, 37.
54. Maria Gulovich, interview, May 28, 1990.
55. Zlamal, *The Partisan Captain*, 38.
56. Maria Gulovich, interview, May 28, 1990.
57. Ibid.
58. Durica, *Slovakia During World War II*, 182.
59. Orwell, *Homage to Catalonia*, 47.
60. Victor Frudenfels, letter, August 5, 1992.
61. Rysovy, *Zilina and the National Slovak Uprising*, 44.
62. Ford, *Donovan of the OSS*, 340.
63. Durica, *Slovakia During World War II*, 171–172.
64. DeLaney, *Harvest of Deceit*, 65.
65. Rysovy, *Zilina and the National Slovak Uprising*, 144.
66. Ibid.
67. Zlamal, *The Partisan Captain*, 67.
68. Rysovy, *Zilina and the National Slovak Uprising*, 144.
69. Kirschbaum, *The Anniversary of the Slovak National Uprising of 1944*, 192.
70. DeLaney, *Harvest of Deceit*, 65.
71. Brown, *Bodyguard of Lies*, 108.
72. Halaf and Tacka, *We Were Not Alone*, 159.
73. Maria Gulovich, interview, May 19, 1990.

Chapter 2

1. Jelenick, *The Parish Republic*, 125.
2. Dunlop, *Donovan: Wartime Spymaster*, 336.
3. Licko, *USA v. Banskej Bystrici rok: 1944*, 3.
4. Brown, *Wild Bill Donovan*, 165.
5. Hymoff, *OSS in World War II*, 183.
6. Licko, *USA v. Banskej Bystrici rok: 1944*, 3.
7. Brown, *Wild Bill Donovan*, 527.
8. Hymoff, *OSS in World War II*, 183.
9. Ibid.
10. Halaf and Tacka, *We Were Not Alone*, 13.
11. Rysovy, *Zilina and the National Slovak Uprising*, 160–161.
12. Persico, *Piercing the Reich*, 117.
13. Ford, *Donovan of the OSS*, 324.
14. Brown, *Wild Bill Donovan*, 209.
15. Dunnigan, *Dirty Little Secrets of World War II*, 26.
16. Hymoff, *OSS in World War II*, 185–186.
17. Ibid.
18. Report of Dawes Orders for Lt. James Holt Green, January 14, 1945.
19. Goldston, *Sinister Touches*, 116.
20. Debriefing report on Lt. John Schwartz, January 14, 1945.
21. Richard Grey, interview, August 8, 1990.
22. Ibid.
23. Ibid.
24. Ibid.
25. Licko, *USA v. Banskej Bystrici rok: 1944*, 5.
26. Col. Gilbert Pritchard, report on flight to Tri Duby Airfield, October 14, 1944.
27. Lt. Howard Dallman, interview, October 12, 1997.
28. Ibid.
29. Hymoff, *OSS in World War II*, 186.
30. Col. Gilbert Pritchard, report on arrival at Tri Duby Airfield, October 14, 1945.
31. Sgt. Kenneth Dunlevy, interview, January 18, 1991.
32. Operational History of Dawes Mission, January 24, 1945.
33. Sgt. Kenneth Dunlevy, interview, January 8, 1991.
34. Licko, *USA v. Banskej Bystrici rok: 1944*, 6.
35. OSS report on capture of Anglo-Americans, January 13, 1945.
36. Hymoff, "The Revolt that Failed," *SAGA Magazine*, 42.
37. Directions from Supreme Headquarters Allied Expeditionary Forces, September 9, 1944.
38. Lt. Green, OSS report to Col. Howard Chapin, September 27, 1944.
39. Licko, *USA v. Banskej Bystrici rok: 1944*, 4.
40. Fedornak, *Partizan*, 39.
41. Hymoff, *OSS in World War II*, 187.
42. Licko, *USA v. Banskej Bystrici rok: 1944*, 4.
43. Ibid.
44. Ibid.
45. Hymoff, *OSS in World War II*, 187.
46. Lt. Howard Dallman, interview, January 1, 1995.
47. Ibid.
48. Ibid.
49. Ibid.
50. Lt. Fred Asconti, report on landing problem at Tri Duby Airfield, October 7, 1944.
51. Lt. Howard Dallman, interview, January 1, 1995.
52. Richard Grey, interview, September 12, 1991.
53. S/Sgt. Steven Catlos and Sgt. Kenneth Dunlevy, report, May 8, 1945.
54. S/Sgt. Steven Catlos, interview, August 28, 1968.
55. Ibid.
56. Ibid.
57. Ibid.
58. Ibid.
59. Ibid.
60. Brown, *Wild Bill Donovan*, 186.
61. Sgt. Kenneth Dunlevy, interview, June 8, 1991.
62. Ibid.
63. Associated Press, news brief on war crimes report, men of Dawes Mission, May 25, 1945.
64. S/Sgt. Steven Catlos, interview, circa January 1970.
65. Hymoff, *OSS in World War II*, 190.
66. Licko, *USA v. Banskej Bystrici rok: 1944*, 2.
67. Maria Gulovich, interview, January 27, 1992.
68. Ibid.

Chapter 3

1. Report of Lt. James H. Green to OSS, declassified January 1, 1994.
2. Fedornak, *Partizan*, 3.
3. Lt. Green, situational report to OSS, 2677th Regiment, January 28, 1945.
4. S/Sgt. Steven Catlos, interview, September 12, 1969.
5. As told to Maria Gulovich by Capt. William MacGregor, circa 1978.
6. Fedornak, *Partizan*, 39.
7. Richard Grey, interview, September 12, 1991.
8. Snyder, *The War: A Concise History*, 194.
9. Richard Grey, interview, September 12, 1991.
10. Operational History of Dawes and Related Teams, January 25, 1945.
11. Snyder, *The War: A Concise History*, 194.
12. Ibid.
13. Maria Gulovich, interview, April 14, 1990.
14. Ibid.
15. Ibid.
16. Ibid.
17. Ibid.
18. S/Sgt. Steven Catlos and Sgt. Kenneth Dunlevy, report to OSS, May 8, 1945.
19. Maria Gulovich, interview, April 26, 1990.
20. Ibid.
21. Sgt. Kenneth Dunlevy, interview, May 8, 1992.
22. Major Walter Ross, OSS, report to Colonel Deranian, October 10, 1994.
23. Licko, *USA v. Banskej Bystrici rok: 1944*, 5.
24. Report of SHEAF to Col. Deranian.
25. Young, *Atlas of World War II*.
26. Keegan, *The Second World War*, 527.
27. Ibid.
28. Agent Anton Novak Report to OSS, January 27, 1945.
29. Keegan, *The Second World War*, 527.
30. Hymoff, "The Revolt that Failed," *SAGA Magazine*, 84.
31. Keegan, *The Second World War*, 507.
32. S/Sgt. Steven Catlos and Sgt. Kenneth Dunlevy, OSS report, May 8, 1945.
33. Ibid.
34. Associated Press, news brief on war crimes, July 16, 1945.
35. Maria Gulovich, interview, January 22, 1990.
36. Hymoff, *OSS in World War II*, 188.
37. Licko, *USA v. Banskej Bystricirok: 1944*, 8.
38. Keegan, *The Second World War*, 507.
39. Maria Gulovich, interview, May 28, 1992.
40. Ibid.
41. Ibid.
42. Ibid.
43. Ibid.
44. S/Sgt. Steven Catlos, interview, August 28, 1968.
45. Incoming message from Dawes to OSS, Bari, Italy, declassified January 26, 1977.
46. Recommendation of Award for Lt. John Schwartz, declassified January 26, 1977.
47. Report #643 by MXS-X Section, CPM Branch, declassified #12356.
48. Hrabak, "Slovak National Uprising of 1944," 37.
49. Fedornak, *Partizan*, 34.
50. Ibid.
51. Ibid.
52. Ibid.
53. Ibid.
54. Lt. James H. Green, report on developments to OSS, October 6, 1944.
55. Recommendation of Award for Lt. John Schwartz, declassified January 26, 1997.
56. Korec, "The Cross in the Snares of Power," *Slovakia Quarterly*, September-December 1954: 94.
57. Edward DeLaney, "I Was In Slovakia," *Slovakia* 1, no. 2, 138.
58. Bethell, *Russia Besieged*, 101.
59. DeLaney, *Slovakia* 1, no. 2, 138.
60. Halaf and Tacka, *We Were Not Alone*, 13.
61. Lt. James H. Green, report on developments to OSS, October 6, 1944.

Chapter 4

1. Maria Gulovich, interview, July 27, 1992.
2. S/Sgt. Steven Catlos, interview, August 28, 1968.
3. Ibid.
4. Sgt. Kenneth Dunlevy, interview, January 23, 1990.
5. Zlamal, *The Partisan Captain*, 150.
6. Sgt. Kenneth Dunlevy, interview, January 23, 1990.
7. Maria Gulovich, interview, July 2, 1990.
8. Ibid.
9. Hymoff, *OSS in World War II*, 194–195.
10. Maria Gulovich, interview, July 2, 1990.
11. Victor Frudenfels, letter, August 5, 1995.
12. Ibid.
13. S/Sgt. Steven Catlos and Sgt. Kenneth Dunlevy, OSS report, May 8, 1945.
14. Fedornak, *Partizan*, 34.
15. Zlamal, *The Partisan Captain*, 62.
16. Maria Gulovich, interview, July 2, 1990.
17. Sgt. Kenneth Dunlevy, interview, March 7, 1992.
18. Maria Gulovich, interview, July 2, 1990.
19. Lt. James H. Green, initial mission report to OSS, September 21, 1944.
20. S/Sgt. Steven Catlos, interview, August 28, 1968.
21. Ibid.
22. S/Sgt. Steven Catlos and Sgt. Kenneth Dunlevy, OSS report, May 8, 1945.
23. Ibid.
24. Maria Gulovich, interview, July 2, 1990.
25. S/Sgt. Steven Catlos and Sgt. Kenneth Dunlevy, OSS report, May 8, 1945.
26. Ibid.
27. Maria Gulovich, interview, January 17, 1992.
28. Sgt. Kenneth Dunlevy, interview, March 4, 1992.

29. S/Sgt. Steven Catlos, interview, September 12, 1968.
30. Maria Gulovich, report to OSS.
31. Ibid.
32. Ibid.
33. Maria Gulovich, interview, April 26, 1990.
34. Sgt. Eugene Yeargin, report to OSS, May 21, 1948.
35. Zlamal, *The Partisan Captain*, 158.
36. S/Sgt. Steven Catlos, taped Dawes Mission details, circa September 1969.
37. Maria Gulovich, interview, May 6, 1990.
38. Sgt. Kenneth Dunlevy, interview, March 8, 1992.
39. Ibid.
40. Ibid.
41. Ibid.
42. Ibid.
43. Maria Gulovich, interview, May 6, 1990.

Chapter 5

1. S/Sgt. Steven Catlos and Sgt. Kenneth Dunlevy, OSS report, May 8, 1945.
2. Fedornak, *Partizan*, 18.
3. S/Sgt. Steven Catlos and Sgt. Kenneth Dunlevy, OSS report, May 8, 1945.
4. Ibid.
5. S/Sgt. Steven Catlos and Sgt. Kenneth Dunlevy, OSS report, May 8, 1945.
6. Sgt. Kenneth Dunlevy, interview, June 2, 1992.
7. Ibid.
8. S/Sgt. Steven Catlos and Sgt. Kenneth Dunlevy, OSS report, May 8, 1945.
9. Lt. James H. Green, situational report to OSS, October 6, 1944.
10. Sgt. Kenneth Dunlevy, interview, June 7, 1991.
11. S/Sgt. Steven Catlos, interview, August 28, 1968.
12. Maria Gulovich, interview, March 8, 1992.
13. S/Sgt. Steven Catlos, taped Dawes Mission details, September 1968.
14. Maria Gulovich, interview, March 8, 1992.
15. Fedornak, *Partizan*, 70.
16. Halaf and Tacka, *We Were Not Alone*, 41.
17. Fedornak, *Partizan*, 70.
18. Ibid.
19. Ibid.
20. Hymoff, *OSS in World War II*, 198.
21. S/Sgt. Steven Catlos and Sgt. Kenneth Dunlevy, OSS report, May 8, 1945.
22. S/Sgt. Steven Catlos, telephone interview, circa October 1969.
23. Ibid.
24. Sgt. Kenneth Dunlevy, interview, March 28, 1992.
25. Hymoff, *OSS in World War II*, 198–199.
26. Ibid.
27. Sgt. Kenneth Dunlevy, interview, January 23, 1992.
28. Maria Gulovich, interview, May 6, 1990.
29. Ibid.

30. S/Sgt. Steven Catlos, taped Dawes Mission details, October 1968.
31. Ibid.
32. Sgt. Kenneth Dunlevy, interview, January 23, 1992.
33. Maria Gulovich, interview, May 8, 1990.
34. Ibid.
35. S/Sgt. Steven Catlos, taped Dawes Mission details, September 1969.
36. Maria Gulovich, interview, July 23, 1992.
37. S/Sgt. Steven Catlos and Sgt. Kenneth Dunlevy, OSS report, May 8, 1945.
38. Maria Gulovich, interview, July 23, 1992.
39. S/Sgt. Steven Catlos and Sgt. Kenneth Dunlevy, OSS report, May 8, 1945.
40. Ibid.
41. S/Sgt. Steven Catlos, interview, circa September 1968.
42. Maria Gulovich, interview, April 23, 1990.
43. S/Sgt. Eugene Yeargin, OSS report, May 21, 1945.
44. Maria Gulovich, interview, April 26, 1990.
45. Ibid.
46. Ibid.
47. Ibid.
48. S/Sgt. Steven Catlos, interview, September 1968.
49. S/Sgt. Steven Catlos and Sgt. Kenneth Dunlevy, OSS report, May 8, 1945.
50. S/Sgt. Steven Catlos, interview, September 1968.
51. S/Sgt. Steven Catlos and Sgt. Kenneth Dunlevy, OSS report, May 8, 1945.
52. Sgt. Kenneth Dunlevy, interview, January 23, 1992.

Chapter 6

1. Hymoff, *OSS in World War II*, 199.
2. Sgt. Kenneth Dunlevy, interview, March 8, 1992.
3. OSS Evaluation report on Lt. John Schwartz.
4. Lt. John Schwartz, debriefing, OSS report, declassi?ed, No. 006627.
5. Hymoff, "The Revolt that Failed," *SAGA Magazine*, 42.
6. S/Sgt. Eugene Yeargin, OSS report, No. 643, declassified June 14, 1990.
7. Hymoff, *OSS in World War II*, 203–204.
8. Maria Gulovich, interview, July 8, 1991.
9. S/Sgt. Steven Catlos and Sgt. Kenneth Dunlevy, OSS report, May 8, 1945.
10. Ibid.
11. Maria Gulovich, interview, July 8, 1991.
12. Hymoff, *OSS in World War II*, 202.
13. Maria Gulovich, interview, July 8, 1991.
14. Zlamal, *The Partisan Captain*, 158.
15. Ibid.
16. Maria Gulovich, interview, July 8, 1991.
17. Hymoff, *OSS in World War II*, 202.
18. Hymoff, "The Revolt that Failed," *SAGA Magazine*, 86.

19. Hymoff, *OSS in World War II*, 203.
20. Maria Gulovich, interview, May 2, 1992.
21. Sgt. Kenneth Dunlevy, interview, March 8, 1992.
22. Maria Gulovich, interview, March 9, 1992.
23. S/Sgt. Steven Catlos, interview, August 28, 1968.
24. Maria Gulovich, interview, April 28, 1992.
25. S/Sgt. Steven Catlos, interview, September 12, 1968.
26. Maria Gulovich, interview, April 28, 1992.
27. Hymoff, *OSS in World War II*, 203.
28. S/Sgt. Steven Catlos and Sgt. Kenneth Dunlevy, OSS report, May 8, 1945.
29. Ibid.
30. Maria Gulovich, interview, April 28, 1992.
31. Ibid.
32. Ibid.
33. Hymoff, *OSS in World War II*, 203–204.
34. Maria Gulovich, interview, April 28, 1992.
35. S/Sgt. Steven Catlos and Sgt. Kenneth Dunlevy, OSS report, May 8, 1945.
36. Maria Gulovich, interview, August 1, 1992.
37. Ibid.
38. S/Sgt. Steven Catlos, interview, September 12, 1969.
39. Hymoff, "The Revolt that Failed," *SAGA Magazine*, 84.
40. Ibid.
41. Ibid.

Chapter 7

1. Maria Gulovich, interview, April 9, 1990.
2. Harvard University records of Lt. James H. Gaul.
3. Alcorn, *No Bugles for Spies*, 138.
4. S/Sgt. Steven Catlos, interview, circa September 1968.
5. Sgt. Kenneth Dunlevy, interview, January 22, 1990.
6. Hymoff, *OSS in World War II*, 204.
7. Keegan, *The Second World War*, 490.
8. Hymoff, *OSS in World War II*, 203.
9. S/Sgt. Steven Catlos and Sgt. Kenneth Dunlevy, OSS report, May 8, 1945.
10. Hymoff, *OSS in World War II*, 204.
11. S/Sgt. Steven Catlos and Sgt. Kenneth Dunlevy, OSS report, May 8, 1945.
12. Maria Gulovich, interview, April 25, 1990.
13. Ibid.
14. S/Sgt. Steven Catlos, taped Dawes Mission details, October 1968.
15. Ibid.
16. Ibid.
17. Maria Gulovich, interview, July 8, 1991.
18. Ibid.
19. Ibid.
20. Ibid.
21. Ibid.
22. Ibid.
23. Michael Fedornak, interview, May 20, 2001.
24. Maria Gulovich, interview, July 8, 1991.
25. Ibid.
26. Ibid.
27. Ibid.
28. S/Sgt. Steven Catlos, interview August 28, 1968.
29. Ibid.
30. Maria Gulovich, interview, May 17, 1990.
31. Michael Fedornak, interview, May 20, 2001.
32. Maria Gulovich, interview, May 17, 1990.
33. S/Sgt. Steven Catlos and Sgt. Kenneth Dunlevy, OSS report, May 8, 1945.
34. Maria Gulovich, interview, May 17, 1990.
35. Lt. James H. Green, OSS report.
36. Mira Mullen, interview, July 7, 1995.
37. Johnson, *Modern Times*, 414.
38. *The Secret State*, 254.

Chapter 8

1. Maria Gulovich, interview, July 23, 1990.
2. S/Sgt. Steven Catlos, taped Dawes Mission details, circa November 1968.
3. S/Sgt. Steven Catlos and Sgt. Kenneth Dunlevy, OSS report, May 8, 1945.
4. Hymoff, *OSS in World War II*, 207.
5. Ibid., 205.
6. S/Sgt. Steven Catlos and Sgt. Kenneth Dunlevy, OSS report, May 8, 1945.
7. S/Sgt. Steven Catlos, interview, August 28, 1968.
8. Ibid.
9. Hymoff, *OSS in World War II*, 206.
10. Ibid.
11. Maria Gulovich, interview, July 23, 1990.
12. Hymoff, *OSS in World War II*, 205.
13. Maria Gulovich, interview, July 23, 1990.
14. Zlamal, *The Partisan Captain*, 104.
15. Maria Gulovich, interview, July 23, 1990.
16. Zlamal, *The Partisan Captain*, 163.
17. Sgt. Kenneth Dunlevy, interview, June 3, 1991.
18. Post-war report on Joseph Morton, declassified June 14, 1990.
19. Maria Gulovich, interview, July 23, 1990.
20. Michael Fedornak, interview, May 20, 2001.
21. Keegan, *The Second World War*, 507.
22. Sgt. Kenneth Dunlevy, interview, May 4, 1992.
23. S/Sgt. Steven Catlos and Sgt. Kenneth Dunlevy, OSS report, May 8, 1945.
24. Maria Gulovich, interview, July 23, 1990.
25. Ibid.
26. Ibid.
27. Ibid.
28. S/Sgt. Steven Catlos, interview, August 28, 1968.
29. Hymoff, *OSS in World War II*, 206.
30. Ibid.
31. S/Sgt. Steven Catlos, interview, October 1968.
32. Ibid.

Chapter 9

1. S/Sgt. Steven Catlos, taped Dawes Mission details, October 1968.
2. Michael Fedornak, interview, May 20, 2001.
3. Hymoff, "The Revolt that Failed," *SAGA Magazine*, 86.
4. Ibid.
5. Ibid.
6. S/Sgt. Steven Catlos, interview, circa September 1968.
7. Maria Gulovich, interview, March 9, 1992.
8. S/Sgt. Steven Catlos, interview, circa September 1968.
9. Fedornak, *Partizan*, 34.
10. Ibid.
11. Sgt. Kenneth Dunlevy, interview, January 23, 1991.
12. S/Sgt. Steven Catlos and Sgt. Kenneth Dunlevy, OSS report, May 8, 1945.
13. Ibid.
14. Hymoff, *OSS in World War II*, 207.
15. Maria Gulovich, interview, January 27, 1992.
16. Ibid.
17. S/Sgt. Steven Catlos and Sgt. Kenneth Dunlevy, OSS report, May 8, 1945.
18. Maria Gulovich, interview, July 27, 1990.
19. S/Sgt. Steven Catlos and Sgt. Kenneth Dunlevy, OSS report, May 8, 1945.
20. Harvard University records of Lt. James H. Gaul.
21. Sgt. James Crookshank, interview, July 1, 2003.
22. Hymoff, *OSS in World War II*, 207.
23. Ibid.
24. Ibid.
25. Ibid.
26. Ibid.
27. Ibid.
28. Hymoff, "The Revolt that Failed," *SAGA Magazine*, pages 86–87.
29. S/Sgt. Steven Catlos, interview, August 28, 1968.
30. Hymoff, *OSS in World War II*, 208.
31. Ibid.
32. Ibid.
33. Maria Gulovich, interview, March 9, 1992.
34. Ibid.
35. Ibid.
36. Ibid.
37. Ibid.
38. Ibid.

Chapter 10

1. Report on Dawes Mission to OSS Signal Section #2677, June 14, 1945.
2. OSS Report on Capt. Edward Baranski.
3. Agent Anton Novak, OSS report on Day Mission, February 14, 1945.
4. Ibid.
5. Ibid.
6. Ibid.
7. Ibid.
8. Ibid.
9. S/Sgt. Steven Catlos and Sgt. Kenneth Dunlevy, OSS report, May 8, 1945.
10. Sgt. Kenneth Dunlevy, interview, June 18, 1991.
11. Hymoff, *OSS in World War II*, 209.
12. Maria Gulovich, OSS report and interview.
13. Ibid.
14. Ibid.
15. Sgt. Kenneth Dunlevy, interview, June 16, 1991.
16. Maria Gulovich, interview, July 8, 1991.
17. S/Sgt. Steven Catlos, interview, August 28, 1968.
18. Hymoff, *OSS in World War II*, 212.
19. Maria Gulovich, OSS report.
20. Ibid.
21. Hymoff, *OSS in World War II*, 209.
22. Maria Gulovich, interview, July 8, 1991.
23. Sgt. Kenneth Dunlevy, interview, June 16, 1991.
24. Maria Gulovich, interview, July 8, 1991.
25. Sgt. Kenneth Dunlevy, interview, June 16, 1991.
26. Hymoff, "The Revolt that Failed," *SAGA Magazine*, 87.
27. Ibid.
28. Ibid.
29. Ibid.
30. S/Sgt. Steven Catlos, interview, September 12, 1969.
31. Sgt. Kenneth Dunlevy, interview, March 28, 1992.

Chapter 11

1. Keegan, *The Second World War*, 506.
2. Eisenhower, *The Bitter Woods*, 586.
3. The History Channel, "The Last Secret of the Nazis," November 11, 2003.
4. Snyder, *The War: A Concise History*, 48.
5. Halaf and Tacka, *We Were Not Alone*, 63.
6. Maria Gulovich, interview, January 27, 1992.
7. S/Sgt. Steven Catlos, interview, October 1968.
8. Ibid.
9. Maria Gulovich, interview, January 27, 1992.
10. Ibid.
11. Sgt. Kenneth Dunlevy, interview, March 4, 1992.
12. Keegan, *The Second World War*, 507.
13. S/Sgt. Steven Catlos, interview, August 28, 1968.
14. S/Sgt. Steven Catlos and Sgt. Kenneth Dunlevy, OSS report, May 8, 1945.
15. Maria Gulovich, interview, July 8, 1991.
16. Ibid.
17. Ibid.
18. Sgt. Kenneth Dunlevy, interview, March 4, 1992.
19. S/Sgt. Steven Catlos, interview, August 28, 1968.
20. Maria Gulovich, interview, January 27, 1992.

21. Michael Fedornak, letter, December 18, 1994.
22. S/Sgt. Steven Catlos, taped Dawes Mission details, November 1968.
23. Sgt. Kenneth Dunlevy, interview, June 18, 1991.
24. Maria Gulovich, interview, March 9, 1992.
25. S/Sgt. Steven Catlos, interview, November 1968.
26. S/Sgt. Steven Catlos and Sgt. Kenneth Dunlevy, OSS report, May 8, 1945.
27. S/Sgt. Steven Catlos, interview, September 12, 1969.
28. Maria Gulovich, interview, March 9, 1992.
29. Sgt. Kenneth Dunlevy, interview, March 4, 1992.
30. S/Sgt. Steven Catlos and Sgt. Kenneth Dunlevy, OSS report, May 8, 1945.
31. Sgt. Kenneth Dunlevy, interview, March 4, 1992.
32. Ibid.
33. Hymoff, *OSS in World War II*, 213.
34. S/Sgt. Steven Catlos and Sgt. Kenneth Dunlevy, OSS report, May 8, 1945.
35. Maria Gulovich, interview, May 6, 1992.
36. Ibid.
37. Sgt. Kenneth Dunlevy, interview, March 10, 1992.
38. Maria Gulovich, interview, April 7, 1992.
39. S/Sgt. Steven Catlos, interview, August 28, 1968.

Chapter 12

1. Maria Gulovich, interview, April 7, 1991.
2. S/Sgt. Steven Catlos, taped Dawes Mission details, November 1968.
3. Ibid.
4. Ibid.
5. Maria Gulovich, interview, January 27, 1992.
6. "Viewpoint," The History Channel, March 10, 2002.
7. Sgt. Kenneth Dunlevy, interview, March 4, 1992.
8. Maria Gulovich, interview, January 28, 1992.
9. Lt. Arthur Zenopian, S/Sgt. Steven Catlos and Sgt. Kenneth Dunlevy, OSS reports.
10. Ibid.
11. Ibid.
12. Ibid.
13. Michael Fedornak, letter, January 6, 1995.
14. Hymoff, *OSS in World War II*, 213–214.
15. Sgt. Kenneth Dunlevy, interview, March 4, 1992.
16. Maria Gulovich, interview, March 9, 1992.
17. Keegan, *The Second World War*, 491.
18. Hymoff, *OSS in World War II*, 214.
19. OSS Report on 15th Air Force air drop of supplies, January 26, 1945.
20. Maria Gulovich, interview, January 27, 1992.
21. Ibid.
22. Hymoff, *OSS in World War II*, 213.
23. Ibid., 214.
24. Ibid., 215.
25. S/Sgt. Steven Catlos and Sgt. Kenneth Dunlevy, OSS report, May 8, 1945.
26. Ibid.
27. Maria Gulovich, interview, March 9, 1992.
28. S/Sgt. Steven Catlos, interview, August 28, 1968.
29. S/Sgt. Steven Catlos and Sgt. Kenneth Dunlevy, OSS report, May 8, 1945.
30. Ibid.
31. Hymoff, *OSS in World War II*, 215.
32. Maria Gulovich, interview, March 9, 1992.
33. Ibid.
34. Ibid.
35. Sgt. Kenneth Dunlevy, interview, March 4, 1992.
36. Ibid.

Chapter 13

1. S/Sgt. Steven Catlos and Sgt. Kenneth Dunlevy, OSS report, May 8, 1945.
2. Jan Kristak, letter, June 6, 2001.
3. S/Sgt. Steven Catlos, interview, September 12, 1968.
4. Keegan, *The Second World War*, 507.
5. Jan Kristak, letter, with photos and documents, June 2, 2001.
6. S/Sgt. Steven Catlos, interview, August 28, 1968.
7. Ibid.
8. Hymoff, *OSS in World War II*, 216.
9. Ibid.
10. S/Sgt. Steven Catlos, interview, August 28, 1968.
11. S/Sgt. Steven Catlos and Sgt. Kenneth Dunlevy, OSS report, May 8, 1945.
12. Maria Gulovich, interview, April 7, 1992.
13. Hymoff, *OSS in World War II*, 216.
14. Maria Gulovich, interview, May 8, 1991.
15. Sgt. Kenneth Dunlevy, interview, June 18, 1991.
16. Maria Gulovich, interview, May 17, 1990.
17. Sgt. Kenneth Dunlevy, interview, June 3, 1991.
18. Maria Gulovich, interview, July 8, 1991.
19. Ibid.
20. Ibid.
21. Ibid.
22. S/Sgt. Steven Catlos and Sgt. Kenneth Dunlevy, OSS report, May 8, 1945.
23. Ibid.
24. Maria Gulovich, interview, March 9, 1992.
25. Sgt. Kenneth Dunlevy, interview, March 4, 1992.

Chapter 14

1. Maria Gulovich, interview, January 2, 1992.
2. Ibid.
3. Sgt. Kenneth Dunlevy, interview, March 19, 1992.
4. S/Sgt. Steven Catlos, interview, October 1969.

5. Ibid.
6. Hymoff, *OSS in World War II*, 217.
7. Ibid.
8. DeLaney, "I Was In Slovakia," *Slovakia* 1, No. 2, 6.
9. Maria Gulovich, interview, May 28, 1992.
10. Sgt. Kenneth Dunlevy, interview, March 10, 1992.
11. Maria Gulovich, interview, May 28, 1992.
12. S/Sgt. Steven Catlos, interview, circa September 1968.
13. Johnson, *Modern Times*, 419.
14. Wilhelm Muller, report on Nazi interrogation and torture of Dawes prisoners and their execution on January 24, 1945.
15. Wilhelm Ornstein, report on viewing execution of Dawes men and Margita Koscova.

Chapter 15

1. Maria Gulovich, interview, January 22, 1992.
2. Ibid.
3. S/Sgt. Steven Catlos, taped Dawes Mission details, circa November 1968.
4. Ibid.
5. Maria Gulovich, OSS report.
6. S/Sgt. Steven Catlos, interview, September 1968.
7. Maria Gulovich, interview, January 27, 1992.
8. S/Sgt. Steven Catlos and Sgt. Kenneth Dunlevy, OSS report, May 8, 1945.
9. bid.
10. Sgt. Kenneth Dunlevy, interview, May 28, 1992.
11. S/Sgt. Steven Catlos, interview, circa September 1968.
12. Keegan, *The Second World War*, 491.
13. Maria Gulovich, interview, January 27, 1992.
14. Ibid.
15. *No Hope for the Wicked*, 7.
16. Keegan, *The Second World War*, 510.
17. S/Sgt. Steven Catlos, interview, September 1968.
18. Keegan, *The Second World War*, 512.
19. Ibid.
20. Maria Gulovich, interview, April 7, 1992.
21. S/Sgt. Steven Catlos, interview, September 19, 1968.

Chapter 16

1. S/Sgt. Steven Catlos and Sgt. Kenneth Dunlevy, OSS report, May 8, 1945.
2. Maria Gulovich, interview, January 22, 1992.
3. Sgt. Kenneth Dunlevy, interview, March 10, 1992.
4. Ibid.
5. Maria Gulovich, interview, January 22, 1992.
6. S/Sgt. Steven Catlos, interview, August 28, 1968.
7. Ibid.
8. Ibid.
9. Maria Gulovich, interview, January 22, 1992.
10. S/Sgt. Steven Catlos, interview, August 28, 1968.
11. Ibid.
12. S/Sgt. Steven Catlos, interview, August 28, 1968.
13. Maria Gulovich, interview, January 22, 1992.
14. Ibid.
15. Ibid.
16. S/Sgt. Steven Catlos and Sgt. Kenneth Dunlevy, OSS report, May 8, 1945.
17. Sgt. Kenneth Dunlevy, interview, March 10, 1992.
18. Maria Gulovich, interview, January 22, 1992.
19. S/Sgt. Steven Catlos, interview, August 28, 1968.
20. Maria Gulovich, interview, April 7, 1992.
21. S/Sgt. Steven Catlos, interview, August 28, 1968.

Chapter 17

1. Sgt. Kenneth Dunlevy, interview, March 10, 1992.
2. Recommendation of Award for Maria Gulovich, May 31, 1945.
3. Ibid.
4. Sgt. Kenneth Dunlevy, interview, March 10, 1992.
5. S/Sgt. Steven Catlos, interview, circa October 1968.
6. Sgt. Kenneth Dunlevy, interview, March 10, 1992.
7. S/Sgt. Steven Catlos, interview, circa October 1968.
8. DeLaney, "I Was In Slovakia," *Slovakia* 1, no. 2, 6.
9. Ibid.
10. Maria Gulovich, interview, May 28, 1992.
11. DeLaney, *Five Decades Before Dawn*, 143.
12. Maria Gulovich, interview, May 6, 1992.
13. Ibid. Russian folk songbook, property of Anastasia Smo, given to the author in October 1995.
14. Maria Gulovich, interview, May 6, 1992.
15. *Hope of the Wicked*, 99.
16. Maria Gulovich, interview, May 6, 1992.
17. Incoming report to Maj. Otto Jakes, March 14, 1945.
18. Lt. Stephen B. Penrose, letter to Vassar College, February 26, 1946.
19. Maria Gulovich, interview, August 3, 1992.
20. Juraj Rajnenic, letter, June 14, 1995.
21. Maria Gulovich, interview, August 3, 1992.

Chapter 18

1. Maria Gulovich, interview, August 3, 1992.
2. Ibid.
3. Ibid.
4. Persico, *Piercing the Reich*, 129.
5. Ibid.

6. Maria Gulovich, interview, August 1, 1992; Persico, *Piercing the Reich*, 139.
7. *The Spear of Destiny*, 326.
8. Persico, *Piercing the Reich*, 311.
9. Ibid.
10. Maria Gulovich, interview, May 6, 1992.
11. Ibid.
12. Barbara Podolsky, interview, September 29, 1995.
13. Keegan, *The Second World War*, 491.
14. Maria Gulovich, interview, May 6, 1992.
15. Johnson, *Modern Times*, 431.
16. Recommendation of Award for Lt. John Schwartz, Hoover Institution, January 21, 1977.
17. Hymoff, "The Revolt that Failed," *SAGA Magazine*, 8.
18. Report by Lynn Neizerling, Associated Press, on prisoner conditions at Mauthausen Prison.
19. As told to Maria Gulovich by Lt. William MacGregor (circa 1978).
20. Maria Gulovich, interview, August 1, 1992.
21. Ibid.
22. Ibid.
23. "The Last Days of World War II," The History Channel, November 11, 2003.
24. Freedin, *The Forgotten People*, 99.
25. Maria Gulovich, interview, May 28, 1992.
26. *Hope for the Wicked*, 98.
27. Maria Gulovich, interview, May 28, 1992.
28. Ibid.

Chapter 19

1. History (from end of World War II, August 1945, to fall of Soviet communism in 1989).
2. Recommendation of Award for Lt. John Schwartz, declassified January 21, 1977.
3. Lynn Neizerling, Associated Press, July 7, 1945.
4. War Crimes Report (August 31, 1945).
5. Neizerling.
6. William McDermott, *Cleveland Plain Dealer*, July 16, 1945.
7. Persico, *Piercing the Reich*, 311.
8. Maria Gulovich, interview, August 3, 1992.
9. "I Was In Slovakia," Edward DeLaney, *Slovakia* 1, No. 2, 44.
10. "The Last Days of World War II," The History Channel, November 11, 2003.
11. DeLaney, *Harvest of Deceit*, 112.
12. Freedin, *The Forgotten People*, 99.
13. Keegan, *The Second World War*, 491.
14. Maria Gulovich, interview, August 1, 1992.
15. Ibid.
16. Ibid.
17. Maria Gulovich re: arriving at Vassar College.
18. Lt. Stephen B. Penrose, letter to Dr. Henry Noble McCracken, February 26, 1946.
19. Lt. Graham Campbell's recommendation of award for Maria Gulovich.
20. Maria Gulovich, interview, August 3, 1992.
21. Ibid.
22. Ibid.
23. Smith, *The Shadow Warriors*, 90.
24. Maria Gulovich, interview, August 3, 1992.

Epilogue

1. *Eclipse*, 662.
2. Mrs. Harriet Gaul's letter to General Donovan (May 8, 1945).
3. Response from Acting Director Charles Cheston, *Eclipse*, 668. Werner Muller testimony.
4. *Eclipse*, 662.
5. War Crime Report on Strategic Services, November 11, 1947.
6. Mrs. Harriet Gaul's final response to Colonel Charles Cheston.
7. Bradley, *Czechoslovakia: A Short History*.
8. Ibid.
9. Freedin, *The Forgotten People*, 70.
10. Kirschbaum, *Anniversary of the Slovak National Uprising of 1944*.
11. Zlamal, *The Partisan Captain*, 285.
12. Freedin, *The Forgotten People*, 99.
13. Maria Gulovich, interview, August 3, 1992.
14. Freedin, *The Forgotten People*, 72.
15. Roy Madden, interview, circa November 1995.
16. Ibid.
17. Ibid.
18. Victor Frudenfels, letter, with *Pravda* article, August 5, 1992, on fate of Generals Rudolf Viest and Jan Golian.
19. Ibid.
20. Ibid.
21. Mira Mullen, interview, July 1, 2000.
22. Ibid.
23. Ibid.
24. Ibid.
25. Hrabak, "Slovak National Uprising of 1944," 14.
26. Joseph Mikus, report of Red Cross International Committee, *Slovakia* 1, June 30, 1947: 645–646.
27. "Murder in Slovakia," speech of Honorable Alvin E. Konski to House of Representatives, April 4, 1947.
28. Epstein, *Operation Keelhaul*, 53.
29. Ibid.
30. Ibid.
31. Zlamal, *The Partisan Captain*, 268.
32. Freedin, *The Forgotten People*, 10.
33. *Operation Keelhaul*, 68.
34. Ibid., 69.
35. Ibid.
36. Ibid.
37. Ibid.
38. S/Sgt. Steven Catlos, interview, August 28, 1968.
39. Ibid.
40. Ibid.
41. Sgt. Kenneth Dunlevy, interview, August 3, 1992.
42. Maria Gulovich, interview, August 3, 1992.

43. S/Sgt. Steven Catlos, interview, circa September 1969.
44. Jan Kristak, letter, June 6, 2001.
45. Habak, "Slovak National Uprising of 1944," 412.
46. S/Sgt. Steven Catlos and Sgt. Kenneth Dunlevy, OSS report, May 8, 1945.
47. Karel Berger, letter, August 15, 1995.
48. Bradley, *Czechoslovakia: A Short History*.
49. Hymoff, *OSS in World War II*, 183.
50. Ibid.
51. Ibid.
52. Ford, *Donovan of the OSS*, 322.
53. G. J. Jason, report on current conditions in Slovakia, July 8, 2003.
54. Rysovy, *Zilina and the Slovak National Uprising*, 162.
55. Luba Macko, letter, June 11, 2003.
56. Brown, *Wild Bill Donovan*, 656.
57. Rysovy, *Zilina and the Slovak National Uprising*, 162.

BIBLIOGRAPHY

Alcorn, Robert Hayden. *No Bugles for Spies.* New York: David McKay, 1962.
Baldwin, Hanson. *Battles Lost and Won: Great Campaigns of World War II.* New York: Smithmark, 1994.
Bethell, Nicholas. *Russia Besieged.* Alexandria, VA: Time-Life Books, 1980.
Bohus, Chnoupek. *America v. Povstani.* Bratislava, Slovakia: Vylacil Lama Press, 1994.
Bradley, John F.N. *Czechoslovakia: A Short History.* Edinburgh: Edinburgh University Press, 1971.
Bradley, General Omar N. *A Soldier's Story.* New York: Random House, 1999.
Brown, Anthony Cave. *Bodyguard of Lies.* New York: Harper and Row, 1975.
_____. *Wild Bill Donovan: The Last Hero.* New York: Times Books, 1982.
Churchill, Winston. *The Second World War, Volume 5: Closing the Ring.* New York: Houghton Mifflin, 1951.
Davidson, Bill. *Cut Off Behind the Bulge.* New York: Stein and Day, 1972.
DeLaney, Edward L. *Harvest of Deceit.* Sacramento: Century Pathfinder, 1971.
_____. *Five Decades Before Dawn.* Pasadena, CA: Deljon, 1969.
_____. "I Met President Tito," *Slovakia Annual* 22, no. 40: 22.
_____. "I Was In Slovakia." *Slovakia* 1, no. 2.
Dugan, James, and Carroll Stewart. *Ploesti: The Great Air Battle of World War II — August, 1943.* New York: Random House, 1962.
Dunlop, Richard. *Donovan: Wartime Spymaster.* New York: William Morrow, 1994.
Dunnigan, James, *Dirty Little Secrets of World War II: Military Information No One Told You.* New York: Viking, 1982.
Durica, Milan. *Slovakia During World War II: The Slovak Republic.* Toronto: Slovakia World Congress, 1973.
Eisenhower, John. *The Bitter Woods: The Battle of the Bulge.* New York: Putnam's, 1969.
Epstein, Julius. *Operation Keelhaul; The Story of Forced Repatriation from 1944 to the Present.* Old Greenwich [Conn.]: Devin-Adair, 1973.
Fedornak, Michael. *Partizan, The Heroic Story of Michael Fedornak; American-Born Rusyn Spy Behind Enemy Lines and the Iron Curtain.* Ellsworth, ME: Downeast Graphics and Printing, 1998.
Flynn, Ted. *Hope of the Wicked.* Sterling, VA: Maxkol Communications, 2004.
Ford, Corey. *Donovan of the OSS.* Boston: Little, Brown, 1970.
Freedin, Seymour. *The Forgotten People: Thomas Masryk and Eduard Benes.* New York: Scribner's, 1962.
Goldston, Robert. *Sinister Touches: The Secret War Against Hitler.* New York: Dial Press, 1982.

Halaf, Dusan, and Ladislav Tacka. *We Were Not Alone.* Banska Bystrica, Slovakia: Museum of Slovak National Uprising, 1994.
Hrabak, Philip. "National Slovak Uprising of 1944." *Slovakia Quarterly* 4, September-December, 1954.
Hronek, Jeri, *Volcano under Hitler: The Underground War in Czechoslovakia.* Czech National Council of America, 1942.
Hymoff, Edward. *The OSS in World War II.* New York: Richardson and Steirman, 1986.
_____. "The Revolt that Failed." *SAGA Magazine* 30, no. 1, 1965.
Jelenick, Yeshayahi. *The Parish Republic: Hlinka's Slovak People's Party.* New York: Columbia University Press, 1976.
Johnson, Paul. *Modern Times: The World from the Twenties to the Nineties.*
Keegan, John. *The Second World War.* New York: Viking Press, 1990.
Kelley, Karol, and Vladimir Mini. *Memories of the SNU.* Banska Bystrica, Slovakia: International, 1994.
Kirschbaum, Joseph. *Slovakia at the Crossroads.* New York: Robert Speller and Sons, 1936.
Kirschbaum, Joseph, ed. *Slovakia in the 19th and 20th Centuries.* 2nd ed. Toronto: Slovak World Congress, 1973.
_____. *The Anniversary of the Slovak National Uprising of 1944.*
Korec, J. Ch. "The Cross in the Snares of Power." *Slovakia Quarterly*, September-December 1954.
Letterich, Josef. *History of Modern Slovakia.* New York: Praeger, 1955.
Licko, Miroslav. *USA v. Banskej Bystrici rok: 1944.* Bratislava, Slovakia: NKV, 1994,
McIntosh, Elizabeth. *Sisterhood of Spies.* Annapolis, MD: Naval Institute Press, 1998.
Miller, William. *Unforgettable Days of the Slovak National Uprising.*
Mikus, Josef. *Slovakia and the Slovaks.* Washington: Three Continents Press, 1977.
Moravian Brothers, *Historical Facts of Czechoslovakia*, Release 200, 1945.
Orwell, George. *Homage to Catalonia.* London: Sacker and Warburg, 1954.
Perrett, Geoffrey. *Eisenhower.* New York: Random House, 1999.
Persico, Joseph. *Piercing the Reich.* New York: Viking Press, 1979.
Read, Anthony, and David Fisher. *Lucy: Most Secret Spy Ring of World War II.* New York: McCann and Geoghegan, 1981.
Rysovy, Vavro. *Zilina and the Slovak National Uprising.* Slovenski Narodne: Universum Sokol Publications, 1981.
Schwartz, Harry. *Struggle for Democracy in Czechoslovakia.* New York: Praeger, 1969.
Simko, Mitchell. *Slovaks in Obscurity.* Middletown, PA: Jednota Press, 1992.
Smith, Bradley. *The Shadow Warriors.* New York: Basic Books, 1983.
Snyder, Louis. *The War: A Concise History, 1939–1945.* New York: Dell Books, 1962.
Toland, John. *The Rising Sun: The Decline and Fall of the Japanese Empire, 1936–1945.* New York: Random House, 1970.
Young, Brigadier General Peter, ed. *The Cassell Atlas of the Second World War.* New York: Berkeley, 1973.
Zlamal, Miroslav. *The Partisan Captain.* Hamilton, ON: Circle B Printing, 1970.

INDEX

Numbers in ***bold italics*** indicate pages with photographs.

abortion 203
airmen, American: awaiting evacuation to Italy ***40–41***; collected for evacuation 44, 46, 64; cover story of search for 35–36; funeral ***36***; hidden by Mullen 252–253; rescue by villagers and partisans 250–251; worsening condition on mountain trek 79, 80, 81, 84, 86, 97, 99
Alexei (Pasternak's nephew) 182
Andrea (ambassador's wife) 207–208, 209, 210, 213, 221, 222
"Apple trees were aflower" song 222
"Arcadia" Allied policy of subversion 20
Arndt (SS torturer) 192, 193, 195, 196, 197
Arnett 95
Ascanti, Fred 46
Asmolov, A.N. 64, 79
Austro-Hungarian Empire, prior to WWI 10

Bachmeyer, Georg 238
Balkans, ceded to Soviet sphere 9
Banska Bystrica: Dawes Mission "headquarters" 42; German assault 59, 60; German reprisals 66–67, 71; Germans and Soviets advancing toward 44–45; help of townspeople for downed airmen 251; Maria based in 23; scramble to escape 68; survivors return for 1964 celebration 258, 259
Baranski, Edward: capture in civilian clothing 145; as energetic, daring, with short fuse 54; gallant sacrifice for Slovakia 262; move Day team to Detvaskae Lazy, then to Piest pri Detve 144, 145; need for batteries for radio 145; no reports of 139, 143; setup of team HQ in Banska Bystrica 58; ties to Slovakia 143; torture by Gestapo 194–195
Battle of the Bulge 126, 154
beauty parlor visit 216
Beneš, Edvard: CFI plan to return to power 27; communiques from Roosevelt in support of revolt 35, 67; convincing Wilson of viability of new state of Czechoslovakia 10; as Czechoslovak president-in-exile 12; death during communist coup 250; promising assistance to CFI 32; returned to power, revenge on Tiso 220; signed Friendship treaty with Soviets 34, 221; vetoing more weapons for revolt 58, 261
Bible, Dunlevy's 160, 161, 175
"Bless them all" song 223
blizzard and "white darkness" 101
Bloom, Sol 249
Bohemia 10–11, 12
bombers, American, heading for Germany 172
Bowery Plan 48, 55, 58
Brezno 57–58
Bronze Star for heroism 244–245
Brown, Robert 38, 108, 140
Bucharest 211
Buchleiter, Margit 228
Budapest 154, 206
Bukowski, Adam 78
Bunker (Death House) at Mauthausen 190, 199

calf 87
Carter, Harry 214, 221, 222
Catlos, Ferdinand (General and Slovak defense minister) 32
Catlos, Stephen: assessing morale of tiny group 109; attending 1964 celebration in Slovakia 256–260; breaks, then discards radio 73; celebrating rescue with shopping and dining spree 216–217; as childhood friend of author's husband 3; concern for airmen on eve of mountain trek 74, 97; decision to remain with Russians, make for Red Army front 169; defense of Maria 218; facing suspicion about escaping capture 215; finds unlikely shelter with family and in forest bunker 173–180, ***188***; gratitude

277

toward helpful villagers 117–118; horror at sight of frozen CFI carcasses 108; illness forces decision to be left behind 171, 172, 173; impressions of train ride 211; initial Dawes "Bowery" assignment 55; intensive questioning by American authorities 218, 219; loss of horse and batteries at unsafe bridge 102, 129; Maria's impression of 174; one of five to escape capture 167; qualifications for Dawes Mission 47–48, 136–137; receives medal for service 258, 259; remaining friends with Dunlevy 260; repeated questioning by Red Army 204; rescue by Romanian patrol 187; sadness at Christmas 162; search for missing Green 136–139; sense of dislocation on eve of mountain trek 80; tobacco juice as beacon lights 152–153
CFI (Czechoslovak Forces of the Interior): abandoning wounded comrades 71; casualties, drunkenness and looting 61–62; casualties of German assault 59; changes after independence 7; deserting group, absconding with food 96; disillusionment 75; entrapped near Banska Bystrica 60–61, 62; escape from Banska Bystrica to hide in mountains 71; formation and objectives 7, 26; Green's requests for aid overruled 43, 45; group found as frozen carcasses 107–108; Maria decides to work for 30; resupply with war weaponry 45–46, 58; warned to keep moving or freeze 101–102
chamberpot incident 19
Chapin, Howard 43
Chebenec "mountain of death" 98
Cheston, Charles 248
Chetniks 34
Christmas celebrations 157–158, 181, 187
Churchill, Winston, reaction to "joke" by Stalin 35
CIA (Central Intelligence Agency), OSS as precursor 3
cigars and cigarettes 184
Clark, Mark 154, 221
clothing: American style 51; buying new, in Bucharest 216; civilian, unobtrusive 42, 62, 73, 104, 144; damp 74, 81, 82; frozen 102; Gestapo affecting civilian garb 23; lice-infested 27, 77, 182; shrunken in wash 202; spies, in civilian clothes (out of uniform) 145; WAAC uniform 230; for winter 69, 73, 74, 77, 79, 81, 97
Cold War, presaged in Slovakia 13
colonel-smuggling incident 25
communism: as objective of some Slovak partisans 27; oppressions of 4–5, 240; Russian distrust of 82; Vlasov's disillusionment with Bolshevism 254; *see also* Soviet guerrillas
corset tomfoolery 158, 161
courier assignments for Maria 27
couriers 23

crisis, importance of action in 17
cryptographers: danger faced if captured 96, 107; Dunlevy 69; radio codes, loss to German patrol 95
Czech Brigade 78, 79, 82, 84
Czech Republic 5, 262
Czechoslovakia: author's visits to 4, 5; ceded to Soviet sphere 9, 221; creation after WWI 10–11; early history 10; internal demographic conflicts 11; invasion by Nazi Germany 12; as relatively undamaged prize of war 206, 249; strategic importance in central Europe 11
Czechoslovak Forces of the Interior *see* CFI (Czechoslovak Forces of the Interior)

Dallman, Howard 40, 41–42, 45–46, 47
Davis, Glenn 245
Davis, Guilliam: celebrating rescue with shopping and dining spree 216–217; decision to remain with Russians, make for Red Army front 169; defense of Maria 181; Maria's impression of 174; one of five to escape capture 167; protecting Maria from lewd attentions 163, 203–204; rapport with Maria, 151; sharing reminiscences with Maria 225–226; SOE team member 139; warning to Maria 150
Dawes, William 36
Dawes Mission, betrayal, attack and capture: betrayed by Slovak partisan 169, 190; cabin and ski lodge burned 169; cabin occupants captured 165–167; decision to remain with Russians, make for Red Army front 169; five escape with Russians 167; transfer to Mauthausen concentration camp 190
Dawes Mission, Catlos, ill, finds unlikely shelter: companions' disapproval of decision to stay 173, 176; demand for American uniform by Hungarian deserter 177; escapes and finds shelter in woods 179–180; hiding in sheep pen loft 178; rescue by Romanian patrol 187; visit from German medic 177; warning of sweeps by Germans 178
Dawes Mission, caught in crosshairs: bathtub and shrunken clothing incident 202; destination Odessa and sealed fate 208; dysentery 203; guards in constant attendance; team treated as prisoners 201; Maria pretends to be married to Davis 205, 207; repeated questioning 204; sent to hospital, Zenopian to different camp 202–203; Siberian soldier's intrusion 207–208; sweater theft incident 201; three to transfer to Odessa, Maria to be held back 207; transfer to center for liberated refugees 206–207; transfer to Soviet headquarters for counterespionage 204
Dawes Mission, diminished group on the move again to Red Army front: Americans, British, Russians and Maria remain 170;

Index

Catlos stays in Rejdova 175; crossing Hron Valley and bridge at night 171; entering villages infested with informers 175; glimpse of American Bombers heading toward Germany 172; Maria urged to stay in Rejdova, decides to accompany team 173–175; pursued by ten thousand troops 170; refused shelter in forester's hut 172; Rejdova villagers welcome Americans 173; shelter in lean-to near Rejdova with Polish partisans 172; supplies airdropped too late, fall into hostile hands 170

Dawes Mission, four proceed to mine shaft hideouts near Hankova: battle rages past; team leaves mine 186; guide Gregor 180; Maria falls, Davis and Zenopian quarrel 180–181; Maria returns to mine with food and cigars 184; Maria seeks food and help in German-infested villages and countryside 182–184; move to Petramanovce mine, crowded with escapees 184–186; near escape from Germans at Rejdova 180; shelling of mountainside 185; Soviet soldiers looting abandoned villages 187

Dawes Mission, freedom's high price: assignment as general's special aides, flight to Bari 219; Catlos' defense of Maria 218; end of war 221; intensive questioning of Catlos and Dunlevy, suspicion of Maria 218, 219; last goodbyes of Maria and Davis 226; loneliness of Maria, left in Bucharest 220; Maria and Davis celebrate end of war 221–222, 223; radio broadcast of executions of other Dawes teammates 219–220

Dawes Mission, Gaul in charge: German attack on camp 132–133; Green found, last radio transmission sent 139–140; heading for Polomka in Dumbier mountain range 133, 134; search for Green, saved by village women spinning flax 136–139; shelter in shack with Jewish partisans 136; shelter in shepherd's barn 134

Dawes Mission, Gulovich joins: reception attended 51; skills aiding espionage 7–8, 32–33, 74, 85

Dawes Mission, "Hail Mary" escape plan works: American G.I.s confront Russians 213; buying new clothing 215–216; Catlos and Dunlevy kept incommunicado 215; escape from train 211–213; facing suspicion about escaping capture 215; hope of reaching American post in Bucharest 211; Maria pretends to be married to Davis 211; Maria's concern as refugee from now non-existent country 214–215; men are dropped off, leave Maria without farewell 214; phone call to American post 212; surprise reunion for shopping and restaurant meal 216; train ride with Russian officers 209–211; women installed in villa, bathe, and sleep on floor 214

Dawes Mission, holed up in Polomka: cabin hideout **160**, 168; Christmas celebration, lonely and troubled 156–164; concerns over lax security, reliance on Soviets 153; food drop by 15th Air Force, near capture of collectors 151–152; hoping for another air drop 164; nocturnal sortie and destruction of railroad tunnel 155; period for rest, recuperation 156; Red Army advance delayed 154; resentment of presence of women 151; tobacco juice as beacon lights 152–153; warning of approach of German and Hungarian soldiers 155

Dawes Mission, horror for captives at hands of Nazis: brutal interrogation by Gestapo 190–198; execution of all fourteen 198–200

Dawes Mission, inception, achievement, and costliness: American pride at contribution to Slovakian Uprising 263; as bold operation at terrible price 262; criticized as ill-conceived and ill-planned 262; intelligence information gained 43, 64, 144; launch from Italy 37, 40; loss of life 3, 8; qualifications and training of volunteers 37, 261; question of Donovan's prior knowledge of Soviet intentions 9; reinforcements brought in 46–49

Dawes Mission, move on to Polomka in two groups: arrival at Polomka cabin, guided by local boy 148; attempt to buy horses 139; capture of Keszthelyi and Mican 140; exhaustion, cold, and hunger 148; Gauls' accusations of Maria; she decides to leave group 141–142; groups led by Gaul and Green 140; Maria and farm boy find shortcut 147; short interlude of recuperation 150; trudging through snowy forests at night 146; warning of approaching Germans 145–146

Dawes Mission, on the run after split-up: blizzard and "white darkness" 101; division, debate, and departure 99–101; encounter with absconding CFI Brigade 101–102; fighting frostbite 103; MacGregor and airmen captured 105; sunshine and rising temperatures 104

Dawes Mission, on the run and on their own: celebrating Thanksgiving 126–127; close call with German patrol 117; encounter with French partisans 108; encounter with suspicious partisans 114–115; exhausted, wet, cold, and miserable 108; final split from CFI brigade 107; finding help in village of Dolnia Lehota 108, 109–114; finds frozen carcasses of CFI 107–108; heading for barracks near Kracova 120; at heart of manhunt by Germans 126; low morale, lost cohesion 106; meetup with SOE team 128–129; recuperation and medical help 122; shelter and sewing circle in farmer's house 116–117, 119; still heading for Red Army front 107

Dawes Mission, on the run toward Red Army

front: across Chebenec "mountain of death" 97; arrival at Soviets' Klement Gottwald camp 77; attack by Nazi Alpine soldiers 97–98; CFI Brigade deserting in night 96; cold, wet, and hungry 83; crowding into crude hut 84; flight to hideouts in mountains 67, 72–73; Germans advancing 78; leaving Klement Gottwald camp for lumber camp 79–84; lost in mountains 81, 82; reconnaisance and capture by German patrol 95–96; separation from Czech Brigade 84; slipping down cliff 83; sorties into villages for food 85; warning not to approach villagers 86
Dawes Mission, related missions: Bowery Mission 48, 55, 58; Day team 53, 54, 58–59, 143, 144, 262; Houseboat 38, 143, 262
Dawes Mission, relative safety with Red Army: crossing Hungarian border; suspicious interrogation by Soviets 189; rescue by Romanian patrol 186–187; reunion with Catlos 189–190; team travels to Red Army camp 187–188
Dawes Mission, threatened with discovery: evacuation from Banska Bystrica 63–64, 66; Germans and Soviets advancing 44–45; position more tenuous 57–58; urgent request for evacuation 59–60
Day team 53, 54, 58–59, 143, 144, 262
DeLaney, Edward 220, 254
Detvaskae Lazy 144
diarrhea 136
diary of Keszthelyi 142, 175, 220
Direlanger brigade 59
Dobrodsky, Josef 31, 70
Dolnia Lehota 109–114
Donavaly 69, 258
Donovan, William B.N. 3, 9, 244, 245, 248, 262
"Don't Fence Me In" song 217
Drezner, John 84
Dulles, Allen 233, 241, 242
Dumbier mountain range 133, 134
Dunlevy, Kenneth: admiration of and recognition of debt to Maria 175; assessment of Zenopian 151; celebrating rescue with shopping and dining spree 216–217; decision to remain with Russians, make for Red Army front 169; deploring plunder taken by Red Army soldiers 210; disgust at Unkrainian soldiers' looting 189; distrust of Soviet guerrillas 80, 162; facing suspicion about escaping capture 215; first meeting with Gulovich 69; impressions of Green and Gaul 76, 134; intensive questioning by American authorities 218; learning of father's death 219; loaning Bible to Gaul 160, 161, 175; Maria's impression of 148, 174; one of five to escape capture 167; opting to stay with mission 100; receives citation for Dawes service *257*;

refuses to attend 1964 celebration in Slovakia 256; relief at split from CFI brigade 107; remaining friends with Catlos 260; repeated questioning by Red Army 204; saved by Gulovich 4; sentry duty, worries about approching enemy troops 162, 163; sorrow at Morton's predicament 125, 146; sympathy for Catlos 173, 176; sympathy for Horvath 156; tobacco juice as beacon lights 152–153; value as cryptographer 49, 107; watchful eye on partisans 92–93
Dymko (Soviet guerrilla unit commander) 155, 159, 165–167, 170
dysentery 123, 176, 177, 203

Eastern Orthodox Church, bishops aiding Jews 22
Eichmann, Adolf 16
Eisenhower, Dwight D. 206, 255, 263
Esenhoffer, Heinz 199
espionage: as dangerous, lonely, hunted calling 5, 9–10; immigrants recruited for 3; qualifications and training of volunteers 37, 47; as weapon of war 5; *see also* OSS (Office of Strategic Services)
Evelyn (English girl at villa) 223

F.B.I. (Federal Bureau of Investigation), position on establishment of OSS 9
Fedornak, Michael 64, 66, 71, 78, 82, 169
15th Air Force: Carrying six Dawes team members to Slovakia 37; carrying supplies to CFI at Tri Duby 45–46; excavating B-17 from muddy airstrip 46; Morton and Paris as guests of 49; precision bombing with information provided by Dawes 43, 59, 144; refusal to deliver more war supplies 58; refusal to evacuate Dawes team 60; refusal to help evacuate Americans 190
Fiola, Frederick 145
food in war zones: beans and horsemeat 108; beans, stone-hard 84; CFI Brigade members absconding with 96; confiscation by Germans 149; confiscation by Soviets 236; countryside plundered by soldiers 206; discovery of stash of vegetables and live calf 87; eligibility for American relief parcels 235; food drop by 15th Air Force 151–152; horsemeat and possible contamination 84, 88; packhorses stolen 83; piglet 121; poor Red Army rations 203; rationing 96; Rejdova villagers provide feast 173; sorties into villages for 85–86, 88–90; stealing authorized 103; stolen flour 84–85; venison 97; villagers providing to mine shaft hideout 182
Fortuni, Anthony 54
Friendship Treaty (Slovakia and Soviets) 34, 221
Fritz (Nazi-hating ex–Wehrmacht twin) 155, 161, 162, 166
frostbite 103, 114, 119, 122–123, 163

Frudenfels, Victor 70

gangrene 122–123, 125
Garrigue, Charlotte 10
Gaul, Harriet 248, 249, 260
Gaul, James Harvey *57*; accusations about money 141–142; attempts to dissuade discontented OSS from leaving group 99, 100; Bowery Mission 55–56; in charge in Green's absence 131; Christmas scavenger hunt 158; disapproval of romance 88, 122; distributes money 78; Dunlevy's approval of 76–77; hiding in woods from Germans 131, 132; impromptu Christmas religious remembrance 160–161; interrogation and execution by Gestapo 194, 196, 196–197, 198; Maria's respect for 8; nocturnal sortie and destruction of railroad tunnel 155; qualifications for Dawes Mission 47, 136; search for missing Green 136–139; special regard for Czechoslovakia 249; Thanksgiving Day prayer 127
Geneva Convention: blatant violations by Nazis 238; Hitler's rejection of 43; naivete of expecting German conformity 261; Roosevelt's warning to Hitler 35
German-ancestry citizens, loyalty to Nazi regime 81
Gestapo 23, 30, 171, 190; *see also* Nazi soldiers; torture
gold and silver mines of Slovakia 239
Goldberger, Julius 16, 18, 21
Golian, Jan 26, 31, 45, 63, 251–252
Gorman, Jack 46
Greece, decimation of resistance movements 26
Green, James Holt *44*, *65*, *91*; attempts to dissuade discontented OSS from leaving group 99; attempts to find food 86–87; authorizing stealing of food 103; capture 169; Christmas scavenger hunt 157; commanding Dawes Mission 8, 37; distrust of Soviet guerrillas 52, 80; doubly betrayed 190; escape from Banska Bystrica to hide in mountains 71; finds potatoes 87; gratitude to Maria 88; interrogation and execution by Gestapo 190, 191, 192, 196, 197, 198; likened to Ashley Wilkes 77, 96; Maria and Davis recall 226; nocturnal sortie and destruction of railroad tunnel 155; ordering "wanderers" to get cleaned up 76, 120; pressing on toward Red Army front 107; request for aid for CFI 43, 45; urgent request for evacuation 59–60
Gregor (guide to abandoned mine) 180
grenade incident 53–54, 143
Grey, Richard 38–39, 47
Gulovich, Anastasia (Maria's mother) 233–234, 250
Gulovich, Edmund (Maria's father): daughters' activities 16; declared "enemy of the people," exiled internally 250; hiding wife and daughters from soldiers 235; kidnap and forced labor 250; lasting influence on Maria 92, 242, 246; possibility of false charges and arrest 240; prediction that Maria would leave 20, 234; punishment for protesting Jewish Codex 18; reassurances to Maria 236; refusal to abandon parish for America 235; refusal to convert to Orthodoxy 250; reunion with Maria 233, 234
Gulovich, Magda 19
Gulovich, Maria, new life in America: awarded Bronze Star for heroism 244–245; life at Vassar 243; marriage and children 260, 261; meetings with families of lost team members 260; question of finances 243, 245, 246; remained on NKVD Most Wanted list 261; troop ship to New York 243
Gulovich, Maria, on the run with Dawes team: attraction to Keszthelyi 86, 88; banishment from homeland 8; concern as refugee from now non-existent country 214–215, 216–217; concern for airmen on eve of mountain trek 80–81; dissention over women's presence, Maria decides to leave 163; forced to spy for NKVD 205–206, 207; gratitude toward Americans 128; love blossoms 113, 115, 128, 141; one of five to escape capture 167; pretends marriage to Davis 205, 207, 211; rape by Velichko 27–28, 128; recruitment for rescue of Americans 7; sores on frostbitten foot 114, 119, 122–123, 163; suspicion, jealousy of Margita 149, 163; throws in lot with Americans 62–63, 72
Gulovich, Maria, qualifications for espionage, praise of work: appearance and self-possession 20; composure building morale 120; decoration for heroism 15, 17, 244–245; Dunlevy's admiration and recognition of debt 175; mention by former OSS agent 4; national identity card *24*; reluctance to revisit painful period 7; skills aiding espionage 8, 32–33, 74, 85, 174–175
Gulovich, Maria, reaching relative safety: American's suspicions of 225; attempts to persuade sister to emigrate 239–240; convoy to safety in Salzburg 241, 242–243; escape from NKVD 241–243; immigration to USA finally approved 241–243; last goodbye to parents and Slovakia 236; learns of executions of other Dawes teammates 227–228; NKVD pursuing 240–241; obtains exit visa, flies to Bari 225; pressing Americans for emigration to America 224–225; recuperation in Rome 230; reporting on Dawes team's travails 230; reunion with family 233–234; sharing reminiscences with Davis 225–226; Soviets refusing to release 225; on special post-war OSS mission with Schwartz 232–239

Gulovich, Maria, works for Soviet guerrillas: dining with and liking Americans 56–57; in disfavor for anti–Nazi sentiments 18; forced to become courier 23–24; undercover of role as student 24;
Gulovich, Marta (Maria's sister) 17, 19, 234, 236, 239–240
gypsies 32

Habecker, Walter 191, 192, 193, 194
Habsburg Empire 10
Haines, Gary 92, 95, 232
Hannah and son Zoltan (sister and nephew of Julius Goldbergber) 16, 17, 19, 21, 23, 25
Hans (Nazi-hating ex–Wehrmacht twin) 155, 161, 162, 166
Hansen, Kevin 100, 105
Harustiak, Pavel 251
Heller, Charles: Dunlevy's worries about, on eve of mountain trek 79; horror at sight of frozen CFI carcasses 108; joke played on Grey 38–39; Maria's impression of 148; Maria's respect for 8; qualifications for Houseboat Mission 38
Heydrich, Heinrich 118, 252
Himmler, Heinrich 59, 190, 198
Hitler, Adolf: failed assassination attempt 26; fury at assassination of Heydrich 252; interest in Czechoslovakia 11; presenting unhappy choice to Tiso 12; Slovakia to be held at all costs 126; suicide 221; *see also* Nazi Germany
Hlinka Guards 19
Hoestler, Charles 230
Holt, James 57
Hoover, J. Edgar 9
horses, packhorses 78, 83, 102
Horst Wessel troops 59
Horthy, Nicholas 16, 54–55, 58
Horvath, Alma 111, 124, 156
Horvath, Joseph *110*; Dunlevy's confidence in, on eve of mountain trek 79; execution with 14 other Dawes members 198–200; gathering information among Banska Bystrica natives 43; last letter to wife 195; longing for wife 90, 92, 195; mistreatment by Gestapo 171; qualifications for Dawes Mission 37; rapport with Maria 149, 156; rapport with nurse 123; sadness at Christmas 161; singled out for punishment 248
hospital: for partisans 123; of Red Army 203
Houseboat Mission, 38 143, 262
Hrinova 18
Hruby, Vratislav 231, 232
Hungary: ceded to Soviet sphere 9; deportations, internment of Jews 16; Germans and Red Army occupying 58; OSS interest in 54–55; Slovakia integrated into 10

Igor (village Casanova and blackmailer) 22
insurrectionists *see* partisan groups

Jakes, Otto 39, 45
Japanese surrender 231
Jason, John, Jr. 3
Jegerov, Alexia Semionovic 27, 28–30
Jewish Codex 16
Jews: deportations 16; Gulovich family rescue of escapee 17–18; joining insurrectionists 32
Josef (helpful farm boy) 147
Jurgen 84

Kaltenbrunner, Ernst 190, 198, 238
Kaminski brigade 59
Keszthelyi, Tibor *74*; aids Maria's escape 62–63; anger over destroyed radio 73, 76, 101; appearance 56; attracted to Maria 86, 88; Bowery Mission 48, 55, 58, 59; brings Maria winter clothing 69; capture during attempt to buy horses 140; close call in Dolnia Lehota 13, 131; diary 142, 175; dinner invitation to Maria 56; execution with 14 other Dawes members 198–200; fever 90; hope for favorable outcome 48; imprisoned in Mauthausen concentration camp 190; infiltrating agents into Hungary 56; last letter to parents 195; love blossoms 113, 115, 128, 141; Maria remembers with longing 223, 224, 246; Maria seeks information on 228; meets Maria 55–56; opting to stay with mission 100; protects Maria from Schwartz 72; saves Maria from icy skid 98
Khrushchev, Nikita 258
Klement Gottwald camp, Dawes group's arrival at 77
Konev, Ivan (General, First Ukrainian Army) 32, 45, 255
Konski, Alvin O. 254
Kora, Stephen 48, 55, 56
Koscova, Margita: American with ties to Slovakia 66, 139; disapproving but enjoying corset caper 158, 161; escaping, vacating hunting lodge 78; execution with 14 other Dawes members 197, 198; interrogation and execution by Gestapo 190, 197, 198; interrogation by Germans 190; joining British as interpreter 139; making contact with Slovak partisans 66; mellowed attitude at Christmas celebration 160; mutual dislike, jealousy of Maria 148–149, 151, 163; Sehmer's gifts of clothing 158; transfer to Mauthausen concentration camp 190
Kozi Chrbat "Goat's Back" 72–73, 78
Kristak, Anna 176, 179
Kristak, Jan 173, 176, 261
Kristak home *174*
Krizan *see* Schwartz, John (Krizan)
Krutel, Anne 23, 62
Krutel, Josef 23, 62

Lain, Kenneth: attending 1964 celebration in Slovakia 256, 257, 258, 259; capture 104–105; gallant effort at heavy toll 262;

Index

leaving Dawes to escort airmen 100; released from POW camp, back in Air Force 233; search for food 88; sets up defense with anti-aircraft guns 69; torture by Gestapo 233; veteran of Anzio, assigned to train CFI on weapons 52, 53, 79
language skills in espionage 3, 8, 32–33
leaflets 144–145
lice 27, 77, 182
Lidice massacre 118, 252, 253
Lieskovce 145
Liu, Maria Gulovich *see* Gulovich, Maria
love blossoms 113, 115, 128, 141

MacGregor, William: attending 1964 celebration in Slovakia 256, 259; capture by German patrol 105; Dunlevy's confidence in, on eve of mountain trek 79; no news of 229, 231; opting to go with airmen 99–100; practical joke by Russians involving anti-tank gun 53; release from POW camp 233; setup of anti-aircraft guns at Sports Hotel 69; Soviet resistance to assignment 52; urging Maria to leave Soviet guerrillas 62–63; warning of German strafing 68
Madden, Roy 250–251
Malinovsky, Rodion 206
Maquisards (Free French) 26
Masaryk, Jan 58, 250
Masaryk, Thomas 10
Mauthausen concentration camp 190, 199, 233, 238
McAuliffe, Anthony 154
McCracken, Henry Noble 243
McDermott, William 238
Mican, Jerry (Jaroslav) *65*; capture during attempt to buy horses 140; Dunlevy's worries about, on eve of mountain trek 79; execution with 14 other Dawes members 198–200; gathering information among Banska Bystrica natives 42–43; hiding in woods from Germans 131, 132, 133; imprisoned in Mauthausen concentration camp 190; Maria's respect for 8; ordered to accompany brigade 84; qualifications for Dawes Mission 8, 37, 39
"Mikhail" (Mikhail Gennady Jahovlivic Stalny) 51, 61, 73, 81
Mihailovich, Draga 34
Miller, Glenn 154
Miller, Lane 135, 168
mine shaft hideout 181–182
mines of Slovakia 239
Moly, Francis 48, 55, 56
money 78, 121–122, 141–142, 206
Moravia 10–11, 12
Morgan, Jack 154
Morton, Joseph *50*; anger at Gaul 146; concern for destroyed film 73; diffuser of tensions 85; horror at sight of frozen CFI carcasses 108; interrogation and execution by Gestapo 196; journalist's credentials, praise from colleagues 238; as last minute volunteer for mission 49; post-war investigations into execution 237–239; question of permission to join Dawes mission 261–262; refuses chance for evacuation 60; sadness at Christmas 161; sharing sulpha with Maria 125, 163; suffering from frostbite and dysentery 123; sympathy for Maria 142, 163–164; tobacco juice as beacon lights 152–153
Mullen (father of Mira and plotter of Heydrich assassination) 252–253
Mullen, Mira 118, 252
Muller, Werner: recounting circumstances of executions 238; as translator at Mauthausen camp 191, 192, 195, 196, 197–198, 198–199, 200
Munich Pact 11–12

national identity card 24
Nazi Commando code 43
Nazi Germany: invasion of Slovakia 31; retaliation against citizens, partisans, Soviets, and Americans 66–67; *see also* Hitler, Adolf
Nazi soldiers: bottled up in Rejdova by Romanian troops 178; crack Alpine corps 97–98; fed rumors by villagers 125–126
Neizerling, Lynn 249
Newburgh, Robert 251
Niezerling, Lynn 238
Nikolai (teams' Soviet guard on train) 211–212, 213, 215
NKVD (Soviet secret police): Maria forced to sign paper, agreeing to spy 205, 217; Maria forced to spy for, interviewing refugees 205–206, 207; presence in resistance movements 107, 169; rounding up girls 240; Slovak church leaders turned over to 235; as threat to Maria's post-war future 224, 231, 241
Novak, Anton 143–144, 145
nurses, Slovak 123–124
"Nuts!" reply by McAuliffe 154

O'Neill, Kelly 238
Ornstein, Wilheim 199, 238, 239
OSS (Office of Strategic Services): creation 9; Gauls' mother's letters to 248, 249; interagency hostility with British SOE 34, 35; interest in Czechoslovakia 12; interest in Hungary 54–55; need for mission into Slovakia 13; plan for mission to Slovakia 35; recruitment of immigrants 3; secret drops of supplies to resistance movements 26; special post-war mission for Maria and Schwartz 232, 237–239

Pachmayer, George 198
Pajedova, Terka (Zuska) 109
Paris, Nelson: fainting spell 148; hiding large camera and destroying film 73; interrogation

and execution by Gestapo 199; Maria's impression of 148; question of permission to join Dawes mission 261; refused shelter by farmer near Myto 135; rescue by Maria and Catlos 132–133; worries about condition of, on eve of mountain trek 81
Pasternak (villager providing food) 182
Patch, Alexander 255, 256
Patton, George 221, 255
Paveltich, Daniel 53–54, 143, 145
Pavlo (guide aiding team) 107, 110, 113, 114, 115, 120, 121, 167, 168–169, 170, 171
Pavlovich, Pavel (captain in Czech partisan group) 25, 30
Perry 131, 132, 133
Petramanovce mine 184–187
piglet 121
pilots, American *see* airmen, American
"Pistol Packin' Mama" song 161
Podolski, Barbara 230
Polak, Milan 22–23
Polana 144
Polish Home Army 26
Polomka 133, 134, 139
Pope Pius VI 22
Prague 221, 255, 262
Prasiva mountain range 71, 72, 79
priests: allowed to marry 20; communists' hatred of 72, 240; large scale post-war arrests of by communists 250; punishment, prohibition of political views 18; risking imprisonment 22; Slovak church leaders turned over to NKVD 235
Pritchard, Gilbert 40, 41, 45, 46
propaganda, German, against partisans and Americans 145
Prykryl, Vladimir 71, 78, 97, 107

radio: depressing news of war in Europe 177; loss of 73, 76, 101, 129; parts pickup assignment to Bratislava 24–25; transmitter 121
radio codes *see* cryptographers
radio message 139–140
rape: females in "liberated" countries subject to 149, 207, 211, 240; of Maria by Velichko 27–28, 128; protection of men against 88, 173; by rampaging Soviet armies 235; by Soviet-controlled partisans 52; of Stella by her partisan commander 203; and syphilis of Andrea (ambassador's wife) 208, 210; women's suicide to avoid 208
Red Army 126, 154, 189, 207, 210
resistance movements *see* partisan groups
restaurant meal 216
reticence of heroes 3
Rimski Sobata 189
Rockefeller, Nelson 9
Romanians (Allies) 186, 187
Roosevelt, Eleanor 245
Roosevelt, Franklin D.: creation of OSS 9; declaring support for CFI as part of Allied armies 35; greetings to Czechoslovak friends in arms 67; reaction to "joke" by Stalin 35
"Rose of Tralee" 162
Ross, Martin 199
Ross, Walter 43, 212, 219
Rozyno 188
Rudinskaya, Maria Radiovna (code name "Tamara") 37, 51, 61
"Russian Revenge" (dysentery) 203
Ruthenia 4, 5, 11
Rypakova, Josephina 252
Rysovy, Vavro 31, 262
Ryzek, Jan 145

Sascha ("Sha Sha," NKVD spy and "guide") 169, 170, 175
Sasewa 95
Sasha (guide) 107, 110, 113, 114, 115, 120, 121
scavenger hunt 157–158
Schell Battalion 59
Schoenseneiffen (SS supervisor) 191, 192, 193, 194, 196, 198, 200
Schwartz, John (Krizan): attending 1964 celebration in Slovakia 256, 259; capture by German patrol 95–96; faint signal heard from 143; farewell to Maria 237; gathering information among Banska Bystrica natives 42; NKVD jail, then release to Americans 232; preference for remaining in Banska Bystrica 66; qualifications and experience 38, 94; resentment of romantic attachment 88; reunion with family 233; on special post-war OSS mission with Maria 232, 237; suspicion of Maria 72; tracking down Nazis for justice 237
Sehmer, Ernest *51, 65, 66*; appearance and cheeriness 139; capture 169; Christmas celebrations 157–158; dynamic leader 150; as genial host at Polomka 148, 149; interrogation and execution by Gestapo 190, 193–194; making contact with Americans 129; Maria and Davis recall 226; nocturnal sortie and destruction of railroad tunnel 155; recognition of USA Navy jacket 128
serenade to Maria 92
sewing circle 116–117
Shukayev, Mikhail 81, 82, 155, 159, 169
Siberian troops 207
"Silent Night" 162
Slovak National Uprising: bloodletting by Germans and Soviets 32; bloodletting by Germans, pro-communists and Soviets 249–250; celebration of 20th anniversary of uprising 256–260; comparison to Yugoslav partisan operation 78–79; costliness 8, 34, 71, 249–250; defeat 70–71; Gestapo searches 30; launched upon invasion by Nazis 31; little present day knowledge of, or interest in 262; opposing aims of multiple groups 27; reasons for failure 261; report of German derision 79; rumors, disorder and

fear 25; Soviet control and subversion 31; Soviet reluctance to discuss 4–5
Slovak Republic 5, 262
Slovakia: bearing brunt of Soviet retaliation 249–250; black market and rationing 16; deportations, internment of Jews 16; early statehood followed by integration into Hungarian kingdom 10; hope of independence 7; independence after fall of communism 8; independence at price of German "protection" 12; map 13; new tyranny of communists 235–236, 237, 239, 250; occupied by Soviets and bankrupt 8, 220, 223, 240; Stalin's eyes on gold and silver mines 239; turmoil and internal discord 15; ultimatum on eve of WWII 11–12
Slovenska Narodne Rada (provisional government) 31
SOE (Special Operations Executive): agents as "forfeited" 9–10; inter-agency hostility with American OSS 34, 35; need for mission into Slovakia 13; plan for mission to Slovakia 35
Soviet guerrillas: capture at Prasiva 79; decimations 26; duplicity and lawless behavior 8, 52, 60, 66, 82, 149; escaping to mountains 61; execution of German diplomatic group 31; map 13; Maria's courier duty to mountain camp 27–28; massacre in barracks near Dolnia Lehota 132; NKVD (Soviet secret police) presence in units 107, 169; raping local women 149; refusal to help evacuate Americans 60; seizure of MC 34s 77; subversion of OSS and British efforts 52–53, 64; war materiel airlifted from Italy *41*; wartime infiltration and sabotage in Slovakia 15, 24, 26
Soviet Intelligence operation in Slovakia, Maria works for 32–33
Soviet Russia *see* USSR (Union of Soviet Socialist Republics)
Special Operations Executive *see* SOE (Special Operations Executive)
Sports Hotel, Donavaly 69
Stalin, Josef: plan for execution of German generals 35; *see also* USSR (Union of Soviet Socialist Republics)
Stalny, Mikhail Gennady Jahovlivic 51, 61, 73, 81
Stefan (Hlinka Guard) 19
Stella (pregnant girl) 202, 203
Stonek (captain in CFI) 51
Studensky, Ivan Skripka: arrival in Banska Bystrica 32; destroying documents 61; encountered again after blizzard 102; first meeting with Americans 55–56; gives Gulovich money for boots 61; Gulovich reports to 32; leaves Gulovich in charge 61; leaving Klement Gottwald camp 79; orders Gulovich to vacate room 69; refusal to help evacuate Americans 60; relocation to another mountain camp 97; warning Maria to avoid Americans 104
subversion, as weapon of war 20
Sudetenland 11
suicide: of "Anthropoids," assassins of Heydrich 252; of Russians to avoid repatriation at end of war 232; of Vlassovites preferring death to repatriation 255, 256; of women to avoid gang rape 208
Sukayev, Mikhail 64, 71
Surkov 120, 131
Svara, John 54
Svoboda, Ludvig 59
Svolenska Slatina, Day team "headquarters" 54
sweater theft incident 201
syphilis 208, 210

"Tamara" (Maria Radiovna Rudinskaya) 37, 51, 61, 97, 103, 104
Taylor, Jack 228, 229
Teheran Conference 9, 15, 34
Thanksgiving Day 126–127
Tibetan prayer mill 192
Tiso, Josef, Monsignor 220; attempt to buy time 30; capture, trial and execution 253; execution called injustice 254; hope of Slovakia becoming U.N. mandate 253; Jewish question 253; rumor of death of 31; taint of cooperation with Nazi Germany 7, 21; unhappy choice presented to 12; victim of events 21
Tito, Josip Broz 26, 34, 35
tobacco: cigars and cigarettes 184; spat juice as "beacon lights" 152–153
Tomes, Emil 54, 143, 144, 145
torture by Gestapo 190–198, 228, 229, 233, 239
Truman, Harry S, commendation from 244
Tuka, Vojtech 16

Ukraine and Ukrainian solders 5, 157, 166, 189, 221, 224
Urban (villager helping Maria) 182, 183, 184, 185
USSR (Union of Soviet Socialist Republics): British and American suspicion of post-war plans 35; Czechoslovakia, Balkans and Hungary ceded to 9; Donovan's early warning as enemy 262; refusal of support for Polish Home Army 26; resistance to Anglo-American presence 13; reticence on Slovakian Revolt 4–5; settling old scores with repatriation, slaughter and Siberian exile 224, 231–232; Stalin's eyes on Slovakia's gold and silver mines 239; *see also* Soviet guerrillas
Uzgorod 5

V-2 Rocket plant bombing 59
Vatican, pressure from 16

Velichko, Piotor Alexjenic 27–28, 31, 52, 77, 259
venereal diseases 149, 208, 210
venison 97
Vienna 206
Viest, Rudof 58, 75, 251–252
villagers: arrival at Polomka cabin, guided by local boy 148; finding help in village of Dolnia Lehota 108; joyous welcome to Americans 173; Maria and farm boy find shortcut 147; preyed upon by thieving partisans 82; providing guides 148, 180, 182; rescue of downed airmen 250–251; search for Green, saved by village women spinning flax 136–139; shelter and sewing circle in farmer's house 116–117; shot by Gestapo 251; sorties into villages for food 85, 182–183; spreading rumor of typhus to Germans 173; warning not to approach 86; warning of approaching Germans 145–146, 155
Vlasov, Andrej Andreevich (Ukrainian general) 157, 221, 224, 254–256
Vlassovites (Ukrainian troops) 157, 221, 224, 237, 255, 256
Vojitossak (Slovak bishop) 16
Vrto, John 145

Wallenberg, Ben 16
Wanderfer, Jack (code name Wilson) 107, 139, 191, 192, 193
war correspondent Morton 49, 50
war's end 221–222, 231
Warsaw, Poland 26
wedding ring 114
Weir, John 249
Weizner, Frank 233, 241

West Point ceremony 244–245
whipped cream incident 216
"white darkness" (blizzard conditions) 101
Willis, James 139, 148, 193
Wilson, Jack (real name Wanderfer) 107, 139, 191, 192, 193
Wilson, Woodrow 10
Winberg, George 44
winter clothing *see* clothing
women: causing dissention in ranks 163; civilizing effect 159; guerrillas' lasciviousness and team's protectiveness 163; resentment of presence of 151; *see also* rape

"Yankee Doodle Dandy" as signal 213
Yeargin, Eugene 75–76, 88, 95, 232
Yegerov 71

Zalenska Slatina 144
Zelzno 157
Zenopian, Arthur: complaints of illness and mistreatment 202; Maria's impression of 174; one of five to escape capture 167; reluctance to keep moving 169, 181; resentment of, accusations against Maria 169, 180–181; resentment of presence of women 151, 163; sings "Pistol Packin' Mama" 161; SOE team member 139
Zhukov, Georgi 206, 240
Ziereis, Franz 191, 192, 193, 194, 195, 197, 198, 199, 229
Zilina 31
Zutter, Adolph 200, 238
Zvara, John 144, 145
Zvara, Vera 144, 145
Zvolenska Slatina 58